ESSENTIALS
of
NURSING
MANAGEMENT

Concepts and Context of Practice

Barbara Stevens Barnum, R.N., Ph.D., FAAN
New York, New York

Catherine O. Mallard, R.N., M.Ed.
National League for Nursing
New York, New York

AN ASPEN PUBLICATION®
Aspen Publishers, Inc.   1989   Rockville, Maryland
Royal Tunbridge Wells

Library of Congress Cataloging-in-Publication Data

Barnum, Barbara Stevens.
Essentials of nursing management.

"An Aspen publication."
Includes bibliographies and index.
1. Nursing services--Administration. I. Mallard, Catherine O.
II. Title. [DNLM: 1. Nursing Care. 2. Nursing
Supervisory--organization & administration. WY 105 B263e]
RT89.B285   1989   362.1'73'068   88-7484
ISBN: 0-8342-0018-X

Editorial Services: Jane Coyle Garwood

Library of Congress Catalog Card Number: 88-7484
ISBN: 0-8342-0018-X

Printed in the United States of America

1 2 3 4 5

Table of Contents

Introduction   vii

PART I—THE CONTEXT   1

Chapter   1—The Nation and the World   3

    Impact on the Consumer   4
    Health as a Business   5
    Marketing to the Consumer   6
    Quality Issues   7
    Effects of Changes on Physicians and Nurses   8
    Summary   10

Chapter   2—The Organizational World   12

    Traditional and Emerging Systems   12

PART II—THE GOALS   23

Chapter   3—Patient Ideologies and Care Standards   27

    Setting the Tone   27
    A Consumer Orientation   29
    Patient Ideologies   32
    Nursing Theories   42
    Summary   44

Chapter 4—Professional Nursing Excellence 46

    Nursing and the Society 46
    Professional Excellence on the Job 55

Chapter 5—Goal-Oriented Management and Strategic
            Planning 60

    Alternative Starting Points 60
    Strategic Planning 66

Chapter 6—Productivity and Managed Efficiency 72

    Effectiveness and Efficiency 73
    Productivity 75
    Summary 84

PART III—RESOURCES: SELF, STAFF, MATERIALS,
SYSTEMS 87

Chapter 7—The First-Line Manager: Role and Responsibilities . 93

    Role Analysis 93
    Responsibilities of the First-Line Manager 99
    Summary 105

Chapter 8—Communications Resources 107

    A Communication Model 107
    The Nurse Manager as Sender and Receiver of
        Communication 109
    Communicating with and through Groups 116
    Summary 127

Chapter 9—Legal and Ethical Implications of the First-Line
            Manager Role 129

    Legal Considerations 129
    Ethical Considerations for the First-Line Manager 141
    Summary 147

Chapter 10—First-Line Supervision **150**

    The Challenge of Managing Professional Staff 150
    The Nature of Supervision 151
    Staff Skills versus Job Design 151
    Orientation of New Staff 153
    Motivation 159
    Summary 164

Chapter 11—Managing People **167**

    Delegation 167
    Direction 174
    The Use of Groups for Management 175
    Committee Leadership Skills 185
    Summary 189

Chapter 12—Managing Care **192**

    Problem Solving Management 192
    Effecting Change 200
    Change or Continuity? 206
    Summary 207

Chapter 13—The Business of Nursing **209**

    Cost-Effective Management 209
    Budgeting 212
    Summary 219

Chapter 14—Management of Materials, Technology,
             and Product Lines **222**

    Inventory Control 223
    Staff Involvement in Materials Management 224
    Materials and Services Provided by Other
        Departments 225
    Product Selection 227
    Product Line Management 228
    Quality Service and Customer Satisfaction 229
    Managing Technology 230
    Technology Moves into Home Care 231

Computers 232
Summary 234

Chapter 15—Management Concepts 238

The Manager's Context 238
Mapping the Domain 240
Summary 260

Chapter 16—Staffing and Assigning of Nursing Personnel 262

Nursing Patient Classification Systems 262
Staffing Decisions 265
Staff Assignment Systems 276
Summary 282

Chapter 17—Systems of Measurement for Nursing Care 285

Nursing Quality Control Systems 285
Selecting the Content To Be Evaluated 291
Constructing the Standards 292
Formats for Quality Control Tools 295
Sources of Evidence 295
Factors That Influence the Quality Control System ... 297
Surveillance and Feedback Systems 298
Summary 299

Chapter 18—Employee Performance Appraisal 302

The Evaluative Process 302
Change-Oriented Evaluation 306
Guidelines for Communicating in Interviews 311
Summary 314

Index 317

Introduction

This book is designed for the nurse manager in a first-line position—that is, a nurse in any organization who has responsibility for managing the direct care of patients and the assignment and direction of staff who deliver that care. The first-line manager holds the bottom-rung managerial position in a care-administering hierarchy. The first-line manager oversees the primary work of a nursing practice: nursing care of patients. While first-line is the lowest level of management, it is also the most critical level; failure of the first-line position signals failure of the total system. Conversely, success at the first-line level assures achievement of the organization's reason for being.

Sometimes there is confusion concerning which nurses are staff and which are managers. The confusion results from the very nature of nursing practice. *All* nurses are managers in one sense; even the staff nurse "manages" the care of patients. The hospital bedside nurse, for example, organizes the care of a group of patients. Her management consists of scheduling her personal time and the institution's resources to meet the cumulate needs of her patient group for a given work period. This requires basic management skills, such as deciding what work will be done, determining the methods to be used, prioritizing and scheduling events, and coordinating with other care givers for immediate and ongoing care.

Similarly, the community health nurse who functions one-to-one in delivering care "manages." She organizes for care in two senses. First, she plans and schedules her visits to clients according to various principles, including patient needs and travel logistics. And, while each visit is a separate unit of production, management of care goes on within each patient visit. Her management includes ongoing assessment of when other health professionals are needed by each client.

All nurses manage care; it is the nature of nursing care that it must be coordinated among many professionals. As long as patients need continuous, sustained nursing, there will be a need for coordination of activities among nurses as well as for coordination of patient-oriented services delivered by other professionals. All nurses are managers in this sense; all nurses coordinate activities for patient care.

This book, however, is written for the nurse with the formal power of management as it applies to staff, not to patients. The first-line manager has responsibility for the outcomes achieved by groups of organized care deliverers. He or she is accountable to higher administration for achievement of organizational goals. This accountable nurse achieves patient care goals by managing the work of other people, i.e., of subordinates who provide direct patient care. Sometimes the subordinates are professional peers; sometimes they are other health care workers. Sometimes the first-line manager gives care right beside those whom she manages. Whether or not she gives direct care herself, she is accountable for the care delivered by the entire work unit. This book is designed for the nurse manager who holds the first level of managerial responsibility in the organizational chain of command.

The book is organized around a basic management model comprising the following components: *context, goals, resources,* and the *interplay* of these elements. This model is only one possible arrangement among a plethora of intellectual schemes that may be used to describe management work. There are many interesting and satisfactory models around which to describe and structure nursing care management, but a model of nursing care management is advantageous only if it can be used to plan the work as well as to describe it. For that purpose, each model has advantages and limitations. The effective manager uses different models at different times, in different circumstances. Part of the work of this book will be to increase the reader's knowledge of potentially useful models. The model used for the overall organization of this book has advantages and limitations, just like any other model. One of its advantages is simply that it provides an orderly way in which to compose a book as well as a systematic way in which to conceptualize the work of the first-line manager.

CONTEXT

The *context* refers to the situation in which the care is delivered; it includes all the important aspects of the environment, those elements of the surrounding world that have an impact on the care and that modify the ways in which it is delivered. Context includes many elements: the character, ethnicity, socioeconomic status, and values of the patient; the particular circumstances of patient and family; the broader nature and values of the community, nation, and even the world in which health care is sought; and the structures and dynamics designed by a given society for the delivery of health care. Context includes the dominant social issues of the patient's society, the prevalent ways of conceptualizing the world, and the methods of interface between and among the social institutions of the age. In essence, context refers to anything that may modify and impinge on the way in which nursing and health care are delivered to individuals where they are located in time and space. At different times, different aspects of context will assume importance in health care management.

There is a reason why context is discussed first: context is slippery, changing, and difficult to predict for any reasonable period of time. Take the present nursing shortage as an illustration. Just a few short years ago there were dire predictions of a nursing glut. The prediction was that institution of the DRG system nationwide would radically decrease the number of job opportunities available for nurses. Indeed many nurses found themselves laid off or reduced to part-time employment at the time of the system's initiation. Now the opposite situation prevails, and our institutions are panicked over their inability to find and hire needed nurses. What in the context has changed? Are there more patients? Fewer nurses? Has the nature of the care required changed? Are there more acutely ill persons, fewer with low-level care needs? Have the expectations for quality of care changed? Or is it simply a state of mind, a nationally accepted interpretation of the situation, that has changed? Whatever the source of the contextual shift, the fact remains that one must plan care of patients differently when faced with a shortage of nurses than when coping with a surfeit of available nurses.

The context for delivery of health care has never been completely stable, but the rapidity of change in our society and in our health care practice systems has forced us to consider context in new ways. A rapidly changing context is a new fact of life for many of us, one that forces us to plan management of care in new and complex ways. This was not always the case in health care. Only a few decades ago, nurses could plan care with a clear vision of the environment in which the care would be delivered years later. The world at the end of their planning phase—say, five years ahead—would look pretty much like the world that existed when the planning began. Prediction, allotment of resources, and planning ahead were rather simple in a stable world.

Today, in contrast, we see rapid and unanticipated changes in the health care systems of the nation, modifications that result from numerous contextual influences: altered reimbursement systems for health, new and expensive technologies, care methods that can only be offered on a rationed basis, increasing life spans for the very old. Additionally, we face surprising changes in the patterns of disease itself. A decade ago, no planner would have theorized that the nation would be subjected to a new and dangerously spreading plague such as the AIDS catastrophe.

Today our ability to look ahead with accuracy is constrained. Today's health care environment may be radically changed overnight. Its responsiveness to changes in other social structures has been enhanced. The pace is quickening.

The burden of context is dual. First one strives for an accurate perception of the context. To be certain of one's discernment is difficult when things change rapidly. Accurately interpreting the nature of the context is thus one burden. The additional burden is simply that of coping with the *fact* of change itself. "Change" has become the status quo, and one manages differently when one stands on shifting sands rather than on cement.

Just to make things even more difficult, the context for planning is not only changing but expanding. At one time, the first-line nurse manager could work effectively if she knew what was happening in her local environment. Indeed, she might manage quite adequately if she simply knew her own organization inside-out. Today, that is not enough. A change in an administrative program at the federal level—Medicare reimbursement policy, for example—may radically readjust the resources that a manager receives to deliver care. Or the policy may affect the way she keeps records, the staff she may employ, or the nature of the patient who is placed with her facility.

One contextual factor that has not changed radically is the sex mix in the nursing profession. Male nurses have been and still are a small minority in the field. Because of this, we ask them to continue to show the flexibility they have already demonstrated by entering a "feminine career." The male reader is asked to adjust once more—to the feminine pronouns that this book adopts in recognition of the statistical norms.

Context, then, must be assessed locally, in one's own organization, on one's own work unit; and it must be assessed in larger environments up to and including the national and international. And it must be assessed with increasing frequency, so that one's notion of the environment is current and on target. The environment that matters is expanding in breadth and is shifting rapidly, but the questions to be posed are the same: What is happening in my environment that has the potential to affect care? What can I do about that environment? What can I change? What are the best ways to alter that environment? What elements of environment are outside of my control? How can I respond to the environment in the most productive manner?

To identify the context in which one works is not an easy task, for, indeed, there are numerous contexts, not just one. Immediately, there is the context in which one's assigned work unit partakes. The nature of the immediate environment will depend heavily on the design of the organization of which the nursing unit is a part. For most first-line managers, the organization will be one in which they are employees rather than owners. Much of the internal context will be determined by the organization's mission, goals, and tone.

While the first-line manager may influence these elements, they are not hers to determine single-handedly. There are many givens in her place of employment.

The manager's organization has its structural context, its emotive context, its web of relationships with other communities and other organizations. The context will be influenced by all the people concerned with the organization—its employees, its clients, its suppliers, its governors, its regulators, its various constituencies. The more knowledge that the first-line manager has of these numerous influencing clusters, the greater will be her understanding of why the organization is as it is.

Context extends as far as its effects reach. If rockets to the moon affect the organization, then they are part of its context. Of course, the context of Huntsville, Alabama, may not be the context of Des Moines, Iowa, but in a shrinking world the rocket set off in Huntsville could affect, albeit circuitously, the budget of the health care organization in Des Moines. One of the overriding themes of context is the increasing interrelatedness of our world.

And that increasing interrelatedness makes it likely that health care institutions will share some common contextual themes, some common demands, some common problems. Nationally, one common theme is the demand for cost control and increased productivity. In this environment, few organizations have been able to avoid a hard self-evaluation in terms of institutional fiscal accountability. Another contextual factor is the growing demand for improving quality of care, a swing away from the fiscal focus that has predominated for the last decade. The simultaneous imperatives of fiscal conservation and quality of care are the crux of most health care management decisions today.

Issues of context may be blatant or subtle; they may range from such pragmatic dictates as the allowable reimbursement for a patient stay to the enigmatic ethical problems created by new technologies of care. It is important for the first-line manager to recognize the predominant contextual variables of the times. And she must bear in mind how rapidly the context in which she practices can change. Today's problem, today's focus, becomes tomorrow's moot issue. Taking frequent stock and making insightful interpretations form an essential part of the effective manager's job.

GOALS

Goals are the formally and informally defined targets of an organization or a department. Goals represent the intentions, the purposes that the unit was designed to achieve. In previous eras, it was adequate to advise the nurse manager to set her goals as a first step in planning. Usually, that nurse manager took the context for granted; it underlay her planning without itself being considered. And usually the assumed context was resource-rich, allowing the manager to select goals based on their internal worthiness alone. Today it is not that simple. The changing context impacts on the ways in which the nurse manager sets goals. The interplay of context and goals is complex; the goals that the nurse manager selects may be partially dictated by the context in which care is delivered. Certainly the ways in which the manager's goals are conceptualized will be affected by the nature of the work to be done and the world surrounding it.

In our changing environment, some nurses are setting new goals for themselves and the profession. Nurses are involved in entrepreneurial efforts that could not have been envisioned in the society of a decade ago. The creating of competition in the health care world has opened new opportunities for the creative nurse with a good head for business.

Other nurses, including most nurse managers in traditional settings, find their goals constrained by the pinch of a society demanding greater cost stringency from the health care community. If cost is a dominant theme of context in health care delivery, quality of care is a dominant concern in the setting of goals.

In determining goals, the nurse manager not only decides what is to be achieved but also defines the standards that are to be met in the achievement of the goals. Standards capture goals in operational terms—that is, they prescribe how goals are to be achieved, they specify levels of achievement, or they offer concrete models against which actual achievement may be measured.

Often in the past, goal setting consisted of writing down idealized notions of care. Today's nurse manager has a better appreciation of the relationship between goals and the resources available to achieve them. She is realistic in selecting goals and standards appropriate to her environment. She recognizes that carefully set goals can be a stimulant to achievement. Idealized goals that represent an impossible dream serve only as disincentives; the noblest desires must be tempered by the realities of a situation. In health care as in other domains, one's vision of the good must sometimes compromise with one's understanding of the possible.

Differences between desirable and achievable goals often revolve around issues of resources. Resources, in turn, are constrained by the context in which they are acquired. Resources are most often reflected in costs. Concerns of quality versus cost containment are not easy to resolve. The friction created by the interplay of cost and quality has long been a problem for nurses and nurse managers desiring to provide quality care. Others in the society are now coming to appreciate more fully the dilemma, the conflict between goals for care and goals for economy. It is the particular challenge of the first-line manager to make clear the linkage between achievable goals and resources provided for their achievement.

The first-line manager sets goals of varying sorts. First there are goals for patients; these are reflected in standards of care and their related action plans. Additional goals are set for staff performance, staff professional growth, and for effective and efficient use of resources. Some goals will be primary, such as patient goals; other goals will be instrumental, or subordinate to higher-order goals. Inservice education, for example, is not provided merely for the inner satisfaction of staff but, primarily, to improve patient care.

Many instrumental goals relate to managerial effectiveness and efficiency. Goals for productivity can certainly not be neglected just because one has primary goals for excellence in care. The institution that neglects productivity goals will soon be bankrupt and in no position to meet its primary goals for patient care.

In today's environment, managerial and professional goals must be flexibly planned. Goals may need to be altered, dropped, or added as contextual and resource elements change. The first-line manager cannot, for example, set five-year goals and expect them to hold good, without modification, for the entire period. Today most first-line planning goals hold for shorter periods of time, and even goals of one year's duration will need to be reviewed periodically to assure that they still pertain. Strategic, or contingency, planning has replaced the more formalized management-by-objectives pattern of the past.

Setting of goals is a major requirement and challenge for the first-line manager. Her goals must be realistic and attainable under the circumstances; they must be worthy, both in themselves and in comparison with alternative proposals that were not selected as targets; and they must be of a level to assure the safety and integrity of those the manager serves. Goals are particularly important in a complex and changing environment. Without them, it is easy to forget where one is going.

RESOURCES

Resources are the physical, intellectual, and structural assets by which the work of an organization or a department is achieved. Resources were necessarily mentioned in the preceding discussion of goals, for goals are achieved through the judicious use of resources. In truth, it is impossible to isolate model elements (context, goals, resources, interplay) except as an intellectual endeavor. Resources of many kinds are combined in the delivery of nursing care—resources of intellect, creativity, manpower, materials, systems, and methods. Resources are the concrete and intellectual tools with which one achieves the job.

Most but not all resources can be equated with their costs for purposes of planning. The expert nurse, for example, costs more than the inexperienced one (or at least that is true if the pay scales are set fairly). Some resources, of course, simply cannot be purchased. The nurse who has a personality that brightens the patient's day has a quality that cannot be ordered and paid for.

The first major resource of the first-line manager is herself. How does the manager enhance her own performance? Specifically, how does she relate to others? How does she get the most from staff while augmenting their professionalism and enthusiasm rather than burning them out? How does the manager use the systems at her command? Does she create efficient means for getting the work done? Does she efficiently allocate her personal use of time by practicing effective delegation of staff? What sort of person is she? What sort of manager?

Staff members are the manager's most obvious and most critical resource. Nursing hours and human talents are the assets that will absorb much of the first-line manager's concern. These are costly resources, to be used with prudence. The subtle balance between meeting the human needs of staff and fulfilling organizational purposes is the responsibility of the first-line manager. It is not an easy balance to strike. The effective manager seeks ways to meet staff needs through achieving patient needs.

Methods and systems are sometimes overlooked as resources. The means whereby care tasks are assigned and completed on a unit are important resources within the control of the first-line manager. The selection of assignment systems, the structures set up for communication with others, the habits of work and interaction within a work group are resources that may be changed and improved if the manager remembers to consider them as resources. All elements of managed care are structural resources that the first-line manager may use to achieve her goals.

Material assets comprise another sort of resource. These include such nuts and bolts as equipment and supplies. Presence or absence of needed materials must be considered as well as the quality of the items. Associated services also affect the availability of such resources. Are supplies replenished when needed, in the amounts needed? Is equipment serviced efficiently when it is in disrepair?

Among the most problematic aspects of providing care at times are the human support services that are provided—or not provided—to nursing. For example, what services are supplied by a dietary department? In what ways do dietary activities interface with nursing responsibilities? Is there a transportation service for moving patients? Does the service work efficiently? What about housekeeping, pharmacy supply, security, laboratory, and so forth? Services provided poorly by others often cause extensive, unplanned extra use of nursing resources. The first-line manager, because of her location at the hub of patient services, must manage interactions with others as much as she manages her own resources. Otherwise, as custodian of the patient she may, ironically, find her staff servicing the units that were designed to assist nursing.

Space and architectural factors may also be considered as material resources. If staff have to traverse a long hall every time they need to reach a clean utility room, for example, nursing hours are affected. If a geriatric center lacks handrails on corridors used by patients, the architectural limitation clearly affects how one uses nursing resources. Even an aesthetically unattractive environment can create a psychological damper, depressing staff energies and achievement.

The general rule for management of resources is quite simple: Human and material resources should be utilized in ways that conserve them, while optimizing their effects. Resources must be husbanded, safeguarded, and used judiciously. But used they must be. When the expertise of a nurse is overlooked because she is not a socializer, for example, a potential resource is squandered. Sometimes a narrow definition of available resources represents limitations in the mind of the manager. Few of us take full account of the resources available in our environments. It is the first-line manager's job to see that staff are acquainted with and use the resources at hand.

The effective nurse manager has a realistic sense of what she can accomplish with a given set of resources. She is also able to determine what resources would be required in order to deliver a requested product, e.g., a given level of patient care, a new client service. Estimating the fit between resources and the task to be done (goal) is part of her job.

Substitutions are possible among and between resources in many instances. For example, nurses often find that creative and emotional resources enable them to excel in a crisis, to meet an emergency situation despite critical lacks of material or staff. Such substitute resources (drawing on critical emotional and energy reserves) might not solve the same problem, however, if the situation were to be prolonged. Different sorts of resources may compensate for the lack of a given resource. For example, a change in assignment system (structural resource) might compensate for an unexpected shortage in staff. Similarly, a move to a facility with improved space arrangements (physical resource) might decrease the number of staff required to complete the same number of tasks.

The effective manager sees resources everywhere: the shape of her patient care ward, the location of her office, the attitude of a department head. She sees and exploits resources where others see only givens or fail to see at all.

The effective manager also learns how and where to get the resources she needs. She learns the gentle art of acquisition. At the same time, she is realistic in assessing when certain resources will not be forthcoming in spite of her acquisitional effort and creativity, and she takes these limitations into account in setting her goals.

INTERPLAY OF MODEL ELEMENTS

It is obvious that context, goals, and resources interact at all times. Sometimes one element is the driving force, sometimes another. Changes in resources call for changes in goals, and vice versa. An altered context may reduce or enhance resources, or simply change the nature of the resources that are available. Striking a balance between the resources available and the goals to be achieved is critical. And both must fit with the given context if the effort is not to be in vain.

Since all aspects of this model are in dynamic movement, the effective manager of health care adopts a contingency model of management, which denies that any absolute rule or way to manage applies in all circumstances. A contingency model asserts that all elements interact and that understanding the circumstances of a specific case is essential to making—not the "right" managerial choice (there are no absolutes), but a *good* choice. To say that "it all depends" is not an excuse but an accurate assessment of the situation. The ability to interpret circumstances accurately is one key to effective management. The objective of the first-line manager is to optimize her resources in a given situation, within an accurately interpreted context, to achieve a wisely selected set of goals. Orchestrating the activity to achieve goals calls for dynamic and timely management. It is hoped that this book, and this model, will help the first-line manager to enhance her effectiveness in meeting that challenge.

part I

THE CONTEXT

Few things in life remain unchanged over time. Individuals, families, communities, and organizations grow and adapt according to events and conditions within the environment. Depending on its pace, and how it is understood, change can be almost imperceptible, taken as a matter of course, or sudden and dramatic, throwing everything into chaos. For example, the emergence of reimbursement for health care as an issue of national concern may be perceived as a new development or considered predictable, depending on one's knowledge of the political and economic factors in operation.

A successful manager is aware of her organization's environment and knows what is key to its continuing operation. The effective manager at any organizational level knows what elements in the environment are important to track. For example, health care executives who watch for Medicare policy changes are able to alert their organizations to legislative actions. In this way they move their organizations forward rather than leaving them unprepared. External forces—societal, political, economic, technological and legal—influence, to greater or lesser degrees, the context of health care.

Health care has moved beyond the control of the individual practitioner; the health care delivery system is affected by the interaction of many contradictory elements. The gradual introduction nationwide of a prospective payment system through diagnosis-related groups (DRGs) is an example. The institutions that assessed their environment and planned accordingly fared better when prospective payment regulations were finally imposed. Hospitals that were unprepared, and thus unable to compete, closed or were acquired by the larger, stronger hospitals or health care chains.

Despite the complexity of the health care system, it is necessary for organizations large and small to understand the factors that influence change. Inferences must be drawn from prevailing health care trends and policies if the organization is to take appropriate action.

1

The shift of patients out of acute care and into home care was a predictable outcome of the DRG system. The organizations that anticipated the trend and developed or expanded home care services successfully adapted to the introduction of prospective payment.

The course for an organization may be charted by its senior executives, but the implementation of organizational policies and procedures at the unit level is the responsibility of the nurse manager. If she understands why policies were developed, the first-line manager can explain their significance and provide leadership to staff in adjusting their practice to accommodate the new initiatives. The staff that is not informed of these changes is made to feel that the organization is acting without regard for them. In this case, they may interpret policy changes as negative detractions from their usual routine.

The first-line nurse manager is central to the control and direction of activities at the patient level. The development of attainable goals requires a knowledge of the nature of the organization and its available resources.

The nurse manager adjusts her strategies according to the context in which she operates. Just as the outside world is context in relation to the total agency, the rest of the organization beyond her own unit is context for the first-line manager. The characteristics of the organization (whether it is centralized or decentralized, controlled and autocratic versus open and participatory) will impinge directly on the nurse manager. Although the fundamentals of nursing care do not change, the specific management of them alters greatly with changes in the internal and external conditions. Assessing contextual realities, internal as well as external to the organization, brings order to what would otherwise be chaos in the delivery of nursing care.

The first-line nurse manager is the bridge between administration and staff. Her management is critical to the success of the organization, whether the setting is a hospital, clinic, HMO, or home care agency. It is under her direction that policy determinations are enacted. It is around this hub that the larger context of health care revolves.

chapter 1

The Nation and the World

First-line nurse managers should be cognizant of the major trends in health care that affect their delivery settings, their staff members, and the expectations placed on those staffs. Without a thorough knowledge of the forces at work in the environment, nurse managers will be hard pressed to provide the dynamic leadership needed to ensure that their staffs are providing quality care in a working environment acceptable to them.

Health care delivery in the United States is in the midst of a quiet revolution. At no time in the history of American health care have there been so many powerful, often contradictory forces exerting their influence. The politics and economics of health care have wrought enormous change in its delivery. The first-line nurse manager, regardless of setting, has experienced the effect of those forces on her environment. The interplay of health policy with the public and private financing of health care is constantly shaping and reshaping the context in which nurses deliver care.

For more than twenty years the federal government and the private sector have been looking for ways to contain spiraling health care costs. Wage controls, price controls, and certificate-of-need requirements for capital expenditures did not work. National health expenditures soared from $42 billion in 1965 to over $300 billion in the early 1980s, accounting for more than 10 percent of the country's gross national product.[1]

The incentives of cost-based reimbursement for patient care had stimulated growth and spending; the more lab tests performed on a patient during hospitalization, the more money hospitals received. Under the Reagan administration that picture changed. The government began to scrutinize closely the entitlement programs, such as Social Security and Medicare, which previous administrations had considered untouchable. To curb escalating costs, in 1982 Congress passed and the president signed the Tax Equity and Fiscal Responsibility Act (TEFRA), on which the prospective payment provisions of the

Social Security Amendments (P.L. 98-21) were based. This act regulates payment of hospital bills reimbursed under Medicare. By paying hospitals predetermined fees for each discharged patient based on diagnosis-related groups (DRGs), the prospective payment system (PPS) places the onus on hospitals to be more efficient.

The developers of the DRG classification system grouped patients according to their medical diagnosis and treatments. Their purpose was to group patients who used similar amounts of hospital resources.

Under the prospective payment system, fixed prices are established in advance for hospital services based on a patient's DRG classification. Medicare does not compensate hospitals for actual costs incurred in services that are in excess of DRG-based system rates. Therefore, if a hospital overspends, it foots the bill. The hospital cannot appeal for higher payments, nor can it charge Medicare patients more than the pre-assigned deductible. If the hospital contains its costs, it benefits from surpluses; if it does not, it suffers losses. Through PPS, the government has greatly influenced hospital activities, providing a powerful incentive for hospitals to create and use internal cost controls.

Monitoring the use of manpower and materials is essential to effective management. Managers who base decisions on an integration of clinical and financial data are more likely to reach a balance between quality of care and sound economics. As in every area of life, there will be winners and losers. Providers who can control costs while maintaining quality will be the winners in the health care market. Prior to prospective payment, hospitals, physicians, and patients were largely unconstrained in their use of resources; now two incentives are well recognized—minimizing the time of treatment per patient admission and expanding the number of admissions.

The push to shorten the length of hospital stays leads to patients being sent home "quicker and sicker." This has a tremendous impact on the home care industry, as patients and providers demand more availability of home care services. An additional consequence is the rapid expansion of high technology into the home. The burden on agencies is to manage the explosive growth and to provide the full range of services being promoted. Home health care has emerged as a viable and, to many, a preferable alternative to hospitalization.

IMPACT ON THE CONSUMER

In the past, the third-party retroactive financing of health care through Medicare, Medicaid, and private health insurance cushioned the consumer from the true cost of health care and led to a demand for increased medical technology and interventions without concern for price. In addition, the public funding of health care through Medicare for the elderly and Medicaid for the indigent fostered the growing belief that health care was a socially ensured right. One consequence was that health care took on a life of its own, independent of cost and income pressures. The cost-containment measures of the 1980s have begun to challenge the perception of health care as a right.

Inevitably the new system has caused displacements and manipulations of the system. Some institutions, in order to keep profits high, discourage admission of the patient who, due to severity of illness, uses a disproportionate amount of resources. This circumstance impacts, for example, on community cancer centers. The cost of treatment for rare cancers far exceeds the government allowance. While the typical cost for a leukemia patient (DRG 403) is between $4,000 and $5,000, hospitalization for a patient with adult myelocytic leukemia, a rare type, is initially 30 days and results in a bill of $35,000 to $40,000.[2] Community cancer centers cannot afford these large deficits. Consequently, patients are shifted to large medical centers that are better able to absorb the losses. These situations present difficult choices, not only to medical staffs but also to patients. Shifting care from community to medical centers may require expenditures for travel and long absences from families and the support they provide.

Cost control may place greater burdens on health care consumers than mere inconvenience. Dr. Schwartz, professor of medicine at Tufts University and an advisor to the Health Policy Program at the Rand Corporation, is concerned that rationing of health care is inevitable. " . . . it must be recognized that any successful and sustained reduction in resources flowing to hospitals eventually will require the denial of some potentially beneficial care to some patients."[3]

Rationing and restricting of available health care is not yet a reality for most patients. In principle, rationing can be forestalled. First, it will require an educated public. Patients have been cushioned from the high cost of hospital care by various forms of health insurance. A lack of concern for price, coupled with an unrealistic expectation that something more can always be done, have created a demanding population. Altering their attitudes will not be easy. There have to be incentives for consumers to economize on health care spending and utilization. Only if consumers pay more directly for health care will they consume fewer health care services.

HEALTH AS A BUSINESS

The federal government and business are the two biggest buyers of health care—the government for the recipients of Medicare and Medicaid, business for its employees. As the two principal payers they intend to contain the rate of growth in health care spending, and it is within their power to do so. In 1985 Medicare disallowed fourteen percent of payments to hospitals in New York City on the grounds that the hospitalizations were unnecessarily prolonged.[4] Hospitals cannot sustain such losses and survive; for them, this means an end to business as usual. Health care has become a commodity, subject to the same fluctuations of supply and demand and pressures of pricing as other goods and services.

Health care organizations are focusing on improving their bottom-line financial statements to attract investors and relying on their associations, such as the American Hospital Association, to monitor political trends and to lobby for more favorable health care legislation. The need to acquire capital has moved hospital financing efforts away from Washington and onto Wall Street, where hospitals and health maintenance organizations search for funds to fuel their mergers and acquisitions. Whether or not DRGs stay as the cornerstone of PPS remains to be seen, but one thing is sure: The nation's health care delivery system will never be the same.

One very clear long-run trend of cost containment is the increasing importance of delivery systems outside of hospitals. Home care agencies are receiving the burden of patients discharged from hospitals earlier than ever before. Indeed, home care is becoming acute care, not just care of patients who are convalescing or those with chronic diseases. In addition to the increased demand for home care, other outpatient facilities have proliferated in competition for the health care dollar. As the competition increases hospitals are becoming more sensitive to the marketplace and its changing conditions. As hospitals try to secure their market share, many are diversifying and developing their own outpatient services. They are establishing day surgery units, alcohol treatment centers, free-standing emergency centers, and mobile mammography and CT scanning units, among other services.

Another commercially profitable tactic is for institutions to expand into new business opportunities. Several large for-profit hospitals are investing in business ventures unrelated to health care, such as real estate development. Johnson, in 1983, predicted that by the year 2000 super corporations, requiring advanced managerial and financial expertise, would dominate the health care delivery system.[5] Already, successful for-profit chains use their competitive edge to make better deals and enhance their standing in the capital marketplace.

MARKETING TO THE CONSUMER

Economic developments encourage health care providers to move to a consumer orientation. Hospitals are embracing marketing programs as they strive to attract new client populations. With more options available, health care is becoming a buyer's market. Consumers also become cost-conscious when they are forced to pay part of the cost, and gradually consumers are assuming more direct payment for health care. Since the onset of cost containment, not only has the government increased the Medicare deductible but private insurers and employers have made similar adjustments.

To market their services more effectively, hospitals are trying to find out what makes consumers choose one institution over another and how their services measure up. While the pressure is on to minimize costs, the competition among hospitals and doctors to attract patients runs counter to that effort. Inguazo and Harju have shown that patients are reluctant to select a hospital based on price and that the availability of state-of-the-art technology is a major factor in their choice.[6] This would support the notion that consumers are oriented toward wanting the best, regardless of cost. Hospitals are thus willing to acquire cost-increasing technologies that are viewed as quality-enhancing by the consumer. The same study analyzing consumer attitudes according to demographic location revealed a difference in attitude in the Western United States, however.

Many individuals in the West belong to health maintenance organizations (HMOs), which offer comprehensive health services for prenegotiated fees. In those areas, consumers were quite sensitive to hospital costs.[7] Health care is being transformed from an industry dominated by professionals to one in which purchaser power wields influence. Attitudes and expectations are being altered as consumers evaluate their options in terms of cost and quality.

Whether their primary interest be cost or quality of services, consumers' interest in health care is growing. The HMO is an appealing organization to many consumers because of its emphasis on wellness. Keeping clients healthy reduces resource use and increases profits in an HMO. It is estimated that HMOs may reduce hospital days for their members by as much as thirty to forty percent. The growth in the HMO segment of the health care industry is likely to influence physician practice significantly. With surplus of physicians predicted by the year 2000, competition for positions will heat up, enhancing the ability of HMOs to recruit physicians as salaried staff.

QUALITY ISSUES

While many critics doubt that the changes in health care have resulted in higher quality of care or better health outcomes for patients, the purchasers of health care are demanding that providers demonstrate how they measure and control for quality. Dr. William Roper, administrator of the Health Care Financing Administration, (HCFA), predicted that

[HCFA is] attempting to define, then to measure, and finally to ensure the quality of care. In fact, I believe that this, the third decade of Medicare, will have quality as the premier issue. . . . The issues of access and costs remain important but now we have a three-pronged agenda for Medicare policy discussion: access, cost, and quality.[8]

To monitor the health care system, HCFA has contracted with local peer review organizations (PROs) to review claims for Medicare services to determine the validity of each diagnosis, quality of care, appropriateness of admissions and discharges, and the handling of outlier and transfer cases. Based on objective performance criteria, PROs have the authority to recommend sanctions if violations by a provider or a practitioner have been identified.

In the absence of a sound measurement system HCFA, as an answer to business and consumer groups, is making hospital mortality data public on a regular basis. It is predictable that such hospital-specific data will be analyzed by consumers trying to assess the quality of their local hospitals.

EFFECTS OF CHANGES ON PHYSICIANS AND NURSES

Mindful of the autonomy of the medical profession, advocates of regulation have aimed at indirect controls through hospitals rather than attempt to dictate medical practice. Tighter controls, necessitated by economics, threaten to change this situation. In a competitive environment the focus is on the bottom line; there is greater incentive to eliminate procedures that yield no perceptible benefit. For example, in the past physicians used extensive diagnostic tests to rule out all possibilities. The physician attitude "If you can do something, do it" has been moderated to "Will it benefit the patient, and at what cost?"

Outside interests are intervening in medical practice. While some feel this is long overdue, physicians express concern about quality being sacrificed for cost control. Further, the physician is caught between the demand that he not do unnecessary testing and the threat of a law suit if he doesn't order a test. It is a difficult era for the physician.

The supply of and demand for health care professionals, especially physicians and nurses, impacts directly on the delivery of health care. Although the U.S. Government Data from the Division of Nursing in 1984 predicted a balance in the supply and demand of nurses, time has not borne this out.[9] Despite the fact that more nurses are in the work force than at any time in the past, hospitals indicate a measurable increase in vacant positions and report that they are staying vacant longer.

It is likely that several factors contribute to this national trend: increased acuity of the inpatient population; increased employment of nurse practitioners in community and home health nursing; employment opportunities outside of the direct care setting, such as in quality assurance; and wage scales not commensurate with the demands of the job.

The National League for Nursing's 1986 nursing student census indicates an overall decline of 16 percent in total nursing school enrollments since 1980. This represents a loss of over 37,000 students in just six years. Enrollments in basic baccalaureate nursing programs dropped from 95,858 to 81,602 in the last six years, while associate degree program enrollments declined 15 percent. The trend away from diploma education has continued, with a report of more school closings. Since 1980 the number of diploma schools has gone from 311 to 238, a drop of 23 percent.[10]

As a female-dominated profession, nursing has been adversely affected by societal forces such as the women's movement. Nursing was once one of the few rewarding careers open to women; now it competes with a growing number of rewarding and more financially attractive options. Strategies to address the nursing shortage are being developed. The outcomes will depend on nursing's ability to influence economic and societal forces and to adapt accordingly.

To deal with scarce nursing resources, nurse managers are asked to adjust staffing patterns that provide for the efficient and appropriate use of nursing personnel. At some major medical centers, differentiated practice models reportedly improve nursing retention and patient care. Nursing groups are contracting with hospitals to provide nursing services, while the nurses employed are offered a share in the profits.

Nurse executives are adopting a business attitude as they compete for their share of the health dollar. Given that nursing generally accounts for 40 percent of a hospital's operating budget, it is increasingly important to document the cost effectiveness of professional nursing care.

With the development of clinical data systems, nurse managers can document how quality nursing care can shorten hospital stays. According to DRG regulations the shorter the stay the more profit accrues to the hospital. Working in concert with organizational goals enhances nursing's position and power; it thus becomes a pro-active force in the organization.

The first-line manager teaches her staff to adjust their practice to the economic realities. Goals are determined based on an assessment of available resources. In an environment where both manpower and material resources are constrained, the nurse must distinguish necessary and achievable tasks from the ideal. Physicians, health care professionals, and patients need to be educated as to their own real and unreal expectations of nursing.

The future of health care holds many uncertainties. However, as new systems evolve, opportunities for nursing continue to present themselves. Nurses are finding their skills suited to a managed-care environment. Directing the total care of patients from admission through discharge to outpatient follow-up allows the nurse autonomy and utilizes her ability to operate as a generalist.

Nurses with administrative, financial, and clinical skills are being employed in management positions as controllers, auditors, and evaluators. In addition, the recent attention to health promotion is stepping up the marketing of wellness programs. It has been demonstrated that individuals can do more to improve their own health than can medical intervention. Califano believes that the 25 percent drop in deaths resulting from coronary heart disease is primarily attributable to such improved habits as healthier diets, regular exercise regimens, and efforts to stop smoking.[11]

Opportunities for nurses in preventive care are increasing. In some organizations nurses are employed as consultants or independent contractors to design and manage health promotion programs. Corporations recognize that wellness programs save them money and reduce absenteeism. Johnson and Johnson's "Live for Life" program is over seven years old and has been operated at no net cost to Johnson and Johnson for over four years.[12] It is estimated that the program has reduced absenteeism by eighteen percent.

The first-line manager, through her intimate knowledge of her immediate surroundings, has a unique opportunity to participate in shaping and implementing policies and procedures for her unit and staff. Issues and conditions that affect the institution as a whole filter down inevitably to the work unit. Health care facilities, and hospitals in particular, are highly demanding environments requiring adherence to set policies and procedures. The pressure is on nurses to accomplish specified patient outcomes regardless of internal and external forces. It is up to the first-line nurse manager to provide an atmosphere that supports and motivates the staff to meet those demands.

SUMMARY

The context of health care is constantly shifting according to prevailing trends. Therefore, all predictions regarding the long-range effects of new policy initiatives are specious. This makes it difficult to identify key indicators in formulating organizational programs and policies. The one thing that is certain is change. Systems and the management of systems have to accommodate change whether it be opportune or not. As Peters notes in *Thriving on Chaos*, "Failure today is failure to change."[13]

NOTES

1. Division of National Cost Estimates, Office of the Actuary Health Care Financing Administration, "National Health Expenditures, 1986–2000," *Health Care Financing Review* 8, no. 4 (Summer 1987): 25.

2. K.A. Fackelmann, "Community Cancer Centers Warn of Hard Times Ahead Under DRGs," *Modern Healthcare* 14, no. 15 (June 1984): 56.

3. H.J. Aaron and W.B. Schwartz, "Hospital Cost Control: A Bitter Pill to Swallow," *Harvard Business Review* 63, no. 2 (March–April 1985): 167.

4. R. Sullivan, "Decline in Hospital Use Tied to New U.S. Policies," *New York Times* (April 16, 1985): 1, B20.

5. R.L. Johnson, "Era of Responsibility: Competition Challenges CEO's To Be Tough-minded And To Take Risks," *Hospitals* 57, no. 2 (January 1983): 56.

6. J.M. Inguanzo and M. Harju, "What Makes Consumers Select a Hospital," *Hospitals* 59, no. 4, (March 16, 1985): 94.

7. J.M. Inguanzo and M. Harju, "Are Consumers Sensitive to Hospital Costs?" *Hospitals* 59, no. 3 (February 1, 1985): 68.

8. William L. Roper, "The Medicare Program of Tomorrow—An Insider's View," *Nursing and Health Care* 8, no. 7 (September 1987): 44.

9. U.S. Department of Health & Human Services, *Fifth Report to the President & Congress on the Status of Health Personnel* (Rockville, MD: DHHS Publications, March 1986), pp 10-67.

10. P. Rosenfeld, *Nursing Student Census with Policy Implications 1987* (New York: National League for Nursing, 1988).

11. Joseph A. Califano, *America's Health Care Revolution: Who Lives? Who Dies? Who Pays?* (New York: Random House, 1986), p. 187.

12. "Wellness Industry Takes New Direction," *McGraw Hill's Health Business* 1, no. 4 (August 1, 1986): 2T.

13. T. Peters, *Thriving on Chaos* (New York: Alfred A. Knopf, Inc., 1987) p. 401.

BIBLIOGRAPHY

Aaron, H.J., and Schwartz, W.B. *The Painful Prescription.* Washington, DC: Brookings Institution, 1984.

Enthoven, A., and Kronick, R. "Competition 101: Managing Demand to Get Quality Care." *Business and Health* 5, no. 5, March 1988.

Perspectives in Nursing—1987-1989. New York: National League for Nursing, 1988.

Roncoli, M., and Whitney, F. "The Limits of Medicine Spell Opportunities for Nursing." *Nursing and Health Care* 7, no. 10, December 1986.

chapter 2

The Organizational World

TRADITIONAL AND EMERGING SYSTEMS

Health care has traditionally been organized around the physician and the hospital. Prior to the onset of prospective payment, hospitals were paid for all costs incurred. Admission, treatments, procedures and tests, and length of stay were determined by the physician. For instance, the common practice of admitting patients overnight for a series of tests such as a gastro-intestinal x-ray series was often based on convenience, not on cost. The assumption, usually correct, was that charges would be viewed as negligible and therefore not questioned by such insurance carriers as Medicare or Blue Cross and Blue Shield.

The onset of DRGs has altered patterns of hospital utilization. Admissions, treatment plans, and discharges are now monitored to assure the most efficient and cost-effective use of resources. Let us look at the previous example under the prospective payment system. First, the admitting physician is required to justify the overnight admission of a patient for a G.I. series based on medical need, not convenience. If the physician does not adhere to this procedure, the hospital will not be reimbursed. Should the admission be allowed, the physician will need to document the reasons for the overnight admission in the record; if the peer review organization does not concur that the admission was medically necessary, reimbursement for the hospitalization can still be disallowed.

Under the new rules, fewer patients are admitted to hospitals, and there has been an overall decline in length of stay. Nationwide, this has resulted in hospitals experiencing reduced inpatient census and higher acuity rates (sicker patients). This in turn has led to competition among hospitals for patients and exploration of the most cost-effective ways to care for those patients. Services such as x-ray, laboratories, and even surgical procedures are moving to outpatient locations, where care can be delivered at lower cost.

In the past, hospitals focused on purchasing the latest technology, without regard to cost effectiveness. This strategy was a means to attract physicians, who would in turn maintain a lucrative flow of patient admissions. The new system has shifted attention to expanding outpatient services and product lines, thus adapting to the restrictions on cost. The aim is to attract and keep consumers who come to an institution for one service and, if satisfied, return for all their health care needs. This has spurred hospitals to offer a broad range of services and quality care at a good price.

The push is on for health care systems to adapt to economic forces. The trend away from inpatient care has health care institutions looking to diversify. Hospitals are reorganizing, forming alliances with home care agencies and outpatient centers. If these services are already contained within the hospital, the strategy is to move them out and establish them as separate subsidiaries of a larger parent organization. This often allows the hospital to charge off costs at a different rate than if these services had remained a part of the hospital.

The Growth of Alternative Delivery Systems

With the current emphasis on outpatient and health promotion services, such organizations as HMOs, PPOs, individual practice associations (IPAs), and multi-hospital corporations are developing as possible solutions to the severely challenged traditional hospital delivery system. The unprecedented choice of health care provider arrangements available is as bewildering to the health care professional as it is to the consumer.

HMOs are probably the most familiar of the several alternative delivery systems that have recently sprung up. HMOs are best described as prepaid health plans in which a full array of health care services is offered to enrollees on a contractual basis for a prenegotiated fee. The contract outlines specific rules and procedures designed to ensure appropriate care and to protect payers against overutilization of expensive inpatient services. There are several variations in the way health maintenance organizations are internally structured. In a staff model the physicians are salaried employees along with nurses, x-ray technicians, and social workers; they do not share in the financial risks nor in the possible rewards.

In an independent practice association (IPA), privately practicing physicians own the HMO plan and contribute to the risk pool (monies to be used if expenses of the plan exceed the budget, or to be shared if costs are less). By the end of 1986, IPAs were the most prevalent type of HMO, representing more than 58 percent of all HMOs in operation.[1] The other types of HMOs are the group model and the network model. The group model contracts with an independent multi-specialty physician group for medical services, while the network model contracts for services with two or more large physician groups.

The preferred provider organization is yet another alternative delivery system that is gaining ground. Here the insurer contracts with providers who offer the insurer a discounted rate for services. The insured consumer, then, is expected to use these providers. The combination of a prepayment plan with freedom of choice as to provider makes PPOs an increasingly popular option with employers. Under these plans, consumers have the option of choosing a physician or hospital not designated by the PPO. However, because the PPO has negotiated a certain fee for services, any difference in cost is borne directly by the consumer. The risk to the employer is relatively limited, and employees are not locked into designated health care professionals and physicians.

In order to compete, hospitals are expanding beyond their traditional roles to become multi-service enterprises. Hospitals may develop these additional health care components as separate subsidiaries or maintain them as divisions within the organizations. These creative financial arrangements are enabling hospitals to diversify, generate new sources of revenue, and attract new patient populations. In smaller communities, hospitals are attracting patients by offering a wide array of services in a variety of settings: traditional home care, respite care for the elderly at a day care center, mobile x-ray units at the shopping mall.

A Managed-Care Environment

These innovative care delivery systems offer a dramatic change from the traditional fee-for-service system, under which increased specialization in medicine and health fostered a fragmented approach to client health needs. Little attention was given to coordinating services between specialists, inpatient and outpatient settings, and different treatment modalities. Consequently, tests were often repeated unnecessarily, and treatments would sometimes overlap or conflict, as when prescriptions received from different providers might be incompatible. This duplication of effort came at a high price, with each sector demanding payment for services given.

Understandably, insurance programs, employers, and consumers alike support less costly approaches such as HMOs. HMOs commit to providing all health care for a set fee. Through a system of contractual arrangements with acute care hospitals, surgical centers, emergency centers, home health agencies, nursing homes, pharmacies, and primary care and specialty physicians, HMOs control, regulate, and coordinate the services their clients receive.

This means more cooperation between providers and payers, more awareness of quality of care as it relates to cost, and, one hopes, better outcomes for the client. According to most HMO plans, clients are restricted to the services provided by the health plan and to the health professionals, hospitals, and agencies that participate in the plan.

With competition on the rise, physicians, hospitals, home care agencies, and freestanding clinics find it advantageous to contract with several HMOs to increase their share of clients. The fear that quality will be sacrificed to contain costs has put HMOs under pressure to measure and display the quality of health care they provide.[2] This may lead HMOs to be more selective about providers with whom they contract. The implication is that HMOs are in a position to demand measurable standards of care and quality.

A 1984 Harris survey of public, employer, and physician opinion revealed that members' overall satisfaction with HMO services exceeded nonmembers' satisfaction with the traditional system.[3] While the attention given to cost containment by both public and private sectors is a major factor contributing to the sizable proportion of Americans now enrolled in HMOs, only as long as HMOs remain attractive to members relative to price and quality of care will they continue to grow.

The emphasis by health insurance programs on noninstitutional alternatives has fueled phenomenal growth in the HMO industry. Since 1984 the number of HMOs has increased by 64 percent, rising from 419 to 688 in 1986. Correspondingly, enrollment grew by 60 percent, with over 26.5 million individuals enrolled in some type of HMO by the end of 1986. It is projected that by 1990 enrollment will be almost 45 million, an increase of nearly 68 percent in just four years.[4]

The Institutional Environment

Hospitals and other health care settings are reorganizing their operations to better advantage. The trend is from a centralized to a decentralized organizational structure along with a participatory style of management that creates an environment conducive to innovation, creativity, and commitment. In the centralized model, control is concentrated and directed along a clearly outlined chain of command. In a decentralized organization authority is extended to many. While a chain of command still exists, individual accountability of each member is stressed; there is broader involvement in developing organizational policies, greater flexibility in the assignment of tasks, and openness in communication is encouraged.

Health care organizations are learning to market their services by emphasizing their vision of what health care can be. An ad for a freestanding emergency center states: "Our commitment is to deliver the highest quality emergency medical care with superior management systems." This is an example in which the statement of the mission is concise, encompassing, and creates a picture of excellence. It challenges staff to deliver quality care and directs management to provide the wherewithal.

The key ideas of the mission seldom change, but the style of delivery undergoes alterations over time. The overall responsiveness of organizational systems to new goals and delivery models depends on staff having a clear understanding of what the organization is trying to achieve. The philosophy, purpose, and objectives of the nursing division are developed in concert with the changing and increasingly competitive health care environment. Together they provide a starting point for the design of managerial structures, and their message should be explicit in the day-to-day operations of the division.

Nursing in a Changed Environment

In the last decade, radical shifts in health care delivery have been dictated by economic interests. The push to revolutionize health care has met with firm resistance; the underlying desire is to maintain the system's status quo. Consequently, changes produced are often erratic and ill-conceived from the perspective of developing a quality health care system at a reasonable cost and with a reasonable profit for providers.

The alternative delivery systems described earlier grew out of economic, political, and structural necessity. These managed-care initiatives are characterized by a high capacity for risk-taking, innovation, and entrepreneurship. They are in marked contrast to the more traditional hospital, which operated in a bureaucratically hierarchial and conservative style.

Nursing's challenge is to keep pace with this evolving and, at times, quixotic health care environment. While nursing must support the overall mission of the organization, its approach should be grounded in nursing's values and beliefs as to what constitutes professional, cost-effective, quality nursing care. The philosophy and goals of the nursing division provide a basis for organizational and intradivisional decision making: They outline the relationship of nursing to the overall organization, define what nursing is, point out its unique contribution to the organization, and affirm its concern with helping people to retain and regain health.

The Nursing Division

The nursing division operates within the broader context of the organization; nursing's structure, management style, philosophy, and objectives should be in congruence with the overall environment. Examples of questions the nurse manager should ask in examining how nursing fits in the broader organizational schema include: Do nurses participate in policy development at the organizational level? What degree of autonomy does the nursing division have? Is authority in the nursing division centralized or decentralized? To whom does the nurse manager report? How often does she interact with the vice-president or director of nursing? What is the philosophy of the nursing division *via à vis* the organization? Does the head nurse have authority to hire and fire? How are new ideas received? How is change implemented?

The major operating practices of a nursing division characterize it within the organization. These practices structure the work of the division and are, for the most part, encapsulated in the division's operating documents. These documents serve as valuable reference sources to the nurses who practice in the organization. Therefore, they should be kept current to reflect the present reality of nursing department operations. Only a few of these will be discussed here; they are the nursing division philosophy, purpose, objectives, policies, and practices. A taxonomy of divisional operations in a typical operating system is shown below.

- philosophy
- purpose
- objectives
- organization structure
- standards of nursing practice
- standards of care
- budget and control systems
- staffing, scheduling, assigning system
- managerial report systems
- divisional policies
- personnel policies and programs
- job descriptions
- performance evaluations
- quality assurance
- patient classification systems
- procedures
- practices (formalized and informal)

This taxonomy is not meant to be comprehensive; it is necessarily incomplete since every nursing division is likely to have unique operations.

Philosophy, Purpose, and Objectives: Goals for the Future

The philosophy, purpose, and objectives of a nursing division provide the framework for all further plans and activities within the division. The philosophy states those values and beliefs that influence the practice of nursing in the particular institution. The purpose states the reason this particular nursing division exists, that is, the intent that it serves. The objectives are criteria that have been identified as necessary and sufficient subordinate goals for achievement of the purpose(s) of the division.

Determining the philosophy of the nursing division usually is the first operational task. The philosophy is an individualized belief system that characterizes the nursing practice in the institution and directs individuals toward achievement of their purpose. Too often, the nursing philosophy is thought of as an abstract, generalized statement. On the contrary, it should be a specific statement that represents the values and beliefs of the given institution. It creates a climate for achieving professional excellence by stressing high standards.

One does not need to be a philosopher to express ideations underlying nursing practice. The philosophy simply represents the central beliefs and values of the division relative to nursing and nursing practice. Philosophies are not right or wrong, and their content varies from institution to institution, depending on what values are perceived as central to nursing. If a specific nursing theory is used in an institution, it should be noted in the philosophy. It is difficult to devise a nursing philosophy without talking about what nursing is perceived to be, whether or not a specific nursing theory is adopted. Philosophies typically address how nursing relates to the patient and to the particular organization. If in-service education is a major goal, the philosophy may include values specific to education. Relation of the division to professional nursing, to nursing research, to other health professionals, and to society in general are often found in nursing philosophies. A clear philosophical statement contributes to its being realized in day-to-day operations; it should pervade the practice environment.

The purpose of the nursing division is usually the next operational determination. Some argue that the order should be reversed, with philosophy determined after the purpose(s) of the nursing division. In practice, the philosophy and purpose interact and influence each other, so in one sense neither precedes the other. As with the philosophy, the purpose should reflect the realities of the institution. One must guard against the tendency to construct an idealistic purpose rather than an operational one. For example, a nursing division that claims "comprehensive nursing care" as its purpose is usually being idealistic. Such an assertion requires that comprehensive nursing care be defined and that evidence substantiate the possibility of giving this level of care within the institution. Without such verification, "comprehensive nursing care" remains a slogan with little impact on actual nursing operations.

The worded statement of purpose may be given from several different perspectives. First, it may state the purpose of the nursing division *qua* organization, that is, the desired *structure* that provides for and controls nursing services. The adoption of this focus could be expressed as follows: "The purpose of this nursing division is to provide nursing services in a cost-effective manner for all patients admitted to the institution." A second option is to word the purpose so as to describe the *process* of nursing desired. In this case, the purpose envisions a particular concept of nursing as its goal: "The purpose of this nursing division is to provide problem-centered nursing care for each patient." Other purpose statements are worded in terms of desired patient *outcomes*: "The purpose of this nursing division is to ensure that each patient attains satisfactory health recovery and optimal health maintenance." Some statements of purpose choose to include all of these perspectives: structure, process, and outcome.

According to the management style of the organization, its size, and its structure, the nurse manager may have more or less leeway in developing the divisions's philosophy and purpose, and in defining the boundaries of nursing's role. For example, in establishing a philosophy for a health maintenance organization, the nurse manager may emphasize the nurse's role as patient advocate.

The nursing division's philosophy and purpose are usually elaborated into a number of specific objectives. Otherwise, they remain good intentions that are not operationalized at the unit level. According to Drucker objectives are commitments through which the mission of the organization is achieved; they set standards against which performance is to be measured.[5]

Objectives allow staff to focus their efforts rather than trying to do everything at once. Hence, certain objectives are selected for special attention, with the aim of improving the related nursing practices. Focus objectives may be selected yearly, and their selection should be based on the present state of the nursing division. Usually these objectives are selected for the purpose of bolstering known weak spots in practice. Some focus objectives may also be selected to improve on strengths or to develop special interests.

It is important that objectives be operational and translate into specific targets and assignments. Suppose, for example, that a pediatric clinic has a focus objective of improving parent learning about child nutrition. The clinic should plan activities likely to bring about attainment of this goal. Identifying critical objectives makes it possible to allocate resources and efforts appropriately. For example, the head nurse is accountable for seeing that all patient care is planned, organized, and directed by a professional nurse. At the unit level, the nurse manager develops goals that achieve the objectives of the division and support the overall mission of the institution.

Philosophy, purpose, and objectives are meaningless if they are not carried down to the level of concrete activities. *Even well designed objectives will not implement themselves.* Given the quickened pace of change, the nursing division's philosophies and goals need regular review to be kept current. Lengthy statements that do not address the critical areas confronting the nursing division cannot provide direction or motivate staff performance.

New Goals

At all levels of the organization, nurses should have planned strategies that accommodate the reality of cost containment without endangering the delivery of quality nursing care. In acute care settings there is pressure to implement cost-cutting measures rapidly with minimal disruption to services. In the community, nurses are required to quantify their care according to reimbursement policies.

Nursing is critical to the operation of health care institutions—herein lies both its opportunity and vulnerability. The opportunity is to prove its worth through innovative adaptations, because when nursing is not part of the solution, it is an easy target for budget reduction.

As institutions reorganize to strengthen and expand their services, nursing has the opportunity to advance its position in the organization. Nursing administrators are examining their departments from a new perspective—a business perspective. Nurses, not unlike the institutions in which they work, are competing for their share of the health care dollar. As one of the most labor-intensive areas, nursing is vulnerable to cost-cutting measures and reduced resources. In both acute care and community health settings nurses are responding to the cost containment imperative.

Various models have been developed to cost out nursing services to emphasize nursing's profitability rather than expense. Research has proven that nursing care can reduce costs by preventing infections and reducing length of stay. Nurses are actively involved in the planning and development of quality assurance programs to identify problem areas and improve patient care. Such measures underscore nursing's significant contribution to the organization.

For the first time nursing is examining how it can market its services, and thereby market the hospital, HMO, or home care agency. Nursing departments are looking at their potential to develop new services and programs quickly. Product-line management is one approach being utilized. For example, nursing can market an innovative in-service program to be packaged and sold to other nursing organizations, and special health promotion programs can be designed for patients and members of the community. Such initiatives creatively allocate limited resources and generate new sources of revenue.

SUMMARY

Nursing aligns itself with the organization by developing a philosophy and objectives that are in concert with the goals of the organization. The philosophy and purpose of the nursing division should be periodically assessed in light of significant trends in health care and their expected impact on nursing and the organization. If the department is to advance and grow over time, the statement should be future-oriented and allow for anticipated change. The message should be clear, concise, and visible in the operation of the division at all levels.

The first-line nurse manager who understands the goals of the organization, and who articulates them clearly and effectively to her staff through her statements of purpose and objectives, will be best able to meet the challenges presented by the chaotic marketplace of health care delivery.

NOTES

1. *Marion Managed Care Digest* (Kansas City Missouri: Marion Laboratories, 1987), p. 8.
2. Peter Boland. "Trends in Second Generation PPOs," *Health Affairs* 6, no. 4 (Winter 1987): 75.
3. H. Taylor and M. Kagay. "The HMO Report Card," *Health Affairs* 5, no. 1 (Spring 1986): 83.
4. *Marion Managed Care Digest*, p. 9.
5. Peter F. Drucker, *Management, Tasks, Responsibilities, Practices* (New York: Harper & Row, 1974), p. 99.

BIBLIOGRAPHY

American Academy of Nursing. Task Force on Nursing Practice in Hospitals. *Magnet Hospitals*. Kansas City, MO: American Nurses' Association, 1983.

Casanova, G. "Developing and Writing Policy." *Supervisor Nurse* 3, no. 4 (1972): 62.

Moore, M.A. "Philosophy, Purpose, and Objectives: Why Do We Have Them?" *JONA 1*, no. 3 (1971): 9.

National Commission on Nursing. *Summary Report and Recommendations*. Chicago: Hospital Research and Educational Trust, 1983.

Okafor, H.I. "Hospital Policies and Procedures: Even the System Needs a System." In *Communicating Effectively*, edited by A.J. Huntsman and J.L. Binger. Wakefield, MA: Nursing Resources, 1981.

Porter-O'Grady, T. *Creative Nursing Administration*. Rockville, ND: Aspen Publishers, Inc., 1986.

Rosenberg, C.E. *The Care of Strangers*. New York: Basic Books, 1987.

THE GOALS

Goals have always been important in nursing management. Often the goals of the first-line manager are self-evident: They are concerned with meeting the day-to-day problems presented by patients and staff. The obvious needs of patients and staff can be seen as dictating—or strongly suggesting—what the goals of the first-line nurse manager should be. These problem-dictated, resolution-seeking intentions are goals in the practical sense. They represent the informal aims of the first-line manager; they stem from the day-to-day pressures that direct her actions and choices. Since the first-line management situation takes place in an environment that is to some degree unpredictable, these many evanescent, changing goals will always be with the manager. They are her heritage because of the nature of her domain. The first-line manager practices in the immediate, in an environment that brings forth pressing needs and predicaments demanding resolutions in the present or short-run future.

The presence of pressing and immediate needs in the work environment does not diminish the need for longer-range goals. Sometimes there is a tendency to forget about long-range goals in the press of the immediate needs arising in the environment. The problem with letting environmental demands set *all* of one's goals is that it precludes much advancement. The first-line manager needs to set a good balance between future-directed goals and goals pressed on her by the immediate environment.

To balance these two sorts of demands is important to successful management. They represent two different dimensions of the job. Nor is the balance between them a static affair. In a time of difficulty, the problem-resolution demands will probably take priority for the manager. One cannot launch new initiatives while the walls are tumbling in all around. The kind of action needed in these circumstances, problem-solving, is reactive; that is, the manager acts in response to the environment and its presses. For these problems, the manager is primarily controlled by the environment rather than controlling it. When the environment is changing rapidly—and that is often the case today—it is logical that many goals will be reactive.

In contrast, long-range goals (and the range may be varied) are applied when one wants to work toward desirable new initiatives. Long-range goals are proactive; they set the course for activities that would not have occurred on their own. Long-range goals set into effect activities that would not have occurred merely in response to environmental presses. These goals, then, are proactive rather than reactive. Much of the leadership function of the first-line manager is involved with just this sort of thing—setting new goals, new horizons for the work group.

Proactive goals arise on many institutional levels. Some of them may be dictated by higher levels of nursing or institutional management, in which case it is the first-line manager's responsibility to see how such goals may be effectively implemented in her own work unit. Additionally, there will be proactive goals that arise from the first-line manager and her staff, goals that are specific to the work of the unit.

Proactive goals, like reactive ones, serve the function of directing actions. If goals are not translated into activities, then they are merely illusory. Inexperienced first-line managers may see long-range goal setting as an intellectual function having little to do with the job. In many institutions, head nurses (or their equivalents) make out attractive lists of objectives for their supervisors and for accrediting bodies. Display is often the only purpose served by such lists—formulations to prove that managers can put goals on paper. All too often first-line managers put such lists aside and go about business as usual until the lists are outdated and need to be revised again. This pattern of creating "paper" goals is a futile exercise and a waste of valuable time.

In today's high-demand environment it is important that the projected, written goals and the enacted goals coincide. Today's context for delivery of health care has become so complex that there simply is not time for exercises inapplicable to actual patient care delivery. Yet, in today's demanding care situations if a manager does not carefully elucidate her goals, she may be without a direction. It is easy to get embroiled in ongoing, urgent but evanescent matters to the detriment of everything else.

The first-line manager, then, seeks to balance proactive and reactive goals, short- and long-term needs of her unit and her organization. Goals will be defined with different degrees of care depending upon their anticipated longevity. However they may be defined and expressed, the first-line manager needs a clear idea of where she is going; otherwise, she won't know when she's "arrived."

Part II of this book looks at the goals of the first-line nurse manager. For convenience it looks at three different types of goals in three separate chapters. These goals include:

- goals for patients
- goals for professional nursing and for staff
- goals for managerial excellence

There are other goals, of course; the selection is not comprehensive. But these goals cover three domains that deserve the thoughtful consideration of the first-line manager, and they merit precise delineation as well as reflection.

Some goals, those that will be reviewed by accrediting and evaluating bodies, require careful grammatical control and artful presentation. The refining of such goal statements was once a major fixation of nurse managers. Indeed, good ideas can get lost in a messy presentation, but the formulation itself must not become more important than how the ideas get applied.

The first-line manager is often in her first managerial post, and her job may be the first one to place expectations on her for production of "paper" products as well as for action products, i.e., actual patient care. Skill in composing written statements demands effort and learning, but not at the expense of patient care or the actions dictated by the formulated goals. That's what goals are for: to direct action, not to lie buried in a notebook. Putting them on paper is done to retain them, to make them stand out, to give people a memory source for their agreements.

In today's frenetic health care environment, goals are not less important; on the contrary, they are more important. They serve as a guidepost in the sea of activity and environmental demands. True, they need to be scrutinized and revised more frequently now than was the case in the past. The paper product, the official formulation of goals, should last only as long as the goals continue to make sense as action dictates. For it is action—the things people do to achieve goals that they have understood and agreed to—that justifies the formulation of goals in the first place.

chapter *3*

Patient Ideologies and Care Standards

Goals for patient care appear in many forms. On the level of the individual patient, they appear in care plans. Either they are specified or they may be inferred from the nursing orders. Sometimes goals are not stated but problems are; the unstated goal, in this case, is to get rid of the problem. It is to the disadvantage of the nonprofessional staff when goals are not specified but carried, instead, in the heads of the nurses designing patient care. The more people who must interact in the care of a patient, the greater the need for specification of nursing goals. Having clear and specified nursing goals for patients also becomes important in helping other professionals and health care workers to understand what nursing is all about.

Goals for groups of patients appear in other tools such as patient standards, criteria in quality control formats, and teaching objectives for patient education programs. There are also goals held in common for all patients. These appear in such documents as a patients' bill of rights, informed consent documents, or in standards established for ethics committees or research designs.

Before one even gets to the level of stating specific goals, however, patient care objectives are affected by subtle, often inferred but unexamined assumptions in the minds of the manager and her staff. Two such influences will be examined here: (1) the tone or attitude set by the leader concerning the work and how it is to be achieved, and (2) the values and goals inherent in one's basic philosophy of nursing.

SETTING THE TONE

The ideology of the workplace is set by the leader of a work group. In most instances the "leader" is also the manager of the group. It sometimes happens

27

that a strong staff nurse will assume the professional leadership of a work group with a weak or absentee manager or when a manager has abdicated all authority in the name of "democracy." However, because of positional power the manager is usually also the leader of the group. Her authority, along with her ability to reward and punish, normally leads staff to follow the manager's guidelines. What is important to the manager quickly becomes important to the staff. Her values become their own, unless values and goals conflict—in which case the difference becomes a source of contention.

The tone (workplace philosophy) set by the leader inevitably filters down to the workers. Indeed, one of the most important functions of a first-line manager is setting a good tone for the work group. Setting the tone means creating an expectation for how the group will work in and react to the environment. Many factors are involved in tone setting: the formality or informality of group interactions, the degree of professionalism, the degree of friendliness and consideration shown to various individuals and groups, the degree of concern for patients that is defined as appropriate, the nature of conversations held, the sorts of rationale that are acceptable and not acceptable for successes and failures, and other subtle aspects of how the work group operates.

As an exercise in capturing the elusive notion of tone, the reader may wish to think of two work groups she has known in the past, perhaps two hospital units. Pick two that are fairly matched as to their official purpose, such as two medical units. Or one might pick the same organizational unit, perhaps a clinic, as it appeared in two different time periods under two different managers.

Now describe the two units to an imaginary friend who is trying to choose between them in seeking employment. Don't compare the units as to their patients and the specific work to be done, but according to the other factors that would be important to your friend in choosing. Inevitably the sorts of things you mention in such an exercise have to do with "tonal" differences. Examine the aspects you brought up; notice how closely they relate to the management style of the leader in each case.

Take a simple negative example as an additional illustration: Suppose a given head nurse on an inpatient care facility expresses continuous frustration because of the staff and supplies provided to her by "administration." Suppose she blames all deficits in care on failures of the institution. It is almost certain that staff will pick up her attitudinal clues and use blame as a tactic for explaining their own failures. Staff will adopt the leader's negative perspective on the institution and see themselves as helpless to change things. The tone set is one of inevitable failure, of constant discontent, and of dwelling on the worst side of all circumstances. Clearly, tone setting deals with context more than with specific goals, but the wrong tone produces the wrong goals in an organizational unit.

To continue our example, suppose the head nurse on a second unit has a different attitude, sets a different tone. Suppose her actions, as much as her words, say: "Things aren't easy here because the organization can't afford half the things we need to do the job right, but my people are survivors and achievers. We will produce miracles with what we have; we will be creative and clever and will be the best unit in the organization. We thrive on challenges." Staff on this floor will also "catch" the attitude of their leader.

Now if you look at the personnel records of the staff on these two hypothetical units, you may find very few differences in background or past performance, but you can be certain that the staff on the second unit will shine while those on the first unit will be seen as lacking. Very likely, the first unit will be seen as a "problem unit." Any way you look at it, people follow the tone set by their leader. People achieve what they are expected to achieve; that's the way it works. The achievement of goals—or the failure to achieve—can be programmed into personnel by the attitude, the tone, set by their leader.

Setting the tone should be a conscious act of the leader, not something that occurs by default. The way in which a situation is interpreted is not cut in stone. People will see what they are told they see. The perceptions and interpretations of the leader form a great part of the "reality" of the workplace. Staff see their work setting much as their leader sees it—as challenging, exciting, growth-producing, or, on the other hand, as overwhelming, unsatisfying, unfair, depressing.

Not only do subordinates tend to interpret the environment in the same way as their leader, but they also see themselves as she does. Staff develop expectations for themselves that match those of their leaders. The tone set by the first-line manager will determine the nature of the staff that she acquires. The manager who finds herself surrounded by malcontents and frustrated people should first look to the messages that she is sending via her own attitude. On the positive side, the leader who treats her staff as if they were special, professional, and productive will soon find that they measure up to her expectations.

A CONSUMER ORIENTATION

When a proper tone is established in a patient care environment, patients benefit. Ultimately, that is the objective of tone setting: better patient care. In today's health care delivery environment, successful first-line managers have learned to include a conception of the patient as consumer in their operating philosophy. This is an accurate reflection of the market-oriented services that health care and nursing care have become.

Competition among health care providers demands a new perspective on the patient. In previous eras, health care institutions functioned with a subtle but pervasive understanding that their chief "customer" was the physician. Institutions were created to service the physician in his practice. The patient was cared for, but the physician was the one to be pleased. The institution's fear was not that the patient would be discontent, but that the physician would be dissatisfied and take his patients elsewhere. The physician was identified as the chief source of income for the institution.

In the newly developing health care system, that image is changing. The physician is no longer the "customer" to be pleased. Indeed, the work of the individual physician is monitored and judged by reimbursing payers and by the health care institution alike. Both view his performance in light of its cost effectiveness. A physician whose work practices are costly to an institution may be asked to modify his practices or take his business elsewhere.

The institution's income is now seen as patient- rather than physician-based. One hears, for example, that patients with condition X are money makers, while patients with condition Y lose money for the institution. And while the shifting and refining of reimbursement systems will continue without cessation, it is clear that the patient has assumed a new importance in the calculations.

These changes in realities and in perceptions have brought about some practical changes in attitudes toward patients. Health care agencies are adopting a consumer orientation like that found in other successful businesses. Nonhealth-related businesses succeed or fail depending upon their ability to draw more customers to their products or services than their competition. Now that attitude applies to health services too.

In the past, the patient's satisfaction with a health care institution's services was subordinated to the pleasures and conveniences of others, namely the providers. For example, in many urban settings, health care institutions were clumped together for the convenience of health care workers. Patients might have to travel long hours to reach them; that was simply too bad. Physician rounds were made at hours that suited the physicians; patients' sleep needs were not considered. Patients were fed food that might be nourishing (if they could swallow it); the fact that it was unappetizing didn't matter. And patients in outpatient services could wait long hours in pain before being seen by a nurse or physician.

Nurses, in spite of their claims to be patient-oriented, often demonstrated similar egalitarian behaviors toward patients. Patients were awakened from needed sleep because certain routines were to be completed on certain shifts; staff members shouted down halls to each other to "save steps," regardless of patients' need for quiet; nurses bullied patients into meeting nursing schedules rather than adapt to patient needs and preferences.

This is not to imply that all these practices have ceased, but where competition for patients exists, institutions soon adopt the notion of patient as consumer. Indeed, the customer-service model may ebb and flow within the same institution, depending on whether or not it is seeking more customers. Where the service model's application fluctuates, the institution is putting its own needs before those of its patients.

With today's reimbursement policies and competition between providers, treatment of consumers can have a direct effect on the income of an institution. Patients, in becoming an economic factor in the equation, have become powerful. When a patient elects to go to another institution, he has made a statement—a powerful economic one—concerning the services of a facility.

More often than not that statement concerns the nursing care he has received. The patient spends more time in interaction with the nursing staff than with any other workers in the institution. This is true in all inpatient facilities (acute or long-term) and in most community and ambulatory health care settings as well.

Consequently, nurses need to learn to see the patient as a consumer. The nursing service must be redesigned to accommodate consumer preferences rather than nurses' convenience. Often this change applies to attitude as much as to essential services. Certainly the patient will be dissatisfied when his light goes unanswered and his requests for nourishment or pain alleviation go unmet. But often the consumer philosophy has more to do with civility: treating the patient as a guest in one's facility. Even when the patient has received technically excellent nursing, he will be dissatisfied if his personhood is ignored, if his sleep is interrupted unnecessarily, if he is subjected to innumerable personal conversations between staff members more interested in their private lives than in their patients' comfort.

It is the responsibility of the first-line manager to see that her staff appreciate the patient as a consumer of services, a paying customer who must be pleased if he or anyone in his family is to return next time. The patient's privacy, his needs for quiet and rest, his right to make decisions concerning his own care—these are basics that shouldn't need to be stressed. In fact they must be emphasized repeatedly, because in the past they simply weren't considered to be terribly important.

Building a consumer ideology means making radical changes in staff behavior, from eliminating the noisy clogs that the night nurse wears because they are comfortable to tempering the ebullient laughter of young nurses who forget that such levity may be disturbing to the anxious patient in pain. To modify staff behavior appropriately the first-line manager must herself become aware of how her unit appears from the patient's perspective. Treating the patient as a consumer, which is what he is, after all, is a start.

PATIENT IDEOLOGIES

Another source of behaviors and goals for the professional nurse is the philosophy of care inculcated by her education and indoctrination into nursing. Goals for patients are implied or described in all educational programs. They appear in care ideologies espoused in curricula, and they are conveyed through the values and behaviors of instructors and other role models. Often goals for nursing care are assumed rather than specified in these philosophies. The nurse's understanding of "what a good nurse does" is a value conception; and values point out the goals for nursing.

Nor should the first-line manager assume that only her professional staff acquire values and expectations for "good" performance during their education. A nurse's aide, for example, may have been indoctrinated in a program that stresses pride in achievement, pride in self as a care giver. The wise first-line manager will foster all positive values that support good nursing care wherever she finds them. Denigrating the sense of pride in one's work among one group of workers never really enhances the status of a "higher" group, as is so often assumed.

It is important for every nurse to look at the values and goals underlying her internalized notions of what constitutes good nursing. It is even more important that the first-line manager know and be able to convey her own values and goals to her staff in a meaningful way. The nurse manager must know, not only her own perspective on nursing, but that of her staff as well. To lead others, one begins by knowing where they stand.

Not all nursing programs build the same expectations into their graduates, but most graduates of nursing in the United States share a general ideology of nursing care. The next section of this chapter will speak about the generally shared values and objectives predominant in this nursing culture. These values and goals are shared, more or less, by education programs for workers with lower-level skills. Not even the poorest of aide-training programs, for example, deliberately instills a "just get by" attitude in its students.

It is important that the nurse manager create an environment where people feel a sense of achievement in their everyday work. If nurses practice in a setting where their expectations of themselves and their actual achievements do not match, there will be job dissatisfaction, self-dissatisfaction, and disillusionment with one's superiors, one's institution, and/or the profession. It is up to the first-line manager to see that this does not happen to her staff.

When expectations and realities do not coincide, there are two possible cures. The first is to change the situation so that one can achieve one's goals. The alternative is to change the goals and expectations so that they will coincide with what is possible in the environment. Either or both of these tactics may be necessary. We will return to this point after looking at the normative goals held by most nurses who have graduated today or in the recent past.

Nursing Ideology

The typical nursing graduate today has been taught a philosophy that makes it her responsibility to meet all her patient's health needs. The nursing care plans that she completed as a student were usually judged inadequate if any detectable care need was neglected. In addition to ascertaining all nursing needs of a patient, the nurse was expected, in her education, to identify the need for referral, i.e., the need for intervention by other professionals. The most obvious example is that of medical requirements. The nurse is expected to identify needs for medical intervention and to bring them to the attention of the patient's physician. This is true for emergency situations as well as for day-to-day assessments.

It is not surprising, then, that the average nurse approaches her job with a notion that it is her responsibility to see that the patient has "everything" his health requires. Some nursing programs go farther than this, assuming that the nurse is responsible for assessing and meeting a patient's total human needs rather than merely his health needs. Graduates from these programs feel an even greater responsibility to each patient.

Seldom, if ever, has the environment of organized health care offered propitious circumstances for a nurse to make good on the comprehensive care ideal for all her patients. However, in recent years the discrepancy between the care envisioned and the care delivered has grown. The demand for economy in care costs has led health care facilities to reduce resources available for nursing care. Sometimes the most frustrating loss is of personnel; often there are cutbacks in nursing experts, support services, and/or supplies as well.

In this environment of reduced resources, the demands on nurses have not been reduced proportionately. On the contrary, as medical and nursing knowledge have expanded, the nurse has been expected to know more and do more. The situation has been exacerbated by unanticipated needs for acute beds just at the time when healthcare planners envisioned a decline in such demand.

In every setting—hospital, skilled nursing facility, and home care—the nurse cares for more patients than in the past, patients who are sicker and receiving more complicated therapies than was previously the case. The situation is a potentially volatile one, one that takes its toll on both patients and nurses. Patients are exposed to failures in access and care, and nursing suffers by nurses leaving the profession as well as by declining enrollments in nursing programs throughout the nation.

Yet this is the world with which most first-line managers must cope. They have to wrestle with the problem of preserving their staffs' pride in nursing while they give care in less than perfect settings, often with inadequate human and material resources.

Not only has the typical education prepared the nurse only to give total patient care, i.e., "the best," but in many cases the nurse has been taught to equate her professional identity with the performance of such ideal care. Quite simply, the nurse feels like a failure if she gives anything less than or different from comprehensive care. Today's health care environment threatens the professional self-concept of any nurse who understands her role as the giving of total patient care.

What does the first-line manager do when her staff face a less-than-ideal situation in which care must be delivered? Usually she takes a two-pronged approach to this situation, as indicated earlier in this discussion. The first tactic is a never-ending attempt to improve the situation in terms of its absolute resources—physical, intellectual, manpower, and emotional. The second tactic involves a reconceptualization of nursing practice.

Difficult as it is to acquire additional resources, that may be the easier tactic. Recently, the cumulative effects of "hard times in health care" have gained national notice. There have been attempts by various publics to improve the conditions under which nurses work. These attempts have resulted not so much from sympathy for nurses as from anxiety over failures of the system to protect the patient. Whatever the motive for the concern, nurses should appreciate any call for improved resources for patient care. However, even if a ground swell of public concern were to develop immediately, it would take years of careful preparation and planning to alleviate the present situation.

It is the job of the first-line manager to struggle unceasingly for the resources that she needs to do an excellent job of patient care. At the same time, it is her obligation to do the best possible job given the resources at hand.

The fact is that improvement in resources occurs only when management has carefully identified which resources are required to produce which results. This fact of life has forced nurses clearly to identify and quantify their resource requirements for the first time in history. The mechanisms of patient classification have helped enormously to quantify the nurse's work. The effects of quantification have been both revealing and beneficial. Nurse managers are less likely nowadays expected to achieve miracles without adequate resources.

Concretizing the relationship between care delivered and available resources is a welcome change. Nurses are no longer expected to compensate for absent supplies, personnel, and expertise with abstract notions of dedication or creativity. This represents an important first step toward discrediting the assumption that a "good" nurse can do everything her patients require in any circumstance. For the first time, it is widely realized that "everything" can only be achieved with time, expertise, and the requisite physical resources.

How, then, does this new realism affect the typical nurse's assumption that she must do "everything" or be a failure? In addition to seeking additional resources, what can the first-line manager do to encourage an appropriate idea of professional practice? Here is where the second tactic comes into play: the purposeful alteration of the nurse's concept of what it means to be professional, to be excellent.

In essence, what is required is to divorce one's identity as a good nurse from the ideal of providing for all possible patient needs. A contextual perspective allows the nurse to judge her performance on a contingency basis, i.e., to judge how well she did under the circumstances that prevailed. Implementation of the resource-driven model of nursing care, discussed in the next section, is one approach to changing the way nurses evaluate their work.

Goal-Driven and Resource-Driven Models

The predominant philosophy of nursing in this society, as noted earlier in this chapter, assumes that the nurse must do "everything" the patient needs. Analysis reveals this to be a goal-driven model of care. First the nurse sets the goals for her patient; next she determines everything that must be done to achieve all the possible goals; and then she goes about the work involved. The model starts with setting the goals. The goals are set independent of the situation and are limited only by the insight and intellectual capacities of the nurse. This goal-driven design is a useful model when applied to a resource-rich environment. In such a setting the goal-driven model leads to excellence in nursing practice. The nurse has access to plentiful resources (of time, expertise, equipment, and supplies), and she draws on them freely for her patients' care.

The problems occur when a goal-driven model is applied in a resource-deficient environment. There the nurse—still driven by notions of comprehensive care—makes plans that will be impossible to carry out because of scarcities in the environment. In this situation, the goal-driven model is a design for failure. The nurse cannot help but feel that she has failed. Worse yet, in her attempts to do "everything" she will be unselective, and those aspects of care that she overlooks in the press of simultaneous demands may be the very things that should have had the highest priority.

If the nurse cannot admit to herself or to others (especially her immediate supervisor) that not everything desirable *can* be done, then she can't prioritize to ensure that the most important things do get done. A goal-driven model allows for arranging all the work pieces, but it does not allow for selecting among potential time investments.

A resource-driven model, in contrast, begins with an assessment of the resources available. From there it works toward a care plan for a given patient or for a group of patients considered together. In a resource-driven philosophy, the nurse realistically assesses her resources in the most concrete way: What supplies? How many work hours? What expertise? She uses this assessment in determining what can be done within a given shift, day, or block of clinic hours.

In other words, she does not start with an idealized set of goals for each and every patient. Instead, she starts with a realistic assessment of the resources at hand. When that assessment is complete, she decides which goals may be set and which activities can be scheduled to achieve the goals. Notice that unlike the goal-driven model, in which decisions are based on quality factors alone, the resource-driven model requires that a quantitative estimate of available resources be included in nursing judgments.

In the resource-driven model there are three broad categories of assets to be evaluated: (1) staff hours, (2) equipment and supplies, and (3) expertise. Usually the primary resource at a nurse's command is her own time or that of other staff working with her. Since most planning is for a given work shift, for predetermined clinic hours, for an average home visit, or for some other finite time unit, the number of staff hours available is easily calculable. In this sense work time is a "clean" resource. No nurse gets more than 24 hours in a day, and no worker gets more than a shift's worth of time without investment of another resource (overtime pay or human burnout, for example). Staff hours are a precious resource in nursing because they are irreplaceable and costly. The salary of a nurse, a nurse's aide, or other worker is paid every time the employee is scheduled. By comparison, most equipment and supplies are relatively inexpensive.

Nevertheless, equipment and supplies are other resources that must be taken into account in deciding what goals may be taken on. There are certain care therapies that just can't be done without the right supplies; others can be done with creative jerryrigging. The chief problem with creative alternatives is that they inevitably take time to devise, thus consuming the scarcest resource of all: nursing hours. The same loss is experienced when supply services that should be the responsibility of other departments or individuals consume nursing time and attention.

A final resource to be considered is expertise. Nurses are usually conscientious about seeking out nonnursing experts when they are required; their greatest failure seems to relate to the use of nursing experts. Often nurses ignore the nursing expertise that is available in their own institution. Unlike a physician, the nurse may feel that calling on an expert reflects on her own level of competency. Yet nursing expertise is an important resource. Properly used, nurse experts can improve everyone's performance and can facilitate getting work done. Suppose, for example, that an inexperienced nurse spends hours wondering how to meet all of the needs of a complex patient. Suppose she tries several ineffective methods of achieving her goals before she reaches a satisfactory system. How much more expedient it would have been to seek the advice of a nurse expert rather than improvise in the absence of experience. No available resources should be overlooked.

In the resource-driven model a first-line manager teaches her staff to

1. estimate the resources at hand for a given work period
2. consider the possible goals that might be taken on for the period
3. select the most important goals that can be attained within the given time period
4. implement plans accordingly

Notice that this model is more challenging than the goal-driven model for several reasons. First, it forces the nurse to make hard choices; it conflicts with the philosophic dictate that the nurse may have internalized to "do everything." In a sense, resource-driven nursing is like battlefield triage: Hard choices are made to achieve the best overall outcome.

There are other demands in this model. Take, for example, the choice of goals to be pursued. In the goal-driven model, the nurse did not have to choose; she simply planned to meet all needs she could think of for each patient. This sort of care was much easier in the sense that it didn't demand as much tactical thinking. Resource-driven nursing, in contrast, forces the nurse to choose among a menu of goals, all "good" in themselves. Here she must decide which goals are more important at any given time.

Not only must goals be selected, they must be weighed in terms of the way they consume resources. A worthy goal that involves excessive use of the nurse's time, for example, might be sacrificed for several other goals that could be achieved with less time investment. Time available is not the only resource to be considered here, but it is an important one.

The resource-driven model is more demanding of professional expertise; it holds more dangers of miscalculation. The nurse may err in taking on more work than the time period allows for, for example, or she may make the opposite mistake: setting too few goals. The tailoring of goals and requisite activities to fit a given work period is a major demand of the resource-driven model.

Additionally, the model forces nurses to recognize that the relationship between goals and related activities is not set in stone. There may be numerous ways to achieve the same goal. Some ways may be more neat, more refined, more effective, more pleasing to the nurse or to the patient, but different methods of achieving an objective may place more acceptable demands on the resources of the unit.

In some cases a review of the resources at hand and the potential objectives to be achieved may lead a first-line manager or her staff to pick a resource-saving method over a resource-expending method of achieving the same goal. Suppose, for example, that the preferred assignment system is a primary nursing design allowing for highly satisfactory one-to-one relationships between nurses and their patients. During an emergency shortage of staff, the manager might sacrifice that ideal method for a modified functional plan on a given shift so as to achieve a larger number of goals, albeit at some cost to the quality of nurse-patient relationships.

In the resource-driven model it is possible to compromise on methods in order to achieve the greater good—the achievement of a greater number of important objectives. This does not mean that one always selects the swiftest method over the most effective one. It simply means that there are tradeoffs in any choice, and in selecting the methods of achieving goals one must assess the total situation.

It is clear that evaluation of nursing performance in a resource-driven design is complicated. To assess the performance of a staff nurse, the first-line manager must ask all of the following questions:

1. Did the nurse accurately assess her potential resources?
2. Did the nurse select the best set of goals to be achieved, given all of the possible goals that might have been selected?
3. Did the nurse pick a logical number of goals, given the quantity of work that might fit in the time period?
4. Did the nurse select logical methods for achievement of the goals selected?
5. Did the nurse achieve the selected goals?

Notice how complex this evaluation is compared to the questions one asks in evaluating applications of a goal-driven model:

1. Did the nurse discover all of the logical goals?
2. Did the nurse achieve all of the goals?

The resource-driven model is only one suggested solution to the dilemma created by a situation in which nurses want to, but cannot, provide all the care needed by their patients. It has limitations, as does any model, but it has the potential to allow the nurse to be satisfied with her performance as a professional, even in less than ideal circumstances. Instead of feeling that she is a failure because she could not complete "everything," the nurse using a resource-driven model can take pride in her professional ability to make the best choices among options presented to her by the situation.

The resource-driven model has more flexibility than the goal-driven model. It can work in a resource-rich environment as well as in a resource-scarce environment. When the situation is rich in resources, the resource-driven model simply allows the nurse to take on more goals. Further, the resource-driven model can be applied to the care of any number of patients. It can be used to determine the care of one patient or the work to be done on an entire unit. It can be a practice model for the individual nurse or it can be a managerial model for the nurse in charge.

Need for a Baseline Safety Guide

One danger of the resource-driven model as formulated above is that it lacks a "bottom line" determination of safety. For example, consider an absurd case where a nurse finds herself the only professional caretaker for sixty critically ill patients. True, the nurse could beneficially apply a resource-driven model, but this would not guarantee the safety of such a large group of ill persons even if she made the best possible application of the method. The comparison with battlefield triage is not far-fetched; on the battlefield, not everyone is saved. The resource-driven model makes the best of circumstances; it does not guarantee a *good* outcome, only the *best* outcome possible in the situation.

Given this limitation in the model, it is up to the first-line manager using the model to develop indices for estimating when resource levels are so low as to preclude delivery of baseline care (however defined). Since the resource-driven model associates care with resources, this will involve critical measures of available resources.

Certainly, patient quality assurance tools indicate levels of care achieved, but they function after the fact. A safety net that takes resources into account enables one to act *before* a situation becomes critical. The indices are developed from an assessment of the relationship between care and resources. Such a plan should also identify the nature of the action to be taken when the baseline is exceeded. A simple example of a safety net and an action plan might be: If permanent staffing on 3 East falls below X full-time nurses, then the unit should be closed until that number is available. Or a nurse-patient ratio might be established, and admissions might be limited once the ratio is reached. In the case of a community health nurse, the ratio might have to do with caseload or types of new cases.

Not all action plans involve limiting patient admissions. Some plans call for radical changes in services rendered to patients instead. For example, in an acute care setting, baths might be given every other day or linens changed less frequently. Other amenities that contribute but are not essential to patient recuperation might be modified in the strategic plan.

Having indices and related action strategies set and approved in advance makes management easier. The nurse manager who has such a system is in a far better position than her peer who simply asserts "on experience" that her unit is in a critical situation. Consider a situation where no safety net has been established: A head nurse complains that there is already "too much work to be done" on her unit and that no additional patients should be admitted without additional staffing. While she may be accurate in that assessment, if she has no data other than her subjective sense of the situation others may not take her plea seriously.

Not only must the indicators be determined in advance, but the head nurse should have a plan for what to do when the determined limits are exceeded. Such a plan may involve adding staff, limiting patient admissions, closing a unit, or switching to emergency nursing procedures. What matters is that the actions to be taken have been determined and approved in advance of the emergency when they are needed. Just as a hospital is required to have a disaster plan by accrediting agencies, a care unit needs its own disaster plan for what will be done if resources sink below the determined critical level. The first-line manager who has such an approved plan will have an easier time than the one who simply argues for emergency measures based on her instincts, however accurate they may be. The objective is to have a plan, a system to manage a resource scarcity that assures that patients will still receive the predetermined baseline care.

Actions that need to be taken during a critical scarcity of resources are often unpopular ones; frequently they are costly to the institution. Cutting off patient admissions will be expensive, and hiring additional staff is also costly. Institutions that are carefully watching their bottom line may be hesitant to implement an expensive solution. That is why it is so important to have agreement on such a plan in advance of the time when it may be needed.

Determining what is meant by "baseline" is another critical component of such a contingency plan. Obviously, no manager is going to set that baseline below life-preserving, function-sustaining levels of care for her patients. Yet there may be differences in the levels of care identified as baseline. In one institution a baseline may be set higher than in another. For example, baseline care may or may not include certain amenities expected by the population served; baseline indicators may "flash a warning" only when danger to life and limb approaches, or long before that point is reached.

What are the signs that indicate resource deficits approaching the baseline condition? Those indicators may be different in every patient setting. The most important index in each case would be a factor associating available nursing hours with work to be done. Ultimately these quantitative ratios should correlate with patient outcomes. Indicators in a nursing home might relate to quality of life factors, while those in an emergency room might have to do with protection of life and limb.

The important thing is that the quantitative indices lend themselves to easy and immediate assessment on a given shift or in an appropriately timely fashion. Baseline evaluation tools must be such that they can be applied conveniently and rapidly whenever required. They must be designed to yield a decisive conclusion in the least possible time. It is important that such tools be prerefined and ready at hand; one must not rely on being able to define baseline care at the time when a dangerous or undesirable situation emerges.

It is not only the inpatient acute care unit that needs such baseline preparation. The nurse managing a clinic, the supervisor of a home visiting staff, and the nurse in a skilled nursing facility have similar needs. Wherever one manages the work of a group of caretakers there is a need for knowing when the resources and the patient needs are out of balance. Indicators may be radically different in different situations, but the need for them is pervasive.

Standards of Patient Care

Whether the first-line manager advocates a resource-driven or goal-driven model for delivery of patient care, it is essential that she have well developed standards for caring for patients. Such standards should be identified for each major patient group cared for by the work unit. (Patients are categorized in various ways, by medical or nursing diagnosis, by shared therapy needs, by DRGs, or by other schemes.) Standards of care for patient groups should be stated in measurable terms or accompanied by measurement tools. Simply put, the first-line manager has a major responsibility for the quality of patient care; to judge the quality of care necessitates having standards to be achieved and criteria by which one can judge the degree of attainment of those standards.

More material on standards is discussed in Chapter 17 in relation to quality assurance. Patient care standards are often developed in conjunction with formal quality assurance tools. Some institutions develop separate statements of standards. The most important standards of patient care are those that specify the desired physical, mental, and emotional outcomes of patients while on given care trajectories. Patient care standards perform for groups of patients the function served for the individual patient by the goals identified in nursing orders or on a nursing Kardex. Patient outcome standards, both individual and collective, are essential tools of the first-line manager.

Patient care standards today include not only patients' physiological and mental states but their legal rights as well. Standards include the patient's right to knowledge about his condition and his rights in decision-making situations surrounding his therapy. Sometimes the standards of legal care for patients are codified in a patients' bill of rights. Such information is often shared with patients and their families via a written hand-out or posted widely in care facilities. However patients' rights are communicated to them, it is essential that these rights be both communicated and observed in staff interactions. Chapter 9 gives additional details concerning patients' legal rights.

NURSING THEORIES

A nursing theory, where it is adopted as a basis for care, clearly affects one's goals for patients. In a sense, a nursing theory is an elaborate patient care ideology. More and more nursing departments or care units are adopting or adapting selected theories of nursing care. Often an entire nursing department attempts to apply the same nursing theory to the care of all its patients. The advantage to such uniformity is the simplifying of communication within the nursing department as well as with other professionals outside of nursing. The disadvantage is that a given theory may fit well with the patient work of one unit but less well with another unit. For example, in an ambulatory care setting the nursing theory that works best with the well child population may be less appropriate to the care of the elderly chronically ill.

The opposite extreme in theory application exists where each primary nurse selects and applies her own favorite nursing theory to her patient population. Here the communication problems are compounded. It is difficult enough for physicians, for example, to comprehend the goals of one nursing theory let alone the goals and tactics employed by numerous nurses using diverse theories in care of different patients. Nor do head nurses in such circumstances always do an adequate job of orienting subordinate nursing staff to the subtleties and nursing differences introduced by the differing theories.

Where care is delivered on a one-to-one basis without the use of intervening nursing personnel, a practice of allowing the nurse to select her theory may work. Sometimes this practice is used in community health settings where each nurse has a private case load. Even here the first-line manager will be imposing some theory elements just by the way her service is organized and by the constraints placed upon the practicing nurses.

Whether the first-line manager has the luxury of selecting the nursing theory to be used on her unit or the responsibility of implementing a theory imposed by a higher organizational level, there are several managerial demands involved. The given nursing theory must be closely examined for its practical effects on patient care.[1] The theory must also be looked at in relation to the standard operating procedures already in effect in the care unit. For example, does the theory require the active involvement of the patient's significant other? Is that dictate confounded by the visiting policies on the unit? Does the theory require evaluative structures that differ from those in the present quality assurance tools? Does the theory require more or less patient independence than that which is the norm on the unit? Does the theory require nursing acts that conflict with the criteria by which the nurse's performance is appraised?

The first-line manager must carefully discover all the ways in which the running of her unit must be changed in order to comply with the theory. Often implementation of a theory will involve wholesale revision of the major documents by which nursing action is directed and recorded. All the following documents and practices will need to be examined for compatibility with the selected theory: nursing Kardex categories, nursing order sheets, nursing charting notes, quality assurance tools, patient classification tools, patient care standards, patients' bill of rights, assignment systems, treatment, medication and hygiene practices, visiting policies, staff-staff interaction practices, staff-patient interaction practices, methods of receiving nursing shift reports, performance appraisal tools, orientation documents.

A theory of nursing cannot be implemented adequately without administrative support. Much of that support falls to the first-line manager. She must be certain not only that the methods of working in her unit are consonant with the theory but that they actually support its application.

Even where a specific theory of nursing is not applied, theory elements creep into practice according to the ways that work is organized. In truth, most theory application today is partial and tied to administrative decisions. Probably the two most common theory elements one finds in practice settings are nursing diagnosis and problem-oriented charting.[2] A concept of holistic nursing is the next most common theory element. Notice the theoretical impact that acceptance of one of these theory elements can have on the practice in a unit. If problem-oriented charting is used, for example, no matter what her personal preference a nurse is forced to view her patient as a locus for problems. If she must do her charting under categories of illustrated problems, then she inevitably imposes a problem-oriented method on her nursing design.

Similarly, where a given set of nursing diagnoses has been accepted as the significant data concerning a patient, the nurse giving care is forced to work within those parameters. The nurse working from a given taxonomy of nursing needs may see different needs in a patient than would another nurse without this prescribed structure.

Even the assignment method selected can have a major theoretical impact on care. A functional, task-oriented assignment system, for example, might be incompatible with a holistic view of the patient. It is up to the first-line manager to see that conflicting theory elements are not imposed on the work group. Clarity with regard to theory application, theory goals, and theory interpretation is her responsibility. Where specific theories or theory elements underlie the care given on a unit, it is the first-line manager's responsibility to see that all members of her staff—not only the nurse professionals—understand the theory's impact on care. It is also her responsibility to explain the nursing theory and its application to nonnurse professionals who have frequent contact with patients under the unit's care.

SUMMARY

The first-line manager is not only a manager of people but a manager of nursing care. She must be comfortable with the clinical ideologies of care as well as with management systems. She must understand that clinical theories and unit management affect each other. She must plan for the effective interface of clinical theory, clinical practice, and management practice.

If the first-line manager does not know the goals for patient care, one may be sure that no one else does. Achieving patient care goals is the chief reason for nursing's existence. To achieve care goals one first has to be able to specify what they are, how they can be measured, and how their achievement may be assured through appropriate use of resources and methods. The first-line manager must develop a view of the whole, a notion of how these diverse elements interact and affect each other. She must understand and interpret patient care ideologies and nursing theories, including how they can and do impact on the work of the group under her leadership, and she must plan accordingly.

NOTES

1. See L.J. Coleman, *Development of an Administrative Protocol: The Relationship Among Nursing Theory, Practice, and Administrative Theory* (Master's thesis, University of Illinois, 1977).

2. B.J. Barnum, "Holistic Nursing and Nursing Process," *Holistic Nursing Practice* 1, no. 3 (1988): 27.

BIBLIOGRAPHY

Baer, E. "Making the Most of Today's Economic Climate." *Nursing & Health Care* 8, no. 3 (March 1987): 142.

Benner, P. *From Novice to Expert.* Menlo Park, CA: Addison-Wesley Publishing Company, 1984.

Betz, M., and O'Connell, L. "Primary Nursing: Panacea or Problem?" *Nursing & Health Care* 8, no. 8 (October 1987): 456.

Brown, P.; Funsch, R.; Seremet, N.; Sloan, G.; Taylor, P.; and Ulloa, A. "Linking Psychiatric Nursing Care to Patient Classification Codes." *Nursing & Health Care* 8, no. 3 (March 1987): 156.

Bulechek, G.M. "Nursing Interventions: What They Are and How to Choose Them." *Holistic Nursing Practice* 1, no. 3 (May 1987): 36.

Chinn, P.L., and Jacobs, M.K. *Theory and Nursing: A Systematic Approach.* St. Louis: C.V. Mosby Company, 1983.

Donnelly, G.F. "The Promise of Nursing Practice: An Evaluation." *Holistic Nursing Practice* 1, no. 3 (May 1987): 1.

Goldsmith, J.C. *Can Hospitals Survive?* Homewood, IL: Dow Jones-Irwin, 1981.

Gorman, S., and Clark, N. "Power and Effective Nursing Practice," *Nursing Outlook* 34, no. 3 (May/June 1986): 129.

Henry, B; Arndt, C.; DiVincenti, M.; and Marriner-Tomey, A., eds. *Dimensions of Nursing Administration: Theory, Research, and Practice.* Cambridge, MA: Blackwell Scientific Publications, Inc., 1988.

Hoffman, F.M. *Financial Management for Nurse Managers.* Norwalk, CT: Appleton-Century-Crofts, 1984.

Meleis, A.I. *Theoretical Nursing: Development & Progress.* Philadelphia: J.B. Lippincott Company, 1985.

Moccia, P., ed. and host. *Nursing Theory: A Circle of Nursing Knowledge.* 2-part video program interviewing Patricia Benner, Virginia Henderson, Dorothea Orem, Martha Rogers, Sr. Callista Roy, Jean Watson. New York: National League for Nursing, 1987.

Rinke, L.T. "Replacing a Failing Old Pattern with a Vital New Paradigm: Home Care." *Nursing & Health Care* 8, no. 6 (June 1987): 330.

Stevens, B.J. *Nursing Theory: Analysis, Application, Evaluation.* Boston: Little, Brown and Company, 1979.

Strumpf, N.E. "A New Age for Elderly Care," *Nursing & Health Care* 8, no. 8 (October 1987): 444.

chapter 4

Professional Nursing Excellence

There are two domains where professional excellence assumes importance for the first-line manager. First, she must be concerned with the broader context of health as it is played out in societal governance and in the world of nursing and health care organizations. Second, she must hold and promote a sense of professional excellence as it applies to the nurses and the care delivered on her managerial unit. The first-line manager's involvement in her profession and in the social governance process should be a vital demonstration for those nurses under her supervision. Role modeling for professional excellence is the obligation of any nurse who assumes a position of leadership and authority. Since the first-line manager has influence over so many nurses giving hands-on care, it is essential that she live up to this responsibility.

This chapter begins by looking at professional excellence in the larger context of society. The final portion of the chapter addresses professional excellence in the first-line manager's own unit and institution.

NURSING AND THE SOCIETY

Professional responsibility cannot be achieved in isolation, either by the nurse or by the profession. It involves accountability within a greater social context. Social ends are achieved through the efforts of groups and organizations of people working together to make and enact decisions. This section will look at social accountability as it applies to the first-line manager herself.

Social Accountability

In order to fulfill her responsibilities as a citizen and professional, the first-line manager must necessarily become a learned person. Not only is she responsible for constantly updating her clinical and managerial knowledge, she also has a responsibility to be knowledgable about her society and the world around her. She has a civic as well as professional responsibility to make informed choices and to act in concert with others to support those informed choices.

Nor is it enough for the nurse merely to focus on social change related to health care. Health care decisions interact with other choices made by a society. Health care policy involves political decisions concerning how a society will invest its limited resources. Health care is one value among many (e.g., education, freedom, artistic expression). Choices are negotiated and managed by the political process. Monies devoted to health are not available for other "goods" that the society may envision. It is not enough, therefore, that a nurse merely favor every inherently worthy proposal for health care. She has the obligation to analyze and selectively champion health and health care improvements in the context of the society as a whole.

Ironically, the scientific and technical nature of a nurse's education often limits her exposure to a broader context of understanding. She tends to know a lot about medicine and nursing but less about other aspects of the world. This limitation, if it exists for a first-line manager, can be addressed in several ways. The simplest start is daily, thoughtful reading of a balanced and responsible newspaper. The next ingredient is involvement in the political process at some level, be it local, state, or national. Experience with the democratic political process is an education in how our society runs, how it makes decisions, how it administers decisions once they are made.

Because of her expertise, it is likely that some of the nurse's political involvement will concern health matters. Local peer review organizations (PROs), as an illustration, offer opportunities for the nurse to see professional involvement in a broader context. Other groups not having a health-related focus can be equally enlightening, however. For example, if the nurse were to serve on a local school board she would see the same processes of negotiation, special interests exercising influence, and competition among advocates of certain expenditures. Participation in a political party is another useful form of social involvement. In many localities there are organized groups of nurses working to affect the political process; these groups offer additional opportunities for participation in the larger context.

The nurse also needs to know about the administrative branches of the federal government that are concerned with health care and the nursing profession. She will want to learn the functions and powers of such bodies as the Department of Health and Human Services, including the Health Care Financing Administration, the Health Resources and Services Administration (with its Division of Nursing), and the Public Health Service; the Veterans Administration; the Consumer Product Safety Commission; and the Home

Economics and Human Nutrition Division of the Department of Agriculture. These are just a few federal agencies that deal with various aspects of health. She will want to learn of the Center for Nursing Research at the National Institutes of Health; she will want to understand the functions of the Centers for Disease Control and of the Alcohol, Drug Abuse, and Mental Health Administration.

It is also important to understand the mechanics of how bills, including those related to health, are introduced and worked through the political process. A good workshop in government legislation may be the best source for this sort of information. Some texts on nursing trends give the basics of such "how to" information.

Whatever her selected political activity, it is important that the first-line manager be vitally involved with the society around her. A nurse who elects to be uninformed and uninvolved in the social order should not take upon herself the leadership of others.

Health-Related Organizations

Whatever choices the nurse makes for her political activities, she should also allot time and attention to those social organizations that control, influence, and affect health care delivery. As health care specialization grows, the number of health-related organizations increases. Sometimes the proliferation presents a confusing array of agencies even to the well-informed nurse. The nurse manager will want to be active in one or more organizations that flourish in her local area.

In addition to her active participation in organizations of her choice, the manager also needs to develop an understanding of how the world of health care organizations functions. She should be familiar with the most powerful national organizations and their purposes, biases, and constituencies. Being aware of the brokers and power players in the overall health care environment makes for an informed leader. Space allows mention of only a few of the more powerful health-related organizations.

The National Health Council is one of the few organizations in which the total health care industry finds representation. This is an organization of organizations—that is, its members are organizations rather than individuals. Its importance lies in the fact that the Council provides a forum where diverse interests can meet and plan together for the advancement of national health care. Members include: (1) voluntary health agencies such as the American Lung Association, the American Red Cross, and the National Easter Society; (2) professional associations such as the National League for Nursing, the American Medical Association, and the American Public Health Association;

(3) nonprofit organizations with an interest in health, such as the Paralyzed Veterans of America and the National Urban League; (4) government health agencies such as the Public Health Service of the U.S. Department of Health and Human Services and the U.S. Consumer Product Safety Commission; and (5) insurance and business companies with an interest in health, such as Smith Kline & French, Pfizer, and Eli Lilly from the drug industry or Metropolitan Life, EQUICOR, and Blue Cross and Blue Shield Association from the insurance industry. The National Health Council is important in that it enables providers, payers, suppliers, and consumers to share problems, perspectives, and goals regarding health matters of the nation.

It is important that the nurse/leader gain experience with some group that is not limited to nursing concerns, some organization where the interests of consumers and/or diverse providers are shared. The voluntary agencies, such as those holding membership in the National Health Council, often have local groups that can give the nurse such organizational experience. She might explore such groups as the National Society to Prevent Blindness, the American Diabetes Association, or the American Cancer Society. Such groups are always delighted to have the participation of health professionals.

Within the health care community there are several powerful organizations that have major impact on health care professionals, their practices, and their clients. The first-line manager should be familiar with the major ones. The Joint Commission on Accreditation of Healthcare Organizations (Joint Commission) is one such organization. (This body was formerly the Joint Commission on Accreditation of Hospitals.) The Joint Commission has the authority to accredit hospitals that meet its standards for patient care. While submission to the accreditation process is voluntary, there are many pressures on a hospital to seek such accreditation. An unaccredited hospital will not qualify as a recipient for various funds and reimbursements that may be seen as essential for its financial health. Hence, the "voluntary" process is not quite so voluntary as it might first appear.

With or without accreditation, a health care institution must be licensed by the powers of the state. However, most state licensure standards are lower than those set by the Joint Commission. For the hospital that is accredited by the Joint Commission, licensure is virtually assured.

Organized nursing has long sought to gain greater influence and power within the Joint Commission, and that struggle is likely to continue. Nevertheless, there are opportunities, local and national, for nurse managers to be involved in the Joint Commission through standard setting and evaluation of health care facilities.

Accreditation of home care providers is not yet formalized as is that of hospitals. At present various organizations, including the National League for Nursing and the Joint Commission, are contending politically for deemed status as accrediting agency. The group that is accorded this status will be authorized to perform functions of standard setting and review for home care similar to that presently performed for hospitals by the Joint Commission.

The American Hospital Association (AHA) is another organization of particular interest to the nurse manager. This organization sets standards for the hospital industry and exerts a major influence on national and state politics affecting health and health care delivery. At present the major power brokers in this organization are hospital administrators and physicians. As is the case with the Joint Commission, nurses (nursing administrators in particular) are seeking to develop a stronger influence within the organization.

The AHA has a number of committees and structural units concerned with nursing. The most important is the American Organization of Nurse Executives (AONE). Members of this group are primarily nurse executive officers of health care organizations across the nation. The first-line manager has the opportunity to join this organization as an affiliate member by individual membership in the Council of Nurse Managers. She qualifies for membership to this body whether or not her own facility's nurse executive belongs to AONE.

Some nurses have mixed feelings concerning nursing's participation in nursing councils and groups that are formulated within nonnursing groups such as the AHA. (The Nurses' Association of the American College of Gynecologists and Obstetricians or the Public Health Nursing Section of the American Public Health Association are other examples of this structural form.) The argument against such nursing subgroups is that they provide opportunities for others to exert excessive influence over nursing. The argument for such groups is that they provide linkages whereby nursing can exert influence on how others perceive and interact with nursing. Additionally, such bodies give nurses the opportunity to see a larger picture, to see beyond the health care dimension of nursing alone. Such nursing subgroups often develop a healthy give and take with the parent organizations; in other cases, conflict management may be a way of life between the parent organization and the nursing component. The advantages of having nurses participate with other care givers and providers usually outweigh the benefits of isolationism.

Of the non-nursing professional organizations, none has a greater impact on the health practices and policies of the nation than the American Medical Association (AMA). The relationship between the AMA and various nursing groups has been testy over the years, primarily because the AMA perceives medicine as subsuming all other health care professions. This perspective is clearly at odds with nursing's contention that it is a separate profession with its own goals, its own subject matter, its own domain. Simply put, nursing does not concede that the practice of medicine prepares one to understand and practice nursing.

Given the philosophic differences that exist between the two professions, it is not surprising that relations have periodically been strained between AMA and its counterpart nursing organizations. Unilateral pronouncements by the AMA about what nursing will or won't do have not helped the situation, even when such pronouncements, if properly negotiated, might have been welcomed.

Nevertheless, in the present era nursing cannot afford to operate merely within its own narrow confines; constructive professional relationships with peer health workers are critical to health care delivery in the nation. Indeed, nursing must seek more active involvement with the AMA and other nonnursing professional groups. Establishing effective communication between professional nursing and other health professionals (e.g., American Optometric Association, American Psychiatric Association, American Society of Allied Health Professions, American Society of Hospital Pharmacists) is an important goal—an essential one if truly collegial relations are to be developed.

Whatever her views, the nurse who elects to fill a leadership role (and that includes the first-line manager) should be ready to take an informed and active part in the larger society and in the wider health care community.

Nursing Organizations

While the nurse manager functions in the larger context of society, she still has a major obligation to look to the welfare and advancement of her own profession as well as to the ongoing improvement of the care that it offers to citizens. This means that she must be a member of the American Nurses' Association (ANA) and any specialized nursing bodies that affect the work of her unit. Many nurses also consider individual membership in the National League for Nursing (NLN) a must.

The nurse belongs to these groups partly for the benefits she receives from them as a member, but that is not the chief reason. Her first purpose in belonging is to assume her share of the financial support required to represent nursing in important constituencies and to "be counted" in the organizations' efforts on behalf of nursing. Nursing's major professional organizations have long suffered from a general lack of support among nurses. As long as a few nurses are bearing the burden for the many, nursing will be hampered in what may be achieved. Supporting one's professional organizations is an obligation as well as a privilege.

Membership in a specialty group, therefore, does not absolve the nurse of a responsibility to belong to the major organizations that represent all nurses. Often it is the specialty group, however, that the nurse finds most personally rewarding for its relevance to her job. The specialty groups in nursing are numerous and growing, and most of them do an excellent job of meeting the unique needs of their membership. There are organizations based on functional position, nursing clinical specialty, and technological interests, to name but a few categories. The following organizations illustrate the sorts of groups that exist: the American Association of Spinal Cord Injury Nurses, The American Association of Nurse Anesthetists, the National Alliance of Nurse Practitioners, the Oncology Nursing Society, and the American Association of Critical Care Nurses.

ANA serves as the link for a large number of the specialty organizations through the National Federation of Nursing Specialty Organizations. Others are free-standing (e.g., Council on Graduate Education for Administration in Nursing) or located within the NLN (e.g., the National Forum on Computers in Health Care and Nursing and the Council of Community Health Services). Many of the larger organizations publish valuable journals or newsletters for members.

In addition to the ANA, the NLN, and the various specialty nursing organizations, there are several other powerful nursing bodies. One of the most influential is the American Association of Colleges of Nursing (AACN). Its membership consists of the deans or chairpersons of collegiate nursing programs. Along with the NLN, this organization is instrumental in setting the direction of nursing education in the U.S.

The elite of nursing's organizations is the American Academy of Nursing (AAN). Fellows are elected to the Academy on the basis of significant contributions to nursing. Membership is limited to 500 nurses nationwide. This organization has the largest collection of "nursing notables": directors of major nursing schools and nursing practices, authors, legislators, researchers, and prominent clinicians.

One of the most important groups in nursing is a small organization called the Nursing Tri-Council. This body consists of eight persons, the presidents and executive officers from four major nursing groups: ANA, NLN, AACN, AONE. (The Tri-Council was established by the trio of ANA, NLN, and AACN before AONE joined the group—hence its name.) The significance of this group is that it provides nursing with a forum for united decision making among its major organizations. This mechanism for reaching consensus is critical if nursing is to advance the health care of the nation and preserve the vitality of nursing as a profession.

Whatever nursing groups the first-line manager joins, she will also want to seek membership in one or more groups of nurse managers. She will benefit greatly from meeting her role peers in other organizations. Such managerial groups offer the opportunity for sharing and comparing of nursing management problems and solutions. Managerial groups differ from region to region, but groups often arise under the aegis of the local or state nurses' association or under local or state units of the NLN. Local units of the American Hospital Association are another source of active nurse manager groups. In some cities, unaffiliated groups of nurse managers form associations.

To socialize and confer with peers in similar managerial positions may be the best education for the manager's role. These groups also give the novice manager a chance to see how her more experienced peers function in roles similar to her own. Additionally, such groups often become the foci for shared management tools or research projects. Belonging to the appropriate groups is part of one's obligation as a professional; using the groups for one's own and others' professional development is a leadership responsibility.

Active work on committees is one way to start making an impact on one's profession, on the health care environment, and on the nation. Enlarging one's scope of understanding is a rewarding endeavor from which the first-line manager gains as much as she gives.

Knowing which organizations exist is not, of course, the same as knowing which issues are being debated at any given time. Issues change; the manager needs to stay on top of them. Organizations are good places to learn the issues and the merits of all cases, but to develop informed judgments, the nurse must look beyond the perspectives of a single group and the limitations of self-serving agendas.

Goals of Professional Organizations

Organized nursing groups endeavor to contribute to the health care of the nation in at least two ways. One is by directly tackling selected health problems. Another is by continually upgrading nursing's own standards.

Organizations work toward the first goal in diverse ways. In the present AIDS crisis, many nursing organizations have taken on projects related to AIDS prevention and education. Other groups tackle local or national health problems of their choice. Specialty organizations, of course, focus on health problems within their own domain.

One of the criticisms aimed at organized nursing by other health care professionals is that nursing is often more concerned with its own internal politics than with the health problems of the nation. This is a criticism that should be seriously heeded by nursing organizations wishing to keep their credibility with the public.

Often issues of public interest are raised when nursing seeks to upgrade its own standards. Nursing is sometimes accused of benefitting nurses at the expense of the public's need for nurses. The philosophic debate concerning more nurses versus better credentialed nurses has a long history. Often, in the past, the nursing profession has sacrificed its own upgrading goals in attempts to meet "quantity" demands for nurses. Few other health professions have made such sacrifices, and many nurses question whether this is an effective tactic for the public welfare in the long run.

Nursing is again embroiled in an upgrading furor at present. The major organizations of the Tri-Council as well as many specialty organizations support the concept of two levels of nurse registration, of which the higher level requires a baccalaureate degree in nursing. Beyond that general agreement, few organizations presently agree on how such a program should work. Further, many organizations and individuals feel that the requirement of a baccalaureate degree would disenfranchise too many nurses.

Since all of the serious proposals include a mechanism for grandfathering present RNs into the "professional nurse" category, this fear would seem to be misplaced. The hard fact of life is that no occupational group in the history of this nation has come to be regarded as "professional" without requiring that its members earn the baccalaureate degree. Nursing has somehow failed to educate its own membership to this fact, however. Often the debate is couched in terms of which "type" of nurse performs better. Such arguments as to the content and quality control in one type of program versus another miss the point, which is a political and strategic one.

The inability of the nursing profession to make a firm decision and act upon it in this matter limits our ability to affect health care in the nation. The overlong internal debate leaves us open to the charge of ineptitude by others. The prolonged dissension allows others to accuse us of putting self-interest before the nation's health.

Since the debate concerning nursing status focuses on changes in licensure, some states have imposed their own resolution by changing their nursing acts independently. Licensure is a state's right, so there is no doubt that states can do this. Reciprocity of licenses for RNs in this mobile society will inevitably be affected as individual states depart from the past uniformity of licensing RNs and LPNs. The nature of licensure itself (as a state prerogative) complicates the issue and makes unilateral action by the states problematic for all nurses. It is certainly a major failure that organized nursing has not yet "gotten its act together" on this vital issue.

Accreditation of educational programs is another method of securing quality in nursing. Just as the Joint Commission accredits hospitals offering nursing practice, the NLN accredits all programs offering nursing education. As is the case with the Joint Commission's accreditation of hospitals, NLN accreditation is nominally "voluntary," though in fact, accredited status is less voluntary than it might appear. Student enrollments in most programs are vulnerable if accreditation is not achieved and maintained.

We have, then, a complex process of checks and balances that affect nursing education and practice. Licensure of individuals and institutions is the first process. Accreditation of practice and education settings is the next step. A third mechanism, certification, allows individual nurses to verify advanced achievements in specialty areas. Certifications complement academic degrees as indices of attainment. Examinations for certification are often offered through specialty organizations or through the ANA.

Two certification programs in nursing administration (regular and advanced) are presently available through the ANA. To qualify for the basic examination, the nurse must already hold a position in middle management.

While professional excellence is the aim of all programs of licensure, accreditation, and certification, this short discussion illustrates that issues and processes involved in assuring the quality of nursing care are never simple. Nevertheless, the nurse manager has a responsibility to herself and to others to grow in her understanding of and commitment to professional excellence.

PROFESSIONAL EXCELLENCE ON THE JOB

The first-line manager is selected for her position because someone higher in the organization believes she can produce excellence in patient care. Sometimes excellent clinicians are promoted who turn out to be failures at managing the work of others, but seldom is a nurse given a management position if she fails to demonstrate excellence in her own performance.

The assumption, then, is that the first-line manager is first and foremost an excellent clinician. Role modeling of skilled, caring nursing is part of promoting clinical excellence in others. This does not necessarily mean that the first-line manager does a lot of direct nursing care, though she may in certain settings. What it does mean, in every case, is that she is clinically informed and up-to-date, that she is on top of the clinical nursing demands in her unit, and that she works to bring others up to the same standards of excellence.

The question to be asked is how the manager can foster professional excellence among her staff? This aspect of leadership was partially addressed in the last chapter: the leader sets the tone. The manager's expectation of professional excellence tends to be a self-fulfilling prophecy when her staff understands her demands.

In addition to role modeling and setting the tone for professional excellence, the first-line manager has other administrative tools and strategies available for encouraging excellence.

Education for Excellence

In order to achieve professional excellence the first-line manager supports ongoing educational advancement among her staff. Again, role modeling is one of the best techniques, but she should also be an informed educational advisor for her subordinates and learn what opportunities for ongoing education are available in her community. In addition to pinpointing educational opportunities, the manager will show flexibility by making necessary hours available for those interested in improving themselves.

An assumption that the manager makes in fostering education is that a nurse who extends her nursing education will be a better, more informed worker. This is usually the case, but the first-line manager sometimes has to walk a fine line between patient needs and staff needs for self-actualization. The first-line manager's job is to provide patient care; that is her primary responsibility. Helping staff to get on with their careers is important, but it must not overshadow the primary objective of providing care.

While formal education leading to advanced degrees represents one avenue for improved staff performance, the manager should also be mindful of informal educational opportunities. The effective manager builds links in the nursing community so that information on educational offerings comes to her attention. Sharing such information with staff is important.

Sometimes the best way to encourage others is to communicate opportunities via specific individuals. A brochure about a relevant educational program that is circulated to a whole staff may be ineffective, but if a particular nurse is singled out and asked to attend and report back to the group, more interest may be engendered.

Sometimes needed educational experiences may be arranged in the home institution. Most institutions of any size have a continuing education department charged with meeting educational deficits. In smaller institutions, inservice education may be one job assignment among others for a given category of nurse.

Wherever it may be found, continuing education of the right sort can promote professional excellence. That occurs when the learning opportunities relate specifically to the work to be done. For example, it would be hard to justify sending a medical-surgical staff nurse to a seminar on obstetric care occurring during work hours. Here the manager would have to consider the trade-off seriously. What would she be getting in return for the sacrificed hours of patient care? If the only benefit were to be the nurse's augmented knowledge (desirable enough in its own right), it would be difficult to justify. Inservice education should prepare the nurse for better performance on the job.

It is also important that educational opportunities be offered to the right staff members. Determining who will best benefit from an educational opportunity can be tricky. Sometimes education is offered as a reward. A conference day, for example, may be given to the best nurse performer in recognition of her achievement. Certainly successful performance merits rewards, but it is also the case that sub-par performance may be improved by education. The constraint should be that anyone going to an educational experience on duty time must understand that she is to bring back to the entire work group new ideas, new methods, new ways to improve performance. Education must be seen as something to be applied, not simply as a day's easy assignment.

Clinical Ladders

Like job-supported education, the clinical ladder concept can do much to promote clinical excellence. The clinical ladder evaluates and rewards nurses based on their clinical performance. Sometimes the tools used for nurse assessment are well designed; sometimes they have flaws. One of the common flaws is that the evaluative techniques rely too heavily on knowledge rather than performance. Clearly, one cannot apply what one does not know, but not all people apply knowledge with equal effectiveness.

Some clinical ladders have educational stipulations as well as performance requirements. For example, a nurse may not be able to go beyond level two— or three, or four—unless she holds an appropriate degree. Other clinical ladders focus exclusively on performance, rewarding what one does rather than what credentials one holds. Both approaches can achieve worthy goals, depending on the philosophy of the institution and the intent of the ladder.

Well designed clinical ladders are structured so that rank on the ladder and rewards (status, pay level) coincide. If a ladder offers no rewards for advancement, then it is hard for staff to take it seriously. Remuneration is the reward for excellence in this society; nursing excellence should not be an exception.

The existence of a clinical ladder is an important incentive to professional excellence. The first-line manager's responsibility is to use it both to encourage nurses who deserve advancement to apply for it and to prompt others to higher levels of performance. If the clinical ladder tools are not capable of accurately discriminating levels of performance, then the manager should work to improve the tools.

Nursing Research

Another mechanism that encourages a mind set of professional excellence is the implementation of nursing research in the practice setting. Even if the research involves simple field studies testing one method of nursing versus another, the presence of clinical nursing inquiry reminds nurses that they are professionals. Discussions of recent research and of how research findings might be applied to the first-line manager's unit can also foster professional excellence.

Most nursing organizations have access to one or more nurses who have research expertise. In some organizations the first-line manager might herself have to locate the experts she needs. The manager must be aware of the level of expertise and the level of enthusiasm or anxiety shown by her staff in relation to research. Sometimes creating enthusiasm for this exciting aspect of the nursing profession can be as important as the research project itself.

Summary

The nurse's notion of professional excellence can be severely tested in today's stressful practice environment. When quality of care conflicts with availability of resources, the first-line manager must help staff deal with the conflict in a productive way. The last chapter discussed the resource-driven model of care as one mechanism for dealing with this conflicting demand. The creative manager may find her own solutions.

Building an expectation of professional excellence is the first step toward making it a reality. First and foremost, the manager must herself demonstrate this trait. It is up to her to indoctrinate her staff in the desirability of professional excellence, and it is up to her to find ways to support the staff who seek to excel.

BIBLIOGRAPHY

Aroskar, M. "The Interface of Ethics and Politics in Nursing." *Nursing Outlook* 35, no. 6 (1987): 268.

Aydelotte, M.K. "Nursing's Preferred Future." *Nursing Outlook* 35, no. 3 (1987): 114.

Benner, P. *From Novice to Expert: Excellence and Power in Clinical Nursing Practice.* Menlo Park, CA: Addison-Wesley Publishing Co., 1984.

Boggs, D.; Baker, B.; and Price, G. "Determining Two Levels of Nursing Competency." *Nursing Outlook* 35, no. 1 (1987): 34.

Courtney, R. "Community Practice: Nursing Influence on Policy Formulation." *Nursing Outlook* 35, no. 4 (1987): 170.

del Bueno, D.J., and Freund, C.M. *Power & Politics in Nursing Administration: A Casebook.* Owings Mills, MD: National Health Publishing, 1986.

Hegyvary, S.T.; Duxbury, M.L.; Hall, R.H.; Krueger, J.C.; Lindeman, C.A.; Scott, J.M.; and Scott, W.R. *The Evolution of Nursing Professional Organizations.* Kansas City, KS: American Academy of Nursing, 1987.

Kelly, L.S. "The Ethic of Caring: Has It Been Discarded?" (editorial). *Nursing Outlook* 36, no. 1 (1988): 17.

Murphy, E.K. "The Professional Status of Nursing: A View from the Courts." *Nursing Outlook* 35, no. 1 (1987): 12.

O'Connor, A.B. *Nursing Staff Development and Continuing Education.* Boston: Little, Brown & Co., 1986.

Reverby, S.M. *Ordered to Care: The Dilemma of American Nursing, 1850-1945.* Cambridge: Cambridge University Press, 1987.

Schlotfeldt, R.M. "Reflections on Nursing, 1987." *Nursing Outlook* 35, no. 5 (1987): 226.

Styles, M.M. "The Tarnished Opportunity." *Nursing Outlook* 35, no. 5 (1987): 229.

Wieczorek, R.R., ed. *Power, Politics, and Policy in Nursing.* New York: Springer Publishing Co., 1985.

chapter *5*

Goal-oriented Management and Strategic Planning

Chapter 3 looked at the difference between two different ideologies of patient care: goal-driven and resource-driven. The tension concerning "where you begin," i.e., what drives the model, is also reflected in this chapter. Here we look at the ideologies as they apply to management processes. As with many aspects of management, the result will not be the advocacy of one method over another for all times, in all circumstances. Rather, the key will be to ask which tactic suits the immediate contingencies—which approach or combination of approaches may be effectively applied.

ALTERNATIVE STARTING POINTS

Mintzberg long ago described three different managerial approaches; his perspective holds as true today as when he first recognized it. Indeed, the differentiation helps to explain why today's management looks very different from the forms advocated a mere decade or two ago. Mintzberg identified three styles or approaches predominant among managers: the planning mode, the adaptive mode, and the entrepreneurial mode.[1]

The Planning Mode

When Mintzberg made his observations, the planning mode predominated in health care management as well as in industry as a whole. In the planning mode, the manager devises finely drawn, carefully conceived plans for a given period, often three to five years or longer. Logical goals are set, detailed systems are devised to achieve them, resources are dedicated to the systems, and evaluation procedures are specifically determined to measure achievement.

60

MBO (management by objectives) typifies this approach. Notice that MBO is the managerial equivalent of the total nursing care model discussed in Chapter 3: one starts with goals, and all other activities flow from these selections.

MBO captivated the health care world when it was imported from industry, where it had been popular. MBO was a model that reflected the times, i.e., the context, and it became popular at a time when change was less rapid, when one didn't have to be a visionary to see three, five, or even ten years ahead. The future could be predicted from the status quo. In that era it was not illogical to take a highly rational "plan ahead" approach to management.

Notice that even though MBO is oriented toward the future, it is still based on the present. That is, the manager using MBO sets goals for the future based on her knowledge of the present. Further, she assumes that the means of achieving those goals (the methods, the tactics) are stable enough so that she can select appropriate tactics for achieving the goals within the range of presently available methods. In this sense, MBO assumes a static (or at least stable), predictable world, where change is slow in coming and so easy to forecast that it can be taken into account in one's planning.

MBO was marketed as proactive, a descriptor seen as "good" in that originating era, as opposed to reactive, a label then applied with some disdain by many managers. MBO was seen at the time as a permanent way to manage, as *the* way. As is the case with almost every solution offered as the apex of some line of development, MBO's advocates were blind to its limitations. In this case the blindness involved the failure to see that MBO requires a world that is easily predicted, moves slowly, and is not subject to radical shifts of the environment. Also, MBO, as typically applied in that era, was a low-risk form—the goals set in such rational plans were seldom earth-shaking. The structure of the method itself, with its reliance on the known, is incompatible with searching for brave new worlds.

The mark of a good MBO system, so many of its advocates said at the time, is that one can compose the evaluation tool in advance just by knowing the initial objectives. Notice that this system is highly logical and assumes a rational world. The rationality of the system was reinforced by the creation and adaptation of many mathematical models of decision making.

As with many systems that stress planning and stability, it is not surprising that in MBO much attention was devoted to paperwork. Since the plans that were made were to last and direct the work for many years, the documents identifying the objectives and their plans for achievement were labored over almost as much as the tasks themselves.

As MBO was applied in most hospitals and many nursing departments, it followed a rigorous design, with yearly or longer-term objectives set in stone (or at least committed to paper). Goals, modalities for achievement, and expected outcomes were often neatly set out in coordinated columns. Following the industrial model typical in this nation, most MBO models in health care were top-down distributions. That is, the higher organizational levels set objectives that were transmitted down the line until they reached the lowest levels. Faithful to this model, nursing administration often set divisional goals that were transmitted downward to its departments and units.

The attempt to follow a pure top-down model has usually failed in nursing, primarily because the goals of the different levels of a nursing organization diverge. While a vice president for nursing, for example, may be engrossed in creating systems to distribute resources and work load, the head nurse is concerned with the everyday need to provide care to a body of patients.

Nursing soon became flexible in its use of the MBO model: overall goals were set at the top levels, with lower organizational units (including individual patient care units) given the authority to set objectives that were specific to their own patient populations or functional assignments. This combination of top-down and bottom-up MBO worked effectively for many organizations for many years.

The planning model is still the approach of choice for some tasks in the nursing organization, namely those that are slow to change, easily predictable, and amenable to logical analysis and detailed planning. For example, if a nursing division of a hospital were planning a move to a new facility, the planning mode would probably be the one of choice in preparing the highly detailed logistic plan that would be needed to achieve the move.

The Adaptive Mode

An alternate managerial approach is the adaptive mode. As Mintzberg described this mode of managerial planning, it was in many ways the opposite of the planning mode. First, it was characterized as being reactive rather than proactive. That is, managers do most of their planning, make most of their decisions, in response to things happening in the environment. (The planning model, in contrast, tries to control its environment to a greater degree, or simply takes a stable environment as a given.)

Since it is reactive, the adaptive mode cannot make plans that extend irrevocably into the future. Further, there is little opportunity for all-encompassing plans, since each managerial adjustment is made in response to some unanticipated change in the environment. Hence the goals of an adaptive approach tend to be different from MBO goals; they tend to help the organization reduce conflict, negotiate with major power brokers in the environment, solve immediate and pressing problems. The emphasis on method in the adaptive mode is greater than the emphasis on the substance of the changes to be made.

Adjustments in the adaptive mode tend to be incremental rather than broad-scope—just enough change to solve this problem, then just enough reorganization to solve the next pressing need. Unlike the planning model, there is little rhyme or reason as to what problems are addressed. The old adage of the squeaky wheel getting the oil probably applies as well as any.

The management literature describes one management form, management by exception (MBE) that might, depending on how it is interpreted, be seen to fit the reactive, adaptive mode. If the exceptions, i.e., irregularities, are environmental presses, then MBE can be seen as a reactive model. Many authors, however, discuss MBE in a different sense: "exceptions" are deviations found during the ongoing evaluations of the MBO model. Here the notion of MBE is more that of making subtle adjustments toward previously established goals.

For many nurses the adaptive mode looks much like the problem-solving method they once studied as a clinical approach. In the problem-solving method, the nurse responds to the clinical problems presented by the patient; in adaptive management, the first-line manager responds to the environmental presses of the moment. Many head nurses and other first-line managers feel that this format fits better with the reality of their environments than did the prior planning mode. For example, a head nurse on an inpatient unit might perceive that the needs of her unit fluctuate widely depending on the conditions of its patients at any given time. The same could be true in a community health care agency.

In the era when MBO predominated, an adaptive mode tended to be viewed as uninspired, lacking leadership, and lacking direction. When the future was easy to predict and the health world was relatively stable, that was a position easy to defend. All that changed when radical influences (interferences, if you will) from the outside society began to have a severe impact on how the health world did its business.

Numerous environmental factors have played a role in this revolution; many of them have been described in the first few chapters of this book. Only a few of the major influences will be mentioned here as illustrations. What they share is the fact that, singly and in combination, they rocked the health world out of its smug complacency and its neat predictability.

The imposition of the DRG system by the federal government was one of the first shock waves. Suddenly the reimbursements received by institutions depended on their following someone else's rules—rules unlike those used by the industry in the past, rules which forced radical belt-tightening and changed the health care system virtually overnight.

A subtle change that accompanied the DRG system was the instantaneous computerization of the health care industry. It wasn't even possible for small hospitals to play in the ball park without the equipment that could collect and correlate essential data. This change, now been passed down to the community health industry, has tended to bring an old-fashioned business into the twentieth century with a jolt.

Along with the reorganized payment schemes arising throughout the nation (not merely in federally controlled reimbursement), a new pressure was introduced into the health care industry: competition. Until this conscious thrust was started by the federal overseers, the health care industry had never been concerned with selling itself; it had a captive purchaser for its services. The novel necessity to sell one's goods required a whole new expertise. Suddenly the health care industry was talking about consumers rather than patients.

At the same time, medical technology confronted the health care world with at least two problems. First, technology outreached the managers' abilities to predict its development. Technology was changing too rapidly to be set in five- or even three-year plans. One simply didn't know what kinds of equipment or new therapies would affect next year's budget, let alone a budget for longer periods. Rational planning was no longer so rational. Technology was a player who no longer abided by the rules.

The second problem involved the interplay between technology and cost; technology hit a financial wall. Much of the new technology was very expensive, and it arose in a system no longer able to finance every new device or therapy by raising fees for patients. For the first time, the health care industry was faced with the notion of care rationed because of its costs.

In such an environment the adaptive mode of management no longer looked so strange. Indeed, it was a fortunate health care agency that managed to keep up with the diverse changes in its environment. Simply interpreting the incessant changes in the here and now (forget the future) required a different set of skills than those normally found in the health care executive.

And the executive who could estimate what changes in social policies or medical advances would mean for his institution was a "winner" in the growing competition among institutions. It was, and continues to be, a high-stakes game, since there are no winners unless there are also losers.

As of the present time, the radical and unexpected shifts occurring as health care becomes a corporate business are not over. Nor can all of the ongoing changes be attributed to changing business practices and legislation. The AIDS epidemic, for example, has contributed to overturning the predictions of most prognosticators that we would need fewer hospital beds in the future.

For the first-line nurse manager, the adaptive mode may offer a model that fits, to a large degree, with the environment around her. Problem solving and adapting are important managerial methods when the environment (1) consists of unpredictable and fluctuating aspects, (2) contains many novel situations that are difficult to interpret, and (3) has diverse elements that require separate rather than uniform treatment. In an environment with these characteristics it may be foolhardy to set too many rigid goals in advance; the goals may arise more naturally from the immediate problems that confront management.

Yet it is inadequate to use only an adaptive approach in circumstances other than those demanding crisis management. A balance between adaptive and planning behavior may be the best solution for most first-line managers. The balance may shift from time to time between these two strategies. Flexibility in managerial approach is clearly the key.

The Entrepreneurial Mode

Mintzberg's final managerial approach is the entrepreneurial. In this mode there is a search for new opportunities that have not been grasped in the past. Unlike both the planning and adaptive modes, the entrepreneurial model does not "play it safe." It is more likely to occur in situations where there is a chance of scoring a major "win" if the manager guesses correctly. Obviously, entrepreneurial management also runs a greater risk of encountering failure. High risk for a high gain is the game with this approach.

Unlike the adaptive model, the entrepreneurial model is proactive. It strives to look ahead and to influence or shape the future in the desired direction.

It is not surprising that we see increased entrepreneurial behavior in the health field today. Like adaptive behavior, the entrepreneurial model tends to arise when things are in flux. The very fact that the health care field is unsettled makes it possible for creative managers to see new prospects, new opportunities.

Entrepreneurial vision has introduced such innovations as the corporate care delivery model, the free-standing one-day surgery or emergency care center, and the community day care center that provides relief time for the full-time caretaker tending an invalid family member (for example, a wife caring for a husband afflicted with Alzheimer's disease). The reader will be able to think of many more entrepreneurial tactics that have affected health care in the present era.

Nursing has had its share of members who have ventured into entrepreneurial enterprises. Often these efforts have involved establishing small businesses that specialize in some sort of patient care or nurse education. Some nurse entrepreneurs have successfully offered services that had not been sought by earlier generations. Some have started businesses dealing with aspects of well care that relate to life style. Those who saw this need before it became a trend did very well with their businesses, at least until their efforts were diffused by others trying to market similar services to the same publics.

The entrepreneurial mode requires not only that one be the first to spot an opportunity but also that one be innovative in keeping ahead when others try to capitalize on a good thing. Nurses marketing continuing education once had a distinct advantage. Now every institution and agency markets continuing education offerings. The effect, of course, has been a dilution of the potential market for everyone. The highest form of flattery may be imitation, but too much imitation may swamp an entrepreneurial effort. Some of the latest entrepreneurial efforts by nurses have dealt with the production of tools and computer services that facilitate nursing evaluation or other aspects of management.

Much like the adaptive mode, the entrepreneurial mode involves analyzing change and seeing how it may be used to advantage. In health care, meeting a new health need or meeting an old need in a new way are common tactics.

The opportunities for entrepreneurial efforts in a first-line management position will vary from place to place. A first-line manager, by definition, functions in an organizational structure of which she is not the architect. Nevertheless, the institution may be willing to back a creative manager who sees a new opportunity for progress or profit.

Sometimes entrepreneurial initiatives concern small things rather than big ones. For example, some nursing care units have solved shortage problems and met convalescent needs at the same time by turning units into spouse education wards that teach spouses how to care for a husband or wife about to be discharged.

Whether or not the first-line manager will use an entrepreneurial model depends on many factors; her ability to see things in atypical fashion and her experience in the first-line role are two of them.

Mintzberg's models for management provide three different strategies for addressing the management task. The approaches may be used separately or in judicious combination. Certain aspects of the management role may fit more comfortably with one approach than another. The three modes have three different starting places. The planning mode begins with the goals to be achieved, the adaptive mode starts with the problems to be solved, and the entrepreneurial mode starts with the opportunities recognized in the extant situation.

STRATEGIC PLANNING

Strategic planning, as the term is commonly used, is a managerial tactic that combines some aspects of Mintzberg's adaptive and entrepreneurial modes. Perhaps it is best characterized as an aggressive approach to creative adaptation. Strategic planning is this era's answer to the limitations of the MBO model. In a sense strategic planning itself represents a contingency approach to management, because it has arisen in response to the changing environment of the times. The approach is prevalent in other industries as well as in health care management.

Strategic management is an approach designed to work in an environment subject to rapid and unanticipated changes. It is designed to keep one eye on the changing environment and another on the real and potential competition. It builds in flexibility just as the older MBO system built in stability. Its time dimension, unlike MBO, is the eternal present with an eye to the future, but its notion of the future may change from day to day, and its planning may change accordingly.

At the corporate level, the process of strategic planning goes something like this. Strategic planning starts at the beginning by looking at the mission and goals of an organization, none of which is assumed to be immutable. A goal or even the mission may be revised if analysis shows it to be outmoded. Mission and goals are examined, not in the abstract, but through several screens, the first of which is the place of the organization in its multiple environments.

One of the most important environments considered is that of competition. Who are the competitors? How does the organization compare with its competitors? How is it different? Techniques of marketing are brought to bear on these questions. The objective is to identify the ways in which the organization is better than or different from its competitors. If it is difficult to define differences, then the primary aim is to establish a clearer mission and goals. One major value of the strategic planning approach is that one may define how an institution is unique, what special purpose it serves, or how it serves a common purpose in a different manner than the rest. Creating a unique identity is an important aspect of strategic planning.

The purpose of defining how an organization is different is twofold. First, it is easier to "sell" one's services if appealing aspects can be highlighted for the prospective consumer. Second, being different constitutes a nucleus around which a staff may build pride and enthusiasm.

Competition is one environmental aspect to be considered in strategic planning; the customer is another. Here again an aggressive marketing perspective is taken: Who is my present customer? What new consumers might I cultivate? What customer opportunities am I missing and why?

Notice that just as the final mission and goals might be influenced by the competition, so might they be influenced by the customer. There is much more back-and-forth movement among the pieces in strategic planning than in MBO. For example, a group might reformulate its central mission in order to capture a new consumer group that would not have been attracted by the earlier mission.

The "back-and-forth" negotiating among elements is a prominent characteristic of strategic planning. The MBO system, in contrast, does not change its objectives just because someone thinks of an unserved group. The movement in MBO starts at the beginning and moves to the end in an orderly fashion. Strategic planning is messier, with more sudden adjustments. Anything can be changed if a new opportunity is seen.

In addition to analyzing the competition and the customer, the organization doing strategic planning also analyzes itself. This involves, in the best of circumstances, a forthright analysis of its strengths and weaknesses. Unlike some systems, strategic planning makes no attempt to deny weaknesses. Every business has them; the aim here is to identify them. When one knows one's strengths and weaknesses, then one can build plans on that knowledge. Goals are selected to capitalize on the inherent strengths of an organization. Knowing what one is good at makes it possible to put one's best foot forward.

Another aspect of strategic analysis concerns knowing which actions in which environments may affect how one does business. In health care, for example, one might consider such diverse things as anticipated changes in federal reimbursement policies, constraints imposed by a state board of health, demographic changes in the population using the institution, and changes in corporate tax laws. The challenge is to identify the aspects of the environment that are likely to have the most direct impact on the organization in the upcoming management period. Since the notion of environment is open-ended, it is a challenge of the first order. Even though planning periods are usually conceptualized in smaller blocks of time than is the case under MBO, it is still a challenge to identify the elements that will have the greatest impact on the enterprise.

The organization's mission and goals are roughed out after considering all these factors. The mission and goals devised in strategic planning may look a little different than those established under an MBO scheme. First, they tend to be dynamic rather than comprehensive. An organization engaging in strategic planning won't take on every possible worthy goal, nor will it adopt every virtuous mission. Instead, it is likely to identify a few broad thrusts, a focus or two for its upcoming activities.

The notion is to invest one's energies in a few major areas rather than try to distribute mission and goals over the whole organization like tinsel over a Christmas tree. It isn't that nothing else will happen during the planned period, but it is assumed that many functions will continue outside the focus of attention. The purchasing department will continue to purchase, the dietary kitchen will continue to prepare meals, and if they aren't at the center of planned activity no time will be spent constructing lists of goals for them at the top managerial level.

Strategic planning, then, focuses on where the action will be. It sets the goals for those few endeavors that are identified as critical. Action is concentrated on the several areas of change that are expected to have important payoffs for the organization. Once the broad thrusts for the planning period have been determined, then discretionary resource allocation can be used to support those thrusts.

Once the broad thrusts are determined, the group using strategic planning moves on to determining the methods to achieve the goals, just as MBO planners would. Unlike MBO, however, strategic planning may develop several methods, several scenarios, several alternative tactics. Often these are in the form of "If X happens, we'll do Y; if Z happens, we'll do Q." Flexibility of a new order is built into the approach. Although methods take into account possible changes in the environment, they are tentative and may be changed if they are not working.

Nor are strategic goals inviolable, as are those of MBO. Often strategic planning offers alternatives: "If we can't succeed in bringing about X, then we'll try to achieve Y." Once again, flexibility is the key.

Nevertheless, the corporate group keeps its eye on the targets. Evaluation of one's success in achieving targets is an important step. Unlike MBO, evaluation under strategic planning is a continuous process, not a culminating activity. And the result of a less than desirable evaluation may be the dropping of a goal, the formulation of a new goal (not necessarily related to the old one), or a new scenario using different approaches to the same goal.

In strategic planning there are always goals, but they may be updated and changed at a rapid rate depending upon the success factor, which in turn may depend on how well and how accurately the planning group anticipated important environmental changes. One advantage of strategic planning over the MBO model is this ability to make rapid changes if the situation requires it. Strategic planning enables even the large institution to act with alacrity as things change.

Under MBO it is a major failure if a corporation or division fails to achieve its objectives. With strategic planning there is more acceptance of error and miscalculation; the worst mistake is to stay too long with a losing hand. The sooner one recognizes an error, the better the opportunity for revising the strategy. The sooner one sees a change in the environment, the quicker one acts to modify the strategic plan.

Strategic Planning and First-Line Management

The first-line manager may be involved in strategic planning in at least two ways. As a manager in a nursing division she may be expected to participate in the setting of divisional goals for an upcoming planning period. If she does participate in this process, it will be important for her to understand which model (strategic planning or MBO) dominates in her organization. If MOB dominates, resources are likely to be equally distributed, and the plan is unlikely to change.

If strategic planning is the model of choice, however, she should know that the manager who presents new ideas and bold new programs may receive special funding. When one's unit or activities are not the focus of strategic planning, it is important to be able to explain strategic planning to one's staff, who need to understand why the attention and resources are directed elsewhere. Understanding this planning strategy will help staff to reconcile perceived differences in treatment among various organizational units.

In addition to participating in strategic planning at an organizational level, the first-line manager may have the opportunity to apply the concept to her own level of management. For example, strategic planning may affect the way in which she manages her budget. Since strategic planning is flexible, it is seldom tied directly to line items, as is often the case with MBO. The first-line manager may have the opportunity to use a given budget allotment at her own discretion. For example, the head nurse of an inpatient unit might have the freedom to determine what levels of staff to employ, provided she does not exceed the total figure budgeted for personnel. Similarly, she might have the opportunity to put some of her budget into projects of her own choosing.

Strategic planning gives the creative manager a chance to shine. Departments using the strategic planning model are usually more flexible in their approach to care delivery. An administration committed to strategic planning should be willing to fund exciting new trial programs. A first-line manager in such an organization may have the opportunity to try new methods without fearing censure if they fail.

NOTE

1. H. Mintzberg, "Strategy Making in Three Modes," *California Management Review* 16, no. 2 (1973): 44.

BIBLIOGRAPHY

Alward, R.R. "A Marketing Approach to Nursing Administration—Part I. Journal of Nursing Administration 13, no. 3 (1983): 9.

Alward, R.R. "A Marketing Approach to Nursing Administration—Part II. *Journal of Nursing Administration* 13, no. 4 (1983): 18.

Fox, D.H., and Fox, R.I. "Strategic Planning for Nursing." *Journal of Nursing Administration* 13, no. 5 (1983): 11.

Gluck, F.W.; Kaufman, S.P.; and Walleck, A.S. "Strategic Management for Competitive Advantage." *Harvard Business Review* 58, no. 2 (1980): 154.

Goertzen, I.E. "Making Nursing's Vision a Reality." *Nursing Outlook* 35, no. 3 (1987): 121.

Lukacs, J.L. "Strategic Planning in Hospitals: Applications for Nurse Executives. *Journal of Nursing Administration* 14, no. 9 (1984): 11.

Pilpel, R.H., coordinator. *Preserving the Quality of Health Care in a Changing Environment.* New York: National Health Council, 1987.

Smith, G.R. "The New Health Care Economy: Opportunities for Nurse Entrepreneurs." *Nursing Outlook* 35, no. 4 (1987): 182.

Sowell, R., and Alexander, J.W. "A Model for Success in Nursing Administration." *Nursing & Health Care* 9, no. 1 (1988): 24.

chapter *6*

Productivity and Managed Efficiency

Previous chapters discussed the first-line manager's goals for patients and for staff. This chapter focuses on her goals for the management process itself. Managerial goals are easier to describe than to achieve. In essence, the first-line manager wants to accomplish the greatest number of clinically desirable goals for patients with the lowest possible use of resources (human and material). Secondarily, she wants to achieve this while enhancing the professionalism and job satisfaction of her staff.

Such an achievement requires success in two long-recognized areas of managerial work: (1) human relations, and (2) task orientation. In attending to human relations in her unit, the first-line manager must be cognizant of her own relationships with staff members and the interpersonal relations among staff as peers and coworkers. Both aspects of human relations are important, and both are affected by the approach of the first-line manager. The human relations aspect of managerial work is discussed in Part III of this book.

Task orientation also has two components. The manager is interested in the quality of the work itself as well as in the way that the unit is structured to bring about the work. The first aspect deals directly with goals; it concerns the quality of care given to patients and the patient outcomes attributed to that care. The second aspect has to do with how efficiently the manager arranges for work to be completed. The assignment systems, supply systems, reporting systems, and other mechanisms for work planning, implementation, and evaluation are involved here.

Sometimes nurses have philosophic objections to working in resource-scarce situations. They argue that deficits should not be allowed or encouraged in an arena of life as vital as health care. While the nurse has a right to hold such a position, others would argue that the notion is a naive one that fails to take account of the present dictates of the society. Society has given health care providers a clear message in recent years to cut back on the resources used in health care.

The nurse who rejects that position is obligated to work within the political domain to bring about changes. Meanwhile, of necessity she functions in a world where scarce resources are a fact of life for most nurses and most first-line managers.

EFFECTIVENESS AND EFFICIENCY

In a resource-scarce environment it is important that the first-line manager make the most of her human, material, and organizational resources. Two managerial criteria will help in evaluating her success in that endeavor: effectiveness and efficiency.

One is effective if one's goals are achieved. Hence effectiveness deals primarily with quality. Did the patient progress as desired? Did the care come up to standard? Were the outcome goals for various groups of patients achieved?

Efficiency, on the other hand, asks whether or not the goals are achieved with economical use of resources. Sometimes efficiency is simplistically associated with how fast or how cheaply something is done. For example, a nurse might claim efficiency if she increases the number of clinic clients seen per day by twenty percent. If this were achieved with the same number of staff, it might seem to be an efficient move on the face of it. However, if one were to discover that few of the patients left the clinic with a clear understanding of how to meet their own care needs, the "improvement" would turn out to be illusory. Processing more people with fewer objectives achieved is a false notion of efficiency. For purposes of this discussion, efficiency will refer to the achievement of one's objectives (i.e., effectiveness) with the lowest possible expenditure of resources.

The goal-driven model of total patient care discussed in Chapter 3 aims primarily for effectiveness—that is, achieving all goals set for a patient. The resource-driven model of care, in contrast, focuses mainly on the efficiency factor by considering the interplay of resources and goals and then aiming for the greatest total payoff from the final activity choices.

Management Models

From a managerial perspective, MBO (management by objectives) is equivalent to the goal-driven model of total nursing care, while strategic management (see Chapter 5) is the structural companion of the resource-driven model of patient care. The same methods of operating can be applied, in essence, to the two different domains: patient care and management.

Under MBO the manager sets goals, plans for their achievement, acquires the necessary resources, implements the plan, and evaluates the success or failure to achieve the original goals. The steps are identical to those of "total nursing care," i.e., the goal-driven model.

Strategic planning, in contrast, applies the same methods of operating that underlie resource-driven care. The environment is carefully surveyed to determine what resources it holds, goals are picked and constantly redefined in light of that environment and its changes, methods are selected in light of the resources, and achievement is judged on the basis of the interaction of goals, resources, and environment.

Financial Models

Just as there are managerial correlates of the goal-driven and resource-driven models of care, there are financial planning and evaluation methods that follow each pattern. The first-line manager may need to use one or the other in costing out projects that she plans for her unit. The first, the *cost effectiveness* model, is used to compare the expense of two or more different methods of achieving a given set of desired outcomes.

For example, a head nurse of a coronary care unit might consider two different methods of providing advanced knowledge and procedures training for her staff. The goals (level of knowledge, degree of command of procedures) would be set in advance; i.e., the outcome is held to be fixed, unvaried. One option might be to send staff to a program outside of the home institution. An alternative might involve buying educational hardware and software designed to teach the same information in self-tutorial sessions.

Assuming that the head nurse had accurately assessed the two alternatives as equally satisfactory in meeting her objectives, this manager might make her choice based on various criteria other than the objectives that were held constant. In some cases, cost might be the dominant factor. In other cases, she might also weigh the negative aspects of each option (e.g., numbers of staff gone from the institution for several weeks versus lack of a human teacher/role model). Positive aspects above and beyond the achievement of her objectives might also be considered. For example, with the second option the institution would own the hardware and software after the program, and it might be used in the future should staff changes occur. A cost effectiveness model is designed to allow the manager to compare alternative means of reaching a predetermined set of goals.

The second model, *cost-benefit* analysis, like the resource-driven care model, does not have objectives set in stone. The cost-benefit model compares different actions or projects whose objectives differ. Cost-benefit analysis compares programs (projects, proposals) with different inputs (costs, resources) and different benefits (objectives).

A first-line manager in an ambulatory care clinic, for example, might have funds and personnel hours available for a new project. However, she may not have enough resources for all of the projects that would benefit her clientele. She might need a method that fleshes out the advantages of one option versus those of another. Suppose she has narrowed the choice to two projects. She may wish to compare the advantages of an educational program for prevention of teenage pregnancy and a program for hypertension control in an older age population.

To make the determination, each project must be described as to the resources it would require for its implementation and maintenance. These inputs are then balanced against the goals that each project would be expected to achieve in the community. In this case, the two programs do not share the same objectives, nor would their costs be identical. Nevertheless, to spell out the costs and the benefits for each proposal gives one a better basis upon which to compare apples and oranges.

One question that the first-line manager must ask herself is which program will give her the highest ratio of benefit to cost? In some cases the question can be reduced to a dollar amount, but in most cases, like the one above, intangibles will also enter into the decision. In the present case, the manager would probably need some estimate of the seriousness of the two problems in her community before she could estimate either cost or benefit potentials. She would also need to estimate the number of persons likely to be reached by each program.

Like the resource-driven model of care, cost-benefit analysis considers the ratio of benefit to cost; it is thus a productivity model. Obviously this model calls for more complex decision making than that involved in the cost effectiveness model. And it is clearly possible that two evaluators might come to different conclusions. Nevertheless, a clear comparison of cost with anticipated benefit for each alternative will give the manager a basis for making a sound decision.

Table 6-1 compares the effectiveness and efficiency models as applied to first-line management. Aspects of both care and management are specified.

PRODUCTIVITY

In an environment where resources are scarce it is important to get the most out of every available resource. The manager is productive if that goal is achieved, unproductive if she fails. Productivity can be quantified as a ratio between input and output. In nursing, input is primarily measured in

Table 6-1 Comparison of Effectiveness and Efficiency Models

Effectiveness Model	Efficiency Model
PHILOSOPHY	
Ideal world, unlimited resources	Real world, limited
IMPETUS	
Goal-driven	Resource-driven
PATIENT IMAGE	
Each individual patient's needs	Constellation of patients and their needs
VALUES	
Ideal care, total nursing	Best constellation of care choices
MANAGERIAL MODEL	
Management by objectives	Strategic management
ECONOMIC MODEL	
Cost effectiveness	Cost benefit
FLEXIBILITY	
Method not explored if it achieves goals	Method evaluated for productivity
QUALITY-QUANTITY DIMENSIONS	
Quality goals	Quality and quantity considerations
EVALUATION	
Goal achievement	Goal achievement, selection of goals, productivity ratio

resources of personnel hours, expertise, supplies, equipment, organizing structures, and even in the layout of the plant (i.e., its architectural and functional use of space). Output is described as some measurement of the product. In business the product may be goods or services. In nursing the product is usually a unit of service rendered to a patient or group of patients.

Productivity is not an absolute value but a relative one; it increases or decreases as the input relates to the output. Suppose, for example, we were comparing the input of nursing hours to the output of care services. Productivity increases if (1) the same services can be delivered in fewer nursing hours, (2) the same nursing hours produce more services, (3) nursing hours increase slower than services increase, or (4) nursing hours decrease slower than services decrease.

The appropriate output measures are different for different nursing services. A clinic might measure output in number of patient visits, number of clients, or number of patient "cures." An acute care unit might measure the number of patients served, the number of patient days, or some more sophisticated variant such as the number of patient care units (Us) delivered.

Productivity increases as input declines or output rises. Productivity is often calculated in numerical ratios so that changes can be tracked over time. The first-line manager will want to identify her own productivity indices if none is dictated by her institution. Productivity indices should be derived from data that can be gathered easily on her own unit.

Productivity Indices

Productivity indices need not be exacting and complicated. Sometimes the easiest index is the best. The oldest productivity index, still in use by some places, is probably the measure of nursing hours per patient day. Here, nursing hours worked make up the input, and patient days hospitalized form the output. For many years this index was the primary measurement tool of nursing productivity nationwide.

The limitations of this simple index are easy to identify. Any first-line manager can report the radical variation in daily care needs from patient to patient. The notion that all "patient days" are equivalent is misleading. As the acuity of patients in many institutions increased, the patient-day index became less meaningful. The frustration of nurse managers with the nursing-hours-per-patient-day index led to the derivation of more precise indices of nursing productivity. The research behind many of the newer nursing management tools (patient classification systems in particular) focused on identifying data that might serve in productivity indicators.

The following section of this chapter suggests data sources for productivity indices. They are available in most care delivery settings. Yet the selected indices must be taken merely as illustrations. Each first-line manager will want to consider which data best illustrate productivity in her own situation.

Staffing (S) as simple cumulative nursing hours is a definitive input measure that is easily obtained. In its simplest form, staffing may be calculated as the total number of work hours of a given staff for a given period of time (as was the historical practice). If the productivity figure is to be calculated for a longer period than a given shift, then work hours can be averaged.

In the simplest input-output ratio, staffing might be compared with patient census figures (C), i.e., patient days—S:C. Obviously, if the staff hours remain constant while the number of patients increases, the productivity ratio improves.

A more sophisticated derivation of staffing could be arrived at by factoring in a multiple representing each worker's level of skill (e.g., higher points for an RN hour than a nurse's aide hour). A weighted figure of this sort would represent two variables, staff hours (S) and average skill level (L). We might represent this derived factor as S/L. Here our ratio of input to output becomes S/L:C.

A more sophisticated output figure might further enhance this ratio. We might calculate total patient care units (Us) for the ward or clinic rather than use the simpler census data. Total patient care units enable the nurse manager to reflect a situation in which the correspondence of work to be done with number of patients varies. In this circumstance a manager might want to use the productivity ratio S/L:U.

Notice that the variables identified above (S,L,C,U) primarily represent quantity. If the first-line manager wanted to ensure that the notion of effectiveness, i.e., quality of care, was included, she might perform an additional mathematical manipulation. Patient care units (us) or patient-days (C) might be modified by multiplying them by an averaged-out score from the unit's quality assurance results (Q). The productivity ratios resulting in these cases might include the following:

- S:C/Q
- S:U/Q
- S/L:C/Q
- S/L:U/Q

The first-line manager might decide that she wants aspects of quality to be represented on both sides of the equation. The quality control scores (Q) on the output side might be balanced by average performance scores of a unit's staff (P) on the input side. This added variable would require a sophisticated method of performance appraisal scoring, but the manager might end up with an equation such as S/L/P:C/Q or S/L/P:U/Q.

These data might be very interesting if used to compare care units. Assuming the validity of the measurement tools used, one could answer such interesting questions as whether "better staff" deliver "better care," or whether "better staff" give "better care" under all circumstances or only when there is a certain level of input (resources)?

Comparing data such as those suggested above with inservice education hours offers another source of productivity information. Does inservice education (attendance hours or grades) improve performance (quality assurance scores before and after)? Or does it only improve performance under certain conditions?

It is likely that a first-line manager will use several productivity indices. When the work of her unit is perceived in different ways, she gains more information with which to make managerial decisions. This is what is meant by managed efficiency—management in which care delivery is streamlined according to available facts and figures as well as by experienced intuition.

Variations would occur in the indices selected depending on the setting. In a clinic setting or in a home health care operation, patient visits or patient visits modified by a time factor might be the output instead of patient care units, for example. In a nursing home, quality of life factors might need to be included in deriving indices. Each setting, however, has elements that lend themselves to the creation of productivity indices. It is the first-line manager's job to find those that best represent her own unit.

Variations on staff time, levels of expertise, and quality of performance are not the only inputs that may be used in deriving productivity indices. Supplies are inputs amenable to quantitative manipulation. On a surgical floor, for example, the use of certain staple supplies such as four-by-fours or hot wet dressings might be telling. On a medical unit, the use of underbody pads might serve the same purpose. Is there a relationship, for example, between the number of pads used and the number of patient care units for the same time period?

This example illustrates another advantage of keeping productivity statistics. Sometimes nurses are reproached for using too many supplies, but close observations may show that the increase in input (use of supplies) may be closely tied to increases in output (more or sicker patients). Thus, productivity figures can be used not just to control but to justify the use of resources.

Note that the thrifty retention of materials is not always to be desired. Take a community asthmatic clinic, for example, where extensive distribution of a pamphlet on management of childhood asthma is a desired output. To hoard the copies to "save resources" would defeat the purpose.

Nor is it always the case that "more is better" when it comes to resources. At least one first-line manager using productivity indices found that production actually decreased when her unit was overstaffed. The discovery led this particular manager to identify what she termed a socializing factor. When staff had free time they tended to use it as personal time instead of taking on more patient goals. This discovery led her to change her management style and her staffing patterns.

While the initial scores derived by comparing input and output figures are not meaningful in themselves, they become meaningful as the same measurements are taken over time. From cumulative data one can detect trends in productivity.

This is what is meant by managed efficiency. The first-line manager cannot be responsible for improving management and efficiency if she has no way to assess where she stands. Productivity ratios tell her how her unit performs in comparison to how it performed previously. Additionally, if the health care organization has two or more nursing departments or units that are similar in most respects, it may be possible to compare productivity ratios between and among units. Of course this is not a simple task, and there may be good reasons why one unit is scored less productive than another that superficially resembles it. But the inquiry into why 3 East is less efficient than 2 East can itself be a rewarding study of management or a way to find clinical differences that were not obvious at the start.

If nurse managers collect good productivity data, especially when the data includes measures of quality, they may begin to answer such age-old questions as:

- Does quality of care decrease proportionately as staff time decreases?
- Do sicker patients engender (or receive) better care?
- Do more experienced staff give better care?
- Can more experienced staff give care to more patients?
- Does a better educated staff give better care?
- Does the expert clinician deliver better quality care in the same time allotment than the regular practitioner?
- Can the expert clinician deliver more care (quantity) at better quality in the same time allotment than the regular practitioner?
- Does use of supplies increase with an increase in quality of care?

Only when the manager knows how the variables of her unit interact will she be able to manage care in the direction of efficiency and effectiveness. Only when reliable indices have been developed will that task be achieved in a meaningful way.

Productivity Tactics

The first-line manager can do much to encourage productivity on her unit. The first essential, however, is that her staff appreciate the need for productivity. Creating a positive philosophy of productivity is the first-line manager's obligation. If the staff come to see her demands for increased productivity as a whip over their heads, a situation in which they are always asked to do more and more, then they will reject the notion and indeed may sabotage efforts at productivity.

The manager must make clear that increased productivity is achieved by finding better and easier ways to accomplish objectives. Productivity as streamlining is an acceptable notion to most, while productivity as increasing the work load has little appeal. Productivity is a positive goal, and one that should appeal to a nursing ethic. Most nurses want to provide their patients with the best possible service.

Nevertheless, that nursing ethic can get lost along the way. There is a need to make clear to all employees the fact that they are hired to do a job, not to self-actualize and tend to personal needs on the job. If personal needs happen to be met while the work is achieved, all the better, but the paycheck is given for doing a job. Strange as it seems, this is often a novel concept to new nurse graduates. Programs of education often strive to inculcate professional goals (self-improvement, increased knowledge) at the expense of the concept of work obligations (earning one's way). Sometimes orienting the new nurse employee to the world of work may be a joint project for first-line managers and others responsible for staff education. However it is achieved, the new nurse needs an orientation to the world of work and of productivity. Even veteran employees can benefit from a renewal of respect for the obligations of holding a staff position.

The first-line manager often manages a heterogeneous group of employees, not all of whom are likely to be nurses. Nor can she assume that they all hold a positive work ethic. It is up to her to convey the expectations of the institution as its closest managerial representative. The first-line manager must remember that, to her employees, she *is* the institution.

The most important thing a manager can do to enhance productivity is to create a high-performance culture. When high expectations for performance are set by the leader, others usually accept them. Keeping the group results-oriented is the key to achieving high productivity. Feedback from productivity assessments will also serve as a motivating factor if it is presented in a positive way.

There is a danger that productivity will be sacrificed if the atmosphere of the work place is too informal. There are exceptions, of course, and some highly professional, highly motivated work groups function effectively in an informal atmosphere. These are the exceptions, however, and it is more difficult for a first-line manager to maintain control in such informal circumstances. For the inexperienced first-line manager, there is probably safety in running a unit that focuses on professionalism rather than on breezy, easygoing relationships. There is a risk, if the first-line manager allows a pattern of informality, that it may deteriorate into excessive merriment at a cost to productivity.

Once a positive employee attitude toward productivity has been developed, then the first-line manager can look at other pragmatic ways to improve productivity on her unit.

Structures

Structures are the organizational systems in place to distribute work and resources; they include all routine practices and procedures that are followed on the first-line manager's unit. They include such things as daily routines of care, distribution of nursing tasks, methods for prioritizing patients who need a service, methods by which nurses interact with others, and the systems that deliver, treat, and remove supplies.

Sometimes the place to start is with the structures that deal directly with patients. Are there "routines" that use much time with little payoff? Are there cases where routines are substituted for spontaneous judgments that would decrease the total time taken for the work? Look, for example, at the pattern of taking the temperatures of all patients on a ward. On certain units the need for monitoring temperatures is so apparent that few patients could be safely omitted. In such a case it may conserve time to take all temperatures rather than use the time required to make individual decisions. On another unit, however, time might be saved by making those discriminations and taking only those temperatures that are necessary. For every standard routine the first-line manager can ask: Does the routine save time and resources or does it expend them unnecessarily? Should the routine be eliminated? If so, what alternative will achieve the goals intended by the old routine? Or are the goals unnecessary?

Patient care productivity may be enhanced by leveling out the peaks and valleys of the work day. Often the manager can eliminate occasions when staff stand around, unable to do any work. It may require staggering physician rounds, tray delivery, or visiting hours. It may require changing the time when nursing therapies are normally completed. For example, a less pressured evening staff may be assigned some baths. In a community health setting the changes may pertain to when clients are seen versus when staff meet or confer with each other. Or the logistics of how patients are geographically distributed among staff may be altered.

The next structures to be examined are those that control the indirect work of the unit. Paperwork routines can often be streamlined. Systems for creating, recording, and initiating nursing and medical orders are often inefficient. Systems for supply management also need attention. These may entail negotiation with other organizational departments in order to improve efficiency. Changes in interaction procedures often produce miracles.

The first-line manager must also protect her own efficiency when other departments make unilateral decisions that increase the work expectations for her nursing staff. This does not mean that she obstinately refuses any changes that add to the work load but instead that she builds up reciprocities with other department managers, so that total productivity within the institution may be achieved to everyone's advantage.

One system that demands attention is the one devised for productivity tracking. Has the first-line manager instituted routines so that productivity data will be collected, interpreted, and used? How effective are the methods that track productivity? Has the first-line manager set up productivity indices to tell people "where they stand?" Has she set and communicated productivity goals? Does she give staff feedback concerning their productivity?

The first-line manager must be willing to try different methods, to experiment with new systems. New ways are not always better; old ways are not necessarily wrong. But all systems can be examined and questioned. The manager will want to identify the goals behind every system and procedure. Are they essential, or has their purpose been long since completed? Are they carried on due to tradition rather than any useful purposes they may serve?

The first-line manager should be committed to goals rather than to methods. She should be flexible, never refusing to try a new method "because we've always done it this way." Rational management allows for careful, considered experimentation with change.

All sorts of structures must be examined, even the physical plant. Could methods be streamlined by certain changes in the use of space? Are designated areas used by all workers centralized, while those needed by fewer persons are given less desirable locations? What rearrangements would facilitate use of heavily traveled paths? What alterations would make for better use of entrances and elevators?

Personnel Management

Personnel policies and practices often inadvertently decrease productivity. Illness and tardiness policies should be examined and streamlined where necessary. Are they designed to pay for work that is not delivered? For example, does the illness policy actually encourage use of sick days?

Sometimes the problem is not with the policy but with its application. Disruptive patterns can arise among employees if policies aren't enforced. For example, is a worker given a hard time by peers if he doesn't take a long lunch hour? A policy is no better than its application and enforcement by the first-line manager. She should watch for "unwork" patterns that shorten work hours insidiously: lunch breaks growing longer, coffee breaks increasing in number, early leaves becoming a norm.

The manager should look for distorted beliefs among her workers. For example, there is a frequently observed assumption among hourly-paid employees that they "owe" only certain tasks rather than a full shift of work. "I finished my patients; I'm done." "I won't transfer to 3 West; I already did a full day's work here."

Often staff are the people who know best how productivity may be improved. Is there an incentive for them to share productivity ideas? Many institutions have suggestion boxes for this purpose, and others offer a bonus consisting of some portion of the cost savings engendered by a productivity suggestion.

Another productivity issue in personnel management involves selection and retention of staff members. In a time of resource scarcity the first-line manager can't afford to back an unsatisfactory employee, no matter how much that person needs a job, no matter how much the manager may need staff. Even though staff might voluntarily take up the slack caused by an inept fellow worker, they will resent the person they are "covering for" and they won't really regret her dismissal. On the contrary, they are more likely to resent her retention.

Productivity can also be built into personnel tools. Orientation documents, performance appraisals, and incentives can all be used to encourage it. When productivity affects employees' own interests, as in their evaluations, raises, and privileges, then it will be taken seriously.

Does the first-line manager really know how her employees use their time? Monitoring is essential. Are night employees trading times for naps? If so, is it a price the institution is willing to pay? Does the manager think she should be getting more on-duty hours from staff? How closely are work hours monitored? Are there certain abusers of the system? What uses of time are valid? Which are not? Is library research seen as an on-duty function for nurses? What about conferences with others? There should be a clearly written policy that tells the employee which activities are within the scope of on-duty time and which are not.

The manager must look carefully at her own use of employees' time. Are they sent to appropriate educational programs or to programs that may be interesting but have little application to the work unit? The latter practice is a luxury in a time of scarce human resources. Is excessive time spent in meetings? Are people included who could better be achieving other goals with their time? Are the right jobs assigned to the right employees? The first-line manager may also have some discretion in the numbers and kinds of employees she elects to hire. Is her situation best served by an all-professional staff? Or would she be better off with mixed levels of personnel and more of them? All these questions ultimately have to do with the efficiency as well as effectiveness of care.

SUMMARY

Today's health care environment calls for special attention to productivity. The first-line manager should demonstrate a commitment to productivity and develop a staff culture that supports it. A regard for productivity will enable the manager to deliver more and better care to her patients, whatever the circumstances in which she finds herself. All aspects of the work environment may be examined with an eye toward assessing productivity. Creativity, a fresh eye, may help to free a work group from disabling patterns of behavior. The first-line manager needs to keep her goals firmly in mind. From that perspective she'll be able to assess which aspects of the work enhance efficiency and which inhibit it. Efficiency cannot be considered apart from effectiveness. Productivity is streamlining to a qualitative end, not merely for its own sake. Increased productivity means improved patient care.

BIBLIOGRAPHY

Channon, B. "Dispelling Productivity Myths." *Hospitals* 57, no. 19 (October 1, 1983): 103.

Corriveau, C.L., and Rowney, R.H. "What IS a Day's Work?" *Nursing Outlook* 31, no. 6 (November/December 1983): 335.

Grant, S.E.; Bellinger, A.C.; and Sweda, B.L. "Measuring Productivity Through Patient Classification." *Nursing Administration Quarterly* 6, no. 3 (Spring 1982): 77.

Haas, S.A. "Sorting Out Nursing Productivity." *Nursing Management* 15, no. 4 (April 1984): 37.

Meisner, T.R.; Frelin, A.J.; and Twist, P.A. "Sampling Nursing Time Pinpoints Staffing Needs." *Nursing & Health Care* 8, no. 4 (April 1987): 232.

Prescott, P.A. "Nursing Intensity." *Nursing and Health Care* 9, no. 1 (1988): 16.

Vail, J.D.; Norton, D.A.; and Reider, K.A. "Workload Management System Highlights Staffing Needs." *Nursing & Health Care* 8, no. 5 (May 1987): 288.

Welch, C.C. "A Window of Opportunity." *Nursing Outlook* 35, no. 6 (November/December 1987): 282.

part III

Resources: Self, Staff, Materials, Systems

The term "first-line manager" indicates a management position that is one step above the workers. In nursing, first-line management positions may be filled by head nurses, charge nurses, team leaders, and clinical coordinators. While the degree and duration of responsibility may vary among these positions, all involve managerial responsibility for staff workers—that is, for managing personnel.

In addition to the responsibility for managing personnel, the first-line manager is concerned with (1) the materials necessary for completion of the work, (2) the systems that regulate and turn out the work, and (3) the accomplishment of unit and organizational objectives. The first-line nurse manager is responsible for the provision of equipment and supplies and for the systems that delegate and control the work. The primary objective of the first-line nurse manager is the attainment of desired patient health outcomes during the course of illness, injury, or health-related adjustment. The principles of first-line management are the same regardless of the setting, though the specifics of the role may be modified and tailored to different circumstances.

In industry the first-line manager works close to the actual steps of production, being responsible for turning out the desired product through effective use of personnel, materials, and systems. In nursing the first-line manager is responsible for producing desired patient states and health outcomes through use of nursing staff, equipment and supplies, and systems that organize the work to be done.

First-line management is the critical linchpin in the nursing organization; if it fails, all higher-level planning becomes meaningless. If the nursing division's objectives never filter down to the patient care level, then the planning is futile. The first-line manager works at the juncture where administrative plans are converted into action. This is what makes the role so exciting. Indeed, many head nurses refuse upward promotions for just this reason; they prefer to stay "where the action is."

The first-line manager juggles several critical tasks: monitoring unit productivity; maintaining quality care standards; allocating the appropriate use of resources; budget planning; and selecting and evaluating staff. Depending on the prevailing conditions, she may be required to manage patients with higher acuity levels with less professional staff or to increase productivity in spite of fewer resources. It falls to the head nurse to strike a balance between the conflicting demands of management, staff, and patients.

The first-line nurse manager's primary task is to bring together the staff and other unit components into a working whole that provides the best patient care possible. To accomplish that objective, the head nurse builds on the strengths and neutralizes the weaknesses of the individuals and the systems. It is more helpful to focus on staff abilities than to dwell on their deficiencies or the problems in the system. A negative attitude can be corrosive and undermine the spirit of the unit. A clear understanding of staff limitations is essential; the manager needs to know what they can do in order to challenge them to do better. Knowing the capabilities of one's staff is the first step in helping them develop beyond that point. Working with staff and systems requires a subtle balance in which the manager weighs the immediate and long-range consequences of her decisions.

As health care institutions decentralize their management systems, the head nurse's role grows more complex. Hers is an essential and valued position that carries a large share of the responsibility for organizational performance. There is a danger in assuming that systems such as utilization review and quality assurance will automatically result in quality care. Quality cannot be accomplished by any one component in a system; the responsibility extends from higher administration to every member of the staff.

The goal of providing quality care is not as easily accomplished as one would like. Quality is a complex concept that may represent different things to the patient than to the nurse or physician. Depending on who is defining quality, it may even differ from administration to staff.

The head nurse may rely on established standards of care as a starting point toward achieving quality. However, delivering excellence extends beyond those limited parameters. The means to achieving quality can be as elusive as the definition itself.

In formulating her own sense of quality and what is needed to achieve it, the nurse manager moves from the immediate to the future. She has to evaluate the unit and organizational environment to identify the factors that contribute to or diminish the delivery of quality care. On her own unit she needs to promote a climate conducive to achieving excellence.

The first-line manager may perceive her work as taking place along two special continuums: (1) the real to the ideal; (2) the programmed to the unprogrammed. Each of these continuums will be explored, and the two poles of each continuum will be contrasted in order to make explicit the major dangers in first-line management. In actual practice, the manager will seldom deal with polarized alternatives. Instead, she will ask herself to what degree her thinking is characterized by the real or the ideal, to what extent a problem is dominated by programmed or unprogrammed knowledge.

THE REAL VERSUS THE IDEAL

One of the most important tools of the first-line manager is her direct and personal knowledge of each patient and each staff member. This knowledge enables her to temper general management principles according to the realities of the situation. It enables her to utilize the unique talents and abilities of each staff member and to match these talents and abilities to the unique needs of patients as well. It allows her to manage staff weaknesses and situational limitations.

The inexperienced first-line manager often has trouble reconciling her concept of the ideal employee with actual workers on her patient unit or team. According to textbooks, all employees cheerfully give their all, do every assigned task, and are generally paragons of virtue; the task of the first-line manager is simply to provide proper guidance. The new manager is usually surprised to learn that (1) she is not skillful enough to provide such guidance, and (2) even if she is a skilled leader, some employees will not turn in star performances.

The first-line nurse manager soon learns that, while aiming to build an ideal work team, her assignments must fit the employees she has. In management, one must plan around the real, not the wished for, capabilities of staff members. Management realism may clash with nursing idealism, but the effective first-line manager begins with her staff members as they are, not as they should be.

While the manager must be careful to make her direction, supervision, and assignments fit the real, not idealized, abilities of her staff, she cannot afford to underestimate staff abilities. Bright and capable staff members must be challenged to practice exemplary professional nursing. The first-line manager who overemphasizes control may stifle the performance of her best staff. Indeed, if staff members are continually underestimated, they are likely to resign and seek positions that will make use of their full abilities.

The first-line manager can seldom afford to treat all subordinates alike. For some employees she will use highly directive supervision and continuous monitoring of performance. In contrast, she will allow other employees considerable freedom, autonomy, and latitude for independent professional or role performance. Learning to treat "unequals" differently is a difficult task for some new managers, particularly if they are imbued with the notion of one "right" managerial approach for all cases.

Inexperienced first-line managers can rely too heavily upon a few unusually talented workers. This may cause resentment in all workers, for some will see it as favoritism while others will feel overburdened by an increased work load. The first-line manager must be careful not to "penalize" the unusually talented or willing worker with too much work. Determining a challenging work assignment is different from overburdening a capable worker with a too demanding work load. Nor should the manager deny to the less capable worker the opportunity to acquire further skills through appropriate practice challenges. Rewarding below-average performance with a lighter-than-normal work load is another danger to be avoided.

The nurse manager may find that not only her employees but also her environment and its resources are far from ideal. If the manager acts as if she were in an ideal setting when in fact she is not, she will set unrealistic goals, frustrating her staff and accomplishing little. If, instead, she perceives the environment and its resources realistically, then she will set achievable goals and reasonable priorities.

The real versus the ideal polarity may also influence the first-line manager's relationship with patients. Some first-line managers act upon the unspoken assumption that the patient will respond ideally and achieve all the goals formulated by the nurse. But in cases where the nurse's goals, however well intended, are beyond the present capabilities of the patient, the patient is likely to feel her expectations as an additional burden upon an already diminished capacity for self-care and autonomy.

THE PROGRAMMED VERSUS THE UNPROGRAMMED

The first-line manager deals with both programmed and unprogrammed nursing knowledge and application. Some nursing knowledge is programmed, that is, well accepted by the nursing community and supported by nursing research. Other nursing knowledge is unprogrammed; it is in the early stages of investigation and is not yet validated by research or generally accepted by the nursing community.

The application of nursing knowledge may be similarly programmed or unprogrammed. For example, a nursing unit may have a routine teaching program for obese patients. Yet that program may not be adequate for the needs of an obese patient with a language problem. Hence, the nursing knowledge must be applied to such a patient in an innovative, unprogrammed manner.

Clearly, the greater the proportion of programmed knowledge and programmed application used, the simpler the job of the first-line manager. However, the manager has a particular responsibility when an unprogrammed situation arises. It is her responsibility to chart a course of action, to problem-solve, in these circumstances. This does not mean that she will make all unprogrammed nursing care decisions herself. Indeed, the wise first-line manager will use her best resource people for this purpose. Resource people can include clinical specialists, experienced staff nurses, or nurses from other units or institutions who have special expertise. While it is not up to the first-line nurse manager to make all decisions, it is clearly her responsibility to be creative and effective at finding the best resource people for each unprogrammed situation.

When certain methods of patient care are given general consensus, they may be formalized in procedures, policies, and practices. These elements then become standard operating procedures merely to simplify the work. Diverse methods are often equally satisfactory, but efficiency may be achieved by uniformity of practice.

Many inexperienced first-line nurse managers make staff assignments purely on the basis of the difficulty or simplicity of each patient's care needs. In making assignments, it is suggested that the manager also consider what aspects of that care are programmed or unprogrammed. For example, the care of a given patient may be complex but relatively well programmed; in such a case, a competent LPN may be able to offer care just as satisfactorily as could an RN. The RN might be assigned to a "simpler" case that requires some thinking, planning, and searching for new ways and means.

It is also the responsibility of the first-line manager to document new approaches and new theories of care as they are tested in the clinical area. Whenever satisfactory results are obtained from a new course of therapy, it is important that the findings be preserved and shared with other nurses. Results obtained in any given case are shared in order that a similar plan of care may be tested again in a similar case. In this way programmed nursing knowledge grows and is verified.

First-line management is an exciting role because it offers the ideal synthesis of management and nursing. It offers the nurse a chance to observe the effects of her direction, and, through the careful use of her staff, it enables her to accomplish more than she could ever do alone.

chapter 7

The First-Line Nurse Manager: Role and Responsibilities

In a period marked by rapid change and uncertainty, the first-line nurse manager fills one of the most critical and valuable roles in the administration of nursing practice. The majority of objectives for any nursing service relate to what happens to the patient, and the first-line manager is the administrative channel through which these objectives ultimately succeed or fail. Planning of objectives for the division is in vain if the head nurse (or her equivalent) cannot translate the goals into concrete action. To perform effectively as a first-line manager requires that one have clear ideas of that role and how it relates to other roles in the organization. This chapter explores the first-line managerial role as it is typically enacted in an acute care setting. After the role is examined, the chapter goes on to look at the responsibilities of the first-line manager.

ROLE ANALYSIS

The head nurse is pivotal in linking nursing management to nursing care. Inherent in the role is the conversion of plans and concepts into action, one of the most difficult tasks of management. For example, the reliability of a nursing staff instrument based on a patient classification system depends on the accuracy of the data input, and that means accurate assessment of each and every patient. It is critical that staff understand what is being measured and use the instrument correctly. Typically it is the function of the head nurse to explain such a system and implement its accurate use. The head nurse has to ensure staff acceptance of new management systems and to apply policies, practices, and procedures of the institution and its nursing division to the concrete situations on a given patient unit. She must do this in a way that achieves her own objectives and goals as well as those of higher management. Such application demands clear perception of the concrete situation and good judgment in applying those concepts in each instance. To be successful, the head nurse must be able to conceptualize and apply those conceptualizations to the realities of her unit.

Because the head nurse has one foot in the work and the other in administration, she needs a wider scope of abilities than is required by most positions. First, she must have clinical nursing experience in order to direct her staff and to maintain their respect in her as a leader. In addition to nursing ability, she also needs management skills to direct the work of others effectively.

One reason why management can be difficult for the head nurse is inexperience. Typically the head nurse role is the first permanent management position in the individual's nursing career. High turnover in the nursing profession, unfortunately, is also evident in head nurse positions, thus contributing to the problems of inexperience. The practice of promoting nurses without preparatory education into head nurse positions further compounds the problem. It is recognized that adequate preparation of the first-line manager is critical to the effectiveness of nursing care.[1,2] A report by the Institute of Medicine contended that more nurses with graduate education would be needed to handle society's increasingly complex health care needs; nurse managers were among the specialists requiring more advanced preparation.[3] Additionally, a poll of nurse executives indicated that the head nurse role is the most valued in the nursing organization and that, when possible, they would prefer to hire master's-prepared nurses because of the multi-dimensional aspects of the first-line manager's job.[4]

Another complexity specific to the head nurse role is that of interaction with multiple persons, departments, and divisions. Staff nurses practicing in a primary nursing model are increasingly autonomous. They view themselves as being in control of their professional practice and as influencing unit level decision making. It is necessary that the head nurse work out acceptable role relations with these professionals. The assumption that things will gradually work themselves out can leave the head nurse's role blurred and undefined. It should be clear, whatever the nursing care delivery mode, that the responsibility of the head nurse for decision making is not diminished. Under a philosophy of participative management, staff are included in the discussion of problems and professional issues, but it is the responsibility of the head nurse to ensure that solutions are reached.

In an organizational structure from which the erstwhile supervisory layer has been removed, the dimensions of the first-line manager's job enlarge. She may find herself increasingly involved in activities that take her away from the unit. In this situation the need to maintain a clear system of accountability is all the more important. Staff should always know where to reach the head nurse, and there should be no confusion as to who is in charge in case of an emergency on the unit.

For the new nurse manager the switch from a staff nurse's role to a managerial role may be difficult, especially if she is filling the new role in the presence of people already accustomed to her as a staff member. Staff often resent perceived changes in peers who are promoted. Often they fail to recognize that such changes are necessary to fill the new role and do not represent a character change in the new manager. Moreover, it is difficult for a new manager to learn the new behaviors necessary for successful role enactment when she is being subtly or unsubtly coerced to retain the behaviors of her past role. Sometimes friends will unconsciously exert pressures on the new manager "not to change." In other instances, attempts to regulate the behavior of the manager represent efforts to subvert or take over the power of the role from the new role holder. Seldom does a new manager escape this testing of her ability and will to act in the new role. If a new nurse manager is able to assume her management duties among staff previously unknown to her, the role assumption is likely to be easier.

A staff nurse filling a temporary management role—for example, as charge nurse for a single day—faces a task not unlike that of a new manager in a permanent leadership role. If the temporary charge nurse knows that tomorrow she will again be a peer staff nurse among those she is directing today, that knowledge may limit the amount of authority she feels free to exert. At the same time, some staff who also alternate in leadership roles are supportive of the temporary manager, knowing they will need that person's support when they are asked to fill a managerial role. Since great versatility is required to fill different roles in a single setting, it is usually preferable not to alternate in leadership roles but rather, if possible, to fill them on a full-time basis.

The first-line manager who is sensitive to aspects of role enactment will appreciate the role-related behaviors of all who are in her environment. For example, she might expect the nurse's aide to be slow to share her knowledge and system know-how with a new aide. (Since the aide has so little power in the typical institutional hierarchy, she might be more zealous in protecting that modicum of power than would a staff nurse orienting another staff nurse.) The first-line manager should be cognizant of how all aspects of role behavior interact. She will be careful to know the job descriptions for every staff member under her direction, so that she may feel secure concerning the technical limits and boundaries of each role. She will also be sensitive to the role-specific expectations held by herself and others. If she is aware of these expectations, she can use them to facilitate her adaptation, in her new role, to her staff, or she can systematically work to change those expectations that distort others' perception of various roles. Similarly, she will be able to appreciate individual coloring of a role, including her own, and to recognize when such effects are productive and when they are manipulative and destructive. Developing insight into her own motivations and those of others will help the new manager to understand better the behavior of patients, physicians, and the health care professionals with whom she must interact in the work setting.

Professional Relationships

Whether in relation to physicians or to other health care professionals in the organizational setting, nurse managers are recognizing the importance of asserting the power of their management positions as well as the autonomy of their profession. In an environment where resources are limited and competition keen, it is not unusual to find professional differences. Social workers, physical therapists, respiratory therapists, and physicians all play a significant role in patient care and want to be accorded recognition. The strength of the staff nurse, whether in the acute care or outpatient setting, is that she is a generalist, able to care for patients with diverse diagnoses and needs ranging from total physical dependency to a need for emotional support.

Nursing, in many settings, has 24-hour accountability for patients. This often requires performing a variety of tasks normally within the purview of other health care professionals. For example, respiratory therapy may become the nurse's responsibility outside the hours of 9 to 5, Monday through Friday. The same may be true for physical therapy, diet therapy, and numerous other services. It is no wonder that nurses become frustrated when other professionals dictate how and when treatments are to be given without recognizing the nurse's own contributions to specialized care.

Professional respect, status, and income tend to be positively correlated with perceived independence of practice. As nurses strive to control their own practice, interprofessional relations may become strained when nursing's contributions are not fully recognized. The head nurse can assist her staff and other professionals to understand the interrelatedness of their roles. Nurse managers foster mutual respect when they encourage collaboration between their staff and other disciplines by defining it as an opportunity to achieve better health outcomes for the patient.

The nurse manager should recognize her role as representative of both management and professional nursing. As first-line manager she must maintain smooth coordination with all other divisions and departments concerned with direct patient services or nursing support services. It is essential that this coordination be smooth, because when there are breakdowns the problems revert to the head nurse as custodian of the patient. Indeed, the patient care unit may suffer more from a poor interface with laundry or dietary services than does the service that is technically at fault. Because of the high number of interfaces per shift, the head nurse role is subjected to more sources of potential frustration than are most management roles.

Seen in its full scope, the head nurse role (or its equivalent in other settings) is that vital management position through which the patient-related objectives of the nursing division are concretized in first-hand direction of nursing activities. The head nurse role is also the management position with the greatest responsibility for day-to-day coordination with all other departments and divisions that relate directly or indirectly to the patient.

Effects of Organizational Structure on Role

In a highly centralized organization the head nurse's responsibilities are confined to her unit, and her primary aim is to see that rules are followed and that orders from the top are carried out. The extent of her decision making is limited to immediate unit activities such as staffing schedules, patient assignments, and supervision of unit personnel.

Indeed, some nursing divisions encourage the head nurse to undervalue her management role by using her as a fill-in worker. When a nursing division chronically uses its head nurse to fill in for absent staff nurses, it is clear that the division sees her management as unessential, something to be done only when there is lots of help. This attitude by higher management certainly does not encourage the head nurse to appreciate the significance of her management role; nor does it encourage her subordinates to look on her as a manager.

A nursing division with a clear appreciation of what good management can do will know that a manager is needed more on an understaffed day than at any other time. Appropriate head nurse management will assure the institution of optimal output from all employees.

Not only the institution but the head nurse herself may need to adjust to the concept that her time "away from the bedside" contributes just as much to patient welfare as does direct care. Once the head nurse has developed administrative skills, she will be able to see the impact that good management has on patient care.

The job dimensions of the first-line manager expand considerably in a decentralized organization. The first-line manager has authority over her budget, which includes the responsibility to operate within budgetary limits. Research, policy issues, staff development, peer review, and patient care evaluation are often unit-based. The head nurse in a participative management model exercises minimal management control; instead she focuses on involving her staff and developing their capabilities to manage the care of their patients effectively and efficiently. She balances the immediate concerns of her unit with the needs of the overall organization.

Shifting from a centralized, hierarchical nursing structure to a decentralized, participatory philosophy takes commitment from all of management. It cannot be achieved by fiat or by replacing the organizational chart. Eliminating traditional reporting structures and delegating authority downward succeeds only if everyone involved is ready and able to meet the challenge. The actualization of decentralized authority must begin with the support and cooperation of nursing administration. Staff need to be educated to the role change and involved in the process of decentralization. It is an ongoing process by which staff gradually extend and develop their professional autonomy.

Nurses seek personal and professional fulfillment in their jobs. It has been shown that decentralization enhances job satisfaction and professional role enactment.[5,6] The head nurse focuses on the tasks of human relations, and, in the best of situations, she is a mentor who encourages and supports her staff. Staff, in turn, are free to contribute ideas for programs, patient care, and work schedules. Head nurses have the requisite authority to affect change at the unit level and to decide which ideas are to be implemented.

Similarly, the head nurse role will vary with different care delivery systems. For example, a primary nursing assignment system calls for different head nurse activities than does a functional assignment system. In a primary nursing system, the head nurse will be heavily involved in evaluation of the quality of patient care. In a functional system, in contrast, the head nurse serves primarily as a logistic coordinator of all tasks, since she is the only person with a view of the whole.

Resources of the First-Line Manager Role

The head nurse role is more complex than the staff role in both its responsibilities and its resources for action. The head nurse may share the same concept of good nursing with the staff nurse, but she has more means at hand for implementing that concept. The staff nurse has essentially one resource for accomplishing her job, and that is herself. The systems she will use and the assignments she will fill are set. The judgments made by the staff nurse have to do mainly with how she functions within the prescribed systems and practices of her environment.

The head nurse has a larger number of resources at her command. She has at least three potential variables: use of self, use of staff, and use of delivery systems. The head nurse has the right to determine the most effective use of her own time. She decides how and when she will relate to her staff and her patients. In addition, she has the right to determine and regulate those systems that control the day-to-day delivery of nursing care on the unit. She can determine the nature and timing for such routine events as hygiene, bathing, and temperature checks. Most importantly, she can establish systems for evolving and implementing nursing care orders. She also has the freedom to use her staff in the way that is most appropriate to produce the objectives of her unit. She can determine methods of staff assignment, set criteria for performance, and design programs for staff education.

The head nurse has an extensive array of resources for patient care, staff management, and administration of organizational and nursing division policies. In institutions that have centralized authority as well as in organizations marked by staff participation, the first-line manager is accountable for using those resources to uphold quality standards of patient care, provide an environment conducive to professional excellence, and conduct all activities within organizational policies.

Management of Staff

In their management of staff, many nurse managers fail to make optimal use of their own resources. It is easy for them to rely on management systems such as staff assignments and personnel evaluations to manage staff. If the head nurse is new to the job, she may fall back on the power of higher administration rather than exercise the authority of her position and take responsibility for her actions. Over time, the manager who is unwilling to use her authority risks losing the confidence and respect of both her staff and higher administration.

RESPONSIBILITIES OF THE FIRST-LINE MANAGER

When the first-line manager thoroughly understands her role and resources, she can apply those concepts to meeting her many and varied responsibilities. Responsibilities of the first-line manager include: setting objectives, planning and organizing, communicating and motivating, measuring and evaluating, develop staff, ensuring patients' welfare, and administering policies. Each of these aspects will be discussed briefly.

Setting Objectives

All planning rests on the assumption that the first-line manager has a clear idea of the goals to be achieved or the products to be created. The head nurse is likely to have unique objectives for her unit, formulated according to the types of patients for which she is responsible, the characteristics of her particular environment, and the overall goals of the nursing division. These objectives direct her activities, although they are supplemented by interim and ad hoc objectives formulated on the basis of the day-to-day situation. They incorporate ongoing changes dictated by strategic planning. Thus, for an eight-hour shift a head nurse may plan a mix of activities, with some directed toward formalized unit objectives and others directed toward interim objectives arising out of the particular state of the institution, the unit, or its occupants at a given time. Setting objectives leads logically to the next responsibility: planning and organizing for their achievement.

Planning and Organizing

Reaching an objective entails making a plan concerning what has to be done. The plan must assign responsibilities, and it must be communicated to staff. The challenge of first-line management is to convert planning into action by way of organizing. Because her plans are immediately put into action, the first-line manager must deal with the realities of nursing care delivery. There is no way that a first-line manager can escape by flight into nonrealistic planning. The plans of the first-line manager are tied to their everyday results, and these results provide loud and clear feedback.

One danger in first-line management tends to be an overinvolvement with immediate problems and a relegation of planning to the backburner. The first-line manager, working in the midst of many people and events, can easily spend all of her time responding to the here and now. But the greatest pitfall in the path of first-line managers is acting without a plan.

Planning requires a definition of goals and the imposition of one's plans upon the environment. Because nursing takes place in a very complex environment, inflexible plans have little chance for realization; the environment may well require some alteration of goals and plans. Unanticipated events will occur on the patient unit, in the outpatient clinic, and during the home visit. Courses of illness and recovery can be anticipated but never entirely predicted. Working as she does in a coordinated system, the first-line manager should not rigidly regiment the behavior of others. Her planning must be flexible and open to revision as circumstances may require.

The nature of planning will depend upon the responsibilities of the nurse manager and the capabilities of the person filling the position. For example, the head nurse's planning will involve long-range projects, while the planning of an inexperienced charge nurse may include nothing more than short-term completion of all designated nursing care programs and therapies for the day's patients. In either case, the manager must know what is to be accomplished by the end of the shift or project period so that she may organize and reorganize toward that end.

The first-line manager analyzes which activities need to be done, sets priorities, and plans the best means to achieve the desired ends. In the past it was possible for the nurse manager to decide what was needed (e.g., staff, supplies) and to request it from administration. However, when resources are limited the decision falls to the head nurse how best to use what is available to derive the fullest benefit.

One of the important tasks of first-line management is to recognize when a plan must be altered, postponed, or even scrapped in favor of an alternative one. Changing a plan, however, is far preferable to operating without one.

Communicating and Motivating

It seems absurdly simple to suggest that the head nurse tell her staff what she expects of them. As simple as this sounds, it is a step often neglected. The head nurse may assume that her staff will envision the same goals she does. This assumption, unfortunately, is often faulty. Even if all staff members are highly motivated to give "good patient care," there is no reason to assume that they all mean the same thing by this phrase. Therefore, the head nurse has a critical obligation to make clear to her staff the kind of performance she wants.

As the acknowledged head of the unit, the nurse manager lays the groundwork for the exchange of information related to patient care issues, organizational matters, and health care trends. The way information is articulated to staff has a direct bearing on the way it is used and processed. For instance, distributing a memo outlining new policies for discharge planning is not as effective as having a staff meeting to review the policies, explain why administration has instituted them, and to discuss policy implementation and its impact on staff and current practices.

Communicating does not consist of lectures by the head nurse to staff, with the head nurse controlling the situation. Effective managers keep communications flowing between all members of the nursing division. Because of her vital role in the organization, the head nurse's ability to *listen* to staff and administration is as important as her being a good spokesperson. Staff members have a healthy sense of self-preservation, so they soon learn the real interests of the head nurse. If her professed interests—what she says—do not coincide with her behavior, she should not be surprised if those verbalized interests are ignored by her staff. Nurse managers create an environment conducive to professional behavior when they solicit staff suggestions and act on them.

The head nurse should habitually assess her communication with staff, meaning the messages she gives to staff by her behavior as well as in words. Her expectations and her own enthusiasm for patient care can be motivational to others if communicated appropriately.

Measuring and Evaluating

The head nurse makes her expectations explicit and does not assume that staff will share her standards for performance. Staff need to set personal goals that correspond to the unit objectives, and the manager provides the yardstick against which the individual measures her performance. While periodic written evaluations are an essential management tool, they should be supplemented by routine feedback on what staff is doing right and what areas need improvement.

The danger in not setting standards is that minimal standards, if any, will prevail. The delivery of quality patient care depends on each staff member striving for excellence. The nurse manager understands that everyone won't perform equally well, but she establishes what to aim for, what is required, and what is acceptable. In addition to staff performance appraisals, quality assurance reports form a basis for judging how well a group is performing.

Developing Staff

Ultimately the first-line manager is a developer of people. She develops her own skills as a manager and provides opportunities for staff to enhance their clinical competence. The new environment in health care gives nurses the chance to expand their roles and to develop and plan new ways of doing things.

Staff development is a broad concept involving inservice education, informal teaching opportunities, and role modeling. Whatever means are used, its objectives are to improve patient care while enhancing staff members' own effectiveness.

Ensuring Patients' Welfare

One step in meeting the manager's responsibility for patients is to scrutinize the delivery systems carefully—their successes, their limitations. The assignment of staff is one such delivery system, and one in which the head nurse has great latitude. Even if she works in an institution committed to a specific care modality such as team care or primary care, there are still many variations possible in the interpretation and application of the selected method.

Some delivery systems are not so immediately obvious as the assignment method. The system of communicating new orders is one example. This system, like many others, usually evolves by circumstance and is passed on by tradition rather than resulting from a considered decision. Hygiene routines as well as routines concerning vital signs and treatments are systems. There are systems for reporting on and off duty, for transmission of information regarding patients, for interacting with physicians who visit patients on the unit, for coordinating with various practicing students, and for permitting exchange of shifts.

All of these systems and others like them have an impact upon patient care. They determine how staff will spend their time; they regulate many of the safety and comfort factors of the environment; and they channel relevant information to, from, and about the patient. It is important, therefore, that the head nurse identify the systems in effect in her unit and subject them to rational scrutiny. Are the existing systems appropriate for attaining her patient care objectives? Should some systems be eliminated as serving no valuable purpose? Should others be added to streamline the work or complete it more effectively?

In looking at the delivery system as they relate to her patient goals, the head nurse can streamline and choreograph the activities of her staff. Once such systems are subjected to intelligent scrutiny, one should not find much absurdities as nurses passing morning basins to up-and-about patients when they do not have enough time to do the teaching these patients need, and nurse assistants taking unnecessary temperatures of afebrile patients who would have benefitted more from skin care. Nor would patients who need optimal rest be awakened at an early hour for baths they do not need. Most of the well publicized absurdities of institutional nursing care are defects in the delivery systems rather than acts of individual incompetence.

The first-line manager is ultimately responsible for and to every patient assigned to her jurisdiction. This means that she must know the status of each patient on an ongoing basis, including achievements and the goals yet to be reached. She should also know the challenges and problems that each patient presents to her staff. She is assisted in acquiring such knowledge by quality assurance measures and by review of patient data on charts; but first-hand observation and communication with each patient is an essential part of meeting her responsibility for patient welfare.

Administering Policies

A final responsibility of the head nurse is administration of nursing division policies. The head nurse must recognize that she is part of the administrative team and that interpretation of administrative nursing decisions to staff members is a crucial part of her job. She is responsible for communicating nursing division goals and for translating those goals into actions. The head nurse is the major implementer of nursing policy.

As an administrator, she must remember that all her employee-related decisions carry the weight of precedent-setting judgments. She cannot afford to make a hasty decision that gives one employee an advantage that would not be offered to another under similar circumstances. She must recognize that all her decisions and actions have to be consistent with general administrative rules and policies. The new head nurse should be assisted by her supervisor or director to develop this sensitivity to the administrative role.

An important member of nursing administration, the head nurse should accept responsibility for contributing to and participating in administrative decisions. This includes not only committee participation but also communicating to her supervisor or director any information or opinion important to administrative decision making. Becoming a first-line manager necessarily involves participation in the larger organization beyond the confines of one's unit. One advantage of this expanded participation is that it allows the first-line manager to learn of other resources available to help meet the needs of her own unit.

In accepting the administrative role the head nurse also accepts the obligation to learn the craft of management. Some institutions are able to offer the head nurse a management course; others are not. When such a course is unavailable, the head nurse should seek help in the form of guided reading on basic management so as to equip herself for her function. The supervisor or director of nursing should be able to provide an appropriate reading list as well as opportunities for discussing and sharing ideas.

The head nurse will need to consider how management principles apply to nursing. She should apply management knowhow, for example, to the basic concepts underlying all common forms of assignment of staff—functional, team, modular, and primary nursing systems. She should apply management concepts to staffing and its strategies, such as cyclical plans and flexible staffing. She should study management systems as they apply to assessing the quality of patient care and to estimating patient work load and patient classification. Broad management themes must be considered along with nursing-related management practices. They will need to be accommodated to the head nurse's theory of nursing as well.

The head nurse will discover that her own role will vary depending on the nature of her staff and her care delivery systems. For example, if her staff are primarily new graduates, she will need to spend much time in mentoring, role modeling, teaching, directing, and evaluating. If, on the other hand, her staff are highly experienced, she may need to challenge them to attain a more advanced level of independent nursing practice or to design and carry out controlled research projects that test new patient care methodologies.

SUMMARY

It is most important that the head nurse fully understand the scope of her role and her responsibilities. Since her education seldom prepares her for the management aspects of that role, the head nurse often needs assistance in developing management skills and perspectives. The nursing division should assume some responsibility for management development by providing educational programs or resources and by making clear its expectations for managers. Adjustment to the head nurse role is facilitated if the head nurse can use a role-descriptive framework by which to identify and order her functions. The head nurse needs to recognize that translating concepts and goals into concrete activities is her unique responsibility.

NOTES

1. National Commission on Nursing, *Summary Report and Recommendations* (Chicago: Hospital Research and Educational Trust, 1983), p. 7.

2. American Academy of Nursing, Task Force on Nursing Practice in Hospitals, *Magnet Hospitals* (Kansas City, MO: American Nurses' Association, 1983), pp. 86–87.

3. Institute of Medicine, *Nursing and Nursing Education: Public Policies and Private Actions* (Washington, DC: National Academy Press, 1983), p. 45.

4. L.C. Hodges, R. Knapp, and J. Cooper, "Head Nurses: Their Practice and Education," *Journal of Nursing Administration* 17, No. 12 (December 1987): 39–43.

5. D. Przestrzelski, "Decentralization: Are Nurses Satisfied?" *Journal of Nursing Administration* 17, No. 11 (November 1987): 23–28.

6. American Academy of Nursing, Task Force on Nursing Practice in Hospitals, pp. 20, 88.

BIBLIOGRAPHY

Alexander, E.L. *Nursing Administration in the Hospital Health Care System.* 2d ed. St. Louis, MO: C.V. Mosby Co., 1978.

Barker, M., and Ganti, A.R. "An In-Depth Study of the Head Nurse Role." *Supervisor Nurse* 11, no. 11 (1980): 16.

Carter, K.A. "Managerial Role Development in the Nursing Supervisor." *Supervisor Nurse* 11, no. 7 (1980): 26.

Clark, C.C. "Assertiveness Issues for Nursing Administrators and Managers." *Journal of Nursing Administration* 9, no. 7 (1979): 20.

Courtade, Sr. S. "The Role of the Head Nurse: Power and Practice." *Supervisor Nurse* 9, no. 12 (1978): 20.

Curry, J.L. "Assertiveness Training for Supervisory Nurses." *Supervisor Nurse* 9, no. 9 (1978): 43.

Dooley, S.L., and Hauben, J. "From Staff Nurse to Head Nurse: A Trying Transition." *Journal of Nursing Administration* 9, no. 4 (1979): 4.

Douglass, L.M., and Bevis, E.O. *Nursing Management and Leadership in Action.* 3d ed. St. Louis, MO: C.V. Mosby Co., 1979.

Drucker, P.F. *Management: Tasks, Responsibilities, Practices.* New York: Harper & Row Publishers, 1974.

Gerschefske, L. "Assessment and Development for Head Nurse Positions." *Supervisor Nurse* 11, no. 2 (1980): 21.

Heimann, C.G. "Four Theories of Leadership." *Journal of Nursing Administration* 6, no. 5 (1976): 18.

Hinckle, J. "Priorities of the Charge Nurse—Part I." *Supervisor Nurse* 8, no. 11 (1977): 47.

Holle, M.L. "Staff Nurse Yesterday: Nurse Manager Today." *Supervisor Nurse* 11, no. 4 (1980): 52.

Holloman, C.R. "The Nurse Enters Management." *Supervisor Nurse* 2, no. 4 (1971): 54.

Jenkins, J.W. "Good Nurse or Good Manager—What's the Difference?" *Supervisor Nurse* 9, no. 11 (1978): 48.

LaRocco, S.A. "An Introduction to Role Theory for Nurses." *Supervisor Nurse* 9, no. 12 (1978): 41.

Miller, N. "How To Succeed in Nursing Management." *Supervisor Nurse* 8, no. 10 (1977): 18.

Minehan, P.L.; May, L.; and Deluty, L. "Training Biocultural Leaders." *Journal of Nursing Administration* 11, no. 3 (1981): 37.

O'Donovan, T.R. "Leadership Dynamics." *Journal of Nursing Administration* 5, no. 7 (1975): 32.

Pardue, S.F. "Assertiveness for Nurses." *Supervisor Nurse* 11, no. 2 (1980): 47.

Porter-O'Grady, T. *Creative Nursing Administration.* Rockville, MD: Aspen Publishers, 1986.

Ruan, M.A. "Professional Survival." *Supervisor Nurse* 12, no. 2 (1980): 47.

Schweiger, J.F. "The Indecisive Leader." *Supervisor Nurse* 9, no. 11 (1978): 54.

Silber, M.B. "Nursing Management Starts and Succeeds with Self Esteem." *Supervisor Nurse* 12, no. 3 (1981): 42.

Spitzer, R. "The Nurse in the Corporate World." *Supervisor Nurse* 12, no. 4 (1981): 21.

Stevens, B.J. "The Role of The Nurse Executive." *Journal of Nursing Administration* 11, no. 2 (1981): 19.

Wilsea, M.M. "Nursing Leadership Crisis: Proposal for Solution." *Supervisor Nurse* 11, no. 4 (1980): 47.

chapter 8

Communications Resources

A COMMUNICATION MODEL

The nurse manager achieves through her interactions with others. Managerial communications must be understood from two perspectives: basic principles of communications and the communication function within an organization. The basic principles of communications include the need for effective communication techniques in all endeavors. Appreciation of the role of communication as an organizational function helps to improve the efficiency and effectiveness of organizational management.

It is most important when communicating to realize that not everyone is alike and that the recipient of communication most likely has different interests, backgrounds, beliefs, and feelings than those of the person initiating the communication. Failure to recognize these differences impairs communication from the outset.

Various communication models have been developed to explain the nature of communication. Whether one uses a simple checklist approach (e.g., Who is involved? What is the purpose? What is said? In which medium? With what side effect?) or a more sophisticated one, communication has to be considered within the total context. One approach to understanding the nature of communication is to identify and examine the simple components of every single communication exchange.

The system in its simplest terms consists first of a sender with certain goals. The sender encodes (translates into symbols) those goals to form a message. That message is transmitted via some medium (audiovisual-sensory input system) to the intended receiver. Upon its sensory intake, the receiver decodes the message (interprets its symbols) and responds to its perceived content. How the receiver interprets the message and responds to its perceived content are influenced by the receiver's own goals in relation to the sender and in relation to the message's subject matter. When the response includes communicating feedback to the sender, the receiver assumes the sender role, and the communication sequence begins again.

The Function of Communication

The sender always communicates for some purpose, to have some effect upon the receiver. Common purposes include to inform, to entertain, to inquire, to persuade, to command. The goal may be to evoke a particular attitude or a particular behavior, verbal or actional.

The success of a communication is judged in terms of the goal-response relationship. Organizations usually define a good communication as one in which the goal of the sender is attained. This definition has a limited perspective, however, because it assumes that only the goals of the sender have relevance in receiver response. The receiver may also have goals that modify the receiver's response to the message. This consideration leads some authors to define a good communication as one in which both sender and receiver achieve goal satisfaction.

The Structure of Communication

Communication can take place in two ways: by direct action and by symbolic activity. A pat on the back or the opening of a door are examples of direct communication. Even these, however, are subject to possible misinterpretation. Most communication is of the symbolic type. Verbal communication is the most common form, with words standing for meanings. When symbolic communication is used, the level of common understanding achieved between sender and receiver depends on their degree of agreement concerning what the symbols mean. For example, telling a person in the street to do something "stat" might not produce the same effect as using that term with a nurse. Of course, the person in the street might pick up the meaning of "stat" from other direct signals, such as the urgency in the voice of the speaker or the apparent seriousness of the situation. The word's meaning might also have been learned from such symbolic sources as novels, movies, or television shows. The point is that an adequate level of common understanding of the symbols used must be reached between sender and receiver if communication is to take place.

The act of putting meaning into a symbolic form is called encoding, and the act of extracting meaning from symbols is called decoding. The degree of agreement between the message sent and the message received will depend on the degree to which the symbols have the same meaning for the two parties. In the diagram (Figure 8-1), arrows branch from the goals of the receiver toward both the decoding and the response, indicating that goals can affect not only the receiver's response but also the receiver's interpretation of what is being conveyed.

Methods of Communication

There are many different methods of communication: talking, writing, showing, and all the various possible combinations of sensory input. These sensory messages can be delivered face-to-face or via the communicator's medium of choice. Properties of the medium itself, such as proximity, distance, warmth, and coolness, add overtones of meaning to the message.

These, then, are the primary components of a functional communication system: sender/encoder, goals, message, medium, receiver/decoder, goals, and response. The parts as well as the relationship of the parts to each other are important in analyzing or constructing a communication.

THE NURSE MANAGER AS SENDER AND RECEIVER OF COMMUNICATION

The nurse manager is constantly interacting with others. Her underlying personal, cultural, and professional biases influence how she formulates a message and how she delivers it. Depending on who the receiver is, the nurse manager may alter her style as her role changes. Issuing a directive may be appropriate for staff but inappropriate for the vice-president of nursing. Emphasis is often placed on downward communication—from superior to subordinate—but equal consideration should be given to receiving upward communication from staff. Coming from different perspectives, the staff nurse and the head nurse may see reality differently. The expectations of each other's role and degree of responsibility for the job are likely to be different. The nurse

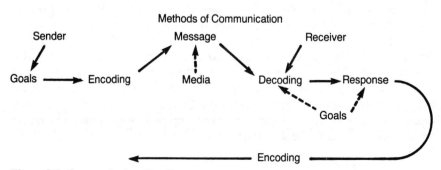

Figure 8-1 Communications Paradigm

manager must recognize that the receiver also has personal and cultural biases that color that person's decoding ability. It is important that the nurse manager know about the values, beliefs, and opinions of her audience in order to encode her messages appropriately.

As a communicator the nurse manager must monitor how she is being understood and interpreted. Communication is not simply the sending and receiving of messages, but encompasses the total encounter between individuals: their personalities, cultural backgrounds, and professional preparation, as well as the location, the subject matter, and the feelings and attitudes surrounding the situation. For instance, consider the head nurse counseling a newly hired nurse regarding a medication error—a situation that can have very different outcomes depending on the variables. Let us assume that the head nurse conducts the meeting in the nurses' station with several other staff present. The new nurse will "hear" the content of the message, but because it is embarrassing to be openly counseled she may be distracted and unable to concentrate fully. The head nurse's intent, to counsel the staff nurse regarding an error, may have been achieved from her perspective; however, the staff nurse may have gotten a different message—"Don't expect understanding from the head nurse." Managers must be sensitive to how listeners may be affected by their messages. In order to communicate effectively the manager must repeatedly ask herself such questions as: What do I want to achieve? How much investment does the listener have in maintaining the status quo? Communication aimed at changing attitudes or behavior demands more of the receiver than information devoid of personal content.

In effective communication the content of the message is clear and organized; the terms used have the same meaning for the receiver as for the sender. Failure to use clearly understood symbols is probably the most common problem in communication.

Nurse managers need to watch the tendency of staff to use professional jargon indiscriminately. Speaking in medical jargon may be a tactic to enhance a sense of belonging, as an exclusionary device, or as an assertion of power over another. A common miscommunication occurs between staff and patient when the message is not phrased so as to be clearly understood by the patient. For example, the nurse who says, "Mrs. Jones, your doctor has ordered sitz baths for you, T.I.D. Please get ready and I'll be back shortly to help you with the treatment." Unless this is explained, the patient may well wonder how she is to get ready. She may not know what a "sitz bath T.I.D." means. Using symbolic language becomes habitual, it is true, but one should be aware that people sometimes have unconscious reasons for not considering their audience when formulating their messages. Persistent patterns of miscommunication on the part of staff should be sensitively explored.

Another sender problem is the common failure to communicate to all who need to know. For any communication instituting a change in policy, practice, or procedure, the nurse manager should carefully identify all individuals who need to receive the message. The manager should consider not only the face value of the message but the implications it may have, both for her own staff members and for other departments in the institution. Poor personnel relations are bound to follow if changes are instituted without proper communication.

Problems of Message Reception

Not all communication problems are sender problems; many are problems of message reception. In examining her own tendencies as a message receiver, the nurse manager can become aware of receiver deficiencies in others. The following are common receiver defects.

Selectivity

There are three related processes that are constantly involved in communication. These mechanisms are known as selective attention, selective perception, and selective memory.[1] They indicate how people select from the flow of communication those messages that fit their attitudes, values, or existing ideas. At the same time, people ignore, dismiss, or forget what doesn't fit.

People tend to see, hear, or remember messages in which they are interested, and to miss messages that do not interest them. Selective attention, then, involves the degree of attention given to a message because of the subject's inherent interest or uninterest. Selective perception allows the receiver to select those parts of the message that conform with his desires or expectations. Such focusing on parts of the whole can cause either incomplete or distorted interpretation of the message by the receiver. What is remembered and what is forgotten involves a similar mechanism. A familiar experience for many nurses is the postoperative patient who does not "remember" the preoperative instructions.

Anticipation of Content

People sometimes assume that they have grasped the essence of a message before completely hearing it out or reading it carefully. Occasionally we all "tune out" the rest of a message once we think we have understood the thrust of what is being communicated.

Thinking Ahead into the Sender Role

Some persons become so preoccupied with their upcoming response to a message that they mentally formulate their answer instead of digesting the message being sent. Persons who think ahead into the sender role are often guilty of interrupting the speaker and responding to incomplete messages.

Receiving Skills

Receiving skills are seldom given sufficient attention. Conscientious effort should be made to apply such basic listening techniques as the following:

- Give the speaker your full attention; try to hear what the speaker is saying, not what you expect the speaker to say.
- Do not interrupt or begin to formulate your answer mentally until the speaker has finished the statement.
- Listen for both facts and feelings. What has the speaker said, and how does the speaker seem to feel about it?
- Tell the speaker what you think has been said; see if that is really what the speaker meant.
- Use questions to clarify meanings.
- Suspend judgment until the speaker finishes talking.

Reading skills should follow similar patterns:

- Read for what the author says, not what you expect the author to say.
- Periodically summarize in your own words what the author is saying and doing. Where does the author seem to be leading?
- Differentiate your own conclusions, assumptions, and inferences from what the author has actually written.

The manager must be a sensitive message receiver because of the nature of her job. At times, messages to her may be somewhat distorted by the attempts of her staff to please. Her receptivity to messages must be such that staff do not feel inhibited when delivering unfavorable reports.

Message Content

The message itself is the next factor the nurse manager must consider. In a face-to-face communication, clarity is usually attained by feedback and interaction between the two individuals. The manager, however, does some of her communication in written form, where direct corrective feedback is not possible. Before dissemination, messages should be carefully checked for clarity of meaning, accuracy of content, and completeness of detail. The manager who has problems with written communication may find it useful to have such messages read by a disinterested party before publication, so as to allow for needed revision. Usually, self-discipline in message evaluation satisfactorily serves the purpose.

Communication Forms

Managers find that a great percentage of their time is spent on communication in one form or another. Organizational communication ranges from a one-to-one relationship to one-to-many. A common error is communicating in one-to-many fashion content that should be expressed one-to-one. Disciplining an employee in front of her peers, for example, is seldom an appropriate form. Nor is it appropriate to waste the time of a group of persons by discussing issues that are pertinent only to one or a few members.

Another defect occurs where the nurse manager chronically communicates with some of her immediate staff to the exclusion of others. The manager must be extremely careful not to penalize some staff members by accidental withholding of necessary information.

The one-to-small-group situation is a communication form that is most useful when the message affects the group as a whole more than as individuals. This form provides an opportunity for immediate clarification, feedback, and reinforcement within the group that will have to function with a common understanding of the message.

Communication may be face-to-face or mediated. A mediated communication is any message presented through some device, such as films, slides, or projected visual material. Although face-to-face and mediated forms are intrinsically different, it is possible to combine the two forms. Showing a movie and then discussing its content represents such a combination of techniques.

Here again, selection depends on the goals of the communicator. Person-to-person communication has several advantages, such as

- focusing the receiver's attention on the issue;
- providing immediate feedback and clarification;
- enabling the message to be adapted to the specific audience.

Mediated forms also have their advantages:

- The message can be given to different groups with no alteration in the presentation or meaning.
- Use of more than one sense (combining visual and audio) may have more impact than speech alone.
- The mediated form allows a complex idea to be edited and tested until the presentation has optimal clarity.
- Mediated communication has the effect of formalizing and recording a decision.
- Mediated forms can be retrieved for future reference to the subject.

Again, communication is sometimes most effective when two forms are combined: e.g., face-to-face communication followed by written reiteration of the message. This form is particularly useful when communication requires specific actions on the part of the recipient.

It is also possible that several alternative modes may be viable for a given communication. An innocuous policy change might be announced at a mass staff meeting, published in a general memo, or discussed with small groups (one team at a time). A different policy, one that more drastically affects workers, however, might require careful selection and staging in order to announce it most effectively. Selection of the proper mode of communication can be very important in effective leadership.

Factors to be considered in selecting a mode of communication include the message content and the anticipated audience response. A Christmas bonus may easily be announced in a printed memo; anticipated layoffs announced in this manner would not only be insensitive but would represent the worst of strategies.

Some questions to consider in selecting a communication mode are:

- Is the message easy to understand, or does it need a mechanism for feedback? Is the feedback needed immediately or will delayed response be adequate?
- What is the audience's anticipated response? What is the intensity of the issue? Will it cause a change in routine practices?
- What need is there for formal documentation of the message? Is the content appropriate to a policy or procedure statement, memo, meeting, or other form?
- What are the abilities of the nurse administrator? With which mode of communication is she most comfortable and most adept?

• Who is the targeted audience? Will the message reach all who need to know?

Directional Flow

Another factor to consider when discussing communications in an organization is directional flow. Communication is necessarily influenced by the structure of an organization. Communication lines between the manager and all relevant persons in or closely associated with the organization are presented in Figure 8-2.

It is usually easier for the nurse manager to evolve effective outgoing communications than incoming communications, because outgoing communications are perceived as more directly under her control. If the nurse manager learns to express herself and to consider "who needs to know" for all communications, her outgoing messages have a greater likelihood of success. There are, however, many ways in which she can foster good incoming communication. For example, many nurse managers use the daily report to gain information about staff, patients, and unit concerns. Her availability to

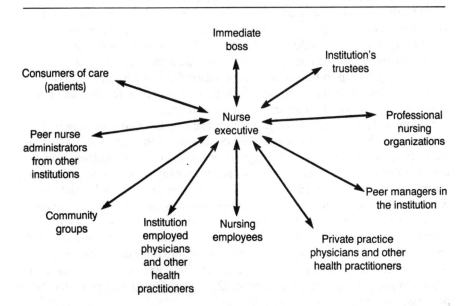

Figure 8-2 Communication Lines

meet with individual staff members and having their trust will allow for more open and useful communication.

Head nurses may evaluate nursing care plans as sources of nursing staff input, that is, as incoming communication. The nurse manager should carefully examine both the written and informal parts of her communications system to ensure that it facilitates incoming as well as outgoing communication with her office.

COMMUNICATING WITH AND THROUGH GROUPS

The effects of group membership comprise another factor that has an impact upon organizational communication. Much of the nurse manager's communication is directed toward groups rather than toward individuals. Even when communication is directed to an individual, that person still reacts partly on the basis of group membership.

Blumer, in his description of symbolic interactionism, notes that all things derive their meanings from social interaction.[2] Humans act toward things on the basis of the meanings those things have for them, and those meanings are social products. For Blumer, even a physical object is a symbol and a social creation; its meaning comes from the society, not from the object itself.

This concept has important implications for the nurse manager. Work groups are also social groups. Therefore, she must consider group responses to her messages as well as individual responses. If the group as a whole places a certain meaning on a communication, there will be pressure on the individual member to conform to the group interpretation. In many instances it is more productive for the manager to deal directly with collective feelings and reactions rather than focus on group members as individuals.

In approaching organizational communications the manager may find it useful to see herself as the center of a communications network. Indeed, a major portion of her time and energy is devoted to one or another form of communication. This fact of organizational leadership causes some analysts to claim that all organizational problems are really communication breakdowns. Although this view ignores the existence of many real problems of other types, there is a partial truth to the perspective. Certainly the nurse manager can eliminate many unnecessary problems by appropriate use of communications and communication techniques. Several important communication lines will be examined next, namely (1) collateral relations with other persons and groups in the patient care environment, (2) collegial relationships with other professionals, and (3) consumer relationships.

Collateral Relations

The first-line manager has collateral relations with many groups and individuals. Indeed, the patient service unit is the hub of most activity in a health care institution, and the number of interactions required of the first-line manager may be overwhelming. Collateral relations are those relations entered into by parties who do not relate to each other as superiors and subordinates but who interact in the patient care environment out of necessity and whose activities require coordination in order that all parties may achieve their goals.

In some instances collateral relations may involve persons who work in the same department or in different departments or divisions of the same organization; in other instances such relations may extend beyond the organization into other networks.

Not all collateral relations can be examined here. Instead, three major areas of collateral relations will be selected to illustrate problems and to suggest solutions to those problems. The three areas involve the first-line manager's collateral relations with (1) managers of support services, (2) physicians and other health professionals, and (3) patients and their families. Not all collateral relationships are alike, but all are similar in that they are external to the hierarchical lines of authority of the typical health care organization.

Support Services and the Negotiated Order Model

What sort of management model will be effective in dealing with collateral units and departments in this sort of environment? Clearly an authoritarian approach will not work, because the nurse manager does not have the power to enforce her decisions. The best model seems to be the negotiated order model, by which the nurse manager negotiates with the managers of other units or departments for those things that she wants. These negotiations usually result in compromises, allowing all of the parties involved to achieve some of their goals. When mutual goals can be identified and agreed upon, the negotiations are more likely to be successful. In a negotiated order model the nurse manager strives to make the other parties accept her goals as their own. Often the nurse manager is successful at this, since her goals are patient-related, and patient needs have a strong moral influence on management decisions in health care institutions. For example, if the head nurse can make the head of the laundry department realize that the department's system of distribution works to the detriment of patients, she is likely to get cooperation in altering the system of distribution. Thus, the establishment of mutual goals is an ideal tactic for one using a negotiated order model of management.

In negotiations with others the nurse manager must take into account their goals as well as her own. She must learn the art of compromise and insist on "all-or-nothing" solutions only when total compliance with her position is really important. She must be careful not to place herself in the win-lose position too often. In an environment where others also hold legitimate powers, the nurse manager who employs only win-lose tactics is likely to incur a great number of losses, while the one who knows the art of compromise usually manages to achieve her goals through a series of negotiations. The nurse manager must also learn to use trade-offs in negotiation. A trade-off occurs when the nurse manager gives the other party something that party particularly wants in exchange for something she herself needs. In fact, trade-offs and compromises dominate the collateral relations of successful nurse managers today. The negotiated order model is necessitated by the organization of the typical health care institution, where multiple sources of authority and power reside side by side.

As the first-line nurse manager's power in the organization declines—that is, as alternative sources of discretion and authority are created—her ability to bargain and coordinate with others becomes critical. Who are the collateral persons with whom the first-line manager must bargain and coordinate? High on the list are the directors of those departments that provide essential support services and supplies. Laundry, pharmacy, material management, admitting, and dietary departments are major examples in the acute care setting. In some facilities, probably out of frustration with the time and energy required by multiple collateral relationships, some directors of nursing are seeking to regain control of support services that directly affect nursing care. Hence, one may find institutions in which departments providing such services as unit management, transportation, or housekeeping are within the nursing division. Where this pattern prevails the head nurse may find that she is the immediate superior of nonnursing staff. By having line authority over such personnel the head nurse will enter into fewer negotiations over goals and tasks. As she gains in power and control, the scope of her managerial responsibilities obviously increases. Since support services are numerous and complex, there will always be persons who remain collateral to her first-line managerial authority and who will thus keep her negotiating skills well honed.

Health Professionals

The relations of the first-line managers with other health professionals usually resemble relations with support staff. Since most of these health professionals are employees of the same organization, mechanisms for the internal settlement of disputes can be utilized. The other health professionals also have the patient's welfare as their central objective, and this shared goal often facilitates negotiations when conflicts arise.

Often the relationship of the first-line manager to another health professional is one of generalist to specialist. The respiratory therapist, for example, has greater knowledge of a given, albeit narrow, area of patient care. The first-line manager must learn to use rather than compete with such specialists, to the benefit of the patient.

Discharge planning, for example, requires the collaboration of nursing and social work. Each discipline contributes crucially to the process, with neither being clearly in charge. Often the social worker will come to the head nurse to seek information and develop a plan of action. The head nurse, alert to the potential conflict that might ensue if she usurps the staff nurse's role, includes the staff nurse in all planning sessions. Should there be a communication problem between social worker and staff, the nurse manager facilitates their communication. She might schedule routine discharge-planning meetings that include social service, nursing, and medical staff. Nurses are not always asked for their evaluation of the patient's ability to carry out the activities of daily living or to learn and comprehend medication regimens; their identification of potential problems that will affect the discharge might also go unsolicited. The nurse manager must reinforce the responsibility of the staff nurse to participate actively in the patient's total plan of care.

Collateral relations must be conducted with many individuals and groups. Good relations should be established before problems emerge. Inviting representatives of other departments to attend nursing unit meetings is one way to strengthen communication and coordination between groups that must work together. Indeed, good collateral relations are the first step toward problem resolution.

Nurse-Nurse Collegial Relations

The nature of relationships between and among nurses is changing because of the development of nursing as a discipline and because of changing economic and power structures in health care delivery systems. In examining relations between nurse colleagues it is important to differentiate professional and administrative relationships. Administrative relationships are dependent on lines of command in the organization. Hence, the nurse executive can give directives to the head nurse by virtue of her position and the authority accorded to that position. In contrast, professional or collegial relations do not rest on organizational lines of authority; they rest on interactions made possible by shared professional knowledge. Professional relations among nurses are based on shared nursing knowledge as well as on respect for one another's area of nursing expertise. When collegial and administrative relations are confused, there is the potential for nonproductive communication.

Nurses need to develop a professionalism that is reflected in respect for each other. In the past, nurses were often made to feel guilty if they lacked any part of "nursing knowledge." In such situations they often perceived that the need to consult with another nurse was an admission of deficiency in their own performance. Contrast this with the practices of the medical profession: An orthopedic surgeon has no qualms about consulting with a neurologist if a given case falls within the realm of the latter's expertise. Nurses today are beginning to use similar patterns of peer interaction. Now a staff nurse is likely to call a cardiovascular nursing specialist if she needs such expertise. The use of other nurses for care consultation develops mutual respect for nurses as professionals. Additionally, such actions identify nurses rather than physicians as the arbiters of nursing expertise. Frequent peer interaction and consultation also build for the nurse a network of professional colleagues—a network that increases the resources at hand for any nurse involved.

First-line managers sometimes feel themselves to be competing with clinical specialists for power within nursing. When clinical specialists work in staff positions, a dangerous behavioral cycle may develop between the specialist and first-line manager:

1. In order to protect her own authority and power, the first-line manager fails to consult the clinical specialist about care problems.
2. The clinical specialist, frustrated over her lack of input into the care system, makes a bid for administrative power, trying to supplant the first-line manager.
3. The first-line manager responds to this threat by even greater exclusion of the clinical specialist.

Such a cycle of behavior involves a confusion of two sorts of power: professional power and administrative power. The first sort of power derives from professional expertise and knowledge. If the first-line manager (who holds administrative power) uses the clinical specialist's professional power appropriately, her administrative power is seldom threatened. The first-line manager must perceive her job as one of using scarce resources appropriately. Certainly the clinical specialist's knowledge is a scarce resource, one that should be tapped to the fullest degree possible. When the first-line manager takes full advantage of the clinical specialist's expertise, there is seldom a problem of power. Indeed, failure to use the knowledge of the clinical specialist reflects poor management.

As nurses come to realize that they have much to offer each other, a new mutual respect develops. This mutual respect helps nurses to bridge the psychological gaps that previously separated diverse groups, such as education and service groups. The growth of collegial relations among nurses has thus fostered the development of new nursing roles that transcend previous barriers. Today many new joint or dual roles are being created and tested in nursing. Some nurses may combine staff nursing and student education. Others may combine administration of service and educational units within a single university or corporation. Still others may combine teaching of students with inservice education.

Joint roles require careful planning and testing. How much time should the nurse spend on actual care delivery? How much time, and of what sort, on student education? If a director of nursing combines patient care with her managerial job, what happens if she leaves a critical meeting to administer care to one of her patients?

It is not as easy for nurses to combine care with another role function as it is for physicians. Medical care is intermittent, while nursing care must often be sustained over long periods of time. While it is difficult to work out the distribution of tasks and roles over joint and dual appointments, such appointments have much to offer. Practice, for example, will keep faculty members updated on skills and appreciative of changes in the care delivery setting. Similarly, teaching responsibilities will keep the clinician appreciative of the complexities of education in a developing discipline such as nursing. Joint and dual roles will foster shared respect and communication among nurses.

Typically the term "joint role" refers to a job that has two or more diverse subroles but is played out in a single institution. In some instances, nurses may fill two different roles (dual roles) in separate institutions. Those institutions may have arranged a trade-off system, or dual role holders may actually work for both institutions. Sometimes the arrangements are informal, with less mixing of tasks but with ample exposure to both service and education (or service and administration). For example, an institution may ask that the faculty who monitor the clinical experiences of affiliated students volunteer to present some inservice education for the personnel of the clinical facility. In turn, the clinical facility may offer to provide some expert clinical preceptors for advanced students. In these informal relations what counts is that a sense of reciprocity be created. Each partner to the agreement must benefit from the exchange of services. Sometimes informal trade-offs later become formalized into job descriptions.

It is not essential to create joint or dual roles in order to establish collegial relations among nurses. It is possible that nurses who fill traditional roles may learn to share their knowledge, perspectives, and skills more often. Collegial relations really evolve from a state of mind, a state in which nurses recognize the abilities and talents of their nurse peers and assist each other in a cooperative rather than competitive manner.

Professional relations occur between colleagues, and they stand apart from administrative relations. Thus a head nurse has the right to refuse to follow an administrative order from her supervisor if the order compromises her professional ethics or the canons of professional practice. Similarly, in keeping with the difference between professional and administrative relations, a director of nursing would feel perfectly free to ask an expert nurse clinician (her administrative subordinate) for professional guidance and direction in establishing protocols of clinical patient care. Collegial relations are based on professional expertise: they enable administratively unequal persons in the same field to act as professional peers and equals.

Relations with Patients as Consumers

Some readers may find it strange that collateral relations with patients should be discussed. Yet patients are persons with whom agreements are required. A refusal to engage in collateral relations with the patient reflects an unacceptable tendency to objectify the patient. When patients are treated as objects, there is no need for collateral relations; objects are to be manipulated and used. To say that such manipulations are carried out "for the patient's own good" is not enough to justify ignoring the personhood of the patient. The growing sensitivity of both patients and nursing staff to this problem is manifest in the demand for a "patient's bill of rights." It is sad that a bill of rights should have been made necessary by staff behaviors.

Negotiation represents one approach to relations between the first-line manager and the patient. The sensitive first-line manager will see to it that her staff plan nursing care regimens *with* patients. Patients have a right to know what alternatives exist in care planning and what results are likely to be achieved with each alternative. The professional presents alternatives and gives expert advice, but patients ultimately have the right of choice concerning their own bodies, their own actions, and the actions of others toward themselves.

The consumer movement of the 1980's has had a significant impact on health care. Reports of health care discoveries make front page news and educate the public as to the latest medical findings. Armed with information, consumers want to participate actively in health care decisions.

The first-line manager should respect the patient as a person with final decision-making power. Obviously, patients vary in their ability to participate in decision making. For some patients the "choice" may be to leave all decisions to others. Such a choice is less common than might be expected, however. Certainly one should not assume that patients routinely divest themselves of autonomy. They may, however, need help in expressing their rightful autonomy in the confusing health care environment. Nurses are in a position to align themselves with clients and to advocate on their behalf.

Regardless of setting (hospital, nursing home, health maintenance organization, home health care agency), the nurse powerfully influences client satisfaction with the facility. Clients will likely have more encounters with nurses than with any other health care professional. A positive attitude can go far to promote patient satisfaction.

Educating the public as to what they can expect during their hospitalization or clinic visit will influence patient attitudes and responses as well. The goals of nurses and consumers should be in concert to assist the client to achieve the best health outcome possible.

Nurse-Physician Collegial Relationships

Nurses have long sought collegial relations with physicians. Physicians, in both subtle and not so subtle ways, often have resisted these overtures. It is important to analyze the underlying dynamics of this situation if collegial relations are to be established in today's health care delivery system. Physicians have often chosen to eschew such relations with nurses, preferring to maintain a relationship in which they are dominant rather than collaborative. Historically, physicians held such relationships when nursing was subordinate and not yet striving to establish its own separate identity. Now nursing is establishing its unique identity as a field with its own subject matter, different from the subject matter of medicine. In the most simplistic formulation of that difference, nursing is the science of caring for a person undergoing a health-related experience, while medicine is the science of diagnosing and treating a pathological state. Whatever the distinctions between the two disciplines, however, it is obvious that nursing is the newly emerging field without a long history of scientifically based practices.

This difference in age is not nursing's only disadvantage in pressing for equality with medicine. Assertiveness on the part of nursing threatens what medicine regards as its turf. Like any other discipline, medicine does not want to yield territory that it presently controls. Indeed, even today a physician is entitled by law in every U.S. state to practice nursing. Every nursing practice act defines nursing as dependent on medicine. Nurses are striving to change this legal dependency, but legally medicine still maintains control. Nurses, as one would expect, have tried to stress the independent aspect of nursing in their interpersonal relationships with physicians. This is by no means the rule, however; there are still many nurses who overtly assume a subordinate position to physicians and who receive their psychological rewards from physician approval.

Physicians have several advantages in defending their superordinate position. First, the fact that they leave "orders" on charts gives the impression that they have an administrative relationship with the nursing staff of an institution. In fact, that is seldom the case. Most physicians do not have line authority for nurse employees; most nurses report to head nurses and to a nursing hierarchy. Nevertheless, the physician is likely to try to exert administrative authority as a power tactic. If nurses act as if they were employees of the physician, then for all intents and purposes administrative control has been effected.

Why would the physician wish to establish this pseudo-authority? Not all physicians excel in human relations, and an authority position reduces the need for negotiation. Physicians can also simplify their work if they can regard patients as their "private property," for then they need not consider the goals and values of others. Some physicians also fail to understand the nature of collegial relations between disciplines, which does not establish an absolute "equality" between nurse and physician. Physicians who have this misunderstanding of the collegial relationship may argue that "there is no way in which her baccalaureate degree is equal to my years of undergraduate school, graduate study, and residency." Such an argument fails to recognize that nurses are not trying to establish their equality in the practice of medicine. They are simply trying to say that they are as professional and competent in what they do as are the physicians in what they do.

The best way for a nurse to establish collegial relationships with physicians is to exhibit excellence in her nursing care. She need not hesitate to make this excellence visible to others, nor can she fail to communicate it. Nevertheless, the nurse manager must be aware that there are many sociological factors that inhibit collegial relations and support a subservient nursing position. These factors include the following:

- Most physicians are male and most nurses are female in a society that is still male-dominated.
- Many physicians have a "class" advantage insofar as they may come from generally wealthier segments of the population than do nurses.
- Most physicians have had more years of education than the nurses with whom they interact.
- Society has accorded to the physician greater rewards of both status and compensation.
- Age and experience usually work in favor of the physician.
- Traditional patterns of interaction often reinforce a subordinate-superior dichotomy.

In spite of these psychological edges in favor of physician dominance, the pattern of nurse-physician relations is changing. Nurses are asserting their own rights as independent practitioners of nursing. If the nurse refuses to be fooled into a spurious superior-subordinate game, then the physician is forced to act on the real relationship: that of two professionals caring, though with different foci, for the same patient.

In the past, when a contest of authority took place between a physician and nurse, the physician was likely to win the support of the hospital administration because the physician was recognized as the source of patients, hence of income for the institution. That situation is shifting today because of the critical shortage of nurses. When the shortage of nurses causes income-producing floors to be closed, nursing is soon recognized as a source of institutional income. This is now happening in numerous facilities. Administrators and physicians are recognizing that an environment must be created in which the nurse wishes to remain. Administrators are reconsidering their financial compensation packages, and physicians are being forced to reconsider their human relations with nurses. Many are beginning to change, or trying to change, their behaviors to foster retention of needed nursing staff. Collegial relations foster retention.

The change in long-established patterns of interaction does not come easily. Nor is the curbing of imperious behavior by physicians the only behavior change that is needed. The change must be two-way; the nurse must demonstrate pride in herself, in her profession, and in her ability to make appropriate decisions and recommendations concerning patient care. This means eliminating the "doctor-nurse game" in which the nurse obliquely words her request so that it may appear that the physician initiated it.

In establishing parity in nurse-physician relationships, the nurse must not feel a need to compete for the physician's turf. She does not have to catch a medical error or inconsistency to prove her worth. What she has to prove is her ability to manage nursing and nursing judgments. Much of the old ethos of nursing worked against such behavior. For example, nurses were encouraged to qualify all judgments: "Appears to be uncomfortable" rather than "Patient is uncomfortable" and "Abdomen appears to be distended," when there is no doubt of the assessment. This tendency to circumvent instead of make judgments was ingrained in traditional nursing patterns of behavior, and it encourages abnegation of nursing decision making and action. One positive effect of the use of nursing diagnostic taxonomies is the breaking down of this aura of tentativeness.

If the nurse truly wishes to establish collegial relations, she not only must excel at her own profession but she must refuse to accept behaviors in herself or others that deny an equal relationship. This means that she will not accept immature behavior in the physician. She will not allow herself to be lectured to like a child; she will not accept blame for the errors of others or allow herself to be manipulated into immature behavior by the immature behavior of others. Nor will she hesitate to participate fully in patient-centered discussions with mixed professional groups; she will recognize that her nursing input has a valid and estimable place in discussions of patient status.

A study conducted at George Washington University Medical Center concluded that the most important factor affecting patient survival in intensive care units is the quality of nursing care. The quality of the communication between physicians and nurses was especially significant, while sophisticated technology was found to play a smaller part in lowering mortality rates.[3,4] At the best hospital, nurses operated semi-autonomously and were able to cancel elective surgery if nursing resources were particularly stretched. At the worst hospital, doctors and nurses were in open conflict about the number of patients nurses could reasonably and safely care for. Such disputes work against positive patient outcomes.

Usually the nurse has little trouble recognizing overtly negative behaviors that are destructive of relations with colleagues. She may, however, have more difficulty recognizing the more subtle forms of "putting her in her place." The physician who calls the nurse by her first name, while expecting her to call him "Dr. Jones," exemplifies a subtle form of discrimination. A "nurses' week" celebration that resembles "secretary week" is another case in point.

Of course, a collegial relationship with physicians causes new problems for the nurse. For example, what does the nurse do when a physician fails to inform a patient of all possible consequences of a projected surgery? What if the physician fails to meet patient teaching needs while making it difficult for the nurse to meet them? The changing relationship creates situations where the nurse feels a professional obligation to act on her own nursing judgment rather than mechanically follow a physician's orders concerning aspects of nursing care. Collegial relations are neither simple to achieve nor always peaceful. They bring with them added responsibility to assume one's own professional obligations at all times. To merit collegial relations one must assume the burdens as well as the rewards of full professional accountability.

Such relations enable the practitioners to collaborate in a way that enables both to respect one another's expertise in their own disciplines. Obviously, such respect is not without its evaluative aspect. Nursing and medicine, for example, share enough common elements that an observant and discriminating nurse will be relatively accurate in distinguishing excellent, mediocre, and poor medical practice. Similarly, an observant physician will be relatively accurate in differentiating good and bad nursing practice. Evaluations of the professional expertise of others (in one's own or in a related field) will color collegial relations. Indeed, truly effective collegial relations would require reporting of the inferior practice of others for the protection of patients. Normally, in beginning a professional relationship one assumes competence on the part of the other professional. Confirmation of that competence goes far toward cementing the collegial relationship.

SUMMARY

An important function of the first-line manager is to be an effective communicator. To do this she must be aware of methods of communication and be able to use them comfortably. An understanding of the theories of communication helps the first-line manager to assess the effectiveness of her communication skills.

The style and technique of a manager's delivery set an ambience within the work unit. An awareness of the impact of one's own communication patterns is necessary, as is sensitivity to the receiver. Communicating clearly and listening attentively are essential for a successful manager.

Collaboration and collegiality are required in communication patterns if the health care organization is to operate as an integrated whole. Professional relations among colleagues help to optimize the use of human resources. They stress the building of respect for professional competence and expertise rather than foster counterproductive competition.

Nurse managers must recognize the importance of partnerships and value the unique contribution of other health care workers. In an acute care setting the role of the dietary department is no less relevant to achieving quality patient care than is the role of social services or surgery. In home health care the relationship between the family, the physician, and the nurse is critical in managing the client's continuity of care and treatment.

The first-line nurse manager must identify all those individuals and groups that impact on her delivery of nursing care. The interplay between groups is inevitable, and it will be handled more effectively if the first-line manager actively plans for it. Good relations should be established before problems emerge. Effective collaboration requires sensitivity to the goals, tasks, and resources of all who are involved.

NOTES

1. Louis Forsdale, *Perspectives on Communication* (New York: Random House, 1981), pp. 113–130.
2. H. Blumer, *Symbolic Interactionism—Perspective and Method* (Englewood Cliffs, NJ: Prentice-Hall, 1969), pp. 2–6.
3. David Holzman, "Intensive Care Nurses: A Vital Sign," *Insight* (December 1, 1986): 47.

4. W.A. Knaus and D.P. Wagner, "When Is ICU Care Appropriate?" *Business and Health* (January 1987): 31–34.

BIBLIOGRAPHY

Baird, John E. "Changes in Nurse Attitudes: Management Strategies for Today's Environment." *Journal of Nursing Administration* 17, no. 9 (September 1987): 38–43.

Cotton, C.C. "Measurement of Power-Balancing Styles and Some of Their Correlates." *American Science Quarterly* 21, no. 2 (1976): 307.

Culbertson, R.A. "The Governing Body and the Nursing Administrator: An Emerging Relationship." *JONA* 9, no. 2 (1979): 11.

Doona, M.E. "A Nursing Unit as a Political System." *JONA* 7, no. 1 (1977): 28.

Harriman, B. "Up and Down the Communications Ladder." *Harvard Business Review* 52, no. 5 (1974): 143.

Keenan, T.; Aiken, L.; and Cluff, L.E., eds. *Nurses and Doctors: Their Education and Practice.* Cambridge, Massachusetts: Oelgeschlager, Gunn & Hain, 1981.

Likert, R. *The Human Organization: Its Management and Values.* New York: McGraw-Hill Book Co., 1967.

Longest, B.B., Jr. "Institutional Politics." *JONA* 5, no. 3 (1975): 38.

Malkiel, B.G. "Productivity—The Problem Behind the Headlines." *Harvard Business Review* 57, no. 3 (1979): 81.

Uyterhoeven, H.E.R. "General Managers in the Middle." *Harvard Business Review* 50, no. 2 (1972): 75.

Webber, J.B., and Dula, M.A. "Effective Planning Committees for Hospitals." *Harvard Business Review* 52, no. 3 (1974): 33.

chapter 9

Legal and Ethical Implications of the First-Line Manager Role

This chapter considers the legal and ethical obligations of the first-line manager. Legal and ethical issues, while overlapping, do not encompass one another. Legal issues, which will be discussed first, can be seen as the minimal requirement for ethical practice. Abridgement of legal responsibilities results in actions in which the nurse is held liable at law. Ethical issues are broader and include areas that, if ignored, would not necessarily result in legal action but might be considered censorable under professionally approved standards. Ethical issues are broader and often less clearly defined. As ethical debates are resolved in a nation, they tend to be codified in the laws of the land. The area of legal and ethical behavior is extensive and changing, and so only the broadest guidelines can be offered here. This chapter should be seen as an introduction, not as an exhaustive examination of this complex area.

LEGAL CONSIDERATIONS

The first-line manager's legal responsibilities may be classified as (1) responsibilities to and for the organization and its employees, and (2) responsibilities to and for patients. While these obligations interact and overlap, they will be separated here for purposes of discussion.

Responsibilities to and for the Organization

The first-line manager has organizational responsibilities in several directions. At the upper end of the hierarchy, it is her responsibility to bring serious deficits in the care program to the attention of administration. At the other end, she has numerous responsibilities to and for her staff.

Assuring Staff Competence

The first-line nurse manager is responsible for those individuals performing under her supervision and is accountable for the assignment of staff within her unit. An effective head nurse knows her staff and their areas of strength and weakness. Involvement in the hiring and orientation of new personnel affords the nurse manager an opportunity to evaluate an individual's knowledge and skills prior to her joining the unit. Once on the staff, the new member will continue to be observed until she is determined to be a safe practitioner. This is especially essential when hiring new nurse graduates, who may lack sufficient clinical experience.

It is expected that nurse managers will use their professional judgment and knowledge to ensure that no harm comes to patients as a result of substandard care. This requires the head nurse to observe her staff routinely in practice and evaluate them according to established standards.

In the eyes of the law, it is understood that there is an element of risk for patients/consumers receiving health care. While it is the goal of the health care professional that the patient achieve the best health outcome, there can be no guarantee that it will be achieved. Treatments and medications are prescribed with the knowledge that there may be side effects. It is the nurse's duty to be aware of the potential for harm and to assess the patient accordingly. It is important that the nurse realize and understand her legal responsibility and her accountability in relation to her practice. The head nurse should serve as a resource for staff in this respect.

The employment of agency nurses by hospitals to supplement unit staffing poses a potential liability problem. Nurses unfamiliar with the patients, the unit, or even the hospital require close supervision. Before assigning them any duties the nurse in charge should verify their credentials and their professional skills. This information should be documented. It is dangerous for a first-line manager to assume competency based solely on the fact that the nursing department assigned the nurse to the unit. The employer, in this case the hospital, shares responsibility; but the head nurse is accountable for ensuring that patients are given care by competent practitioners.

The prospective payment system has resulted in patients being discharged "sicker and quicker" from hospitals. Another result of this practice is an increase in high-tech nursing in community health care. This has placed an additional learning burden on the community health nurse whose past practice was primarily low-tech. Home health care nurses must be knowledgeable and competent to supervise and handle the equipment that is becoming a part of home health care. Nurse managers in this area must ensure that the nurses under their supervision have the necessary education and experience before assigning cases to them. The legal vulnerability of the manager is even more apparent in the home health context, because, unlike the head nurse in an acute care unit, she is not likely to be present to observe her staff nurse giving care.

Legal Safeguards in Nursing Practice

Nursing practice is governed by regulations and laws. Laws are enacted to protect the rights of individuals from being violated. Regulations are the rules of procedure by which laws are implemented. All laws concerning professional practice are based on standards of conduct; laws and regulations establish means for enforcing those standards. The state boards of nursing have been given broad rule-making authority by their state legislators. The right to regulate nursing practice rests with the states, not the federal government, by virtue of the U.S. Constitution.

State boards of nursing enforce the nursing practice acts in their state. In accordance with the authority granted to the state board, it can impose certain sanctions when there is clear evidence that standards have been breached. For example, the board may suspend or revoke an individual's license to practice. Questions related to professional conduct are determined in adherence to accepted standards of nursing practice. At the national level, the American Nurses' Association, as well as the various nursing specialty organizations, have established and promulgated standards of nursing practice.

When Are Nurses Liable?

The entire health care industry has been barraged with liability claims charging injury as a result of substandard care. Consequently today's clients and patients are worried and watchful of the care they receive. The watchdog function is an important aspect of the consumer movement, as is the consumer's desire to participate actively in decisions related to his treatment plan. Although medicine has borne the brunt of malpractice suits, as evidenced by physicians' escalating malpractice fees, nursing is equally vulnerable to liability.

Legally the nurse, as a professional with a defined scope of practice, is expected to function within that defined scope and to exercise independent judgment within it. Nurses are therefore liable for their actions if they practice beyond that scope or if they make wrong judgments within the scope of practice. The old defense that they were "following doctor's orders" is invalid. Kelly states that "one who undertakes to perform the services of a professional nurse . . . is under a legal duty to use that reasonable degree of skill, knowledge, and care ordinarily possessed by nurses acting under similar circumstances."[1] Thus a nurse's actions will be measured against the accepted standard of nursing practice, and a nurse's failure to act accordingly is considered to be professional negligence.

There are four elements, all of which must be present before liability can be established: (1) a legal duty to the patient, (2) a breach of nursing standards, (3) injury to the patient, and (4) proof of damage.[2]

Within the relationship of nurse and patient a legal duty exists holding the nurse accountable for her professional conduct. She must perform according to a reasonable standard of care. The patient bringing suit, i.e., the plaintiff, may look to the ANA standards of practice, the state's nurse practice act, the Joint Commission on Accreditation of Healthcare Organizations (formerly JCAH), or the written policies of the hospital or community health agency for standards by which to judge the nurse's performance.

Next, in a malpractice claim, it must be established that the nurse acted in a manner that a "reasonably prudent" nurse would not adopt. Some examples of errors or omissions that could constitute nursing negligence are

- failure to monitor and report patient's condition and to take appropriate action;
- failure to protect the patient from a dangerous condition;
- failure to attend the patient;
- failure to exercise independent judgment.[3]

The nurse is expected to ensure that the patient receives proper care. She is not absolved of her responsibility when she notifies the physician. For example, if the nurse reports a patient's worsening condition and the doctor does not respond, she is still expected to act on the patient's behalf and take proper measures. She is also culpable for failing to report observed negligent behavior on the part of another.

A commonplace "failure to attend the patient" occurs when siderails are left down on the bed of a confused elderly patient. If the patient were to fall out of the bed and fracture a hip, a case could be made that the nurse failed adequately to attend the patient. It may be argued that any prudent nurse would raise the siderails as a precaution to protect the patient from a foreseeable danger. In fact, hospital policy often dictates that patients over sixty-two are to have the siderails on their beds raised.

Next, it must be proven that the patient sustained injury as a direct result of the nurse's negligence; the legal term for this is "causation." In the previous example, if the patient were to fall out of bed without suffering injury, there would be no liability. If, over time, the patient developed back pain, it would have to be proven that the patient suffered back pain as a result of the fall and that the back pain would not otherwise have occurred.

The patient must prove that damage has actually occurred as a result of the nurse's negligence; the possibility of some future loss is considered insufficient.

Persons suffering property loss or personal injury can bring suit for damages resulting from negligence. The court awards damages to compensate for pain and suffering or economic losses caused by an injury.[4,5]

The nurse manager has many other responsibilities to and for her staff. For example, she needs to see that their rights as employees and citizens are not abridged.

Managing the Impaired Nurse

Among the most difficult and sensitive situations the nurse manager must confront is the staff member suspected of substance abuse. Often the newly promoted head nurse is unprepared and ill-equipped to handle the problem. The information included in this section is meant to increase awareness regarding a serious management issue and provide general guidelines for beginning managers.

The misuse or abuse of alcohol and drugs is as much a problem for health professionals as it is for the general population. Over half of the disciplinary actions taken by state boards of nursing are related to abuse of alcohol or controlled substances.[6] The nurse manager needs to be a skilled observer, alert to the possibility that there could be a problem and knowledgeable about what to do. She must know the policies and procedures of her organization regarding substance abuse; and, equally important, she must know the laws that dictate her actions concerning cases of abuse.

The nurse manager, through her daily contact with staff, comes to know and expect certain behaviors based on her experience with each individual. This knowledge is one of her best tools in dealing with an impaired professional. Certain signs and symptoms may appear over time in the substance abuser. Physical symptoms include tremors, slurred speech, a persistent runny nose, dilated or constricted pupils, and an unsteady gait. A change in behavior often occurs as well. The employee becomes easily irritated and isolates herself from friends in the workplace; her relationships become problematic, and her performance on the job deteriorates. Absenteeism increases, as do the frequent unexplained absences during work hours.

The nurse manager has a responsibility to educate her staff, as well as herself, regarding the potential problem. She needs to know what to watch for. Even with an aware staff, behavioral and/or physical changes in a nurse or staff member may go unnoticed for some time. Nurses often fail to "see" that a friend has such a problem. Recognition that something is seriously wrong usually follows an incident such as missing narcotics or patient problems, after which staff nurses are often the ones who notice an emerging pattern. Narcotic counts are increasingly incorrect; or, on particular shifts, patients report pain medication as ineffective, or records show changes in patient usage of pain medications. When inappropriate behavior is evident, not only concern but action is required. The overriding professional responsibility is to protect the patient from potential harm.

Once an incident has occurred or a staff member has voiced suspicion, the nurse manager has the responsibility to intervene in the situation. The nurse manager facing this situation for the first time is advised to seek help from higher nursing administration or from the employee assistance program (EAP), if one has been established in the organization. Confronting a nurse suspected of substance abuse should not be undertaken lightly or attempted without guidance.

Intervention. The seriousness of the incident may require notifying outside authorities. In a case of narcotics being stolen, federal authorities are called in to investigate. Some states have regulations requiring that nurses suspected of using or abusing alcohol or drugs be reported to the state board of nursing. The policies and procedures adopted by the nursing department provide guidance to the nurse manager; policies should be closely adhered to and documented each step of the way.

It is important that the head nurse be clear in her own mind as to what she wants to accomplish. The goal should not be to punish the employee but to help her and make her aware of the inherent danger that her behavior poses to patients and to herself. The goal is to have the employee seek treatment. The close working relationship between the head nurse and her staff can be both an asset and a hindrance. The nurse manager may have difficulty being objective when confronting the nurse. She may feel angry and betrayed or blame herself for not acting sooner. These emotions may adversely affect her ability to counsel and to understand the staff member's needs in the situation.

Whatever the former relationship, it is predictable that the staff member will deny any untoward behavior and become angry at the accusation. The head nurse needs to frame the interview carefully and to maintain control of the situation. Some points should be considered: (1) Allow sufficient time for the meeting (up to two hours), so that the anger, shame, fear, and guilt that the nurse may experience can be worked through. To end the interview prematurely, before arriving at some resolution, would greatly diminish chances for a successful intervention. (2) Schedule a time when there will be no interruptions. (3) Be patient and understanding, but do not waver. Regardless of how adamantly the nurse denies the problem, keep returning to the facts of the case and to your own determination not to allow further endangerment of patients. (4) Know what resources are available for the nurse (EAP on site, treatment options outside the organization), including what costs are covered by employee benefits. Know the organization's policy regarding continued employment. (5) Be clear as to the consequences of her behavior and her decision regarding treatment. This should cover whatever disciplinary action may be taken by the employer and any reporting required by law. (6) Bring written documentation of the incident, including direct observation of the individual's behavior and performance, pertinent dates, times, and witnesses. (7) Do not procrastinate concerning the interview, but schedule it as quickly as possible.

Although the course of the interview will be influenced by several variables—recognition of the problem or lack of it by the impaired nurse, her amenability to treatment, and the interviewer's own attitude and skill—the range of possible outcomes can be reduced to several common scenarios. In the first scenario, the impaired nurse admits that she has a chemical dependency but refuses assistance. Sometimes she claims that she can cope with it herself or that her personal behavior is not the concern of the first-line manager.

The troubled nurse may argue persuasively that she cannot afford to enter treatment, that others are reliant on her economic support. Regardless of how sympathetic the nurse manager may feel to the plight of the chemically dependent nurse, her primary responsibility is to protect the patients under the nurse's care from potential harm. If the problem is serious enough to warrant dismissal, it should probably be reported to the state board of nursing regardless of state regulations. In some cases the nurse will choose to resign her position rather than face disciplinary action. While this may resolve the immediate problem of the employing organization, it does not resolve the question of ethical responsibility that arises if the impaired nurse continues to practice elsewhere, thus exposing the public to potential danger.

A more common scenario is one in which the nurse admits to a chemical dependency and agrees to participate in an employee assistance program or seek appropriate treatment. Often the troubled nurse is relieved when she is confronted, because she no longer has to be afraid or to hide or deny the problem. The nurse manager should then lay out a detailed plan for specific treatment, including what will happen if the nurse drops out of treatment. The treatment may require a temporary leave from the work situation for a specified time period. The nurse manager should arrange the necessary referrals for evaluation and follow-up to be sure that the impaired employee has acted on the prescribed plan. As mentioned earlier, it would be a mistake to trust the individual's ability to handle her dependency problem on her own.

Whether or not to notify the state board of nursing will depend on the state regulations and the gravity of the problem. In some cases the reporting is deferred if the nurse agrees to participate in treatment and exhibits satisfactory compliance with the prescribed treatment plan. The employing organization has a responsibility to monitor the nurse's participation, while protecting her right to confidentiality. (Re-entry of the impaired nurse into the work environment will be discussed later in the section.)

The next possible scenario revolves around the impaired nurse who denies the problem and refuses any evaluation. The consequences of the person's decision should be clearly stated. These will, in all likelihood, include the nurse's removal from the work situation and the initiation of disciplinary action against her. It is not necessary to prove that the nurse is drug- or alcohol-dependent, only to document the actions and events as they occurred. Obviously, the head nurse should have sound evidence that the relevant actions or events took place before initiating the employee interview.

In all these cases some thought should be given as well to informing the individual's family or significant other about the interview outcome. This may depend on the nurse's response to the intervention, especially if there is any question of suicidal tendency. Should the nurse be intoxicated or under the influence of drugs at the time of the interview, she should be escorted home and not simply sent home.

Re-entry. The goal of intervention and treatment is to enable the impaired nurse to resume her career. The employer has a commitment to work with the recovering nurse, and the manager should develop a trusting and open relationship with her. The circumstances surrounding the impaired nurse's re-employment require careful planning along with ongoing monitoring. Although employers would often prefer not to hire impaired nurses, federal law protects these nurses from discrimination as handicapped individuals. A method for monitoring that has proven increasingly successful is a contractual agreement that clearly outlines the responsibilities of the returning employee and the expectations of the employing agency.[7,8,9] The areas delineated in this contract include: agreement to abstain from all alcohol and drug use; voluntary cooperation with random urine and/or blood tests to check for chemicals and/or alcohol; documentation of regular attendance and participation in a prescribed plan of treatment, which may include EAP, Alcoholics Anonymous and/or Narcotics Anonymous; agreement as to when and under what conditions she will administer narcotics; consequences if terms of agreement are not adhered to, including notification of the state board of nursing; actions by employer in case of resignation; duration of the contract.

Other issues that should be considered prior to the nurse's return to duty include proximity to drugs, area of practice, availability of supervision, shift rotation, and the employee's right to privacy. These issues need to be weighed, case by case, in the light of each individual's circumstances. It is generally considered to be in the best interest of the impaired nurse that she not have immediate access to mood-altering drugs on her return. A period of readjustment, such as six months, may be established during which she will not be allowed to give narcotics. Additionally, it may be stipulated that her narcotic administration will be supervised for a set period beyond the initial probation.

The responsibilities of the nurse's position and the stresses of her practice area should also be examined. Stress should be minimized during recovery, since it will have a direct bearing on the impaired nurse and her ability to cope. Work with a consistent and supportive staff is preferable to a float assignment, which would make monitoring difficult if not impossible. The returning nurse's work schedule should also allow her to attend meetings of her support group. In those facilities where a "buddy system" pairs the recovering nurse with a peer who works with her during the re-entry phase, scheduling both together will be an additional consideration.

The impaired nurse has a right to expect that circumstances related to her alcohol or chemical dependency will be kept confidential. The restrictions that may limit her professional practice, i.e., the ban on administering narcotics, may require some explanation. The nurse manager may want to discuss this with the recovering nurse and her counselor, since it is the decision of the impaired nurse whether or not to disclose her situation. Sometimes the impaired nurse feels comfortable sharing the fact that she is recovering from a dependency problem. If not, it is up to the nurse manager to ensure her privacy to the extent that it is practically feasible and consistent with the welfare of patients.

The head nurse should be clear as to her accountability in the re-entry process. Usually, to guard the nurse's privacy, a separate file is established. Here it should be documented that the nurse is abstaining from mood-altering substances and is complying with the agreed-upon plan of aftercare.

Responsibilities of the Nurse Manager. While confronting the issue of the impaired nurse may be difficult, ignoring the problem has far worse consequences. The nurse manager has an overriding responsibility to patients and staff to provide a safe and effective work setting.

Even in community health or clinical situations where nurses work more independently and exercise autonomy over their practice, the nurse manager has the duty to know her staff and watch for any behavioral change. Lack of appropriate intervention is dangerous for patients as well as a disservice to the impaired nurse, and it erodes the confidence and trust that should exist among colleagues. Confronting the impaired nurse with the facts of the situation in a supportive and understanding manner can provide the incentive for her to seek appropriate help, maximizing her chances for full recovery.

First-line nurse managers should avail themselves of abuse-related resources within the institution, agency, community, and profession. Employee assistance programs are institutionally based and staffed by trained counselors. The EAP has the responsibility to set policy and to conduct education, outreach, referral, and monitoring activities. Community resources include Alcoholics Anonymous and Narcotics Anonymous.

Nurse managers have the opportunity to effect early treatment and facilitate rehabilitation of employees with substance abuse problems. Through staff education, professional support, consultation with employee assistance programs, and involvement at the organizational level, the nurse manager develops a comprehensive approach to the problem that includes early identification, effective intervention, and ultimate re-entry. Impaired nurses are suffering from a disease, in some cases of life-threatening proportions. They deserve concern and caring from their fellow professionals. Nationally, there are several organizations that provide valuable information regarding this issue. These include:

Drug and Alcohol Nursing Association, Inc.
P.O. Box 6216
Annapolis, Maryland 21401
(301) 263-1131

National Nurses Society on Addictions
Impaired Nurse Committee
1020 Sunset Drive
Lawrence, Kansas 66044
(913) 842-3893

Legal Issues and Institutional Policies

The first-line manager is not only responsible for her employees, she is also responsible for seeing that her unit meets the legal obligations of an institution providing health care. In the present legal and health care environment, that is not always an easy thing to do. New administrative tactics are being tried by institutions in an attempt to cope with a health care industry that borders on a crisis state. Often these tactics represent the best *available* way—not necessarily the best way—to deal with a crisis situation. Often case law does not yet exist to clarify the legal status of such administrative actions. Let us examine one such instance.

In the face of a shortage of nurses some hospitals have adopted a policy of mandatory overtime, which requires that nurses remain on duty if there is no registered nurse to relieve them. It becomes the staff nurse's responsibility to find another nurse to cover if she is unable to fulfill the duty. Nurse managers may want to investigate their legal responsibilities in relation to this policy, given the ambiguity of the situation. The legality of mandatory overtime will be tested if and when any cases are brought forward involving the policy.

Other cases of legal ambiguity involve assigning nurses without special expertise to areas requiring it. Suppose, for example, that a nurse from a general medical floor is assigned responsibility for a shift on a small pediatric intensive care unit. Clearly this is an unsafe practice, and if at all possible a more qualified nurse should be found. Yet circumstances like this have occurred in recent years, and there have already been some court cases. In general, when an institution has proved that it had no better alternative, the courts have ruled favorably—i.e., that *any* nurse is better than *no* nurse.

In general, the first-line manager and her organization must strive to do everything possible when faced with a crisis situation. If the manager and her institution have done their utmost, they should be safe under the law. Nevertheless, shortages of nurses or nurse specialists are increasingly becoming issues in court cases.

The nurse manager should also be aware that hospitals have been penalized by regulating agencies in some states for keeping care units open that were not properly staffed.

One of the nurse manager's most important administrative responsibilities is to see that patient records are accurate, adequate, and timely. The patient or client record, regardless of the health care setting, is meant to document accurately and completely the care administered to the individual within the organization. Each institution determines the format of its records. However, several elements are common to all: patient history, physical exam, diagnosis, treatment, and progress notes. Several national organizations dictate standards for documentation. For example, there are federal conditions for participation in the Medicare program. Home health care agencies are required to keep clinical records that include "identifying information, name of physician, drug, diet, treatment, activity orders, signed and dated clinical notes, progress notes, copies of reports sent to physicians, and a discharge summary."[10]

The written record of care can significantly influence the outcome of any liability claim. First, any omission of care in the charting allows the presumption that the care was not done. For instance, when medications are not charted, the assumption is that they were not administered—not that they were administered but not noted.

It is important for the manager to instill in nursing staff the habit of accurate and concise documentation. The use of ambiguous statements ("Patient ambulatory, appears comfortable. Having a good day.") is absurd and belies the nurse's ability to act as a professional. It would be more accurate to write "Patient ambulated with walker for 10 minutes in the morning and afternoon. Patient stated, 'I have less pain in my left knee today than anytime since surgery.' Patient has regained 60% of his full range of motion for his left knee."

Nurses' notes are expected to be accurate, timely, and legible. They should clearly and concisely describe the patient's condition and any nursing actions taken. The chart is a legal document, and nurses should be held to charting accordingly.

For the home health nurse, documentation is also the basis for reimbursement to the agency. In addition to the comprehensive notes required for legal purposes, the record should accurately reflect the tasks performed that are covered by insurance. It is important that the community health nurse, as the patient's fiscal intermediary, familiarize herself with eligibility requirements of Medicare, Medicaid, and private insurance plans such as Blue Cross and Blue Shield. As an illustration, describing a patient as "ambulatory" may limit his insurance eligibility, since some policies only service clients considered "homebound."[11,12] This does not mean that a nurse should falsify records for insurance purposes but that she must accurately record the reality. Suppose that in our illustration the nurse casually applied the term "ambulatory" to a patient she assisted from the bed to the nearby bathroom. Here the imprecise use of the term could disqualify a legitimately homebound patient.

Laws change, and new rules and regulations may affect practice. In 1987 the federal government enacted several measures to ensure quality in the area of home health care. For instance, agencies participating in Medicare are now required to provide clients with a Patient's Bill of Rights, and nurses will need to document that they complied with the law.

Similar regulations are in effect for hospitals as well. The nurse should be aware of the origin of policies and procedures. Recent legislation, the Omnibus Budget Reconciliation Act of 1986 (OBRA), has a direct impact on the first-line manager by requiring hospitals to have discharge planning programs and to provide a notice of discharge rights to patients upon admission.[13]

Legal Obligations to Patients

In addition to responsibilities for staff management and institutional administration, the first-line manager has responsibilities to and for patients.

Patients' Rights

The nurse has traditionally acted as patient advocate, helping individuals and their families to cope with the complexities of the health care system. Over time, the legal aspects of this role have expanded and become quite intricate. Nurses have a responsibility to themselves and to the public to learn more about the rights of patients receiving care. Sensitive areas include: rights of patients to informed consent, confidentiality, and privacy; rights of children to protection from neglect and abuse, parental consent, and visitation; right of terminally ill patients to self-determination; the legal status of living wills; and legal requirements for "do not resuscitate" orders. States vary in what their laws permit on these matters. For example, many are going through changes at present concerning the legality of the living will. Nurses need to stay informed regarding how these laws affect their practice.

Informed Consent

An especially important area of nursing responsibility is the obligation to inform patients fully about their care. One aspect of importance is the doctrine of informed consent. Nurses are often called upon to witness or to obtain a patient's signature on a "consent to treatment" form. At a minimum, the patient must have adequate information to make an informed decision regarding his care. The patient must understand: (1) the nature of the problem or condition to be treated; (2) the type of treatment proposed; (3) potential risks accompanying the treatment; (4) alternative therapies, if any exist; and (5) the expected outcome or prognosis for the patient. The nurse has a sensitive obligation in this area. She must not sign a consent form unless these procedures have been followed. A nurse is often approached by patients for further information, or through her relationship with the patient the nurse may evaluate that the patient is not fully informed. It is her legal responsibility to see that informed consent is achieved in such cases.

In summary, the nurse has a responsibility to protect patients in many ways. She protects them from personal injury, she assures the confidentiality of information, and she assures that they have given informed consent to treatment.

The nurse also has an independent duty to use her skills and knowledge to protect the patient against substandard care. The nurse's failure to act in a given situation may constitute liability for the nurse and hospital. Again, it is imperative that the nurse manager educate staff as to the increasingly complex legal implications of nursing practice. She must also help staff to explore how they can protect themselves from liability through correct and careful action.

ETHICAL CONSIDERATIONS FOR THE FIRST-LINE MANAGER

Ethical perplexities confronting health care professionals are proliferating as health care technologies expand and as health care services are more and more influenced by costs. There is an ever increasing number of ethical questions and few definitive answers. The first-line manager should be aware of ethical issues along several dimensions. First, she should try to understand why ethical problems are suddenly in the news after years of virtual quiescence. She should also know the types of moral problems facing the health care world today. Next she must become sensitive to the issues that may confront her and her staff in the everyday work situation. Finally, the first-line manager must be able to identify efforts that can be made in her organization to cope with the burden of health care decisions having major ethical implications.

Why the Explosion of Ethical Quandaries?

Ethical quandaries arise when changes in the environment confront people with new choices that involve judgments about what is right or wrong, about where one's duty lies. Ethical issues arise when decisions on such matters have not yet been codified into generally accepted laws and regulations. Today's health care environment abounds in ambiguous situations.

When new technologies increase the range of health care options, choices must be made about which technologies will be developed for a society and which will not. When a given technology seems to promise a self-evident "good," the issue seems easier than when the technology offers mixed results. Compare, for example, two advances: the artificial heart and improved neonatal therapies that save more and more premature infants.

At first glance the artificial heart appears to be an inherent good. The person needing such a heart can be saved by an implant and is likely to die without one. The issue at stake is life versus death. The quality of the life offered by the artificial heart may be somewhat limited, but it is usually seen as an improvement over the patient's quality of life before the implant.

The value of new neonatal technologies is more mixed. Often the techniques that save the lives of infants cannot protect them from deficits that they may carry throughout life. Mental and physical impairments may be extensive in some cases. Here the decision makers cannot deal with a simple "good" versus a "bad." There is no simple answer to the question of whether it is better to save a newborn with major physical and mental impairments than to let the infant die. There can be no "right" answer to such a question. People, all of whom consider themselves to be highly ethical, will reach very different conclusions if they reason from different principles.

For that matter, ethical issues raised by the artificial heart are not as simple as would first appear. The cost of such surgery at present is staggering. For the same amount of money that is invested in one artificial heart, the quality of numerous lives could be improved. Or the same resources could be applied to development and application of another technology that might save the life of another patient with a different condition. What appeared to be a simple "good" suddenly isn't so simple anymore.

Additionally, we soon see that the number of people who could be helped by artificial hearts far exceeds the number of hearts available. Suddenly we are faced not only with the issue of whether or not the technology should be developed, but with the added problem of rationing. If there is not an adequate supply of artificial hearts, who should receive the available ones? Rationing rears it ugly head. Once again, well intentioned, "ethical" people will disagree on the principles by which such rationing decisions should be made.

This brief example illustrates some of the reasons why ethical decision making is a weighty issue. Basic ethical dilemmas include: (1) rationing (Who should get scarce resources?), (2) choices among alternative goods when the costs preclude the development of all choices, and (3) choices when outcomes of therapy are mixed as to quality of life.

Quality of life is a relatively new consideration in health care. Medicine as a profession has a long history of regarding life, whatever its quality, as better than the loss of life. Others, including patients and often nurses, debate this point. Is mere prolongation of life in the case of a patient with a terminal disease, for example, a good? The issue of the quality of life lived under medical therapy is presently being reconsidered in our society. Quality of life has become an important factor to be weighed against the mere retention of vital signs.

Nurses are often more comfortable than are physicians with decisions to allow certain patients to die. These life and death decisions, however, are typically in the hands of physicians rather than nurses. Patients and their families are also starting to demand their rights in the decision-making process. What was once a "simple" matter settled in an authoritarian manner has become a complex negotiation in which many persons have a stake, not all of whom recognize the rights of the others involved. The ethical dilemma is further fogged when a legal issue is involved, i.e., when a court has the authority to be involved in making a life-death, treatment-no treatment decision.

Today's Ethical Issues in Health Care

Numerous technological, rationing, and cost factors can be identified as raising new ethical issues in health care today. For the most part, issues are dealt with at policy levels beyond the influence and control of the first-line manager. Of course, if she is a political activist, like other citizens, she may add her influence to the social decision process. Only a few illustrations of ethical problems will be offered here, since each week seems to bring a new series of health-related quandaries.

Let's begin with the issue of equity. Most reasonable people would agree that health care should be equitable, yet the issue of equity is difficult to resolve in individual cases. What about the self-paying patient in New Jersey who was charged an exorbitant price for minor care simply because his diagnosis fell into a costly DRG category? What about the Pennsylvania religious hospital that verges on bankruptcy because it has a philosophic commitment to take the poor whom other institutions reject to maintain their profit curve? What about the elderly New York wife who is made destitute because her husband's nursing home is legally entitled to reclaim its costs from his dwindling finances? One person's equity is another's deprivation.

What about the inequity of two sets of parents seeking a scarce resource such as a liver for a dying child? How much equity exists when one couple has access to public media and the other doesn't? What about the rights of a financially stressed surrogate mother versus the rights of the wealthy contracting father? What about the rights of their child? What about the rights of the voluntarily aborted fetus that is born alive in spite of the fact that it has not reached the age of legal viability? What about the terminal patient seeking to discontinue life support in the face of family opposition? What about a reduced population of young people carrying the tax burden for a disproportionate number of elderly in the general population? What about those who are denied health care access because they lack the ability to pay?

The cases and the issues are numerous, but in each case we may ask: Who decides? Who pays? Who has rights? Who has obligations? What is equitable? The problem with most of the decisions to be made in today's society is that the choices are not between the good and the bad but instead between opposing goods.

On-the-Job Issues

Ethical issues may arise in at least two ways for the first-line manager on the job. Issues may arise concerning the care of certain patients on her unit, and issues may arise in the management and assignment of her staff. It is also possible that professional and institutional values will conflict in the work setting. The first-line manager must be concerned not only with issues that present ethical quandaries for her, but also with those that present ethical problems for her staff.

Nurses, because of their position in the organizational structure of the health care setting, may experience a tension among their responsibilities to patient, physician, and organization. They may receive conflicting demands or requests, or they may simply face time pressures that inhibit their ability to do what they perceive to be needed.

It is critical that the organization facilitate resolution when nurses are caught between opposing moral dictates of this sort. In at least one study, nurses report having been caught between physician demands and what they believed to be right for the patient.[14] In such a situation the nurse may feel pressured to yield to the physician's decree because of his perceived power within the institution. Yarling notes that there is no logical reason for a nurse to consider herself morally inferior to a physician,[15] but nurses report that they are often intimidated in such circumstances.

Furthermore, some nurses fear that their organization and their manager may not support them if they take an ethical stand on a disputable issue. In some cases, unfortunately, the dominant norms of the organization hold that nurses are not expected to challenge medical or organizational decisions. In such circumstances nurses often feel powerless to exercise control, even over their own behavior.

Consequently, nurses may fail to act when circumstances do not present clear, patent wrong-doing. Sometimes nurses are unsure of their own beliefs and values, further complicating ethical decision making. Naturally they are indecisive when ethical questions arise. Sometimes nurses unthinkingly adopt a patient advocate role without a clear understanding of the ethical position the advocacy involves.

Nurses need a forum in which they can discuss and analyze moral dilemmas with others. They need practice in resolving such dilemmas. The first-line manager can see that opportunities for this sort of learning and values clarification are made available on an ongoing basis. She can be particularly helpful in seeing that proper assistance is at hand if a complex ethical issue arises on the unit.

Every nurse manager must be vigilant to see that no staff member is ever given an assignment that conflicts with the staff member's own ethical code and personal values. Some scrub nurses, as an illustration, must be excused from assisting at abortions, even though the procedures are legal.

Most institutions form an ethics committee to decide upon the best action to take in serious cases with ambiguous ethical ramifications. Such committees prevent arbitrary and premature decision making in complex cases. Even with a committee, however, there may be honest moral disagreement over the best way to handle a given problem. An institutional review board serves as another clearing house for ethical problems—those that may arise in medical, nursing, and other research using patients. Even though such committees may contain people who hold different beliefs, there is merit to the deliberations that finally lead to joint decision making. The quality of the decision is certainly enhanced by the deliberation process.

Whenever possible it is best to codify policies that relate to ethical issues before they are actually needed. Most institutions, for example, will have an official policy concerning how "do not resuscitate" orders are derived and implemented. Similarly, institutions that, because of religious or other beliefs, withhold certain medical procedures, will have policies that express what may and may not be done in the institution.

In regular nursing practice there are several issues with ethical implications that surface with regularity. They include: "do not resuscitate" orders; policies for suspected child, spouse, or parent abuse; policies for drug abuse; the patient's right to informed consent; and the right to refuse treatment. None of these issues can be entirely resolved by a policy statement. For example, reasonable people may disagree as to how much information is adequate for patient decision making and preservation of autonomy.

Some of the ethical problems arising for nurses relate not to decisions they must make but to options forgone because of limitations on staff and resources. As prospective payment systems and other fiscal pressures have mounted in the health care industry, hospitals and nursing homes have adopted more businesslike practices. Financial stringency may be necessary for an institution's survival, but it may frustrate the caring values of the nurse. Nurses have ethical problems when they see needy patients turned away from emergency rooms, when situational demands allow insufficient time for each patient, when the stress of a work environment is such that people become hardened to the human needs of others. The first-line manager has an ethical obligation to see that simple caring does not get lost along the way.

Financially dictated changes in patient care have caused concerns in many places. Consumer groups as well as health professionals have raised serious questions as to the ethics of hospitals prematurely discharging patients for economic reasons. In many cases, such patients return home with limited access to the essentials of care. Further, when such patients have no financial resources—suppose Medicare eligibility is lost—then another moral problem arises. Home health care nurses are placed in the position of either discontinuing visits or continuing to provide necessary care "off the books," i.e., not documenting their visits. The nurse's only other available tactic may entail adjusting data to fit the necessary criteria for reimbursement. No choice seems to fit the ideal notion of ethical professional behavior. Which choice represents the lesser evil? Which, the greater good?

The nursing profession, like most other professions, has a code of ethics. The *Code for Nurses*, adopted by the American Nurses' Association, provides guidelines for nurses concerning their obligations to patients, colleagues, and the larger society. It does not, except in the broadest of terms, address specific ethical dilemmas such as access to health for the uninsured and homeless, abortion, "do not resuscitate" orders, medical experimentation, distribution of scarce health resources, and allocation of expensive technology. Nor can it tell the nurse what to do in particular situations. The code is a useful guide, but ethical decisions must still be puzzled out in light of the unique situational variables of each case.

It is up to the first-line manager to see that the personal ethical values and beliefs of her patients, her staff members, and herself are not transgressed. She should have input into the procedures by which her institution supports ethical decision making on the part of all staff and clients.

SUMMARY

This chapter has given an overview of complex and controversial subjects: legal and ethical responsibilities of the first-line manager. Both subject areas include a wide spectrum of cases, problems, and changes. Both areas are also in constant flux, as scientific and political changes bring new social dilemmas into being.

Legal considerations were presented as general principles and guidelines. The manager is cautioned to remember that neither case precedents nor legal codes apply universally. The manager needs to know which regulations pertain to her own jurisdiction.

The nurse manager who knows her legal responsibilities can protect herself, her staff, and her organization from legal liabilities. This, in turn, protects the patients under her care. Prevention of an actionable situation is far easier and far preferable to the defense of a suit after an unwanted situation has occurred.

The situation of the impaired nurse was presented in some detail for three reasons. First, it is a difficult problem for all involved. Second, it touches upon areas of both legal and ethical concern. Finally, it is a situation that falls clearly within the manager's jurisdiction.

Ethical considerations have been presented rather sparsely here, merely to sensitize the manager to the sorts of situations she may encounter. Unlike legal precedents, ethical judgments do not have to do with absolutes. Perhaps the closest one can come to an absolute obligation is to say that the manager should make every effort to ensure that no one under her jurisdiction—patient or staff—is placed in a situation where he cannot follow his own ethical code for behavior. It is up to the manager to see that the system is designed to foster rather than thwart the employee and the patient who are trying to be true to internalized moral principles.

NOTES

1. Cynthia E. Northrop and Mary E. Kelly, *Legal Issues in Nursing* (St. Louis: C.V. Mosby Co., 1987), 40.

2. Sheryl Feutz, "Diminishing Liability: Laws and Regulations," *Journal of Nursing Administration* 16, no. 10 (October 1986): 13–14.

3. *Legal Issues,* p. 110.

4. Ibid.

5. Feutz.

6. E. Sullivan, L. Bissell, and E. Williams, *Chemical Dependency in Nursing* (Menlo Park, CA: Addison-Wesley Publishing Co., 1988), 16.

7. Ibid., 79.

8. M.S. White, "On the Scene: University of Cincinnati Hospital. The Disease of Chemical Dependency: Recovery to Restoration," *Nursing Administration Quarterly* 9, no. 2 (Winter 1985): 39.

9. Collette E. Robbins, "A Monitored Treatment Program for Impaired Health Care Professionals," *Journal of Nursing Administration* 17, no. 2 (February 1987): 18.

10. *Legal Issues,* p. 211.

11. Helen Creighton, "Legal Implications of Home Health Care," *Nursing Management* 18, no. 2 (February 1987): 16.

12. *Legal Issues,* p. 204.

13. Omnibus Budget Reconciliation Act of 1986, Section 9305(c), P.L. 99-509.

14. R.J. Zablow, *Preparing Students for the Moral Dimension of Professional Nursing Practice: A Protocol for Nurse Educators* (unpublished dissertation, Teachers College, Columbia University, 1984).

15. R.R. Yarling, "Ethical Analysis of a Nursing Problem: The Scope of Nursing Practice in Disclosing the Truth to Terminal Patients," *Supervisor Nurse* 9, no. 5 (May 1978): 49.

BIBLIOGRAPHY

Applegate, M.I., and Entrekin, N.M. *Teaching Ethics in Nursing: A Handbook for Use in the Case Study Approach.* New York: National League for Nursing, 1984.

Aroskar, M.A. "The Interface of Ethics and Politics in Nursing." *Nursing Outlook* 35, no. 6 (November/December 1987).

Backus, L.V., and Inlander, C.B. "Consumer Rights in Health Care." *Nursing Economics* 4, no. 6 (November-December 1986).

Binder, J. "Value Conflicts in Health Care Organizations." *Nursing Economics* 1 (September-October 1983).

Daniel, Irvene Query. "Impaired Professionals: Responsibilities and Roles." *Nursing Economics* 2, no. 3 (May-June 1984).

Feutz, Sheryl A. "Preventive Legal Maintenance." *Journal of Nursing Administration* 17, no. 1 (January 1987).

Fry, Sara T. "Moral Values and Ethical Decisions in a Constrained Economic Environment." *Nursing Economics* 4, no. 4 (July-August 1986).

Huckabay, L. "The Troubled Nurse: A Conceptual Framework for Resolving Problems." *Nursing Administration Quarterly* 9, no. 2 (Winter 1985).

Hull, Richard T. "Codes or No Codes." *The Kansas Nurse* 55, no. 10 (November 1983).

Luckenbill-Brett, J.L., and Stuhler-Schlag, M.K. "Mandatory Reporting: Legal and Ethical Issues." *Journal of Nursing Administration* 17, no. 2 (December 1987).

MacMillian-Scattergood, D. "Ethical Conflicts in a Prospective Payment Home Health Environment." *Nursing Economics* 4, no. 4 (July-August 1986).

Murphy, Ellen R. "Health Care: Right or Privilege?" *Nursing Economics* 4, no. 2 (March-April 1986).

O'Connor, P., and Robinson, R.S. "Managing Impaired Nurses." *Nursing Administration Quarterly* 9, no. 2 (Winter 1986).

O'Neil, Eileen A. "A Gavel Falls for Nursing: Sermchief V. Gonzalez." *Nursing Economics* 2, no. 2 (March-April 1984).

"On The Scene: The Troubled Nurse at the University of Cleveland Hospital." *Nursing Administration Quarterly* 9, no. 2 (Winter 1985).

Reinhardt, U.E. "Rating the Health Care Surplus: An American Tragedy." *Nursing Economics* 4, no. 3 (May-June 1986).

Wette, T. "The Ethical Dimensions of Aging." *Business and Health* 1, no. 1 (November 1983).

chapter 10

First-Line Supervision

THE CHALLENGE OF MANAGING PROFESSIONAL STAFF

Nursing takes place in a labor-intensive and knowledge-intensive field; hence the first-line manager's greatest resource for achieving effective and efficient patient care is her staff. Effective use of equipment, supplies, and systems will assuredly improve nursing care delivery, but these materials will never supplant the nursing staff in importance. Indeed, comparison of dollars spent on personnel versus dollars spent on equipment and supplies will convince anyone that nursing is a labor-intensive field.

Well defined standard operating procedures will aid the head nurse or her delegate, but they are not to be confused with the application of professional knowledge in each care action and decision. Patient needs are not so standard as to be amenable to an assembly-line type of management. The first-line manager functions in a situation that requires management of knowledge workers, people who base their work activities upon a compendium of knowledge, skills, and attitudes too extensive to be translated into a routine, standardized pattern of behavior.

Knowledge workers, it is well known, are a difficult group in some respects. They expect more than mere wages from their work; they expect to derive a sense of satisfaction and self-esteem from work well done. And they may be quite determined about holding to internalized goals and values that dictate how they will proceed in their work.

Getting the most out of knowledge workers requires special managerial skills. Those who are enthusiastic and perform exceptionally well in their jobs usually feel challenged by the work itself and take responsibility for their own jobs. Managing professionals requires more than overseeing; managers serve as guides and teachers, providing information and setting standards. Because of the professional's individualized perspective, management tactics aimed at

150

increasing nursing efficiency by assigning and moving people, equipment, and supplies sometimes produce inefficient results.

Staff management calls for a unique combination of interpersonal skills and managerial technology. This and the following chapters discuss how the nurse manager can best achieve high-quality performance from her staff.

THE NATURE OF SUPERVISION

One of the major functions of the first-line manager is supervision of staff members. Often supervision is perceived as checking to see that staff complete their assigned work. This is a narrow conception of supervision, representing only the lowest level of what supervisors do. Supervision includes all aspects of getting the most from people. People are the most important resource in any organization, and when they are treated as such they are likely to be motivated, creative, and committed to their jobs.

An important element of supervision is placing people where they can perform most effectively. This requires that the nurse manager assess staff members astutely as to their strengths and weaknesses, which are then weighed against the requirements of the job assignment. Employees do best when they know how to do the job, are motivated to do the job, are not frustrated in attempts to do the job, and receive recognition when the job is well done. From examining the needs of the worker we can derive the characteristics that define a good first-line nurse manager.

STAFF SKILLS VERSUS JOB DESIGN

The nurse manager must be especially sensitive to the skill levels and knowledge of each worker, but first she must know which knowledge, skills, and functions are required for each job under her supervision. For example, the primary nurse cannot begin to assess the capabilities of a licensed practical nurse until she knows what expectations are set for LPNs in her institution. This information should be available in a job description.

The Job Description

The formalized description of a job should contain the following elements: a title; required qualifications; all reporting relationships; a general description of the position with its key functions; a detailed list of tasks and responsibilities; and hazards of the job. The job description is critical to the healthy functioning of the organization. Besides structuring the work that needs to be done, it provides the basis of future performance evaluations. A job description should be given to each employee upon hiring and periodically reviewed. Staff members need to know what they are expected to do and at what skill level they are expected to perform. Failure to establish clear job expectations promotes unsatisfactory performance.[1]

Skills Assessment

After the head nurse learns the skills required for each position, she must assess each employee's suitability for a position. Unlike machines, human resources never fit specifications perfectly. Any given employee is likely to exceed some job requirements and to fall short of others. It is up to the nurse manager to identify areas of excellence, competence, and deficiency for every worker under her supervision. Clearly it takes many hours of observation to identify workers' abilities and deficiencies with any degree of accuracy.

This ideal may not always be feasible. For example, a nurse in charge of a work group for only a few days will not have time to learn about each group member. When she does not have personal knowledge of each individual, the nurse manager must rely upon the generic job descriptions in determining assignments.

Abilities may be identified in part by discussing an assignment with a given employee, but the manager cannot rely entirely upon staff members' reports of their own abilities. Some staff members will be fearful of admitting ignorance or inability; others may claim ignorance merely to avoid unpleasant work.

It is important that the first-line manager differentiate between performance and ability. It is often tempting to assume, simplistically, that poor performance indicates a lack of knowledge or skill. If this *is* the case, it is the manager who must see that the employee acquires the needed skill. The first-line nurse manager must recognize, however, that not all problems of performance are problems of education. There are other factors accounting for poor employee performance. Any one of the following might account for defective performance in an employee who has the requisite knowledge and skills:

- The employee deliberately performs the task poorly for personal reasons (such as distaste for the process or disbelief in its therapeutic effects).
- The systems by which the unit is organized make it difficult to do the task as directed. (For example, the employee may not have experience with a primary nurse care model.)

- The employee's total assignment may be too heavy, and the employee has insufficient time to do all tasks appropriately.
- The task is considered to be of little importance to the head nurse. (One task may be neglected to free time for tasks that are more heavily rewarded.)
- Assignment to the task represents a loss of status to the employee, who fears a loss of esteem if required to perform it.
- Poor performance may represent a rebellion against the manager.

The head nurse must ensure that tasks are clearly assigned. For jobs to have meaning, individuals need to take responsibility for their work. If work is assigned to a group, it is likely that no one member of the group will necessarily feel responsible for completion of the task. The simple practice of giving each employee clearly defined assignments will avoid many problems.

In community health settings and in hospitals where primary nursing is practiced, the nurse may have considerable autonomy in her practice. This requires that the nurse have adequate knowledge and decision-making skills to take appropriate action when called for. This relatively independent form of practice adds another element of responsibility to the manager when evaluating staff for these positions. It is highly doubtful that a newly licensed nurse would have the necessary ability to function autonomously in such circumstances. Indeed, the first-line manager must be especially familiar with the skills of *all* of her staff engaged in such highly independent practices.

ORIENTATION OF NEW STAFF

The period of orientation to any new work environment is recognized as a critical time of adjustment for a new employee. The method of introducing new personnel into an organization strongly influences not only their initial impressions but their future commitment to the organization. New employees, regardless of their past experience, need to get thoroughly acquainted with the organization they've just joined. They need to learn its rules and procedures, how things operate, and the prevailing organizational culture. If there is a particular emphasis on customer satisfaction, or on marketing of nursing services, this should be addressed during orientation. Innumerable questions will arise: What is the nursing care model used? Is the nursing department's philosophy guided by a particular nursing theory? What is the staff nurse's scope of practice? Is she allowed or expected to start IVs? Do doctors and nurses share the same dining room? Are white uniforms and caps the expected attire?

Starting a new job is anxiety-provoking for most people. A well planned orientation program should ease the adjustment and provide a smooth transition to the work environment. Although the staff development department is normally responsible for orientation, it should be conducted in collaboration with the nurse manager.

The formal orientation may vary in length from organization to organization. A standard orientation is four weeks in length, with the first two weeks spent in formal classes designed to introduce the orientee to the organization, its policies and procedures, and its standards of care. Classes may cover cardiopulmonary resuscitation, fire and safety guidelines, infection control, and quality assurance.

For the remaining weeks of orientation the nurse is usually in the clinical area to which she has been assigned, preferably under the guidance of the head nurse. The orientation phase is an opportunity to teach the new employee how things are done on the unit or in the agency. The nurse manager should pay attention to introducing the new nurse to her colleagues and to developing a welcoming atmosphere. Clinical experiences during the orientation should be structured to provide reinforcement of classroom education and to maximize the nurse's ability to deliver effective nursing care.

The role and responsibility of the nurse manager during orientation should be clearly defined. Often responsibilities are negotiated between the education department and nursing management. A written evaluation of the orientee should be done at the end of the orientation period. This provides management with baseline data and allows the nurse manager to arrange appropriate work assignments and further learning experiences, if necessary.

There is no way to retain all nurses. However, inadequate socialization into the system, inadequate training, and lack of professional and peer support are often cited as reasons for premature termination. The nurse manager can successfully combat staff turnover by supporting a comprehensive orientation program, which can even serve as a marketing tool for the organization in its recruitment of nurses. Nurses are more apt to choose an organization that has an extensive orientation program. The nurse manager should be integrally involved in the planning and implementation of the orientation program to ensure that the newly hired nurse experiences a smooth assimilation into the unit.

Newly Licensed Nurses

The newly licensed nurse may require additional assistance beyond the routine orientation phase. Kramer has documented the experience of new graduates starting practice and has termed it "reality shock" to express the difference between their expectations of nursing practice and what they encounter on the job.[2] A newly licensed nurse, overwhelmed by the demands placed on her, may be unable to seek help comfortably. Peers may not recognize her difficulty as they go about their own work. If the situation continues unchecked, both the newly licensed nurse and the patients she cares for may be at risk. It is especially important during those first weeks and months to monitor the new graduate's level of coping. The nurse manager should identify not only the learning needs of the new graduate but also her degree of adjustment to the general stresses of nursing practice. With the help of the inservice instructor, the manager can develop strategies for assisting the new nurse with her adaptation.

At times when the work load is exceptionally heavy, staff may resent the novice because they cannot fully rely on her. She may not yet be ready to carry a full patient assignment; she may still need special help from them. Nurse managers need to guard against contributing to any feelings of inequity that may arise in these circumstances. One strategy is to schedule more staff for the shifts when the new nurse is on duty, with the understanding that everyone will help out with the new member's adjustment. This gives staff the benefit of reduced patient assignments and fosters cooperation among staff members to achieve the best overall outcome. The nurse manager has a responsibility to create a supportive environment for all, to be available to her staff (especially the new employee), and to help resolve any problems that may arise during this sensitive period.

Preceptor Programs

Many hospital nursing departments have developed clinical preceptor programs to provide an individualized, unstressful, supportive transition for the new graduate. Usually the program is based on the premise that a one-to-one relationship between the new graduate and the unit preceptor provides the orientee with a role model and a primary resource person on the unit. In addition, it provides better continuity and consistency throughout the orientation, enhances socialization of the new employee, allows earlier identification and resolution of problems, and increases the orientee's competence as a professional nurse.

The preceptor program is a team effort in which the clinical instructor, head nurse, and preceptor all cooperate. Choosing the preceptor wisely is the key to the success of this program. The preceptor program requires staff nurses who demonstrate clinical expertise, effective interpersonal skills, knowledge of the teaching-learning process, interest in professional growth, a positive attitude, and willingness to give time to the preceptor role. It is recommended that the preceptor have a minimum of two years of clinical experience; ideally she should have extensive experience. Workshops may be planned to prepare preceptors for their new responsibility. Principles of adult learning, effective communication, leadership skills, and evaluation are typically included.[3]

Under a preceptor program the new graduate will typically attend classroom instruction given by the orientation instructors as well as work with the preceptor. Upon assignment to a unit she will be paired with the preceptor for a period of four to eight weeks. The orientee will follow the same schedule and shift rotation as her preceptor and, depending on staffing, may share the same patient assignments. During these weeks the preceptor should receive guidance from the clinical instructor and head nurse. Learning experiences for the new graduate will be planned according to the skills and attitude she demonstrates. To achieve the objectives of such a program the roles of all those participating must be clearly defined.

All staff should be included, to whatever degree possible, in the planning and implementation of a preceptor program. They should be aware of its ultimate benefit for the unit and the organization. Preceptor programs have been shown to be highly cost-effective by reducing the rate of new-employee turnover. Reports indicate that it can take anywhere from thirty to ninety days to fill a vacant nursing position. The costs to the organization when nurses terminate within the first year are exceptionally high. The cost of recruitment, marketing, orientation, and overtime must all be considered; estimates range from $6,000 to $20,000, depending on the setting.[4] When nurses leave prematurely, it is often the remaining staff who are left to cope with providing coverage until a new nurse can be hired. Preceptor programs produce another benefit as well: they enhance the image and esteem of the staff nurse who acts as preceptor. Although this is an additional responsibility for the individual nurse, the chosen staff member will recognize the selection as a tribute to her clinical expertise and professionalism. In some cases, preceptors receive additional reimbursement for this activity.[5]

First-line managers will be wise to give preceptor programs their full support, for such programs have been credited with enhanced job satisfaction, increased staff productivity, improved retention, and improved quality of care rendered by the new graduate. Moreover, they provide a successful marketing device for the hospital.

Mentoring

Mentoring is an informal process by which a nurse's professional development may be guided or influenced by another professional who has more experience in the field. Education and business have long recognized the benefits of mentoring for the individual and for the organization. In academia it has long been a way to develop a talented student and guide her career. Mentoring in business contributes to the development of managers and facilitates the process of managerial succession and promotion; it also assures continuity of corporate culture by inculcating the skills and knowledge of veteran employees. Peters and Austin, in *A Passion for Excellence*, describe the process of mentoring in what they call "coaching":

> Coaching goes far beyond the short-term need to help someone with mechanics. . . . [Coaches] perform five distinctly different roles: They educate, sponsor, coach, counsel, and confront . . . always toward the same goal: to facilitate learning and elicit creative contributions from all hands to the organization's overarching purpose.[6]

Although this strategy focuses more on the organizational goals than on the individual's goals, it should be helpful in achieving both. Most importantly, it stresses the contact that should take place between the mentor and the younger learner. Often the first-line manager becomes a mentor for some of her staff. Mentoring cannot be done from a distance; the first-line manager cannot absent herself from the scene day after day and expect to develop mentoring relationships with her staff. Relationships need to be nourished and built over time. In some settings the nurse manager finds herself more involved with upper-level management than with her staff. This may be inherent in the structure of the job and its functions, or it can be the fault of the nurse manager herself. If she is uncomfortable in her mentoring role, she may welcome reasons to "escape" the unit.

To be a mentor to another person requires experience and the maturity to give of oneself by investing in another's career development. The nurse manager who chooses to guide others has an opportunity to develop skills and values in her staff that will serve them throughout their careers. She can identify learning opportunities, provide access to people and information, encourage involvement in special projects, give useful feedback regarding performance, enhance confidence and commitment, and help staff to understand and overcome their unique problems. She can also share her own learning experiences, which will probably be her most effective lessons.

Supervising the Part-Time Nurse

An important aspect of management for many first-line managers is the supervision of part-time nurses. Always a mainstay of hospital staffing, part-time nurses are being utilized in other health care delivery settings as well.

These nurses may be employed directly by the organization as permanent or irregularly scheduled part-time nurses, or they may be supplied through an outside supplemental staffing agency. The distinctions between these categories of part-time nurses are relevant to the supervision that they require.

Ideally, the part-time nurse should be familiar with the organization, with its policies and procedures. In most cases this will be true only for the permanent part-timer. Many home health care agencies, nursing homes, and hospitals require their permanent part-time staff to participate in a full orientation program. When this is possible, the part-time nurse will be more likely to assume a full membership role in the organization. Nurses who identify themselves as being "on staff" are likely to be more loyal and to feel more responsibility for their jobs.

Irregularly scheduled part-time nurses, while employed by the hospital or agency, are less likely to develop the same commitment. A nurse's familiarity with the facility, its practices, and its staff depends on how frequently she works. Nurses employed under this arrangement work only on a request basis and have the right to refuse work when called. Their scheduling may be sporadic, and many employers do not feel inclined to invest resources in the orientation and development of these workers.

The nurse from a supplemental staffing agency has no affiliation with the hospital or home health agency. She is an employee of the staffing agency and is directly paid by that agency. While she may work a forty-hour week, it may not be spent at any one institution.

In settings where part-time nurses are used, the first-line manager should consider institutional policies and her management practices as they relate to these employees. In the hospital setting part-time nurses are often given a quick tour of the unit, receive patient reports, and are left on their own. Their assignment, as seen in typical practice, varies from the most difficult and demanding patients to patients requiring routine care. Part-time nurses should be able to handle a full work load, but this work load is best planned once the nurse's skill level and abilities are known. It is important to recognize that in most cases the part-time nurse is at a distinct disadvantage, since she is likely to be unfamiliar with the setting, the patients, and the staff. Some special consideration needs to be given to orienting her and integrating her into the unit's routine. Regular staff often consider these activities to be too time-consuming and burdensome to bother with, especially for a temporary nurse who is "here today and gone tomorrow." When this attitude prevails, it is evidence of poor management and a waste of resources. Failure to orient and assist the part-time worker affects everyone's productivity negatively. Part-time as well as full-time nurses need to know exactly what their roles are and what results they are expected to produce.[7]

It is the responsibility of the nurse manager to maintain an environment that is conducive to communication and cooperation, and to ensure that quality patient care is delivered. It is a demanding job, but productivity is highest when nursing skills are as well matched to patient needs as available resources permit. It would be important to know, for instance, how frequently a part-time nurse works and where (i.e., setting, specialty, shift), what her credentials are, and—if she is a permanent part-time nurse—when she was last evaluated. One managerial strategy to increase productivity and improve continuity of care is to work out a staffing arrangement that puts the same part-time nurse on the same unit whenever possible. This gives management more control over the nurse's practice. Moreover, the more thoroughly part-time staff can be included in the life of the unit, the higher their level of performance.

The use of agency nurses is reported to increase when nurses are in short supply. The average percentage of vacant RN positions in hospitals doubled between September 1985 and December 1986.[8] In light of such statistics it is more important than ever that part-time nurses be viewed as capable contributing professionals who are willing to do their share. They should be given the fullest possible orientation to their new place of work.

MOTIVATION

Motivation is an internal force; it cannot be created by exhortation or coaxing. Sometimes motivation develops in the employee because of an emotional response to a charismatic leader. However, it is futile to expect each manager to be charismatic. How, then, does the typical first-line manager motivate employees? Even if she can do very little to *create* motivation, she can certainly try to increase this subjective trait by appealing to the employee's pride or sense of professionalism.

In its lowest form motivation is simply a desire to draw the paycheck. If a salary is the only motivation, it is the motivation the manager must use. For the employee motivated only by wages the first-line manager must function as a controller, making clear that good performance is requisite for keeping the job, and hence the wages. The threat of suspension or reclassification to a lower-paying position is the ultimate lever for influencing the performance of such an employee.

Fortunately the supervisor seldom encounters an employee who is motivated solely by salary. Most people have, or can develop, some sense of pride in their work. Since pride and improved performance usually go together, the wise nurse manager will try to develop the employee's sense of pride. Many effective leaders arouse pride in workers by making them feel that they are part of a very special and effective work group. This feeling motivates each individual to meet the high standards of the group.

Others try to encourage the development of pride by speaking about the significance of the nursing profession. Professional and vocational nurses alike are indoctrinated with this sense of professionalism during their education, and most have a strong sense of identity with the nursing profession. The supervisor can reinforce this sentiment among such employees, and she may try to indoctrinate other workers with the same notions. Such a tactic is unlikely to be successful with the nonprofessional worker, however. Nonprofessional workers are more likely to take pride in their specific work group on the unit than in membership in some conceptualized group that transcends the job.

Whether the nurse manager stresses the special qualities of the work group or the special nature of the nursing profession, she should be able to stimulate a worker's sense of pride, which in turn stimulates better performance.

Facilitation of Work

The successful manager does not see her job simply as the delegation of assignments and observation of staff work, but also as a facilitation of the work process. She continually monitors the work environment to identify barriers to accomplishment. Barriers include personnel conflicts or conflicts of style between staff members, inadequate support systems, and inappropriate organizational practices. It is the first-line manager's job to create an environment in which people can work up to their capacities. It is also her responsibility to point out to workers when they are creating barriers for themselves by their own behaviors and work patterns. Thus the nurse manager must look for barriers within the worker, the work group, and the organization, with its various support systems.

One of the most important environmental support systems is the communication system. It is important that the supervisor critically analyze both the formal and informal communication modes available to each worker. It is just as important that appropriate communication lines exist for nonprofessional as for professional staff. Indeed, since the education of nonprofessionals tends to be limited, they have greater need for supportive lines of communication.

The formal communication system includes written daily assignments, charts, care plans and other Kardex forms, written supervisory shift reports, and staff work schedules. The informal communication system includes verbal reports and informal exchanges between workers, shift reports, and patient care conferences. The formal and informal components should be viewed together as comprising a complete communications system. The total system should allow for easy communication of all information necessary for effective patient care.

The first-line manager must make sure that communication flows in all requisite directions; every employee needs both information-reporting and information-receiving channels. These channels should extend upward, horizontally, and downward in the chain of command.

What skills does the supervisor need for her own communication with staff members? The supervisor must develop interpersonal communication skills and skills associated with group dynamics and group management. The head nurse is likely to use at least two modes of relating to individuals. At times she is acting as an administrator, making decisions and issuing directives; at other times she acts in a consultative, problem-solving manner. The manager must convey to the staff person which role she is adopting at any given time; otherwise poor communication will result.

Another mode of communication used by the head nurse is role modeling. No means of teaching is quite as effective as exemplary performance. Role modeling is a pleasant way to educate staff members; it requires no commands, and it reminds staff that the nurse manager is capable of dealing with the concrete problems of patient care.

The head nurse is the staff person's means of communication with middle management. She is the channel through which unusual needs are met and unusual problems are solved. As a link between the worker and middle management, the first-line manager connects the worker to the larger goals and designs of the health care institution.

Burnout and Job Stress

Burnout is often seen as a recent phenomenon, but it may be that only the terminology is new. As it is generally used, the term "burnout" is imprecise and ambiguous. It is up to the first-line nurse manager to assess objectively the staff member who seems to be suffering from the effects of burnout or job stress.

Signs of burnout may range from physical symptoms, such as headaches, stomach upset, sleeplessness, and fatigue, to declining interest in the job, boredom, and careless job performance. Because job stress is often cited as a major cause of staff turnover, nurse managers should be alert to negative behaviors.

It is important that the first-line manager not assume that burnout is an insoluble problem; she should instead approach the problem with an open mind and the expectation that a solution can be found. The solution to this problem often depends on the source of the difficulty.

A study conducted by Lobb and Reid identifies the following job stressors that precipitate burnout: "heavy workload, insufficient resources, unpredictable scheduling and staffing, frequent crisis situations, and inability to satisfy conflicting demands."[9] Although these are situational factors that cannot always be avoided or planned for, the nurse manager has a responsibility to her staff and to those under their care to prepare for such contingencies. The head nurse, working together with staff, should share what is being planned and when relief is likely. Simply acknowledging that a problem exists and is being investigated may be enough to alleviate the pressure temporarily.

The first-line nurse manager may also find several different nonjob-related causes of stress, ranging from interpersonal difficulties to substance abuse or other psychological problems.

It is difficult to predict how each individual may react to stress, or what may trigger it. Huckabay suggests that individuals try to ascertain their own stress level by examining stress-producing situations.[10] Awareness of what contributes to stress can be the first step in developing better coping behaviors. Selecting particular goals—such as viewing change as a challenge and renewing one's commitment to nursing and to patients—focuses on positive attitudes that may counteract burnout.

Early recognition of burnout, followed by appropriate intervention, may prevent a valuable nurse from leaving her job or the profession. And, since first-line managers are as susceptible to job stress as are those they supervise, they should examine their own reactions to stress and stressful situations.

Recognition and Evaluation

Recognition of a worker's achievement is one of the simplest means of increasing motivation while simultaneously asserting supervision. Public praise for having done a good job is most meaningful to an employee, for it lets peers know that he or she has succeeded. Public censure, on the other hand, may make the employee resistant to change or impair the employee's ability to work with the group. On some rare occasions, an employee may be subjected to public censure as an example to the rest of the staff; but when the manager does this, she must realize that it could be a devastating experience for the sacrificial employee.

How does the first-line manager obtain the information needed to evaluate an employee's work? Evaluation is a major supervisory function, and it consumes a large portion of each supervisor's time. Evaluation requires that the supervisor observe her employee in all sorts of work situations, so she must devise some means of assessing employee performance that requires a minimal investment of her time while obtaining optimal information.

One observational shortcut rests on the principle of key functions. The nurse manager identifies each employee's key functions and limits observation to this sample of the employee's tasks. A less formal approach to sampling would have the manager observe employees whenever she enters and leaves patient's rooms for other purposes. If the first-line manager always keeps the concept of evaluation in mind, she will be able to observe worker performance even while she is primarily involved in other activities. Observations, whether of good or bad performance, are of little value if they are not recorded, however. It is easy to convince oneself that the incidents will be remembered. At evaluation time, however, that fallacy will become all too clear. Quick but precise notes should be made after each observation period.

After the appropriate observations have been made, the manager must evaluate the worker's performance. For this purpose, the number of sample behaviors is important. It would be unfair to assume that a behavior observed only once or twice typifies the work of a given employee. Some behaviors, however, are so undesirable or so exemplary that they deserve special attention even if they are not repeated. For example, a nursing assistant who talks a suicidal patient out of a threatened jump has performed a critical service, even though it is not likely to be repeated. Similarly, if a nurse is observed (only once) to break all the rules of sterile techniques while applying a dressing, this is a critical incident as well. Incidents are termed "critical" when they are of such magnitude as to reflect upon the future behavior that might be expected of the employee. If a nurse is willing to ignore sterile technique in even one case, for example, the supervisor cannot afford to trust her to apply it in all others.

In order to assess the significance of a worker's behavior, there must be some standard by which to measure it. Often the standard is the manager's own image of "what a nurse should be able to do" or "how an aide should act in these circumstances." A well written job description will provide a more objective standard. For professional nurse performance the supervisor may be guided by the various sets of standards produced by the ANA and its subdivisions. These standards are articulated in terms of the nursing process and are thus applicable to the actions of individual nurses.

Individual nursing units or nursing departments may devise standards that address nurse behavior in addition to standards or objectives set for desired patient outcomes. An effective nursing department will use both types of standards.

Once the nurse manager has assessed the worker's actions, she must advise her about any needed change in performance. Unless the worker is made aware of areas of deficient performance, she is not likely to work toward improvement. When this simple means of informing is not effective, the manager must determine what further steps are to be taken—special education or firmer discipline, for example.

Some managers reserve feedback for formal evaluation periods. Since these periods tend to be infrequent, it is unwise to withhold criticism until the scheduled time for evaluation. Employees who are making mistakes should be told so immediately, so that they can begin correcting them at once. The nurse manager should never assume that employees know they are making errors. It is her responsibility both to make clear the standards of performance and to call attention to any deviation from those standards. The first-line manager who refrains from corrective action due to distaste for confrontation or simply embarrassment is not fulfilling her responsibilities as a leader and a manager.

The manager sets the limits of acceptable behavior; she decides what will and will not be tolerated. It is her responsibility to communicate these limits to her staff and to see that the limits are not infringed with impunity. Once again, staff members should be informed of the limits; they should not have to guess at them.

Some nurse managers find that their own ideals of participative management and their images of professional nursing conflict with their supervisory responsibilities. While some nurses view autonomy as the ideal model for employee behavior, not all employees are comfortable with autonomy. Some employees, even some very good workers, need clear and firm directions set by others. Whether or not she so desires, the nurse manager may have to function as an authority figure for certain workers. Problems arise when the supervisor is not willing to modify her own managerial style to meet work group needs. A team leader, for example, may try to force "democratic rule" on a group that is unprepared for it; when one is not ready to make decisions, "democracy" may be perceived as a burden rather than as a benefit. It is true that other managers err in the opposite direction, maintaining rigid control of a group that is ready for and desirous of greater autonomy. The more common error, however, is a lack, rather than a surfeit, of managerial direction.

SUMMARY

What is the role of the nurse manager in the successful use of human resources? Clearly supervision is not one rule but many, and it requires not one consistent approach but a number of approaches, depending on the needs of the staff and the organizational setting. Supervision involves many diverse activities: communicating, directing, evaluating, coordinating, teaching, planning, and disciplining, to name only a few. Supervision is a primary responsibility of the first-line manager, for her most important resource is her own staff.

NOTES

1. V.D. Lachman, "Increasing Productivity Through Performance Evaluation," *Journal of Nursing Administration* 14, no. 12 (December, 1984): 7–13.

2. M. Kramer, *Reality Shock: Why Nurses Leave Nursing* (St. Louis: C.V. Mosby Co., 1974).

3. M.L. Murphy and S.M. Hammerstad, "Preparing a Staff Nurse for Precepting," *Nurse Educator* 6, no. 5 (September-October 1981): 17–20.

4. F.G. Sabatino, "What's a Nurse Worth?" *Hospitals* 61, no. 19 (October 5, 1987): 10.

5. V.A. Mooney, B. Diver, and A.A. Schnackel, "Developing a Cost-Effective Clinical Preceptorship Program," *Journal of Nursing Administration* 18, no. 1 (January 1988): 31–36.

6. Thomas J. Peters and Nancy Austin, *A Passion for Excellence* (New York: Random House, 1985), 338.

7. Douglas S. Wakefield and Sally Mathis, "Formulating a Managerial Strategy for Part-time Nurses," *Journal of Nursing Administration* 15, no. 1 (January 1985): 35.

8. American Hospital Association, *The State of the Nation's Access to Hospital Services*, second annual report (January 1988) p. 8.

9. M. Lobb and M. Reid, "Cost-effectiveness at What Price? An Investigation of Staff Stress and Burnout," *Nursing Administration Quarterly* 12, no. 1 (Fall 1987): 59.

10. L. Huckabay, "Stress and Leadership: A Coping Mechanism," *Nursing Administration Quarterly* 8, no. 3 (Spring 1984): 17–19.

BIBLIOGRAPHY

Clark, C.C. "Burnout Assessment and Intervention." *Journal of Nursing Administration* 10, no. 9 (1980): 39.

Darling, LuAnn W. "The Mentoring Dimension—The Case for Mentor Moderation." *Journal of Nursing Administration* 15, nos. 7, 8 (July/August 1985).

Douglas, L.M. *Review of Leadership in Nursing.* 2d ed. St. Louis: C.V. Mosby Co., 1977.

Drucker, P.F. *Management: Tasks, Responsibilities, Practices.* New York: Harper & Row, 1973.

Fleishman, R. "Human Resource Motivation." *Supervisor Nurse* 9, no. 11 (September 1978): 57.

Hersey, P.; Blanchard, K.H.; and LaMonica, E.L. "A Situational Approach to Supervision: Leadership Theory and the Supervising Nurse." *Supervisor Nurse* 7, no. 5 (May 1976): 17.

Hertzberg, F. "One More Time: How Do You Motivate Employees?" *Harvard Business Review* 65, no. 5 (September/October 1987): 109.

Hicks, B.C.; Blackmon, S.S.; and Westphal, M. "A Need-Oriented Approach to Staff Development." *JONA* 7, no. 7 (July 1977): 46.

Hinshaw, A.S.; Smeltzer, C.H.; and Atwood, J.R. "Innovative Retention Strategies for Nursing Staff." *Journal of Nursing Administration* 17, no. 6 (June 1987): 8–16.

Hoffman, F.M. "Cost Per RN Hired." *Journal of Nursing Administration* 15, no. 2 (February 1985): 27–29.

Kistler, J.F., and Kistler, R.C. "Motivation and Morale in the Hospital." *Supervisor Nurse* 11, no. 2 (February 1980): 26.

Marquis, B. "Attrition: The Effectiveness of Retention Activities," *Journal of Nursing Administration* 18, no. 3 (March 1988): 25–29.

Moloney, Margaret M. *Leadership in Nursing Theory, Strategies, Action.* St. Louis: C.V. Mosby Co., 1979.

Mooney, V.A.; Diver, B.; and Schnackel, A.A. "Developing a Cost-Effective Clinical Preceptorship Program." *Journal of Nursing Administration* 18, no. 1 (January 1988): 31–36.

Murphy, M.L., and Hammerstad, S.M. "Preparing a Staff Nurse for Precepting." *Nurse Educator* 6, no. 5 (September-October 1981): 17–20.

Oermann, M. "Diagnostic Supervision." *Supervisor Nurse* 8, no. 11 (November 1977): 9.

Patrick, Pamela K.S. "Organizational Burnout Programs." *Journal of Nursing Administration* 14, no. 6 (June 1984): 16–21.

Robbins, S.P. *The Administrative Process: Integrating Theory and Process.* Englewood Cliffs, NJ: Prentice-Hall, Inc., 1976.

Schaefer, M.J. "Managing Complexity." *JONA* 5, no. 9 (September 1975): 13.

Singleton, E.K., and Nail, F.C. "Role Clarification: A Prerequisite to Autonomy." *Journal of Nursing Administration* 14, no. 10 (October 1984): 17–22.

Timmreck, T.C., and Randall, P.J. "Motivation Management and the Supervisory Nurse." *Supervisor Nurse* 12, no. 3 (March 1981): 28.

Ullrich, R.A. "Herzberg Revisited: Factors in Job Dissatisfaction." *JONA* 8, no. 10 (October 1978): 19.

Wadsworth, N.S.; Clark, N.L., and Hollefreund, B. "Managing Organizational Stress in Nursing." *JONA* 16, no. 12 (December 1986): 21–27.

Wakefield, Douglas S., and Mathis, Sally. "Formulating a Managerial Strategy for Part-time Nurses." *Journal of Nursing Administration* 15, no. 1 (January 1985): 35–39.

Warren, J.G. "Motivating and Rewarding the Staff Nurse." *JONA* 8, no. 10 (October 1978): 4.

Zey, Michael G. "A Mentor for All Reasons." *Personnel Journal* (January 1988): 46–51.

chapter 11

Managing People

This chapter looks at some of the managerial processes involved in managing subordinate staff. The processes of delegation and direction are discussed first as they apply in one-to-one relations between the first-line manager and an employee. The last half of the chapter looks at the use of groups for management; issues of committee structure are discussed, as well as basic techniques for making a group work effectively. Committees are important vehicles for delegation and direction within an institution.

Management is often defined as getting the job done through others. This is achieved by working with both individuals and groups. Delegating and directing are two of the essential functions of the first-line manager in her relationships with individuals and groups.

DELEGATION

Delegation consists of several elements: what gets delegated, to whom, how it gets delegated, and how it is monitored or controlled. Effective delegation must be followed by control—that is, making sure the delegation is accepted and complied with satisfactorily.

What Gets Delegated

There are several ways to differentiate delegated elements. One useful distinction is between the permanent and the temporary delegation. Items permanently delegated occur in job descriptions or statements of the functions of various departments or units. Temporary delegations occur in interim assignments; for example, one is assigned as team leader for a shift or one serves on an ad hoc committee planning a career ladder. Permanent and temporary delegations take place at all levels of the organization.

Permanent delegations reflected in job descriptions are of two types: delegation of tasks and delegation of responsibilities. Delegating a task entails specifying exactly what is to be done; it tends to be procedural. In contrast, delegation of a responsibility entails what is to be achieved, not how it is to be accomplished. To illustrate, the taking of vital signs would be a task, while the devising of a management system for the nursing department would be a responsibility. Clearly there are many possible ways to set up a management system, while variations in the taking of vital signs are limited.

As one moves from job descriptions of lower-level positions to those of higher-level positions in an organization, the number of tasks decreases and the number of responsibilities increases. At the executive level, managers may be expected to determine their own responsibilities to a great extent. Few directors of nursing, for example, have a job description given to them at hiring, though many write such a document for themselves.

In delegating tasks or responsibilities it is important for the manager to determine which delegation is right for a given case. Errors occur in both directions. If, for example, a director of nursing consistently assigns tasks rather than responsibilities to her supervisory personnel, she may limit the challenge of a managerial position. She may be faced with resignations from the most capable of her supervisors, those who expect to determine their own work methods. Some insecure managers assign tasks rather than responsibilities as a way of controlling subordinates.

Conversely, the assignment of a responsibility to an employee who is not prepared for that delegation is equally problematic. Sometimes a manager assigns a responsibility to an employee who should be able to accept the level of assignment but shows hesitancy to do so. Such an employee is either not prepared for the level of work or is trying to "pass the buck" with regard to the decision-making elements of the job. In some situations of poor management the employee may have found out from sad experience that such delegations are fraudulent. For example, a supervisor might assign a head nurse to prepare the personnel schedule but then consistently revise it. The head nurse rightly perceives that the responsibility is not truly hers. In such a situation the head nurse may rebel against doing the schedule at all. When an employee refuses a delegated responsibility, the supervisor must accurately evaluate the reason; it might reflect negatively on the delegator rather than on the delegatee.

At the responsibility level, two types of delegation may take place: delegation of decision or delegation of action. Decisions take place on all levels in a nursing division. Even a nurse's aide may have to decide, for example, whether or not to report suspected disorientation in a patient. Most decisions ultimately involve overt action. Effective delegation specifies whether the delegation includes decision, decision and action, or only action (implementing another's decision). Failure to specify the nature of the delegation can lead to disruption of interpersonal relations as well as to impairment of the work to be accomplished.

In addition, the manager must be aware of differences between action and decision as they relate to employee performance. Some employees want to be evaluated only on their actions. This desire is unacceptable for an employee in a job that has inherent decision-making responsibility. Such an employee may complain, "You never assigned a task that I refused to do." Such a disclaimer, although quite possibly accurate, does not explain the employee's failure to generate work goals and activities through decision making. The "clipboard supervisor" who makes rounds but functions only as a supply clerk exemplifies this pattern.

Other employees will want to be judged solely on the basis of their decisions and plans rather than their implementation. The employee who turns out to be "all talk" lacks the follow-through that may be required by the job. Sometimes a nursing manager may misjudge such an employee if her chief source of information is written reports and verbal self-accounts. She may be misled into overestimating the effectiveness of an employee. When an employee is not esteemed as highly by her peers as by the manager, the manager should check out her own estimate of the employee's actual performance in the action domain.

The Content of the Delegation

It is crucial that the content of the task or responsibility be directed to the right person, at the right level of the organization. Errors are common in relation to this factor. For example, for a director of nursing to serve on a committee considering dietary tray service would be an error, for the director normally does not know the details of tray distribution on the units. A head or staff nurse would have more to contribute to such a committee. In setting up committee work many people want to include a higher-level manager than they actually need, assuming that "clout" will be important. If judgment is not used in such cases, the committees will be less than effective, and managers will spend their time in the wrong meetings. If the first-line manager finds superiors attending meetings that could better be served by her level of manager, she should tell them.

Much of the content to be delegated by a first-line manager is often identified in the job descriptions of staff members who report to her. Job descriptions are no substitute for judgment, however, and there will be times when a task normally done by an aide will need to be delegated to a professional nurse. Patients' needs often defy delegation on a simple task analysis basis; a "complex" patient may require that a simple task be done by a higher-level staff member than would normally do it.

Delegation of decision making tends to follow a natural pattern in which strategic decisions, relating the institution to its external environment, take place only at top management levels. Administrative decisions are delegated to top management and, to some degree, to middle management. These decisions involve long- and intermediate-term conclusions concerning internal structures and the use of institutional resources. Operational decisions concerning day-to-day problems and functions are usually delegated to first-line managers with authority for the smaller organizational units. Thus, certain decision-making content is naturally delegated to certain organizational levels.

The nature of the problems to be solved is different for different levels of management. Repetitive problems are delegated to a lower level than are novel, unique problems. Well structured problems, similarly, are solved at lower levels than are those problems that are ill structured—i.e., those that require deciding what the problem really is as the first step toward solving it.

Modes of Delegation

There are two considerations in looking at modes of delegation. The structure of the organization dictates some delegation patterns. Additionally, the *process* of delegating itself needs attention. The act of delegation is the hardest task of management for some new head nurses, team leaders, or other first-line managers.

Structures for Delegation

Hierarchical job descriptions serve as a delegating device. The organizational chart, with its well assigned functions, also simplifies delegation. The organizational chart and job descriptions are the chief tools for delegation of permanent functions.

Similar structures exist for temporary delegations. The daily assignment system typifies this type of delegation. Committee assignments may be either permanent or temporary, depending on the nature of the committee. Work schedules represent another temporary delegation, although cyclical patterns for assigned hours represent an attempt to convert a temporary delegation into a permanent one. If it is at all possible, there is some merit to changing a temporary system of delegation into a permanent one. People tend to accept permanent structures with less debate than is engendered by temporary, changing delegations.

The Process of Delegation

Permanent delegations represented in the job description should be discussed with the employee at the time of hiring. There should be agreement on job expectations before an employee is accepted on the payroll. The performance appraisal represents a mode of reviewing and controlling the acceptance of delegated tasks. To ensure effective delegation, informal evaluations should be performed, since formal reviews occur too seldom.

Sometimes the new manager has problems with making specific delegations to employees, even when those delegations clearly fall within the job descriptions of the employees. In this case, the mode in which the "order" is conveyed is important. A delegation should not be presented as if it were an option when it is in fact intended to be an order. "It would be nice if you cleaned the utility room" is not technically an order, and if an employee wishes to take it merely as an observation, the manager who expressed the thought in this form can hardly object. Additionally, when dealing with employees from other cultures the American nurse must realize that not all societies recognize an order that is conveyed as a "hint."

Sometimes insecure first-line managers seek the consent of the employee when delegating. Take, for example, the new team leader who, near the end of her shift, receives a stat order for an enema. She asks the first nurse on her team, "Do you have time to do this enema?" One need not ponder long to figure out the answer that the team leader is likely to receive. She then hurries to a second, a third, and a fourth nurse with the same question. Each answers predictably. Finally the enema is done by the harried team leader herself, even though she has even less time for it than any of her staff.

In essence, the new nurse manager must learn to give orders (delegations) without guilt. She must learn to delegate with confidence; she must not convey choice when that is not meant. She must communicate clearly what is assigned as well as such constraints on the assignment as time limits or specific techniques. She must recognize that her employees are receiving salaries for services rendered, and she must not hesitate to delegate those services as necessary.

The manager should be aware of the dangers in asking for a volunteer for a task. Who will do the task if no one volunteers? It is very awkward for the manager to have to appoint someone to a task after a long pause in which no one has volunteered for it. One must learn not to ask such questions as "Who will keep running notes of our discussion?" For recurrent temporary assignments—taking minutes, counting narcotics—it may be possible to plan a fair distribution system that eliminates the need to assign people repeatedly or ask for volunteers. When this is not possible, the manager must learn to be comfortable with statements such as "Caroline, please take the minutes for the meeting."

Sometimes the manager has difficulty, not with delegation, but with employees who are clever in avoiding acceptance of delegated work. Suppose an employee continually seeks out the manager for assistance with a task rather than simply doing it herself. What does the manager do? For example, a module leader has great difficulty with making team assignments. Does the head nurse fall into the trap of doing the job for her or routinely revising poor plans? The head nurse must recognize instead that assigning tasks and responsibilities is an inherent part of the module leader role, and that if she continues to do this part of the job for the deficient module leader she helps no one. First, it consumes her own time—time that should be spent on higher-level tasks. Second, she allows the module leader to retain a position without being accountable for its performance. This deceives the module leader as to the nature of her role.

How should the head nurse handle this situation? First, she must make clear to the module leader that the assignment is that person's job, not the job of the head nurse. Second, she must be clear that any help she offers with the assignment is meant to be a teaching/learning experience and not a permanent arrangement. She might say, "Ms. Jones, assignment is part of your job as a module leader, but I will do it this time since you seem to have problems with it. I want to discuss my plan with you as I make it, so that you can grasp the principles of assigning. After I do this plan and we discuss it, I will expect you to do tomorrow's plan. Once you have tomorrow's plan outlined, we can discuss it if you are still not sure about it."

In other words, a manager should not routinely substitute for an incompetent manager or staff person who reports to her. She may do some tasks at first in the interest of role modeling, but not as a regular practice. If an employee is unable to learn with this guidance, then demotion rather than substitution is required. A new module leader must be appointed if the present one cannot learn to function adequately in the role.

Special Problems of Delegation

Decentralization is an institutional system of delegation; it involves placement of responsibility as far "down the line" as possible. To illustrate, staff development and education may be centralized in a staff development department that serves the total nursing divison, or those functions may be delegated to the unit level. In the decentralized plan an instructor is placed on each unit, or regular personnel on the unit are made responsible for the unit's necessary teaching functions. In this instance one can see both the advantages and the disadvantages of decentralization. An advantage of decentralizing the educational function is that the education offered will be specifically tied to the needs of the personnel on the given unit. When the teaching is specific to unit needs, application of learning will be enhanced. The disadvantage of decentralized education is that staff development (a secondary aim compared to the primary aim of patient care) may be lost amidst the hectic demands of the unit. Since the same person, the head nurse, will ultimately be responsible for both of these primary and secondary aims, she may find herself always sacrificing one for the other.

Additional factors may work against this particular attempt at decentralization. First, it is more costly to supply an instructor for every nursing unit than to pay for a centralized education department. Cost may thus make this mode prohibitive. Moreover, if teaching assignments are distributed to regular staff, it is necessary to assess their teaching abilities, which are different from direct care abilities. They will also need decreased regular care assignments in order to make time for the new teaching assignment. Often this is where decentralization fails. New tasks or responsibilities are assigned without creating additional time for their achievement; or new tasks or responsibilities are assigned without first determining whether the assigned employee has the specialized skills required. When this happens, the newly decentralized function is often ignored. One could call this decentralization to the level of incompetence.

Decentralization, then, is a good principle when applied with judgment. A function should not be delegated to a level at which personnel are incompetent to perform the function or simply do not have time for the function. It is logical, however, to decentralize to the level of knowledge. The manager or staff member who knows the most about a phenomenon will usually be the person best prepared to make judgments or to take action concerning it. Additionally, it is sometimes more economical to send functions "down the line" than to use a more highly paid employee. As is the case with many management principles, decentralization is as good or bad as the thinking behind the decision that is made.

One further note concerning decentralization: It diffuses the power base in relation to the function that is decentralized. Hence it is not a good idea to decentralize a responsibility if it requires a strong power base for its enactment. To decentralize a nursing division totally—that is, to turn the director into a consultant and to place total responsibility in the hands of the supervisor(s) of a department—decreases the total power (and united voice) of the nursing division. Such a move would deserve a careful assessment before it were made.

Another specialized form of delegation is the 24-hour role sometimes given to head nurses and/or supervisors. The same 24-hour delegation may be seen in the primary nurse role. In both cases one must ask exactly what is delegated.

Clearly, none of these employees is expected to be present for 24 hours a day, so direct care (or supervision) is not what is actually delegated. In both cases the delegation is of planning rather than acting. Once this is recognized, it is easier to work out interfacing roles. The 24-hour supervisor, for example, should not have functions that conflict with the exercise of shift-by-shift decision making by the night supervisor. Nor should it be assumed that the planning on one shift or in one 8-hour period is a substitute for appropriate administrative action during another 8-hour period. One must clearly differentiate powers that are delegated from those that are not delegated in any 24-hour role.

DIRECTION

Direction of personnel is a function of management that is often overlooked in nursing. When errors in care occur, for example, one often assumes that the cause is an educational deficit. One must understand, however, that education cures only ignorance; it does not cure indifference to an assignment, misunderstanding of what is required, rebellion against authority, or the myriad other causes of malperformance that are not attributable to a failure to know how to do what was assigned. Direction, therefore, cannot be confused with teaching. Direction simply means conveying to subordinates what is to be done, in a way that results in the desired performance.

New managers often tend to assume that all staff share their vision of what nursing should be, what patients deserve, and what standards are to be maintained. This is usually a mistake. If the first-line manager has some vision of standards, methods, and goals, the simplest way to effect the achievement of it is to convey it verbally to staff. Communicate! Tell staff what you want; do not assume that they will intuit your goals. The first rule of directing is to communicate clearly with subordinates concerning what is expected of them. Individual assignments—rather than general orders given to a group—encourage accountability. Direction is enhanced by follow-up of some kind that enables the manager to make sure that her directions were followed. She lets staff know, with praise or correction as indicated, that she has evaluated their performance of assignments. She does not settle for failure to perform, but she is careful to inquire as to why the performance was inadequate. She uses education, disciplinary systems, and individual help as required, but she does not settle for less than she expected.

Direction, clearly, is part of delegation. Often it is the difficult part. The manager must learn not to apologize, verbally or by her actions, for being in a position to give orders; that is what she is paid for. Failure to direct staff is an abdication of the managerial role.

THE USE OF GROUPS FOR MANAGEMENT

Much of the work in a nursing service is done through groups. The productivity of a nursing unit, department, or division is greatly enhanced if groups are used efficiently. The nurse manager needs to know how to select and structure groups for work projects, and she needs to be able to run the meetings of groups effectively. Every nurse manager should carefully scrutinize the use of committees and other groups in her organization, both those she creates and those in which she participates as a member. Good group structures can be as valuable as well thought-out organizational plans. In addition, the committees and other groups that are created reflect the functional definition of nursing that guides the nursing organization.

The term "committee" is used here as a general term to describe a relatively stable group that meets periodically for an identified purpose or purposes, has the official sanction of the nursing organization, and has some established mechanism for maintaining and selecting members as well as for recommending or implementing its decisions.

In determining the types of committees she needs, the nurse manager first examines the objectives and functions of her department or unit. Committees are only one means of accomplishing these predetermined goals and activities. Thus she must decide which objectives and functions can best be achieved through committees and which should be handled by other means.

The committee structure is preferable for two kinds of situations: (1) those that require multiple input for goal attainment, and (2) those in which diverse representation facilitates acceptance and implementation of proposed activities. In the first instance, there are many reasons why multiple input may be required. Some problems require the combination of specialized types of knowledge to be solved. Other problems require different perspectives on how proposed solutions will affect the environment in which they will be implemented. Still other problems simply require extensive brainstorming and focused interaction in order to reach the most satisfactory solution. Diverse representation on a committee may also help with project implementation, lending legitimacy to proposals and encouraging acceptance of solutions by virtue of the committee's "democratic" make-up.

The nurse manager must also be aware of the limitations of committees. Many projects are better assigned to a single individual or a two-person team than to a "bulkier" committee. Projects that require complex research and planning are better planned by a single individual who can become familiar with and sensitive to each aspect of the project.

Furthermore, no committee should be used to supplant the authority and responsibility of line managers. Committees are not designed to handle most day-to-day decisions. Indeed, the dilution of individual responsibility within committees makes them easy places to avoid decision making. Committees are better suited to handling the larger issues, such as major policy changes or long-term plans. Whenever, because of the committee structure, a manager cannot take direct action with an employee in a situation that is impeding the work flow, the committee is assigned to the wrong sphere of activity.

In designing committee structures the nurse manager determines which goals and functions can best be handled by committees, decides which committees will exist, and examines the relationship of the committees to each other. It is impossible to evaluate any one committee of a department or division meaningfully without considering its relation to other committees. The following questions may be used as guidelines in evaluating committee structure and function:

- Are there adequate committee structures to enable the organizational unit to reach its goals? Are there any obvious omissions?
- Does each committee fill a vital need that is not within the scope of any other group or committee? i.e., Does each committee have a clear reason for existing?
- Are the purposes of the nursing committees consistent with the avowed philosophy of nursing?
- Is the total number of committees logical for the size of the organizational unit and the thrust of its objectives?

Committee Powers

The first consideration in examining the effectiveness of a committee is the degree of power delegated to the group. It is important that the group be given enough authority to fulfill its objectives. It is not logical, for example, to expect a committee to evaluate nursing care unless it is given the power to institute selected evaluation procedures on the nursing unit. A committee should not have to rely on persuasion if its directive is to produce action. Even intracommittee factors may be important. Does the committee have the power to delegate assignments to its members, for example?

Giving the committee enough authority to do its assigned job is an issue of power. Another power issue is the committee's ability to implement its decisions. The nurse manager may give a committee power to recommend or power to decide. She may give a committee one standing level of power, or she may give it power options relevant to specific issues and assignments. When the nurse manager chooses to adjust the power level for different assignments, it is important that the committee members clearly understand their powers in each case.

The next power question is, What does it mean to say that a committee has "decided?" There are three major forms of decision making: managerial decision, majority rule, and consensus. The last two, of course, apply to committee work. The manager may decide to accept consensus decisions, or she may be guided by a majority vote. She may agree simply to review the recommendations of those committees she has constituted, reserving decision-making authority for herself. She may wish to adjust the locus of authority according to the problem situation. Once more, it is important that committee members be given a clear directive as to their powers.

Committee Membership

The committee should be viewed primarily as a means of getting work done, not as a means of meeting status needs, as a popularity contest, or as an exercise in the democratic process. There is no logic in appointing a member to a committee if one can predict that the person will not contribute to the committee's objectives. One should "play the best odds" by appointing persons most likely to do a good job. This rationale is largely responsible for the fact that design groups are often more creative and productive than are committees based on organizational position. (A design group is one put together specifically for a given project; its membership is determined by expertise in relation to the subject matter of the project.)

Managers must also be cautious about overuse of the same reliable people on numerous committees. When such participants become a select group, to the exclusion of others, an obstructive "we-they" syndrome may occur.

In selecting members for a particular committee, the manager must consider "who needs to know" in the implementation phase. One often sees a group of higher-level employees planning a change for a lower-level group without any representation from the latter. Representatives should usually be included from the group that is to implement the proposed change. There will be times, however, when confidentiality at a selected management level is needed, particularly in the early planning stages of major organizational changes. In those instances the manager must use discretion in determining appropriate committee membership.

A committee should consist of the smallest number of persons who can meet the committee's objectives. To appoint more is to misuse human resources. Committee membership can be controlled on large projects by designating a small stable nucleus of members and giving them the option to call in others as needed at various stages of the project. When individuals are asked to join a committee with this type of interim membership, the duration of and reason for their participation should be made clear to them.

Committee Feedback Mechanisms

An important facet of committee effectiveness is its structure for feedback to and from nonmembers and administration. If, for example, the committee project is a long-term one and is expected to bring about a change in nursing practice, it may be wise to publish periodic status reports to the nursing groups that will ultimately be affected by the change. These reports will serve to create interest in the project as well as to prevent the resentment that often arises when a plan suddenly materializes full-blown and ready to be implemented.

Periodic status reports are also useful to the nurse manager because they let her know the direction, rate of progress, and general productivity of the committee. She can then calculate any needed redirection, support, or alteration in its membership. The requirement of periodic status reports (as opposed to mere minutes) also pressures committee members to attend to original goals and to evaluate progress toward those goals.

In addition to creating channels of communication from committees, it is important to create channels to committees, whereby organization members who feel that they have something to offer can submit ideas and suggestions. Creating input channels helps to build overall acceptance of committee recommendations and decisions.

Committee Productivity

The nurse manager is responsible for seeing that optimal use is made of staff time. Nowhere is there more danger of unproductive use of time than in committee work. When, for example, ten staff nurses sit around a table for two hours and accomplish nothing, the cost in salaries for those two hours will be hundreds of dollars. The manager cannot allow chronically nonproductive committees to continue to exist simply because the participants enjoy meeting. When a committee is unproductive (comparing member hours to committee output), the cause must be found.

Often a committee is unproductive because it does not really need to exist, as when its objectives are either not attainable or not relevant at the particular time. When the objectives of a committee are judged to be valid but the committee is still unproductive, it may be trying to do the job with the wrong people. A committee leader without appropriate skills may be the problem. A second possibility is an incompatible membership (that is, incompatible with regard to the objectives of the committee, not necessarily incompatible with one another).

Since design groups are single-purpose entities, it is easier for the nurse manager to calculate timing factors for them. She can decide at the start how much time she is willing to invest in a particular task. Design group members can be given this time frame and asked to work within the set limits.

Release time for committee participants is another important timing consideration. Two factors enter into decisions in this area: (1) how much involvement the committee work will require, and (2) how each person's normal job tasks are scheduled. Projects have been known to fail due to resentment on the part of those carrying excessively heavy workloads so that task force or committee members could be away from the work center. Moreover, if committee participation is just another duty added to an already busy schedule, the quality of participation may suffer.

Committee Functions

The nurse manager may find it useful to examine the output of each committee through a taxonomy of committee functions such as those listed in Table 11-1. Such a taxonomy can be useful in committee evaluation. For example, suppose the nurse manager finds a committee in which most activities are socializing functions among members. She may need to question the value of such a committee to her organization, since it neither advances project work nor extends services to those outside of the committee membership.

Important Groups and Committees

It is important that the nurse manager understand the different bases of group formation so that she can select those options most useful to her own

Table 11-1 A Taxonomy of Committee Functions

Functions in Relation to Projects	Functions in Relation to Committee Members	Functions in Relation to Others
Problem solving	Communicating	Communicating
Researching	Expressing	Educating
Standard setting	Compromising	Recommending
Designing	Harmonizing	Clarifying
Implementing	Consensus taking	Summarizing
Monitoring	Reasoning	Encouraging
Evaluating	Socializing	

situation. Even when she is a member of these groups rather than the origi-
nator of the committee structure, her advice will still be important when
committee structure is considered at higher levels. The following four kinds of
groups will be considered:

1. standing committees
2. design groups (task forces)
3. groups based on organizational position and job function
4. interdivisional committees that combine nursing with nonnursing divisions, departments, groups, or individuals

Standing Committees

Standing committees are permanently assigned to make decisions or handle
problems related to a specific area of concern. These committees are of long
duration, often having members who rotate off and on at periodic intervals.
The concerns addressed by standing committees are those that will need
continual monitoring over the lifetime of the organization. Most standing
committees in nursing are located at the divisional rather than the departmental or unit level, but different organizations build committees on different
levels. For example, in one organization each unit may have its own quality
assurance committee, while in another such a committee might exist only at the
departmental level. The organization's conception of nursing is revealed in its
operational standing committees, for these committees are the focal points of
action in providing nursing services. Table 11-2 compares the standing committees of two hypothetical nursing services to illustrate how standing committees reflect the dominant concept of nursing. Analysis is limited to the three
primary standing committees for each organization.

A comparison of the committee structures of the two hypothetical organizations shows some clear differences in their conception of nursing. Organization A divides operations into products (things), procedures (actions), and
patients (people). This is certainly a valid approach to nursing and nursing
management. It tends to be comprehensive in scope. In this approach, each
sector is treated as a separate entity. In each case, the committee has a specific
output that clearly "belongs" to its particular sector (for example, a new
product, a new procedure, a new care plan). There is little if any confusion
about committee tasks; the job of each group is clearly delineated. This is
probably one of the greatest strengths of a division into things, actions, and
people. Under this committee structure a change instituted by one committee
can produce the necessity for a change in the operations of another committee;
a new product, for example, might require a new procedure. But each committee can still determine its own particular function in relation to any given

Table 11-2 Comparison of Committee Structures

Organization A	Organization B

1. Procedure committee:
  • evaluates ongoing nursing practices
  • reviews and updates the procedure manual
  • composes new procedures as needed to accommodate new equipment, new supplies, or advances in nursing
	1. Patient care evaluation committee:
	  • establishes criteria for evaluation of patient care
	  • conducts quality control checks of patient care
	  • conducts periodic nursing chart audits
	  • provides for feedback to the nursing units and to nursing administration

2. New products committee:
  • assumes responsibility for keeping up to date on advances in equipment and supplies
  • arranges for demonstration of interesting new products
  • evaluates utility and cost of each new product and recommends acceptance or rejection
  • implements purchase of selected new products and introduces the products to appropriate staff members
	2. Patient care improvement committee:
	  • uses feedback from patient care evaluation committee, accident reports, and other available data as a basis for instituting changes in patient care
	  • identifies recurrent problems in patient care and seeks means of solving these problems
	    —identifies the care problem
	    —decides the appropriate avenues for solution
	    —institutes change
	  • serves as an advisory group to the nursing staff education section

3. Patient care committee:
  • evaluates ongoing patient care
  • recommends changes in nursing care practices
  • evalutes and promotes patient safety
    —reviews accident/error reports
    —promotes safe working practices
    —promotes a biologically and physically safe environment
  • recommends needed educational programs
  • develops new tools for use in patient care
    —patient data forms
    —nursing care processing forms
	3. Nursing systems improvement committee:
	  • identifies problems in nursing delivery systems (examples: means of giving patient reports, means of assigning staff, means of distributing drugs)
	  • proposes solutions to delivery problems by modifying old systems or creating new ones
	  • plans and coordinates changes in nursing systems within the institution

change. This committee structure views nursing as being composed of a series of separable parts.

Organization B in Table 11-2 example has a different concept of nursing. Here the nurses view nursing as a process rather than as a structure with discrete parts. Committees seem to flow from each other; the work of the care evaluation committee naturally leads to the work of the care improvement committee. Similarly, improvement in patient care will call for changes in nursing systems. All three of these committees may involve things, actions, and people. All three focus on process rather than on discrete entities. Some of the items that were ends for Organization A (products and procedures) become means for Organization B.

For Organization A, two out of three primary committees (new products and procedures) focus primarily on tasks: nursing as a series of activities to be completed. For Organization B, on the other hand, two out of three primary committees focus on the patient. This concept of nursing reflects a patient needs-oriented approach. Organization B starts with patient needs, while Organization A starts with nursing tasks.

This difference can be illustrated by comparing the approach to a new product that each organization might take. For Organization A a product is considered simply because it exists and has come to someone's attention; that is enough reason to evaluate it. Organization B does not approach products this way. When a particular patient need is identified in Organization B, there is provision for a product search (if a product is required to meet the need). In one system, the movement is from the product to the patient; in the other, it is reversed, moving from the patient to the product.

No single mode of structuring standing committees is right or wrong. There can be as many possible ways to organize a standing committee as there are different leaders to think of them. The real question is whether the selected committee structure accurately mirrors the organizational definition of nursing. If an executive tries to indoctrinate her staff in a nusing philosophy, theory, or conceptualization that is not reinforced by the committee structure, she will have difficulty in doing so. For example, an administrator who desires to implement a patient need-oriented philosophy of nursing will have difficulty explaining this philosophy within a task-oriented committee system. Internal consistency among nursing concepts, divisional goals, and committee structure will simplify the work of the entire nursing organization.

Design Groups

A design group (or task force) is an ad hoc committee created to handle a specific problem or task and then dissolved once its task is completed. Major ad hoc committees that handle complex assignments are often termed design groups or task forces. Membership on such a committee is typically earned by virtue of expertise related to the committee's assignment rather than on the basis of organizational position. Design groups tackle many different kinds of problems: administrative, procedural, interdepartmental, or patient-oriented. Indeed, they may be used to address any problem that calls for a select, informed group.

The composition of the design group is dictated by the problem itself. Those persons who have the most knowledge and experience to bring to bear on the subject are appointed to the committee. For example, a staff nurse with broad experience in primary nursing care might chair a committee investigating the primary care system, and head nurses and supervisors might be among the committee members. The goal of the design group is to utilize the organization's best talents for a particular problem. Thus, no two task forces are likely to have the same composition. Some design groups also draw upon resource people outside the nursing division.

Many committees on the unit level will be of the ad hoc variety. Members of the nursing unit are more likely to participate on permanent, ongoing committees at the divisional or institutional level.

Groups Based on Organizational Position and Job Function

Groups based on organizational position and function exist in most nursing divisions. A head-nurse group or a steering committee of nurse managers is an example. In determining whether such groups should be formally designated, the nurse executive needs to evaluate the desirability of providing a vehicle for group cohesion and power. For example, a nursing service director might want her head nurses to meet regularly in order to promote problem solving and acceptance of responsibility by the group. On the other hand, she might not want a committee of nursing assistants if she suspects that it would provide a nucleus for unionization. Even if the power of a group is limited, its existence as a formal body can serve to launch demands and actions.

It is the prerogative of the first-line manager to decide which groups will exist on her unit and how much authority will be granted to them. A group becomes formally recognized when on-duty time is granted for its meetings and its proceedings are recorded.

Most nurse executives find it useful to create an administrative council to facilitate communication and participative management. There are a few factors, however, that should be considered in selecting the membership for such a council:

- A group larger than 10 or 12 in number seldom works as a single unit. Larger groups tend to break into factions.
- A group can comfortably combine persons with different functions if the members share similar objectives.
- The advantages of representation from nonmanagement groups must be weighed against the efficacy of administrative privilege if the council is to be a group that makes administrative decisions and recommendations.

Such administrative councils may or may not include first-line managers, depending on the institution's philosophy and organizational structure.

As with other committees, it is important that groups based on organizational position exist only if they serve a useful purpose. For example, the fact that an organization "has always had a head nurse committee" is not a good enough reason for maintaining the committee. The goals of such groups, however, may be different from the goals of other committees—i.e., broad-based rather than limited to a finite number of projects.

The functions of groups based on organizational position differ from the functions of regular committees. These position-based groups typically monitor and respond to the changing work environment. They tend to be responsive to immediate administrative problems of diverse kinds and to grease the wheels of day-to-day operations. The content with which they deal varies greatly over time.

One function of groups whose members hold comparable jobs is the support, education, and role training of their members. Thus the output of such groups may be measured in the improved performance of individual members as well as in relation to specific group projects.

Evaluation of such a group must take into account the assistance that it offers to individual members. The functions of information sharing, mutual support, and member education are seldom evident in the minutes of such groups. Often such peer groupings provide first-line managers with networking opportunities. It is especially useful for the new manager to learn how others have handled problems similar to those she faces. In urban areas it is often the case that first-line managers with similar specialties but from different organizations may decide to meet regularly to share problems, solutions, and mutual support.

Interdivisional Committees

Another kind of committee is one that crosses divisional lines. Usually interdivisional committees result when (1) coordination of goals and activities is necessary, such as between service and education or among members of a health team working toward a common goal, and (2) recurrent problems arise because of conflicting goals or systems, such as those that may occur between nursing and the dietary or laundry department. Situational problems between two divisions can best be ironed out in interdivisional committees with members who have first-hand experience with the problems that occur when the divisions interact. For example, a head nurse can offer a much more accurate evaluation of a proposed plan for altering tray service than can a nurse executive.

One common problem in interdivisional committees is failure of leadership. Often, in attempting to give equal consideration to each group, a dual leadership is created with one member from each division serving as a cochair. As in other situations, a committee that is the responsibility of more than one person is really the responsibility of no one. It is better to alternate the chair than to divide up the leadership. When working on interdivisional committees, everyone should understand the structure and power of the committee. Seldom will nursing want to bind itself without qualification to the decisions of such committees. Giving such groups the power to recommend is usually a safer policy.

COMMITTEE LEADERSHIP SKILLS

Basic Rules

There are a few basic rules that will help the manager to run committee meetings. Some of the rules concern preparation for the meeting; others direct the leader's activity during the meeting. The following preparation rules are simple and self-explanatory.

In the preparation of the physical environment, the comfort of the participants should be ensured by

- adequate ventilation, light, and heating
- comfortable seating
- good visual arrangements
- adequate space for the writing or reference materials of each participant.

Makeshift meeting places on a busy unit are seldom conducive to effective work (e.g., holding a committee meeting where the nurses can simultaneously watch for patient's lights). One cannot really attend to two things effectively at the same time.

The convenience of the participants can be ensured by

- supplying paper, pencils, and name cards, if indicated
- minimizing interruptions by informing the switchboard of who is in the meeting and who will take messages, and by marking all entry doors to signify what meeting is in progress
- preparing and checking out all necessary audiovisual aids

- supplying agendas and documents to be discussed (do not assume that everyone will remember to bring original copies).

The preparation of the participants should be ensured by

- distributing detailed agendas long enough in advance for necessary preparation or research
- distributing in advance any documents to be approved or analyzed
- indicating any materials that the participants should bring to the meeting.

The leader of a committee should prepare by

- drafting an agenda that clearly indicates the purpose and content of the meeting
- reviewing the status of all agenda topics to date
- gathering all necessary background information and supportive data on agenda topics
- determining who needs to be invited as resource persons for agenda topics
- producing handouts or audiovisual presentation that will facilitate committee understanding of topics
- developing a strategy or strategies for handling the meeting.

Leadership activities during a meeting must also be considered. The leader has two functions to fulfill during a meeting: (1) structuring the business to be done, and (2) directing and controlling members' interaction. Although these will be separated for discussion, it is not always so easy to tell where one function leaves off and the other begins in an actual meeting.

Structuring the Business To Be Done

Structuring the business to be done will be considered as it applies to a single-purpose meeting. The same principles would apply for each segment of a multipurpose meeting. In structuring the business the leader should plan to start each topic with an orientation phase. This should include a summary of past actions and decisions on the topic (if the topic is not new) and a clear statement of what is to be accomplished with regard to that topic in the current meeting. Once the objectives are stated, the leader usually turns the action over to the committee members. The leader should prepare a lead-in question or suggestion for this purpose.

The primary duty of the leader during the meeting is to keep the committee to its task. This requires that the leader remind the group of its objectives when the conversation strays. Another tactic is the periodic use of short summaries of committee progress during the meeting. The leader must be careful not to rush groups into premature decisions in an overzealous pursuance of the meeting's objectives.

At the meeting's termination it is the responsibility of the leader to summarize what has occurred during committee interaction. The leader identifies the decisions reached and reviews the responsibilities accepted.

The structuring of the business to be done varies with the type of communication desired from the meeting. Some meetings aim at information transmittal. In this category, the simplest form is that the leader merely wishes to inform the group of something. This is basically a one-way communication, with information flow from the leader of the group. There may be some slight communication flow from the group to the leader concerning parts of the leader's message that were unclear or incomplete, but essentially the meeting remains in the control of the leader.

In contrast with this type of "tell" meeting, the "sell" meeting is one in which the leader is anxious not only to inform but to convince the group of the worth of a particular idea. When persuasion is the intent, the meeting should be allowed to develop into a three-way interaction. This means that after (1) explaining the idea to the group, the leader (2) invites them to pose questions and give their reactions. In addition, the leader (3) allows time for the members to interact with each other concerning the proposal.

A third type of information transmittal meeting is one in which the leader wants information from group members concerning a particular topic. In this case, there is a simple one-way flow of information from each member to the leader.

Meetings not intended for information transmittal are usually focused on decision reaching. Several different types of decision-reaching meeting can be identified. Brainstorming is the simplest form, because the communication flow is one-way, from each member to the leader. In the brainstorming session, evaluation of ideas is suspended; the purpose is to collect as wide a variety of tentative solutions as possible in a short time. Since no judgment is placed on the suggestions of the members at the time, there is no need for two-way communication.

The advice-seeking meeting is the next type. During this sort of meeting the leader wants to cumulate the opinions and judgments of committee members on an issue. Under strict control the advice-seeking meeting may be restricted to a one-way flow from each committee member to the leader. More often such opinions and judgments create interactions between committee members, and it is likely that the leader will find these interactions to be a useful part of the advice giving.

The highest form of decision-reaching meeting is that in which the members are asked to work together to arrive at a single best solution to the presented problem. This type of problem-solving meeting involves three-way interactions among the leader and group members. Problem solving is the most complex meeting activity; it is also the most time-consuming.

One of the most important leadership activities in structuring the committee's business is to make clear to committee members the communication purpose of the meeting. When the leader fails to do this, most people act on the supposition that problem solving is required. This is wasteful of committee time if the leader is not interested in having the committee come to a decision. Also, when committee members do expend the time to reach a decision, they are resentful if their proposed solution is ignored.

Directing and Controlling Human Behavior

The leader's second function during meetings is the directing and controlling of human behavior. This function will be discussed in relation to the problem-solving meeting, since it involves the most complex human behaviors. The leader has two objectives in relation to the leadership role: (1) to maintain a position of control while (2) still encouraging an active interchange among members.

Part of directing behavior is done by the leader in setting the tone of the meeting. At the start of the meeting, the leader sets the stage for free interaction by seeing that the members are acquainted. If the members of the committee do not know each other, the leader makes the introductions, which should include enough about each member to let the others know what talents and knowledge the member brings to the group's defined purpose. Until the members become familiar with each other, the leader facilitates interaction by directing questions to appropriate individuals.

When the leader is dealing with a committee whose members know one another, she has a different set of problems. She needs to think about the reaction patterns of individual members and about anticipated interactions among members. For the counterproductive reactions that can be predicted, the leader can develop controlling strategies to keep in readiness should those behaviors appear during the session.

The leader both maintains control and promotes interaction by seeing that each member contributes to the work of the committee. This usually involves some degree of suppression of overactive members and a drawing out of timid or reticent members. Another control mechanism the leader uses is restatement and redirection: She rephrases a contribution from a member and uses it as a pivot for changing the direction of the conversation. This is particularly important when a committee has overworked one aspect of the problem and must be moved on to another.

The role of the leader during the committee meeting can be summarized in four functions.

1. focusing the issue
2. refocusing when discussion strays
3. changing the focus when an issue has been covered adequately
4. recapping the status of each issue, the decisions made, and the commitments for action

The best way for the nurse manager to develop expertise at running meetings is to allow time immediately after each meeting for analyzing her own performance. In the analysis she should focus on two questions: (1) Did I meet my objectives for the meeting, that is, did I really get the business done? and (2) Did I facilitate appropriate interactions among the members and divert unproductive interactions? While this material has been presented in relation to committee management, many of the principles identified can also be applied to informal groups. For example, the head nurse might use some of the tactics in ward conferences or shift reports.

SUMMARY

Directing and delegating can be difficult tasks for the new manager, since they often represent her first experience with giving orders to other people. Even when others expect directive behavior, the manager may be uncomfortable in the superordinate role. Many of the values and patterns of behavior in nursing militate against comfort in the boss role.

Nurses, for example, are sensitized not to act "on" patients but "with" patients, to involve patients in planning and decision making. It may be difficult for a new manager to learn that the form of behavior used with one group of persons (patients) may not be appropriate with another group (employees).

Many new managers seek to avoid directing and delegating by the institution of a democratic system of decision making on a unit. Even though basic plans and strategies may be devised by the group system, however, the manager cannot altogether avoid the responsibility for individual decision making and the direction of staff. The manager is still accountable for the overall performance of her unit and her staff. Incidents will occur daily that call for her action; indeed, this is why a manager is needed even under a "democratic rule."

With experience the new manager will grow more comfortable with directing and delegating. Meanwhile, she must practice these skills repeatedly and analyze her own behaviors honestly. Evaluation of factors causing both successes and failures in her direction of others will aid in the role-assimilation process.

Direction, delegation, problem solving, and planning take place in group work as well as in one-to-one relationships. As with directing and delegating, these are many skills that the first-line manager can learn to improve her effectiveness in working with groups of all sorts.

BIBLIOGRAPHY

Baker, K.G. "Application of Group Theory in Nursing Practice." *Supervisor Nurse* 11, no. 3 (1980): 22.

Barrios, W.K. "Toward Optimal Patient Care—The Nursing Conference." *Supervisor Nurse* 12, no. 5 (1981): 28.

Chopra, A. "Motivation in Task-Oriented Groups." *Journal of Nursing Administration* 3, no. 1 (1973): 55.

Clark, C.C., and Shea, C.A. *Management in Nursing: A Vital Link in the Health Care System.* New York: McGraw-Hill Book Co., 1979.

Cooper, S.S. "Committees That Work." *Journal of Nursing Administration* 3, no. 1 (1973): 30.

Davis, L.A. "How Do You Follow-Up?" *Journal of Nursing Administration* 10, no. 2 (1980): 25.

DiVincenti, M. *Administering Nursing Service.* 2d ed. Boston: Little, Brown & Co., 1977.

Fair, E.W. "Be Sure They're Listening." *Supervisor Nurse* 11, no. 7 (1980): 30.

Ganong, J.M., and Ganong, W.L. *Nursing Management.* Rockville, MD: Aspen Publishers, Inc., 1976.

Ganong, W.L., and Ganong, J.M. "Reducing Organizational Conflict Through Working Committees." *Journal of Nursing Administration* 2, no. 1 (1972): 12.

Hamm, S.R. "The Influence of Formal and Informal Organization Within a Modern Hospital." *Supervisor Nurse* 11, no. 12 (1980): 38.

Hill, B.S. "Participative Management: A Valid Alternative to Transitional Organizational Behavior." *Supervisor Nurse* 7, no. 3 (1976): 19.

Jay, A. "The Meeting Chairperson: Master or Servant?" *Journal of Nursing Administration* 11, no. 5 (1981): 30.

Kron, T. "Directing Patient Care." In *Current Perspectives in Nursing Management,* Vol. 1, edited by A. Marriner, 48–55. St. Louis: C.V. Mosby Co., 1979.

Levey, S., and McCarthy, R. *Health Management for Tomorrow.* Philadelphia: J.B. Lippincott Co., 1980.

Marriner, A. "Organizational Concepts—II." *Supervisor Nurse* 8, no. 10 (1977): 37.

McConnell, E.A. "Delegation—Myth or Reality?" *Supervisor Nurse* 10, no. 10 (1979): 20.

Mohney, S.J. "Why Participative Management in the Modern Hospital." *Supervisor Nurse* 11, no. 5 (1980): 36.

Rosswurm, M.A. "A Human Resource Framework for Administrative Practice." *Supervisor Nurse* 9, no. 8 (1978): 52.

Scully, R. "Staff Support Groups Helping Nurses to Help Themselves." *Journal of Nursing Administration* 11, no. 3 (1981): 48.

Stevens, W.F. *Management and Leadership in Nursing.* New York: McGraw-Hill Book Co., 1978.

Volante, E.M. "Mastering the Managerial Skill of Delegation." In *Management for Nurses*, 2d ed., edited by M.S. Berger, D. Elhart, S.C. Firsich, S.B. Jordan, and S. Stone, 30–33. St. Louis: C.V. Mosby Co., 1980.

chapter 12

Managing Change

Managing change is one of the major obligations of the first-line manager. If things didn't need to be changed, there would be little need for managers. This chapter looks at two elements of change. The first is recognizing the need for change (i.e., for action) and determining what that change should be. The reader might be aware that in Dewey's model (presented in Chapter 15) problem solving is presented as the intellectual process that an individual uses when an obstruction stops the ongoing systems—that is, when a change is required. The reader is referred to Chapter 15 for the theoretical structure of problem solving. In the first half of the present chapter, the topic will be discussed in terms of its pragmatic applications.

The second half of this chapter looks at the management of changes implemented in what one's employees or organization will do. Processes for improving and accelerating change will be included. In all cases change is seen as dictated by a problem that needs to be solved. Change for its own sake is seldom justified.

PROBLEM SOLVING MANAGEMENT

As has been indicated earlier, management is a balance of the setting and achieving of goals and problem solving. For the first-line manager problem solving may dominate, because so much of the work on her patient unit is of the unplanned sort. Even when only a specific type of patient is admitted to a care unit or program, there are still many unanticipated elements in the care of any single patient. Even admissions and discharges may be somewhat arbitrary or unanticipated. It is important, therefore, that the first-line manager be a resourceful problem solver. She must recognize when a problem exists, and she must accept responsibility for its resolution if it is appropriate to her level of management. Even if the problem doesn't demand her own attention, she must see that it is resolved.

It may be useful for the first-line manager to consider the elements of problem solving and their relation to the familiar management literature term, "decision making."

Definition of Terms

Most books on management include a chapter on decision making. Levey and Loomba give the following definitions in relation to that task:

A decision is the conclusion of a process by which one chooses among available alternatives for the purpose of achieving a set of desired objectives. Decision-making involves all the thinking and activities that are required to produce a choice among alternative courses of action; it is the central activity of all human beings.[1]

The focus of this definition of decision making is the concept of choice, that is, selecting from among a specified set of alternatives to achieve a given purpose. This chapter also views decision making as one component in a larger process, and that process, problem-solving, is our focus.

The problem-solving process begins long before the decision-making stage; it begins when a person senses that an existing situation needs to be clarified. It begins before the person can say what the problem situation really is.

Decision making is not the final stage of problem solving, either. A decision is not the resolution of a problem. Problem solving is a process that extends beyond a finite decision to the state in which the original problematic situation has been resolved. It is not completed until all the decisions and changes necessary to solve the problem have been executed so efficaciously that the problem no longer exists.

Problem Definition

The most important part of problem solving is defining the problem. The problems that the nurse manager "sees" will determine what solutions (changes) are introduced into the nursing organization. Unfortunately, there are many ready-made solutions simply looking for problems. Hawkers of solutions come in many forms: businesspeople trying to sell a particular management course or computer software program to an organization; other nurse managers who are sure that "their" solution will work for everyone else's problems; consultants with particular approaches to sell; and fads that appear from year to year, such as T-grouping for employees, job enlargement programs, or attitude training.

With "solutions" pressing on all sides, it is not surprising that the embattled new nurse manager is tempted to reach out and grab one. Later, when the effects of that "quick fix" solution are found to wear off after a short period, the nurse executive condemns the solution as ineffective. The truth is, of course, that solutions are effective only when applied to the right problems.

The real danger of ready-made solutions is thus that they dictate what the nurse manager sees to be problems. They create artificial problems; or, worse yet, they distort the perceptions of real problems.

Careful diagnosis of problems must precede any consideration of solutions. Take, for example, the nurse executive who calls in a consultant psychologist to investigate the prevalent interpersonal hostility between RNs and LPNs in her organization. The nurse executive may feel that she has by no means closed off problem definition; indeed, she has called in an expert to help her define the problem. This reasoning is fallacious, for she has called in an expert of a particular kind. Just as accountants find financial problems, psychologists can be expected to come up with psychological interpretations of problems. Thus the nurse executive has already "diagnosed" the problem as existing within the psychological realm simply by the act of calling in a psychologist to solve it.

Suppose, however, that the source of the problem is organizational, that LPNs resent being used to perform RNs' functions at a drastically reduced salary. One can then anticipate that the psychologist's efforts might ease the interpersonal problem temporarily but that the underlying organizational problem will eventually rear its head again.

The most critical step in problem solving, therefore, is that first step, in which the nurse manager classifies the problem, for the classification will dictate (and limit) the solutions to be sought. The nurse manager should learn to avoid premature classification of any problem, and there are several principles that will help her.

The first principle is that the nurse manager should insist on knowing all relevant facts before diagnosing any problem. This principle has become an overworked cliché in nursing literature. The disadvantage inherent in the principle is twofold: (1) knowing the principle does not actually help individuals to ascertain when they actually have at hand all the relevant facts, and (2) the method by which those individuals pick out what is "relevant" is dictated by their tentative diagnosis of the problem.

In the example of LPNs' hostility to RNs, the director assumed that the "psychological facts" were needed to explain a problem of interpersonal relations. If the director had questioned this initial assumption, she might have broadened her search to include other kinds of facts.

The simplest way for the nurse manager to identify assumptions that limit the search for facts is to ask herself, "Why have I picked these out as important facts?" A thoughtful answer to this question will help her to recognize the limitations she has put on her definition of the problem.

There is no easy way to determine whether or not one has all relevant facts, but a practical suggestion can be made. The nurse manager should not rely on a single source of information in seeking the facts. Interviewing four supervisors about supervisor-head nurse problems provides multiple inputs, but it still uses a uniform source of information. One would also have to interview those on the head-nurse side of the argument to derive a balanced view of the "facts."

The second principle for averting premature classification is to recognize that most problems are not problems of facts but of interpretation. The nurse manager should make herself aware of all possible interpretations of facts before classifying them into a statement of the problem.

The third principle is to make a systematic investigation of the scope of each presented problem. Is it a problem in its own right, or is it merely a symptom of a problem that is broader in scope? Accurate assessment of the scope of a problem will determine whether the nurse manager applies her efforts to solving the real problem or merely to plugging one hole in a leaky dike.

Generating Alternative Solutions

A useful principle of problem solving is that of constructing alternative solutions for any given problem. Unfortunately, this is another principle that has become a cliché. Those who "follow the rules" typically identify a few "red herrings," meaning alternatives that can easily be discarded in order to get on with the solution (i.e., implement the original solution). This process clearly defeats the purpose of identifying alternatives.

Alternatives must be viable ones whose merits deserve serious consideration. The identification of alternative solutions is a step that is needed to keep the problem solver flexible and open to the potentialities present in each situation. If the nurse manager's final decision invariably corresponds with her initial proposed solution, it is unlikely that she is generating realistic alternatives.

Failure to generate enough alternatives is not the only possible defect at this stage of problem solving. Some situations simply offer an insufficient range of feasible solutions. Thus a lack of alternatives may reflect the environmental circumstances or it may reflect a lack of creative thought on the part of the problem solver. The problem solver must consider the second of these explanations honestly before concluding that the first applies.

An even more complex situation is one in which there are unlimited potential alternatives. In this instance the problem solver must use categorization in order to select a representative but workable number of alternatives for consideration. When these alternatives can be stated in quantitative terms, it may be possible to make use of a computer program to compare a greater number of alternatives than could be "juggled" by a single reasoning person.

Criteria for Assessing Alternatives

Even after alternatives have been identified, the problem solver must have some standard by which to compare the alternatives. Frequently multiple criteria may be combined. For example, a nurse manager may select an assignment system by weighing alternatives against three criteria: effective patient care, economy, and staff satisfaction. Unfortunately, these criteria may conflict, with each suggesting a different alternative solution. Even so, the nurse manager will be in a better position to make the final decision if she has defined the criteria that will serve as the basis for her selection among alternatives.

Another problem in assessing alternatives occurs when there is limited foreknowledge of the outcomes that may be expected from each alternative. In such cases, even the existence of clear criteria is of little help.

Decision Making

Much of the present literature on decision making focuses on computer-based simulation models designed to make decisions concerning quantitative data. A computer, for example, may be better able to devise a fair work schedule for a large number of employees than is a single person—provided, of course, that the appropriate criteria have been prioritized and built into the control program.

Most of the decisions made by the first-line manager, however, deal with qualitative data. For these decisions, it is necessary to look at decision making as a function of mind rather than as a quantifiable calculation.

One good exercise for improving personal decision-making ability is to analyze the results of key decisions for the previous year. This calls for two discrete activities: (1) identifying those decisions that had the greatest impact on the unit, and (2) analyzing the discernible results of those decisions as compared to the results anticipated when decisions were made.

Both activities of this retroactive analysis may yield surprising results. For example, the nurse manager may find that the most critical decisions were not always seen as being important at the time they were made. The analysis will tell her whether or not she is astute at recognizing critical issues. In comparing actual results of decisions with anticipated results the nurse manager will obtain a measure of her predictive power. One of the best ways to learn good decision making is by such careful analysis of past decision-making activities.

Implementing Selected Alternatives

The "payoff" of problem solving is the effective implementation of decisions. This means that decisions must be passed down the chain of command. A published memo to one's staff, for example, does not necessarily ensure implementation. There are, however, some useful techniques by which to ensure that subordinates will carry out the decisions. March and Simon note that the superior has the power and the tools to structure both the environment and the perceptions of the subordinate.[2]

Control of Perceptions

The superior controls the perceptions of subordinates by (1) setting priorities, (2) controlling the flow of input stimuli, and (3) controlling communication. March and Simon note that the organization's vocabulary screens out some parts of reality while magnifying others. For example, typical nursing vocabulary can be said to magnify patient needs while minimizing economy needs. The vocabulary is attention-directing and cue-establishing; it predisposes the employee to a certain mindset by supplying the accepted categories and hierarchy of thought. Attention-directing and cue-establishing communication is an unobtrusive means of control to which the manager has access.

The manager does not have to change individuals to change their behavior, but only the premises on which they base decisions. If promotions and other rewards go to those who have the "right perspective," for example, ambitious colleagues will soon adopt the desired perspective.

One way to establish a desirable mindset is the directive use of the questioning technique. Staff members take on the purpose of their manager, not through the philosophy of nursing she espouses but through those requirements that are imposed upon them in the everyday work situation. The informal use of the question is one of the best devices for establishing desired work and thought patterns.

The manager who asks her staff member, "How are things going?" misses a valuable training opportunity. She has lost the chance to convey to the staff nurse the kinds of things to be thinking about and acting on. A question such as "What are you doing about the teaching needs of your Spanish-American patients?", on the other hand, is directive.

Subordinates can be taught which issues are important to the nurse manager and which are not through the use of directive questioning. If the conversation of the manager is primarily about scheduling, the staff will think primarily about scheduling. If, however, the nurse manager's questions are primarily patient-oriented, the staff will soon adopt this same perspective. (They have to, in order to provide answers to the nurse manager's questions.) It is in this way that the operative philosophy of nursing and nursing management filters down. Conscious monitoring of the kinds of questions she uses will give the nurse manager an easy informal mechanism for directing staff behavior.

Control of Environment

Establishing appropriate ways of thinking in subordinates is only part of the task of implementing decisions. The implications of each decision for the routine work pattern must be determined, for work patterns are the systems by which most decisions will be implemented. If a decision conflicts with a well established system, that decision is likely to be ignored unless the system is made compatible with the decision.

Suppose a nurse manager decides that qualified LPNs should have the opportunity to maintain their skills in the administration of medications. If such a directive is simply posted on a bulletin board for team leaders on a unit where the ingrained assignment "system" is that RNs administer medications and LPNs give bedside care, it is unlikely that many team leaders will carry out the directive except in a token manner. To regularize the assigning of medications to LPNs the nurse manager will have to interfere with the familiar assignment system.

In establishing controls for implementing any given decision, it is necessary to assess which systems are affected by the decision. The nursing division is such a complex organization that it contains many different types of systems, including the following seven:

1. Provision and regulation of patient care:
   (a) patient assessment systems (nursing interview, nursing history, nursing assessment)
   (b) systems for ordering nursing and medical regimens (nursing orders, physicians' orders, nursing care plans)
   (c) systems for implementing care orders (procedures, policies)

   (d) systems for documenting care (charting and recording plans)
   (e) systems for evaluating care (quality control programs, nursing chart audits, utilization plans)
2. Daily assignment of staff members:
   (a) general assignment plan (functional, team, modular, primary nursing, or other method)
   (b) systems for role assignment (who will manage, who will do bedside care, how will jobs be traded off?)
   (c) systems for distributing tasks (what level of personnel do which tasks in this institution?)
3. Regulation of use of personnel:
   (a) systems for determining workdays and days off
   (b) systems for floor assignments
   (c) systems for shift rotations
   (d) systems for staff priorities on desired positions
   (e) routine practices in use of personnel
   (f) personnel policies affecting use of personnel
4. Management decisions:
   (a) lines of established authority and responsibility
   (b) nature and relationship of job positions
   (c) committee structures
5. Patient placement systems
6. Communication within the division
7. Communication with other departments and divisions

Hundreds of systems can be identified for even the smallest nursing unit. Many of these systems interrelate, combine, and in some cases conflict; but they all contribute to the total output of work on the nursing unit.

Whether such systems are formalized or merely traditional patterns, their existence must be acknowledged, and likely ways in which they will be affected by a given decision must be identified. Clearly, acknowledging and identifying a system is the first step in assessing it or changing it to meet objectives. Next, the function of each system, as the means by which work gets done, must be recognized. Work cannot take place efficiently under a condition of anarchy; systems are tools for the implementing of managerial orders.

This does not mean that the nurse manager accepts existing systems uncritically. The evaluation of systems is one of her primary problem-solving responsibilities. For each system, the objectives that the system was created to meet must be identified. If the system no longer meets those objectives adequately, or if those objectives are no longer important, the system is likely to impair rather than facilitate work. The nonfunctional system should not be made an exception; it should be revised.

An extensive amount of work and planning goes into successful implementation of a new system or the alteration of an old one. If decisions are to be implemented successfully, however, the analysis and appropriate alteration of systems to be affected is an essential step.

EFFECTING CHANGE

One of the primary functions of the nurse manager is to facilitate change. For the nurse manager who uses management by objectives, effecting change is an integral part of the management concept. Management by objectives uses goal-setting and implementation of programs to achieve those goals as a basis for managerial action. For the nurse who uses a problem-solving method, change occurs as the means of solving problems. Even if the nurse manager desires to maintain a static environment, it is rarely possible in today's fluid world. Thus the nurse manager who understands the change process will be all the more effective in her administrative role.

In planning to implement change the nurse manager's first consideration is to evaluate carefully the content of the proposed change, for if the change to be made is poor, no amount of sophistication in the change process will make it worthwhile. Many problems are solvable in the abstract, but determining that X is the best solution for Problem Y is not sufficient. The nurse manager must determine whether or not X is the best solution for Problem Y in this particular environment, at this particular time. The nurse manager must consider not only the desirability of the proposed change but also what resources she has for implementing that change. Resources include equipment, facilities, money for startup and maintenance, and people.

Psychological Aspects of Change

Managers usually calculate resources with reasonable accuracy until they come to the people factor; here they are likely to make mistakes. Common administrative myths about human resources include:

- If one or two people attend a three-day workshop, they will develop enough facility with a new plan to begin successful organization-wide institution of the plan.
- A new plan can be implemented on the basis of inservice education alone, without designing administrative rules, policies, and procedures to support the plan.

- A new plan can be successfully instituted in the entire organization without first testing it to work out the "bugs."
- People will take seriously and obey the "do-better" memo ("There will be no more eating in the nurses' stations." "Colored headbands are not to be worn with uniforms." "Lunch times are to be strictly limited to thirty minutes.") even though it is not accompanied by a planned administrative control system.
- A good plan will work even though the organization can invest only half as many workers as the plan requires.

Once the nurse manager determines that a proposed plan is both desirable and feasible for her institution, she can consider the change process by which the plan may be instituted. An important factor in the change process is the time needed for implementation of a new plan. In general, the larger the unit, the longer the process of change. The nurse manager who moves from one institution to another of a different size needs to adapt to a different pace of change. The time frame for change is also affected by the complexity of the proposed plan, the amount of educational inservice required, and the number of persons involved in the plan. The multiplicity of variables involved prevents the reduction of timing factors to a simple formula, but the nurse manager should strive for the appropriate pacing of changes in her institution.

Resistance to Change

Virtually any change meets some form of resistance. In the change process there are two types of resistance: that incurred by the nature of the change, and that incurred by misperceptions of what the change might mean. Misperceptions can be alleviated to some degree by careful and complete explanation of the change. Such an explanation must include the facts concerning the change itself and how that change will be integrated into the existing system. Since there is likely to be resistance enough to a change on the basis of actualities, it is helpful if resistance based on misperceptions can be avoided.

The nurse managers must anticipate that each and every employee will evaluate any proposed change from all perspectives of self-interest. Through introspection she can easily identify the questions one asks about a proposed change:

- Will the change alter my role in the organization? Will it increase or decrease my power? Will it increase or decrease the status I hold among my fellow workers?
- Will the change alter my job content? Will I be expected to add new activities to my job, or will old activities be replaced by new ones?

- Will the change alter the way in which I do my job? Will it give me more freedom or less freedom to select the means of doing my job?
- Will the change affect the conveniences or inconveniences of my work situation? Will it make life easier, or will it impose additional restrictions upon me?
- Will the change affect my financial status now or in the future? Will it alter my chances for attaining higher-paid positions?
- What net advantages does the change offer me, and what benefits does it threaten to take away?

Few changes can be imagined concerning which every employee will be able to give favorable answers to all questions. Anticipating most questions, however, helps the nurse manager to explain the change in ways that will alleviate groundless fears.

In dealing with resistance the nurse manager will benefit from knowing the typical stages of resistance. These stages vary somewhat according to whether the change is merely being considered or whether it has been definitely authorized. The following stages of resistance are typical of the situation in which a change is first considered and publicized and is then instituted by managerial order:

1. Undifferentiated resistance emerges from various sources.
2. Pro and con sides line up, developing their stands via reasoned arguments or slogans.
3. Direct conflicts take place between the two sides.
4. Those favoring the change "win" when the manager institutes the change.

The nurse manager should not let herself be tricked into making premature and ineffective responses to resistance as it develops. These ineffective responses include defensive self-justification, advice-giving ("What I would do if I were you"), premature persuasion ("Later, you'll see it my way"), censoring (meeting opposition with disapproval), and punishing behavior.

Accepting that resistance is inevitable, the nurse manager will be wise to perform a "force field" analysis for a proposed change to predict which forces will support the change and which will oppose it. Calculation of this balance of forces gives some idea of how much work will be involved in effecting the change and which tools will be needed to implement the change.

Resources for Implementing Change

The tools of the nurse manager exist on a continuum ranging from persuasion to influence to force. Persuasion can appeal to reason, emotion, or both.

Although it is not the exclusive tool of the manager, she does have more communication channels to use for persuasion than do her staff members.

Influence is a stronger force; it is persuasion independent of arguing a cause. The opinion of the individual carries weight because of the esteem in which that person is held. While influence is not necessarily assured by position, it is likely that the nurse manager will have influence equal to or greater than that of others on her staff.

Force, the last alternative, resides in the formal powers of the manager's organizational position. She possesses this option to a greater degree than does any of her staff. The manager should try to use the lowest-level tool or combination of tools adequate to bring about the desired change. To do this requires that she accurately perceive her own powers of influence and persuasion.

The nurse manager also needs to ascertain where her staff stands in relation to the content of the proposed change. The nearer the staff is to acceptance, the easier implementation will be. Stages of acceptance include:

1. awareness of the new idea, practice, or system
2. interest (seeking of more information concerning the new reality)
3. evaluation (sifting of information in light of existing conditions)
4. mental trial of the new idea, practice, or system
5. actual trial, on a small scale if possible
6. adoption and integration of the change into the ongoing operation.

These stages of acceptance represent the steps by which people naturally respond to a change. In making an organizational change the nurse manager may choose to (1) accelerate this natural process by using informational and propaganda techniques, or (2) enforce the desired new behavior, by-passing the stages of acceptance.

The time factor may decisively affect which one of these two approaches the manager chooses. Acceptance of any new idea takes time, although the time required is shorter for ideas that fit the existing attitudes and goals of the group. These attitudes include not only the value systems of the individuals but the institution's value system. Each institution has its own specific areas of pride: "We may not have everything here, but we certainly are tops at. . . ." If the desired change involves considerable conflict with individual or institutional values, persuasion and propaganda alone will probably not be effective.

An important discovery in attitude behavior research is that enforced behavior change can bring about a change in attitude. If the individual is required to adopt a particular behavior, it is likely that cognitive dissonance (conflict between actions and beliefs) will ultimately cause the person to change an attitude. If the attitude is a long-entrenched one, enforced behavior compliance may be the quickest way to deal with it.

Ideally the nurse manager tries to obtain attitudinal acceptance before instituting measures for behavioral changes. However, she needs to be aware that attitudinal change itself does not guarantee the anticipated behavioral change. It is up to her to make individuals aware of attitude-behavior inconsistencies. Cognitive dissonance assists in the adaptation to change only when a person is aware of the conflict between that person's own attitude and behavior.

What, then, are the steps that the nurse manager can take in implementing a change? Letting persons who will be affected participate in the change-planning and implementation processes might well facilitate the change. It is essential to set up good communications. Everyone who needs to know about the change should be identified, including the opinion leaders. The advantage of the change over what it replaces should be spelled out. Both the informational and emotional aspects of the change should be explored. The nurse manager should allow time for those affected by the change to discuss it among themselves and for those who oppose the change to voice their objections to her.

With regard to "who needs to know," the first-line manager must consider how her proposed change may affect other first-line managers in her institution. It is critical that they be informed and prepared to deal with the "fall out" of the change should it affect their own work. Often first-line managers work together to coordinate major changes with a view toward maintaining some degree of uniformity in practice.

During the implementation process the nurse manager should remember that an order to everyone is an order to no one. Some managers issue orders in general memos that are quickly filed in the wastebasket or placed on a bulletin board to be ignored. To be effective, a communication that requires action must clearly state who is to do what, at what time, and in what way. In addition, the manager must be prepared to provide follow-up to ensure that her communication has been implemented.

When the nurse manager expects strong resistance to a particular change, she can take extra steps to ensure its successful implementation. In such instances she should begin with a clear understanding that control rather than persuasion will be the primary implementation tool. Nevertheless, a few steps short of control can be tried to win staff support. The use of an independent change agent may be successful. A resource person from outside the unit and with no personal bias may be called in to serve as a catalyst in the change process. A similar effect may be achieved by use of a design group from within the organization. When a group such as this is to monitor and spearhead the change process, the selection of members is a critical factor. The design group should consist mainly of knowledgeable and strong leaders who favor the proposed change. Other members may be undecided about the issue. Even those who, though against the plan, are openminded and objective can be good task force members. (The latter two member types exert a realistic influence on group planning.) The manager must reserve the right to remove any members who assume outright obstructional roles.

Another method for obtaining staff acquiescence is to assure members that they will have an opportunity to evaluate the new plan after it has been in effect for a specified period of time. When a nurse manager makes this commitment, there are four essential agreements to be made:

1. The trial period must be long enough for the system to become functional and have a fair chance to succeed.
2. The staff must agree to cooperate fully in putting the plan into effect. There can be no "half efforts" or mere biding of time until the end of the trial period.
3. The nurse manager must stick to her agreement and hold the evaluation session as planned.
4. There must be a clear understanding from the start as to whether the nurse manager is to be bound by the decision of the evaluation committee or whether she is merely to consider the committee's recommendations in making her final decision.

When none of the suggested "softening" measures seems likely to work in instituting a change, then the nurse manager must rely strictly on the power and control vested in her administrative office. In such instances she must be prepared for a possible power conflict. She will do well to consider what kind of support she can expect from her own boss if her staff simply say "No." Should she decide to institute the change, it is important that she indicate that she means business. She dare not waver, seem unsure, or yield any ground. She must set and enforce absolute performance standards; she must be willing to take strong action against those who fail to comply with the directive. She must also make certain in her own mind that the issue is important enough to justify such measures.

Implementing a change is only the first step for the nurse manager. She must plan carefully for follow-up if she expects the change to be maintained. She also must be on the lookout for unexpected consequences. No matter how well a change is planned, it is always possible that it may bring about unanticipated outcomes. The follow-up on any change must include a thorough evaluation based on objective criteria that are derived from the goals and objectives of the change project. One of the most important managerial talents is the ability to deal honestly with the knowledge that a change was a mistake. The manager naturally has a great investment in change projects she has originated or supported. She must be very careful that her vested interest does not blind her to the real effects of a plan once it has been put into action.

Most change projects, however, if well planned and well executed, will be accepted with surprising rapidity. Often, by the time the trial period is over, the participants have so adapted to the new system that they will resist a suggestion to return to the old way.

The Logistics of Change

In addition to the psychological and behavioral aspects of implementing changes among staff, one must look at the logistics of change implementation. Even a well accepted change can be undone if the plans for its implementation are inadequate. The manager must be careful to work out the logistics, considering each element of the plan: when it should be phased in, who needs to know, what systems—nursing and others—will be affected, and what adjustments will need to be made in order to accommodate the change.

CHANGE OR CONTINUITY?

Most of the nursing literature presents change as an inevitable virtue, but that is a simplistic view. Indeed, if a system is functioning well it would be irresponsible to implement change for its own sake. The manager should use change as a way of resolving repetitive problems, of implementing new technology and knowledge, or of preventing problems that she anticipates will arise in the near future. Change should not be implemented merely to satisfy a manager's need for "action" within the system. There are times when a manager may decide that a given staff needs a change of operations just to renew their interest in the work process, but this is an unusual situation that applies only to an unusual work group. Even then, there is a reason for the change—a psychological one.

The nurse manager must also be aware that change can produce increased staff satisfaction simply because of its novelty. That is why she does not try to evaluate a change until that change has itself become part of the status quo. Once this state has been achieved, the manager can get a true measurement of the effectiveness of the altered process or system.

Moreover, the nurse manager must evaluate the merits of any change in her own context. Even a good plan will not be good for every institution in every circumstance, and contextual assessment is critical in judging whether or not a beneficial plan has been beneficial for a given work environment. "Bandwagonism" is a danger, especially for the relatively new manager who wishes to be contemporary in all ways. Change is only as good or bad as it is appropriate or inappropriate for a given situation. It is as good or bad as the logistic plan for its implementation; and it is as good or bad as the preparation of the staff who must deal with the change.

SUMMARY

Problem solving and implementing changes are two managerial processes of critical importance in the first-line manager's role. She will be better able to apply these processes if she does so in an informed and systematic way. Problem solving and managing change are vital processes in which the first-line manager can demonstrate her leadership role. Planning, analyzing, and evaluating her own and others' behaviors during these processes will not only yield the most effective results but will enhance the manager's expertise.

NOTES

1. S. Levey and N.P. Loomba, *Health Care Administration—A Managerial Perspective* (Philadelphia: J.B. Lippincott Co., 1973), p. 169.
2. J.G. March and H.A. Simon, *Organizations* (New York: John Wiley & Sons, Inc., 1958), pp. 136–150.

BIBLIOGRAPHY

Daniel, W.W., and Terrell, S.A. "Introduction to Decision Analysis," *Journal of Nursing Administration* 8, no. 5 (1978): 20.

Ehrat, K.S. "A Model for Politically Astute Planning and Decision Making." in D.J. del Bueno and C.M. Freund, eds. *Power and Politics in Nursing Administration: A Casebook*. Owings Mills, MD: National Health Publishing, 1986, 225.

Erickson, E.H., and Borgmeyer, Sr. V. "Simulated Decision-Making Experience via Case Analysis." *Journal of Nursing Administration* 9, no. 5 (1979): 10.

Gordon, G., and Pressman, I. *Quantitative Decision-Making for Business*. Englewood Cliffs, NJ: Prentice-Hall, 1978.

Hatvany, N.G., and Gladstein, D. "A Perspective on Group Decision Making." in D.A. Nadler, M.L. Tushman, and N.G. Hatvany, eds. *Managing Organizations: Readings and Cases*. Boston: Little, Brown and Company, 1982, 213.

Hofing, A.; McGugin, M.B.; and Merkel, S.I. "The Importance of Maintenance in Implementing Change: An Experience with Problem-Oriented Recording." *Journal of Nursing Administration* 9, no. 12, (1979): 43.

Kotter, J.P., and Schlesinger, L.A. "Choosing Strategies for Change." *Harvard Business Review* 56, no. 2 (1979): 106.

LaMonica, E., and Finch, F.E. "Managerial Decision Making." *Journal of Nursing Administration* 7, no. 5 (1977): 20.

Levenstein, A. "Effecting Change Requires Change Agent." *Journal of Nursing Administration* 9, no. 6 (1979): 12.

Manfredi, C. "Primary Nursing and Change: A Case Study." in E.C. Hein and M.J. Nicholson, eds. *Contemporary Leadership Behavior: Selected Readings.* Boston: Little, Brown and Company, 1982, 309.

Marriner, A. "Development of Management Thought." *Journal of Nursing Administration* 9, no. 9 (1979): 21.

Mintzberg, H.; Raisinghani, D.; and Theoret, A. "The Structure of Unstructured Decision Processes." *American Science Quarterly* 21, no. 2 (1976): 246.

New, J.R., and Couillard, N.A. "Guidelines for Introducing Change." in E.C. Hein and M.J. Nicholson, eds. *Contemporary; Leadership Behavior: Selected Readings,* Boston: Little, Brown and Company, 1982, 301.

Nyberg, J. "Probing the Change Process." *Supervisor Nurse* 11, no. 5 (1980): 31.

Rains, J.W. "Skills for Social Change." *Nursing & Health Care* 9, no. 6 (June 1988): 298.

Rosen, H., and Marella, M. "Basic Quantitative Thinking for Nurse Managers." *Journal of Nursing Administration* 7, no. 5 (1977): 6.

Roy, Sr. C. "Human Information Processing." in J.J. Fitzpatrick, R.L. Taunton, and J.Q. Benoliel, eds. *Annual Review of Nursing Research,* New York: Springer Publishing Company, 1988, 237.

Sowell, R., and Alexander, J.W. "Model for Success." *Nursing & Health Care* 9, no. 1 (January 1988): 24.

Spradley, B.W. "Managing Change Creatively." *Journal of Nursing Administration* 10, no. 5 (1980): 32.

Stevens, B.J. "Management of Continuity and Change in Nursing." *Journal of Nursing Administration* 7, no. 4 (1977): 26.

Taylor, A.G. "Decision Making in Nursing: An Analytical Approach." *Journal of Nursing Administration* 8, no. 11 (1987): 22.

Thorpe, R. "Sabotage in Nursing." *Supervisor Nurse* 12, no. 24 (1981): 24.

Vroom, V.H., and Jago, A.G. "Decision Making as a Social Process: Normative and Descriptive Models of Leader Behavior." in D.A. Nadler, M.L. Tushman, and N.G. Hatvany, eds. *Managing Organizations: Readings and Cases,* Boston: Little, Brown and Company, 1982, 246.

Welch, L.B. "Planned Change in Nursing: The Theory." in E.C. Hein and M.J. Nicholson, eds. *Contemporary Leadership Behavior: Selected Readings,* Boston: Little, Brown and Company, 1982, 289.

chapter 13

The Business of Nursing

COST-EFFECTIVE MANAGEMENT

The first-line manager often finds herself comparing the purpose, function, and goals of health care delivery with those of business. Nowhere is this comparison more starkly apparent than in the area of material resource management. This is also the area where health care delivery systems, and often managers, are found lacking. Fundamental principles have changed dramatically in today's environment of cost-effective care delivery. Many health care professionals chose their profession because of a desire to alleviate human suffering. The financial costs related to their caregiving are rarely a dominant concern. Under past conditions there was no requirement that the head nurse be particularly skilled in management beyond the rudimentary level. That the head nurse is now more accurately called the first-line nurse manager is a statement of the sophisticated level of management skills required in addition to competence and compassion at the bedside.

The first-line nurse manager should remember that the comparison with business is useful, if not always fair. There are important differences between health care delivery and private enterprise. Businesses exist for the sake of profits and often operate with little other internal restraint except attention to that principle. In health care organizations run strictly according to business principles, quality occurs only when it makes sense from a profit perspective. Quality is subordinated to profit: If the competition delivers a higher-quality product at comparable cost, the enterprise loses business.

A health care delivery system operating with profit as the primary motive may be required to discharge patients who exceed the DRG-approved length of stay. This example, reduced to the absurd, demonstrates the point that health care can never be totally cost-efficient in the same way that a business can be. That is because the mission of health care delivery is more complex. To state the difference in an oversimplified way, the first-line nurse manager must provide care for the sick compassionately, competently, *and* in a cost-effective manner. Business, on the other hand, need only deliver its product cost-effectively.

These differences, however, should not serve as excuses for bad management in health care. Business practices must be examined and explored as they apply to good health care delivery. The first-line manager must see the task of innovative modern management as an important aspect of her professional competence. Materials management and budgeting are areas where business practices are most readily adapted to health care delivery.

The economic reality for most businesses requires managers to watch their costs, maximize resources, increase profits, and beat the competition. Until recently, this philosophy was foreign to health care managers. Retrospective reimbursement allowed relatively free spending by hospitals. Costs incurred by providers were fully billed to the patient and in most cases were paid by a third party, i.e., government or private insurers. However, the prospective payment system has changed all that. Length of patient stays has been reduced, admissions are carefully monitored, home care referrals are on the rise, and competition is everywhere. Hospitals, health maintenance organizations, and home health care agencies are marketing their services to the public, with each trying to carve out its particular niche. With the host of new competitors in the field, the health care industry has drastically altered its behavior and become more businesslike. When businesses experience reduced revenues, the first strategy is to reduce spending and to limit resource consumption. The next strategy is to increase productivity and to find new markets for the products or services produced. Health care is a business, and the same tactics apply. The challenge is to maintain quality services and stay financially healthy.

The prospective payment system, by tying reimbursement to a diagnosis-related group, effectively controls the length of a patient's stay in the hospital. The realization that profits are inversely correlated to length of stay focused hospital administrators' efforts on measuring costs per patient day. One of the most obvious expenses is nursing care. Traditionally included under room and board charges, nursing care was always seen as an expense item. Some hospitals, anxious for a quick fix to their budgetary woes under the new system, look to the nursing department for solutions.

Hospital administrators now scrutinize nursing as an area where expenses can be cut by staffing reductions and/or the replacement of services provided by nurses with those provided by less skilled personnel. Examples of the latter category include ward managers, respiratory therapists, and patient representatives who "help the patient communicate with the health care system." One can easily envision computer specialists, pharmacy technicians, and others chipping away at the traditional areas of nursing responsibility. This could effectively rob the first-line manager and the staff nurse of their professional identity as well as their responsibilities, while reducing the effectiveness of care delivery. The first-line nurse manager must be cognizant of these competitive threats and train herself and her staff to meet them. This requires not only honing her management skills but demonstrating cost effectiveness and, indeed, demonstrating that nursing can be profitable. As an illustration, some nursing departments now package and sell their own innovative quality control techniques.

Several nursing departments have capitalized on the business approach to the problem and seized the opportunity to cost-out nursing services. Under a costed-out model, nursing is a revenue-generating center with patients paying for nursing care costs per hospital day. There has been a surge in the development of various models measuring nursing intensity, productivity, and cost accounting. Most models apply computer technology to process patient data relative to patient classification, nursing care intensity measures, and nurse staffing requirements.

Business-oriented decisions aimed at increasing profits or restricting resources are made at the top, but they are put into effect at the first-line level. Nurse managers are essential to the success or failure of such efforts. Since nursing is labor-intensive, it is not surprising that restrictions often involve decreases in personnel. And when positions are left vacant, first-line managers have to do the job with less. The fact is that nurses can be resourceful and creative when coping with limited resources, but staff need guidance and education regarding hospital, agency, and unit finances. This chapter and others that follow will explore the nurse manager's role as the business manager of her unit. The ordering and allocation of supplies, product selection, and managing the introduction of new technology are all part of the modern nurse manager's job, as is budgetary accountability.

Computers and technically advanced equipment have proliferated in the health care arena. Regardless of the setting, nurses are increasingly responsible for operating equipment of increasing complexity. The evaluation of products and equipment is best done at the unit level. Nurse managers are necessarily involved in purchasing computers and other high-tech equipment, introducing them to staff and patients, and maintaining them properly.

Of growing importance to the nurse manager's planning is her consideration of the patient and his satisfaction with the services he receives. The use of marketing in health care is a recent, but highly influential, development. Nurse executives are learning marketing techniques that promote the value of nursing to the patient as well as to the organization. The first-line manager is closest to the consumer and has the greatest opportunity to influence customer satisfaction. As alternative delivery systems emerge and compete for the same population, customers are becoming more selective in choosing their sources of health care. The quality of health care received in the past is a determining factor in their decision.

A spate of books and articles describe the numerous business-oriented strategies available to nurses in acute care, home health care, and long-term care. Management interventions include costing-out nursing, planning care according to a resource-driven model, marketing nurses as a product-line, and using data to enhance nursing productivity. The nurse manager is ideally situated to identify which activities will yield the greatest return.

BUDGETING

Given the choice, it is likely that the majority of first-line managers would relinquish the budgetary aspects of their jobs. This is due, for the most part, to their lack of instruction and experience with the principles of financial management. Prior to joining the ranks of management, staff members have little practical knowledge of the budget and the business operations of the organization. While the budget literally has everything to do with what they do, they have little to do with the budget before assuming a managerial role. The budget has typically been used as a club to beat off the onslaught of requests for more supplies, more staff, or newer equipment. The simple statement "It's not in the budget" has been heard by every staff member at one time or another. Often, staff develop a negative attitude toward the budget instead of regarding it as a tool that can help them to accomplish their objectives.

With the increased emphasis on reducing the costs in the delivery of health care, nurse managers are at risk if they are not versed in the rudiments of finance. The grim fact is that many nurse managers are not presently knowledgeable enough to comprehend the implications of budget cuts for their work units.

The shift to decentralized systems of governance in health care organizations has given the first-line nurse manager more responsibility and accountability for the financial state of her operation. Although there are still hospitals and agencies that do not involve nursing management in the budget process, the numbers are decreasing. Administration now recognizes that the first-line nurse manager controls significant resources and should thus have input in preparing and managing the budget for her unit.

The intent of this section is to acquaint the reader with basic terminology and to present a general approach to the budget process. It is beyond the scope of this chapter to discuss the different methods by which budgets are constructed, how costs and revenues may be assigned, and how nursing care may be detached from the charges for room and board. McCloskey, Gardner, and Johnson have thoroughly researched articles related to costing-out nursing services and have compiled a useful annotated bibliography that is referenced at the end of this chapter.

Rudiments of Budgeting

Health care organizations are concerned with providing needed services in an economical manner. Basically, the administration selects certain objectives that will assure the continued survival and prosperity of the organization. The budget is usually thought of as a financial plan that assists management to meet its objectives.

Thus budgeting has two prime phases: (1) the planning phase, to determine what is to be done and when and how it is to be done, and (2) the control phase, to bring actual performance in line with the plan.[1]

A sound budgeting procedure provides the mechanism for prompt reporting of actual versus planned performance, e.g., the actual cost of personnel hours versus projected wages. A budget is prepared in extensive detail to identify the costs and revenues for each area. Because budgets are based on estimates that project into the future, there are bound to be differences between planned and actual performance.

Most budgeting starts at the top. An overall operating budget is determined by the administration, with estimates of total income and expenses. Departments are then asked to make financial estimates for the coming fiscal year. These projections may go through several revisions until the targeted figures are reached. Based on these plans a final budget is prepared. As the year progresses, statements are issued that compare actual revenues and expenses with planned revenue and expense. This allows managers to track the performance of their unit and to make adjustments as necessary; for example, a new strategy may be required to deal with unplanned overtime.

Incremental Budgeting

If the organization constructs its budget according to an incremental method, then the first-line nurse manager is expected to base her projections for the upcoming year on current fiscal year data. At the start of the budgeting process, the nurse manager should receive a summary of the financial data for her work unit for the preceding fiscal year. This may include only six months of spending data, since budget preparation is usually started well in advance. There may be assigned percentages by which to estimate changes in base salaries and benefits and the cost of supplies. Most institutions base their budgets on historical data. This form of budgeting, since it relies heavily on prior reports of expenditures, is often called line-item budgeting—i.e., the manager works by examining each line of last year's expenses, category by category.

Zero-Based Budgeting

Less common is the zero-based budgeting approach. A zero-based budget, unlike the line-item model, starts at zero (without reference to past spending) and builds a budget according to the desired outcomes for that year. The goal is to reorient the manager's thinking and to re-evaluate all programs. Much of the same planning is required—first-line managers must still examine the basic work of the unit, including the necessary commitment of resources to accomplish their objectives. However, the nurse manager must then prioritize the tasks according to a cost-benefit rating system.[2] Obviously this process must be carefully designed, and training is essential. For these reasons, along with the fact that it is an extremely time-consuming process, it is not widely used in the acute care setting.

Types of Expenses

An institutional budget comprises two counterbalancing components: expenses and income. Nursing units have traditionally been considered cost centers to which specific expenses are assigned. A cost center accumulates expenses but generates no income. Consequently, budgets for the nursing department have seldom reflected revenue resulting from nursing activities. Recently, in several hospital systems, nursing has succeeded in unbundling nursing care from room and board charges so that it appears separately on the bill. However, this is not yet the standard practice. The following discussion, therefore, will focus on nursing's expense budget, not its revenue budget.

First-line nurse managers involved in budget preparation need an understanding of what constitutes a budget for their work area. Most nursing department budgets, as indicated earlier, are line-item budgets with the types of expenses separately listed. Line items typically include such expenditures as salaries, benefits, overtime, equipment purchases, rental equipment, and maintenance contracts. Since the head nurse is accountable for her budget, she must learn which individual costs are grouped under each line item and why each cost is placed in that category. Although she may not be able to alter the budget allocations significantly, she will have a better grip on the expenses assigned to her unit and what they represent if she knows exactly which costs are assigned to each general category.

Capital Expenses. Buildings, equipment, and furniture are examples of capital expenditures that have an extended life, normally five years or more, and exceed a specified amount, e.g., any equipment over $500 (the institution sets its own figure). These items are separated out for specific purposes, such as depreciation.

Overhead Expenses. The overhead or indirect expenses incurred by an organization include the cost of utilities, rent, postage, and maintenance. These expenses are allocated to all areas by the accounting department according to a specific formula. The most common method is to charge each area based on the square footage occupied. Depending on the system of the hospital or agency, central administration costs, including executive salaries, may be included here.

Operating Expenses. Salaries, supplies, and telephone service typify items considered to be operating expenses. These are the essentials necessary to keep an organization functioning. They may fluctuate depending on census or the number of patient visits made. Some institutions separate salaries from other operating expenses and place them in a discrete category, the personnel budget.

Personnel Budget. The personnel budget is the largest single expense for the nursing unit, if not for the organization as a whole. Therefore, considerable care should be given to learning exactly how the nursing department formulates its staffing pattern and how specific variables affect the work unit. Staffing will be affected by several variables, including the nursing care delivery model in place, the rate of turnover, the acuity of the patient population, length of stay, fluctuations in census, numbers of experienced nurses versus new graduates, continuing education requirements, and staff mix. Nurse managers need to use their judgment when making staffing decisions as they relate to the budget. Enough flexibility should be built into the budget to accommodate the day-to-day reality, as opposed to the ideal staffing plan.

The staffing plan and the budget for staff are interrelated in complex ways. In an ideal world one would first conceive of the staffing plan, selecting the model that best met nursing care needs for the institution's clients. Then the budget would be calculated to provide for the plan. In today's institution, however, the nursing department seldom has the luxury of such ideal planning. The opposite condition would exist if the first-line manager were presented with a given amount to be spent on her personnel budget. Then, if that figure were nonnegotiable, she would have to figure out the best possible staffing (numbers of workers and categories of workers) that could be obtained for the money.

Most budgeting tactics fall somewhere between the two examples given above, with staffing plans and costs being negotiable and influencing each other.

Supply Budget. Supplies are generally those things that are consumed in the course of providing patient care—that is, supplies are one component of the operational budget. Depending on the organization and how it defines capital expenditures, an item will be determined to be a capital or supply expense. It is the practice of most institutions to set a dollar sum over which any purchase is considered to be a capital and not a supply expense. Thermometers, adhesive tape, needles, slippers, and charting forms are all examples of general supplies that are charged to the unit according to usage. However, an order of sphygmomanometers might fall into either the operational or capital expense category, depending on how many are ordered and what the hospital policy is. Notice here that the purchase of a large quantity of items may be classified as a capital expenditure even if the cost per item is less than the preset figure separating capital and supply purchases. For example, a bedside lamp priced at $75.00 costs less than the institution's figure for capital expenses. If the organization is purchasing 200 of them, the total amount of the bulk purchase may be treated as a single capital expenditure.

The first-line nurse manager may have significant responsibility for the ordering and monitoring of materials for her unit. The projected amount to request for supplies in the upcoming year will be based on the spending levels of the previous fiscal year. An effective manager won't wait until budget time to review material usage in her work area. Monthly expense reports, reports on supplies taken from central stores, and reports on supplies ordered directly from vendors provide baseline information for an analysis of material expenditures. The nurse manager should make a habit of reviewing all available reports for the essential data regarding supplies on the unit.

Advances in technology and the preference for disposable goods tend to increase the cost of supplies estimated per patient. In addition, new treatment modalities, the increased precautions taken with AIDS patients, physician preference for a particular, more expensive, brand of a given item—all have a direct impact on supply expenses. Not all of these influences can be predicted. The nurse manager should construct her budget with some leeway for these unplanned factors in mind. There is also a need to factor inflation into the cost of anticipated items for the next year. When limited resources are available, rather than increase expenditures the nurse manager may be expected to scale down her budget. Decisions will have to be made as to what will have priority. The purchase of a new kind of infusion pump may be postponed, while the plan to switch to digital thermometers remains in the budget.

Since accountability for supplies is at the unit level, the head nurse should review the ordering system and how usage is monitored in day-to-day practice. Staff members must be required to follow the correct procedure when ordering supplies and charging patients. Often staff consider these accounting procedures to be unnecessary paperwork that takes time away from patient care. What they fail to understand is that the hospital cannot be reimbursed when supplies are not charged to patients, and the money is then lost to the hospital and to the unit. If the processing of charge slips is in fact inefficient, the nurse manager must investigate new approaches to the problem. It would be interesting to find out how much money is lost because of an inconvenient system. It often proves worthwhile to spend time designing a more efficient means of charging patients for various care products that are used daily.

Direct Expenses. The first-line nurse manager is primarily concerned with the direct expenses that can be identified and assigned to her area. Salaries, benefits, supplies, and the cost of some equipment are considered to be direct expenses. Usually the direct expenses for a nursing unit are the operating expenses. In budgeting practice, institutions usually estimate the capital and overhead expenses at a higher level of budget planning. Seldom will the first-line manager have to estimate these figures.

The first-line manager may have some difficulty in determining her direct costs if the institution does not keep the data she requires. Institutions that purchase their supplies in bulk, for instance, may distribute costs based on the number of beds in a unit rather than on actual usage.

Usually in a larger organization there will be three separate budgets: a personnel budget, a supply or operations budget, and a budget for capital expenditures. Given the high level of interaction and interdependency of departments in an institution, it is essential that there be collaboration on decisions related to equipment purchases and supplies. That is why all departmental and divisional budgets must ultimately be considered together at the institutional level.

Cost Containment

Cost containment is not a new concept. In most industries workers are expected to do their jobs with efficiency and economy. Waste is unacceptable, and everyone is alert to and involved with the effort to economize. However, many health care institutions are thought to be capable of absorbing a certain amount of waste, especially if it can be justified as "better for the patient." Nurses sometimes use their focus on patient needs as an excuse to ignore cost savings.

On the other hand, sometimes supply rationing is so restrictive that it is not economical. For example, placing several extra disposable pads under a patient may accomplish what the staff nurse wants—it may save the nurse from having to change the linen more frequently. Enforcing stricter adherence to frugal usage of supplies may save on disposable pads but, in the long run, cost more in nursing time. The first-line manager needs to determine carefully where real cost savings can be achieved. She should not simply create more rules without considering their larger economic impact.

Budget Planning

The budget represents a best guess, based on key data, as to revenues and costs anticipated for the coming year. Every budget starts with a plan. The plan lays out the detailed activities for the work unit for a given time period, taking into account the relationships of resources to outcomes and of revenues to costs. In order to work, the plan and the resultant budget are formulated in the context of the overall objectives of the nursing division and the long- and short-range goals of the organization. The plan for the work unit should include both objectives and the methods by which to achieve them. Key data include the number of full-time staff equivalents (FTEs), learning needs of the staff, type of care rendered (e.g., critical, emergency, home care, homemaking), equipment needs, number of beds and/or clients serviced, severity of patients' illnesses, and the dominant reimbursement system.

In setting objectives for her unit the nurse manager has to evaluate the immediate needs of her work group and then project future resource requirements. Her objectives should represent realistic and attainable ends, balancing desirable outcomes with the available resources. The objectives should also be well grounded in factual data. A thorough analysis of the environment should answer these questions: What is working? What is not? What can be done to improve the situation? Because the health care environment is anything but static, the answers should be considered in light of future trends in the external environment and their predictable effects on the organization. The purpose here is not to predict the future perfectly but to predict how decisions made now may be affected in the future and what must be done to prepare for possible contingencies.

For example, the growth of the home health care industry has implications for both the manager in acute care and the manager in the community health agency. The "quicker and sicker" phenomenon created by the earlier discharge of patients from the acute care hospital to the home will affect each setting in its own way. The nurse manager in a visiting-nurse association has to anticipate the introduction of high-technology equipment into the home care environment. One of her objectives in this regard might be to provide classes to prepare her staff to deliver better high-tech nursing care. The nurse manager in the hospital may set as her objective to conduct staff-development programs on early discharge planning that focus on evaluating the patient's need to continue with equipment in the home.

Developing objectives for the future often entails committing resources to projects that may not succeed. There is an inherent risk in this approach, but there is greater risk in shortsighted, static planning. It is up to the nurse manager to weigh the risks against possible outcomes and to identify alternative approaches. The home care supervisor must determine the cost of educating her staff on the latest equipment available for home use. She must also determine how the agency will benefit from such staff preparation. The alternative to not planning for the educational course may be that the agency will lose its competitive edge in referrals. An effective manager enables the organization to move forward by charting the course to achieve results. "Any manager can use his or her plan as a lever to nudge the organization, big or small, down the path to success. This is what good planning is all about."[3]

From her objectives the nurse manager can work out a detailed plan of how resources are to be allocated. Such a plan is needed even when the nurse manager is handed a completed budget without her prior input. In fact, a plan is even more essential if the nurse manager is to match and adjust her planned objectives to a given unchangeable budget. Budgeting is the method that translates objectives to be accomplished into financial terms. The budget should help to guide the first-line manager in her decision making. The future is unknown, and so any plan has to be flexible enough to allow for changing conditions. For example, an unexpected shortage of nursing personnel will adversely affect the staffing budget, requiring more overtime and more hiring of agency nurses than were anticipated. In preparing her own budget, the first-line manager uses first-hand observation, discussions with staff, collaborations with other departments, input from top management, and past financial data.

Usually a unit that plans to initiate a special project, such as a preceptor program or a research study, requires additional funding beyond the normal budget. For such a project the manager would be asked to submit a separate request for funding. Depending on the amount of the investment, this might entail a detailed rationale for the project, background material to substantiate the worthiness of the project, analysis of projected costs, and the expected return—financial or other—that would accrue to the organization.

SUMMARY

An effective first-line manager should know the fiscal bottom line for her work unit. This gets easier with time and experience. By reviewing each monthly statement (the comparison of actual expenses to the projected budget) and deviations from previous years, the head nurse can learn to assess her unit's financial performance. While financial data are only part of the picture, they do give a solid indication of where the money is going. It is the responsibility of the nurse manager to provide the "whys and wherefores" of unit expenses. Staff also need to recognize the value of the services they provide and to understand that without organizational income there can be no mission.

At a time when departmental and unit budgets are often cut to ensure the survival of the organization, the nurse manager who knows where cuts can be made without endangering the quality of patient care is invaluable. Drucker believes that cost control can be best achieved by concentrating efforts on a few areas where relatively minor changes will produce major increases in economic effectiveness, rather than by making cuts across the board.[4]

The nurse manager has to be prepared to make trade-offs and to trade wisely. Many health care providers argue that cost control and quality care are contradictory. Another view is stated by Peters: "When quality goes up, costs go down. Quality improvement is the primary source of cost reduction."[5]

NOTES

1. J.T. Willson, *Budgeting and Profit Planning Manual* (Boston: Warren, Gorham & Lamant, 1983), 1–4.

2. P.J. Grant, "Zero Base Budgeting and the Planning Process," *Hospitals* 51, no. 11 (June 1, 1977): 38.

3. J.M. Stengrevics, "Corporate Planning Needn't Be a Strait-jacket," in *The Wall Street Journal on Management*, edited by D. Asman and A. Meyerson (New York: New American Library, 1985), 140.

4. P. Drucker, *Management: Tasks, Responsibilities, Practices* (New York: Harper & Row, 1973), 125.

5. T. Peters, *Thriving On Chaos* (New York: Alfred A. Knopf, 1987), 79.

BIBLIOGRAPHY

Drucker, P.F. *Innovations of Entrepreneurship*. New York: Harper & Row, 1985.

Gleeson, S.U., et al. "The Four Ps of Billing, Credit, and Collection for Home Health Care Agencies." *Nursing Administration Quarterly* 8, no. 2 (Winter 1984): 74–81.

Goetz, J.F., and Smith, H.L. "Zero-Base Budgeting for Nursing Services." *Nursing Forum* 19, no. 2 (February 1980): 122–157.

Hicks, L.L. "Using Benefit-Cost and Cost-Effectiveness Analyses in Health-Care Resource Allocation." *Nursing Economics* 3, no. 2 (March-April 1985): 78–84.

Hoffman, F.M. *Financial Management for Nurse Managers*. Norwalk, CT: Appleton-Century-Crofts, 1984.

Knollmueller, R.N. *The Community Health Nursing Supervisor: A Handbook for Community/Home Care Managers*. New York: National League for Nursing, 1986.

McCloskey, J.C.; Gardner, D.L.; and Johnson, M.R. "Costing Out Nursing Services: An Annotated Bibliography." *Nursing Economics* 5, no. 5 (September/October 1987): 245–253.

Sovie, M.D. "Managing Nursing Resources in a Constrained Economic Environment." *Nursing Economics* 3, no. 2 (March-April 1985): 85–94.

Strasen, L. "Standard Costing/Productivity Model for Nursing." *Nursing Economics* 5, no. 4 (July-August 1987): 158–164.

Tonges, M.C. "Quality With Economy: Doing the Right Things for Less." *Nursing Economics* 3, no. 4 (July-August 1985): 205–211.

chapter 14

Management of Materials, Technology, and Product Lines

Nurses who choose to become head nurses, coordinators, or supervisors do so out of a desire to improve patient care by better management. Although she will certainly apply her experience at the bedside and in the home and community to her new position, the newly hired nurse manager must contend with mastering new skills. Her clinical competencies alone are not adequate to manage the business of the unit. Along with determining staffing requirements and setting performance goals, the first-line nurse manager is responsible for the supplies and equipment used on her unit. When resources are constrained, this takes on greater importance. In today's health care economy there are generally more uses for funds than there are funds. How limited funds are allocated becomes the first-line manager's decision. The first-line nurse manager has to formulate strategies that enable the work of the unit to continue in spite of a scarcity of supplies, and without jeopardizing patient care.

Under a prospective payment system, decisions tend to become cost-driven. Previously, patients could be charged the prevailing price of the services, including the cost of whatever supplies may have been used for patient care. It was not uncommon, for instance, to have specific charges on the bill for bandages. Under current Medicare reimbursement practices, hospitals receive one fee for the hospital stay, and cannot charge for services or supplies in excess of the predetermined rate.

The first-level nurse manager has to be cognizant of these considerations in planning the resource requirements for her unit. The cost of products, as well as their utility and benefit to the patient, are factors that must be weighed in her decision making. Assessment of supply requirements, conservation of supplies, inventory controls, and collaboration with other units could help avoid the necessity for a rationing mechanism. A careful system of product selection assures that the best product will be purchased at the best price.

Materials management has implications beyond the aforementioned financial considerations. The growth in medical technology has added another dimension to this area. As technology becomes more integral to patient care it is quickly moving outside the hospital and clinic walls. The effects of technology on the patient and his or her family—how it is explained, understood, and accepted by the patient and the family—must be managed as well. As if this were not enough, computers are being introduced at all levels of management in all settings. For the first-line nurse manager who has little knowledge of or exposure to computer technology, this may be a daunting experience. However, once staff are well trained and the computers are integrated into an overall managerial approach, the new technology has proven to be an indispensable management tool.

This chapter will briefly describe some approaches to the issue of material resource management that may prove valuable to the first-line manager.

INVENTORY CONTROL

The move to a prospective payment system in the 1980s has led to increased cost awareness in acute care settings. In most health care delivery settings the first-line manager has the responsibility for materials management. Strasen reports that approximately 15 percent of a hospital's "non-wage expenses" are related to supplies; this represents a significant portion of the institution's budget.[1] Inventory management is an internal control mechanism to track supply usage as related to the ordering and purchasing of supplies. The goal of any inventory system is to keep an accurate record of supply usage so that adequate stock is on hand at all times. The challenge is to determine the correct inventory level so that supplies are not ordered in excess of need and yet meet the demand without running low. One hazard of overstocking is having outdated supplies on hand that cannot be used.

Depending on how the system is organized, the head nurse may have the authority to order certain supplies directly from vendors, or she may be required to requisition all supplies from central stock. Regardless, the nurse manager must be able to calculate supply usage on her unit and determine appropriate inventory standards. This requirement pertains to all items that are kept on the unit in quantity, such as intravenous fluids, intravenous tubing, gauze bandages, preoperative kits, even linen. Strasen[2] provides a simple calculation by which to estimate material usage and when to reorder:

Step 1. Identify the average number of items used per day on the unit.
Step 2. Identify the lead time required for ordering the item.
Step 3. Identify the level of safety stock of the item.

Reorder point = average daily use × lead time + safety stock

This calculation is based on usage norms rather than on individual requests. Given the unpredictable nature of the acute care setting, the supply of certain items may fluctuate depending on the rate of admissions, transfers, and discharges on a unit. Therefore, nurse managers need to allow some margin when estimating the level of safety stock for their work area. It is also important for the nurse manager to know what action(s) to take when supplies run out prior to receiving replacement stock. If the system is such that supplies are only available from central stock during the day, even in emergency situations, this will have to be allowed for in the inventory planning.

The laundry service is another variation of this sort of system. Sometimes it is the laundry department that determines inventory levels for the nursing unit. For example, the laundry might calculate linen supply according to various methods: the number of beds per unit; daily census per unit; average patient census per unit; or past linen usage practices of a unit. The nurse manager should ask how the norms are established, since a unit with 28 patients who are up and around will obviously require fewer linens than a unit with 28 bedbound patients. If number of beds per unit is used to calculate norms in an institution with major differences in patient populations from unit to unit, then problems of linen supply might be solved merely by changing the criterion by which supplies are determined. The same principle, of course, pertains to other supply items.

Any system based on norms should have a mechanism built into it that allows flexibility at times when the unit being supplied has requirements above or below its norm. Often a flow chart will show that the norms are adequate but that the system lacks flexibility in coping with fluctuating needs.

In organizations where a unit manager handles inventory and ordering of samples, the nurse manager should not abdicate her responsibility for overall unit coordination. She should work closely with the unit manager and insist that she be kept apprised of materials usage on her unit—especially should any irregularities occur.

STAFF INVOLVEMENT IN MATERIALS MANAGEMENT

As end users, staff members can provide valuable information as to the quantity and quality of supplies and equipment used in the work area. It falls to the first-line nurse manager to educate her staff to the pertinent aspects of resource allocation and usage. As part of their responsibilities, staff are expected to account accurately for the supplies they use. For example, in some institutions intravenous fluids are stocked on the unit but are charged to the individual patient upon use. If the requisition slip is not filled out, the hospital will not be paid for the fluids used, and the unit may have difficulty obtaining replacement stock. Staff need to understand the consequences of their actions in terms of how they are likely to affect hospital and unit finances.

In spite of the pressures exerted by cost containment efforts, hospitals and health care systems in general are thought of as wealthy institutions capable of absorbing a certain amount of loss. Sometimes, in an effort to save themselves time and effort, nurses use supplies injudiciously without realizing the cost implications (e.g., leaving unit supplies at the patient bedside as a convenience, stashing items that are known to run out).

The nurse manager who involves staff members in a review of supply systems will accomplish two ends. First, most staff are good at identifying supplies they use most, what runs short, and how they might economize. Secondly, staff are more likely to cooperate when the nurse manager ties cost savings to the budget than when they are simply told to cut down on supply waste. The nurse manager who takes the time to investigate an item that appears to be "overused" may learn, for example, that the current brand of disposable pads are so small and tear so easily that three times the usual number of pads are being used. This information allows for making changes that are satisfactory to both staff and budget. A positive approach to the staff gives them credit for being professionals who have accountability for the unit and who share in the problem of managing fewer resources.

MATERIALS AND SERVICES PROVIDED BY OTHER DEPARTMENTS

Problems often arise when a material or service is provided by another department. This situation is particularly difficult in today's large health care organization, where multiple departments must integrate their services and supplies to provide patient care.

At one time in nursing's history the first-line manager (as head nurse) had great power and authority in her domain. Everyone working on the unit reported to her; everyone could be dismissed—with minimal justification required—if she so desired. The mop man reported to the head nurse. So did the ward secretary, if one existed. Her nursing staff was hers to command. Supply and support services as well as nursing care came under her jurisdiction. Her staff prepared the patients' meals and cleaned beds between patients. If a patient needed to be taken to another department, it was one of the nurses who wheeled him there. Equipment was cleaned, rewrapped, and even autoclaved in a small unit on the floor. In such an environment, all these support activities could be orchestrated to contribute optimally to the basic function of the unit, the provision of care.

In today's institution these support services and many others are likely to be provided by departments that are often only tangentially connected to the nursing department in the organizational scheme. At first most nursing departments gladly surrendered support functions to other departments because they were "not nursing." This decentralizing movement, when it began, was heralded by nurses as a great advance that was "freeing nurses to do nursing."

No revised system is without flaws, however, and there were unseen pitfalls in the new order of things. The chief flaw is that, while support services are "not nursing," if they are not performed correctly they can adversely affect the quality of nursing. Patient transportation is "not nursing," but poor transportation services cause sick patients to wait too long on uncomfortable stretchers in cold corridors. Dietary services are "not nursing," but late meals, delivered cold, impair the appetites and nutrition of ill patients. Slow housekeeping services may force critically ill patients to wait for hours in crowded admitting rooms for available bed space. The same point may be made concerning providers of materials. Stocking four-by-fours may not be "nursing," but nursing suffers when none is available. Simply put, failures in materials provision lines and support services create failures in nursing care.

When such services are shifted out of nursing's control, it is inevitable that the workers in those services will adopt goals that are not related to nursing. For example, the transportation aide might not be as concerned about the nursing needs of a person whom he transports as he will be about doing the "normal" number of transfers expected of him by his superior. The housekeeping aide sees his job as doing so many rooms, not as allowing Mr. Jones, who needs rest, to get into his bed faster. The supply clerk may actually "punish" nursing for using what he perceives to be "too many" sheets, pads, or suture sets. The same point may be made for all support services that are detached from nursing.

In an environment where critical support services and supplies are removed from the head nurse's control, she must achieve her goals by use of negotiation. Thus her relationship with the heads of organizational units controlling support services and supplies may be critical to achievement of her own goals.

At no time is that coordination more sensitive and difficult than when resources are being cut institution-wide. The laundry, under its own mandate to cut costs, will not greet a request for additional services with pleasure, however justifiable the request. The dietary department will not wish to implement a vastly improved system of tray delivery if it adversely affects the department's budget.

When such services and supplies are ill provided, they become obstructions to care rather than supports. The problem for the nurse manager is double-edged. If her staff are permitted to compensate for deficiencies in service, the negligent departments are "rewarded" for poor performance with less work.

Yet if nursing fails to make up for poor service, then patient care suffers. Wilsea finds support services to be critically deficient in sample hospitals of one large city. She summarizes:

> Participant responses to open-ended questions revealed that nurses performed these "non-nursing" down-skilled activities because of: 1) the time factor involved in an ancillary department's lack of cooperation or responsiveness to unit needs, which might therefore compromise daily unit work flow or patient safety and care needs; 2) inadequate daily unit supplies from other departments; 3) the shortage of staff in an ancillary department; 4) inadequate amounts of unit equipment; 5) malfunctioning equipment; 6) limited or no ancillary services available in the evenings or on weekends; 7) inadequate unit ancillary staff, such as ward clerks.
>
> Nursing interviews further revealed a high degree of frustration associated with non-nursing activities, a verbalized general sense of responsibility to the patient for performance of these activities in the absence of others, and a lack of responsiveness by nursing management to staff nurses' requests for equipment and/or supplies.[3]

Notice that Wilsea found deficits in nursing management's sensitivities to the supply and equipment problems as well as in the performance by support services.

PRODUCT SELECTION

Health care organizations spend billions of dollars a year on equipment and supplies used in patient care. Given the vast expenditures on materials, it is critical that products are carefully selected to meet required standards at the most economical price. In an effort to economize, hospitals, long-term care facilities, and home care agencies are forming buying groups to increase their purchasing power.[4]

When mistakes are made in choosing supplies, they are generally costly. Some institutions have introduced a policy of product standardization to eliminate different brands and variations of the same item within the organization. Selecting products for the institution is a major decision and should be based on objective data. Often decisions are made by the department of central supply without consultation, in which case they may be based on cost alone, with little or no attention to the quality or utility of a product. A better idea would be to make use of nursing staff expertise to evaluate and select new products. One approach is to organize a committee with interdisciplinary representation to review recommendations for proposed products; this provides a more objective and informed evaluation of equipment and supplies.[5,6]

A formal product-review committee should follow a specific format. Often a trial evaluation is done to gather information on a product's dependability, durability, and effectiveness, and to make comparisons with competitive products. If it is a new product the committee will want to determine the purpose and any potential problems involved with the product. Units that participate in a trial evaluation collect data to aid in the decision making. Safety and quality data as well as patient responses to the product will be useful. The committee should consider such data as well as cost-benefit analyses, compatibility with other products, and the deduction of conversion costs, if any, from any potential savings.

Regardless of whether or not such a product selection program is in place, the nurse manager should solicit information from staff regarding new products and channel the information to the proper department. The nurse manager should be aware of any new product to be introduced as well as what it will involve (e.g., new protocols, special training, or disposal of old stock). The goal remains to get the highest value from each product at the lowest cost. The nurse manager is in a position to help ensure that products and decisions concerning staff contribute to high-quality health care.

PRODUCT LINE MANAGEMENT

The push is on in health care to reduce spending and concentrate on revenue-producing activities to bolster dwindling profit margins. Nursing, while considered integral to the overall activity of the health care organization, has not normally been identified as a department that delivers a distinct and marketable product. This is changing, however. The business literature, replete with examples of entrepreneurial success stories, is finding a new audience within nursing.

Nurse executives who have faced severe budget cuts have come to view innovation and entrepreneurism as survival tactics in the newly competitive arena of health care. A recent outgrowth of this strategy is the conceptualization of nursing as a product line to be developed, managed, and marketed to specific user groups.[7,8] Increasingly, home care agencies and hospitals are relating to nursing as a "product to be defined, priced, marketed, and sold."[9] Some have taken this perspective as an imperative to cost-out nursing services as a variable billing item. This effort has entailed defining various dimensions of nursing practice: What is nursing worth? Who uses nursing's services? What strategy promotes nursing to its best advantage?

Other nursing executives have taken a different direction and undertaken such creative ventures as packaging and promoting nursing by-products, including quality assurance tools and continuing education programs.[10] Nursing departments that take this approach create an environment in which creativity and innovation are rewarded. The first-line nurse manager is encouraged to explore new ideas that will enhance nursing care delivery. Peters, in *Thriving on Chaos*, emphasizes the advantages of pursuing fast-paced innovation and advises: "Become a Johnny-one-note: Wherever you go in the organization ask about the small starts on innovative new products or services, or on tools to expand or differentiate (add value to) current products or services."[11]

This is a new orientation for nurses, who are taught to use their knowledge and skills to care for the needs of others. In the past they have preferred to leave the business side of patient care to someone else, even though this has not always proven to be wise. Product-line management may represent an opportunity to take advantage of an adverse situation and to bring about a positive outcome for nursing.

First-line managers have an ideal vantage point for evaluating what will "sell" to the consumer. Often it is simply a matter of changing one's perspective. Kanter describes entrepreneurism as "the willingness to move beyond received wisdom, to combined ideas from unconnected sources, to embrace change as an opportunity to test limits. [Entrepreneurs] measure themselves not by the standards of the past (how far they have come) but by visions of the future (how far they have yet to go)."[12] For example, there may be a need expressed for increased diabetic teaching. Rather than seeing this as another demand being placed on an already overextended staff, an entrepreneurial nurse may see it as an opportunity to develop a profitable self-learning module for patients and their families.

Some maternity centers, in response to a perceived consumer need, have produced videos that demonstrate basic care of the newborn for sale to new parents. This capitalizes on several trends: the increased participation of both parents in child care activities; the consumer's growing receptivity to educational videos; the knowledge that learning is improved with repeated demonstration; and the focus on convenience and customized packaging.

Those nursing departments that have embraced product-line management cite (among other positive outcomes) professional growth, increased visibility and prestige for the department, and new income sources.[13,14]

QUALITY SERVICE AND CUSTOMER SATISFACTION

It has been said that "good service often leaves no trail." Poor-quality work, however, will seldom go unnoticed. Consumer perceptions regarding the care they receive are of growing interest to health care providers. The rise in the number of alternative delivery systems has put health care deliverers in competition for clients. Patients' satisfaction will influence the degree to which they comply with treatment, how often they return to a provider, and which provider they choose. Consumer satisfaction may be shaped by direct experience, expectations, or word-of-mouth endorsements. The emphasis on patient satisfaction reflects a trend in which consumers are increasingly holding health care professionals accountable for their performance.

Health care is beginning to regard patients not as one-time purchasers but as potential lifelong customers. The goal is to develop a continuing relationship with patients so they will come back to the facility for an array of services ranging from home care to a smoking-cessation program. This is in keeping with Peters's description of the customer as an "appreciating asset"—i.e., a source of word-of-mouth referrals.[15]

Studies of patient satisfaction indicate that nursing is the most critical factor contributing to overall satisfaction with a hospital.[16] This should not be surprising given that nurses, on duty 24 hours a day, are the most prominent care givers during a patient's stay in the hospital. However, what is not entirely certain is the relationship between the patient's and the professional's notions of quality care. Patient satisfaction may be determined more by the quality of the personal interaction than by the quality of the clinical intervention. This is not to say that nurses can get away with poor care as long as they are compassionate, but it points out the need to analyze the nature of the impact that nurses have on the patient environment.

Peters emphasizes the importance of the nurse to the organization in monetary terms: "Upon finding that the average nurse managed $2 million in business each day, [one hospital administrator] mounted an aggressive program to enhance the status of the nursing department."[17] That observation should give the first-line nurse manager cause for thought as well.

MANAGING TECHNOLOGY

Nurses, whatever their area of practice, are faced with the rapid proliferation of medical technology. From sophisticated pacemakers, defibrillators, ventilators, and kidney dialysis machines to the more modest infusion pumps and hoya lifts, nurses must learn to master the mechanical devices that populate the health care environment.

In order to provide safe, high-quality care, nurses should have a clear understanding of the equipment in use—its purpose, its potential effect on treatment, and any risks involved. The first-line nurse manager must ascertain that devices are in safe working order and provide staff members with the resources to learn how to operate the equipment properly. As more and more court decisions are holding institutions liable for injuries resulting from malfunctioning equipment, this managerial responsibility becomes all the more crucial.

Medical technology threatens to become so commonplace that it goes unnoticed by everyone except the patient. What may be familiar to the nurse may be quite foreign to the patient and his family. For example, an infusion pump to monitor intravenous therapy may be placed at the patient's bedside without explanation, because the nurse no longer regards it as high-tech. However, if its alarm should sound, the patient is still likely to be frightened. Nurse managers might discuss with their staff how their nursing treatment and care plans should address technology's effects on the patient, what difficulties it may present, and its acceptance by the patient and family.[18] Henderson says this about nursing in a high-technology environment:

> Nursing has never been more important than in this age when the comforting, caring presence and touch of the nurse enables the institutionalized patient to tolerate invasive, often frightening and sometimes painful technology. In home care as well, the nurse is teacher and demystifies the machines and teaches the prescribed regimen.[19]

For a discussion of the ethical dilemmas presented by medical advancements, refer to Chapter 9.

TECHNOLOGY MOVES INTO HOME CARE

Technology and the advanced therapies it offers have expanded into the home care setting. Cost containment pressures have made home care treatment a cost-effective alternative to inpatient care. In the past, the first-line manager in home care seldom had to worry about advanced technology. Now she must adapt to the introduction of intravenous antibiotic therapy, self-care diagnostics, insulin delivery devices, and cardiac monitoring devices, among other technologies now used in the home. The home care manager who supervises older staff must see to it that they are adequately prepared to handle equipment that they have not previously used in their practice or, possibly, even seen before.

In preparing for the advance of new home therapies the nurse manager should investigate the trends in her geographical region. She should find out what the competition is doing in this area. It is likely that she will have to plan to accommodate client demands for the sophisticated devices and technologies being adapted for home use. Budgetary considerations may limit her options for extensive educational programs for her staff, yet not offering them may cripple the agency's ability to compete.

The innovative nurse manager might establish a mutually beneficial relationship with a durable medical equipment (DME) vendor or a pharmaceutical distributor. An arrangement might be made to have the vendors assist in staff education programs or to offer their equipment for demonstration. The agency should also learn what equipment can be leased rather than purchased, the difference in cost to the patient, how billing is handled, what costs are incurred by the patient for whom high-tech treatment is indicated, and what is covered under Medicare and conventional medical insurance plans. This inquiry will provide the agency with valuable information with which the staff can help patients who use these therapies to make appropriate decisions.

As medical technology permeates the home care market, decisions that confront the nurse manager in the acute care setting will also appear in the community. The issue of who can afford these expensive treatment modalities may create an ethical dilemma for the nurse practicing in home care. The first-line manager will have to deal with her own feelings regarding this before she can help her staff to sort out their priorities.

COMPUTERS

The introduction of sophisticated information systems and their integration into a unit's operational routine has accelerated the collection and analysis of patient data. Initially, computer operations were confined to the finance department to automate the hospital's accounting system. Often this included automating the admitting department as well, to allow immediate entry of pertinent patient information. Computerization expanded into other departments primarily in order to enter patient charges more efficiently. For several decades the presence of computers was hidden at the patient care level and certainly did not affect nursing practice.

More recently, some facilities began to automate various aspects of the patient record. Others found it difficult or impossible to justify the cost of such computerization at first, but the onset of DRGs changed all that. Seemingly overnight, hospitals wanted systems in place to track patients according to their diagnosis and to integrate all related data. Without appropriate data collection, institutions could not press for reimbursement under the DRG system. It was thus the need of institutions for financial reimbursement that fueled the frenzy to computerize. Once sophisticated patient data were available they also served as the basis for a new control system. It was possible to identify, for example, which patient cases were profitable and which were not, which physicians had thrifty modes of case management and which did not. Such knowledge led to an unprecedented involvement of institutional administration in the practice of medicine.

The importance of this sudden computerization of the health care industry must not be overlooked. Virtually overnight the whole industry—down to the smallest rural hospital—was drawn into the twentieth century model of business management through information systems.

Nursing has also recognized the need for more complete managerial data. For instance, nursing departments have noted the value of linking staffing patterns and work schedules to patient classification systems. Some directors have developed software to monitor nursing care costs based on the DRG system. As computers become a mainstay of nursing operations, applications involving computers are increasing for such nursing activities as care planning, Kardex systems, charting, and patient assessment. It is predicted that in the near future computers will not only be in the nursing office but also at the bedside. More sophisticated institutions already have such a capacity.

Since much data collection and computer usage now occur on the nursing unit, it is critical that first-line managers be involved when computer systems are purchased or modified. Extensive sunk costs prevent most institutions from changing systems, even if they find they have selected unwisely. First-line managers should make certain that they get the best system their institution can afford at the outset. The first-line manager who must live with the system should be satisfied that the choice will optimize both her management efficiency and the patient care under her supervision.

The rate of change in computer technology has been phenomenal. What may be the state of the art one year is obsolete the next. Health care organizations can ill afford to invest in hardware or software that will not keep up with their information-processing needs. Nursing must also take a cautious approach. Nurse managers who participate on committees that make decisions about computer hardware and software should familiarize themselves with current system capabilities. The ability to integrate clinical and financial data across departments is critical. Compatibility of systems is another important consideration. While operations vary from organization to organization, there is no reason to keep reinventing the wheel. Excellent software packages have been developed for all sorts of data needs, and a thorough researching of what is on the market is essential.

Although staff nurses accept the proliferation of medical technology as enhancements to patient care, they do not always show this same attitude toward computers. The first-line nurse manager is challenged to influence staff members toward accepting computerization in their practice. The most important thing to remember is that everyone can learn to use computers. The myth that computers are comprehensible only to scientific whiz-kids must be dispelled. It is no more necessary for the nurse to understand the internal mechanisms of a computer than to know how an EKG machine works. A useful approach is to think of the computer as a huge file that stores data in various compartments.

The nurse manager herself must be open-minded regarding both the introduction of computers and her staff's response to them. Her ongoing assessment of staff will assist in determining appropriate inservice education for them. If a liaison nurse who is well versed in computer technology is available, she may serve as an expert resource for the head nurse and staff.

The first-line manager and the personnel she supervises have to feel comfortable with a system to use it well. They should have time on the computer when they won't be disturbed, to "try it out." If the head nurse or staff members have a problem or complaint, it should be shared with whoever is coordinating the computerization project. Chances are good that others have encountered it as well.

Once a system has been installed, the first-line manager should assign a particular staff member or members to daily computer operations. Often this is the unit secretary. The nurse manager should also master the techniques of using the computer so that she can better supervise her staff. Key personnel on each shift should be fully oriented, to ensure that knowledgeable back-ups are always available.

Nurse managers also need to know how much and what kind of support is available from the software consultant and from in-house computer staff. Computer support is essential at all stages, but it is especially critical upon initial installation.

Johnson suggests forming a users group to share information with other hospitals that use the same software.[20] This idea may also be helpful within the organization. The internal group could bring together professional staff from different disciplines to get updates on new software applications, to explore solutions to problems that appear, and to brainstorm on possible innovations for the system.

Computers are an everyday tool in most companies today. If nursing is to compete for resources, nurses must be computer-literate. The vast flow of information must be organized into a reliable and accurate database that can be used to support nursing's position within the organization.

SUMMARY

As the pace of change in health care accelerates, the demands on the nurse manager increase. Cost containment and high-technology bring more responsibilities and greater managerial challenges—the economical use of supplies, the introduction of computers, and the education of staff and patients to high-tech equipment. The first-line nurse manager must have an awareness of how these affect the quality of care. This chapter documented several of the wide-ranging activities of the nurse manager.

It is not uncommon in health care facilities for supplies to be ordered by the secretary or ward clerk. In some settings, it may be thought of as simply a matter of restocking the shelves. However, in an era of cost containment, supplies are less plentiful and this simple chore becomes a major responsibility for the nurse manager. Materials management is more than keeping the shelves stock; materials management, when done expertly, can reduce expenses and improve the operations of the unit. It requires the nurse manager to learn the systems in her institution and to understand how they interact with her unit. This will probably include mastering inventory control, purchasing, and accounting mechanisms.

Coordinating support services presents another challenge for the nurse manager who is often in the position of negotiating with other departments. This can range from working with dietary staff to accommodate late admissions to consulting on the purchase of new equipment. While all departments ostensibly exist for service to the patient, it is often up to the nurse manager to ensure that the patient is well served.

The traditional role of the head nurse may not have encompassed any of these tasks, and neither was it expected that she market nursing and the organization to the public. Yet today these activities are vital to a well-managed facility.

NOTES

1. L. Strasen, *Key Business Skills for Nurse Managers* (New York: J.B. Lippincott Co., 1987), 68.

2. Ibid., 245.

3. M.J. Wilsea, *Identification of Nonnursing Activities of Medical-Surgical Staff Nurses: An Observational Field Study* (unpublished dissertation, Teachers College, Columbia University, 1987), 177–178.

4. E. Eusebio, et al., "Product Selection in the Hospital: Controlling Cost," *Nursing Management* 16, no. 3, (March 1985): 44–46.

5. Ibid., 45.

6. M. Dickerson, "Product Evaluation: A Strategy for Controlling a Supply and Equipment Budget," in J.C. Scherubel, ed. *Patients and Purse Strings II* (New York: National League for Nursing, 1988), 465–468.

7. R.A. Anderson, "Products and Product-Line Management in Nursing," *Nursing Administration Quarterly* 10, no. 1 (Fall 1985): 65–72.

8. M. Crawford and M.L. Fisher, "Marketing: The Creative Advantage," *Journal of Nursing Administration* 16, no. 12 (December 1986): 17–20.

9. Anderson, 66.

10. J.E. Johnson, et al., "Financial Management Series: Marketing Your Nursing Product Line— Reaping the Benefits," *Journal of Nursing Administration* 17, no. 11 (November 1987): 31.

11. T. Peters, *Thriving on Chaos* (New York: Alfred A. Knopf, 1987), 194.
12. R.M. Kanter, "Innovation—The Only Hope for Times Ahead," *Nursing Economics* 3, no. 3 (May-June 1985): 181.
13. Crawford, 20.
14. Johnson, 32.
15. Peters, 211.
16. R.W. Lenke, "Identifying Customer Satisfaction Through Patient Surveys," *Health Progress* 68, no. 2. (March 1987): 56–58.
17. Peters, 198.
18. D. Carnevali, "Nursing Perspectives in Health Care Technology," *Nursing Administration Quarterly* 9, no. 4 (Summer 1985): 10–18.
19. V. Henderson, "The Essence of Nursing and High Technology," *Nursing Administration Quarterly* 9, no. 4 (Summer 1986): 7.
20. J.M. Johnson, "Implementing a Computer Software System," *Journal of Nursing Administration* 17, no. 10 (October 1987): 16–21.

BIBLIOGRAPHY

Barone-Ameduri, P. "Equipment Trials Make Sense." *Nursing Management* 17, no. 6 (June 1986): 43–44.

Coddington, D.C.; Palmquist, L.E.; and Trollinger, W.V. "Strategies for Survival in the Hospital Industry." *Harvard Business Review* 63, no. 3 (May-June 1985): 129–138.

Eriksen, L.R. "Patient Satisfaction: An Indicator of Nursing Care Quality?" *Nursing Management* 18, no. 7 (July 1987): 31–35.

Finkler, S.A. "Microcomputers in Nursing Administration—A Software Overview." *Journal of Nursing Administration* 15, no. 4 (April 1985): 18–23.

Innovations in Nursing Service. New York: National League for Nursing, 1986.

Johantgen, M.E., and Parrinello, K. "Microcomputers: Turning the Database into Unit Management Information." *Nursing Management* 18, no. 2 (February 1987): 30–38.

King, D.J. "Designing A Forms Management Program." *Nursing Management* 17, no. 6 (June 1986): 50–52.

Krampf, S., and Robinson, S. "Managing Nurses' Attitudes Toward Computers." *Nursing Management* 15, no. 7 (July 1984): 29, 32–34.

Lafferty, K.D. "Patient Care Systems vs. Financial Systems: The Cost Justification Battle." *Nursing Management* 18, no. 7 (July 1987): 51–55.

Larson, E., and Maciorowski, L. "Rational Product Evaluation." *Journal of Nursing Administration* 16, nos. 7, 8 (July/August 1986): 31–36.

McAlindon, M.N., et al. "Choosing the Hospital Information System: A Nursing Perspective." *Journal of Nursing Administration* 17, no. 10 (October 1987): 11–15.

McMillan, J.R. "Measuring Consumer Satisfaction to Improve Quality of Care." *Health Progress* 68, no. 2 (March 1987): 54–55, 76, 78, 80.

Mikuleky, M.P., and Ledford, C. *Computers in Nursing.* Menlo Park, CA: Addison-Wesley Publishing Co., 1987.

Mowry, M.M., and Korpman, R.A. *Managing Health Care Costs, Quality, and Technology,* Rockville, MD: Aspen Publishers, Inc., 1986.

Naisbitt, J. *Megatrends*. New York: Warner Books, 1982.

Roe, W.I., and Schneider, G.S. "Technology Review: High-tech Moves into Home Care Market with Cardiac, Nutritional Therapies." *Business and Health* 2, no. 5 (April 1985): 52–53.

Stein, R.E. "Providing Home Care for the Seriously Ill Young." *Business and Health* 4, no. 3 (January 1987): 26–30.

Stuerke, N. "Computers *Can* Advance Nursing Practice." *Nursing Management* 15, no. 7 (July 1984): 29, 32–34.

Super, K.E. "Product Line Management Needs Careful Implementation." *Modern Healthcare* 17, no. 10 (May 8, 1987): 99.

Walters, S. "Computerized Care Plans Help Nurses Achieve Quality Patient Care." *Journal of Nursing Administration* 16, no. 11 (November 1986): 33–39.

chapter 15

Management Concepts

Management concepts are discussed throughout this book, but this chapter will summarize managerial principles not addressed in detail elsewhere. The reader is referred to Chapters 5 and 6 for other significant managerial content that is not repeated in this chapter, namely notions of productivity and strategic planning. In essence, Chapters 5 and 6 address newer notions of management while this chapter summarizes traditional management concepts that have been sustained by their continued relevance to the work of the manager in the organizational setting.

Managing in the health care field is both similar to and different from managing in other settings. General principles of management certainly pertain, but the health care field, and nursing in particular, present unique problems and practices. The content in this chapter will review general management precepts, applications of which will relate to the environment in which the first-line nursing manager practices.

THE MANAGER'S CONTEXT

Information on managing in the organizational setting has been categorized and approached in numerous ways over the years. No interpretation is comprehensive or clarion-clear. There are many different ways in which to conceptualize and organize the knowledge. Whether one takes a historical approach or an analytic approach, the task remains complex. There is an advantage in being able to view the management role from various different perspectives. One approach may be successful in a given circumstance when another fails.

Management, briefly, is the complex job of managing people, systems, and materiel within an organization to accomplish defined goals. The manager works in and through others. Managers also work in radically different environments. Every manager is probably convinced that his or her business is the most difficult and the most important, and familiarity with a particular business's challenges and problems reinforces that sort of thinking.

Nevertheless, health care management takes place in an environment with its own unique set of challenges and problems. Our examination of the context in which health care management occurs might as well begin with the beneficial and pleasant components of the environment.

Health care as a field employs many persons who are professional, who work toward internalized standards of excellence in performance, and who generally are—at least once were—motivated to help other human beings in need. On the whole, the first-line manager will work with good people who are positively motivated and trying to do a good job.

Moreover, the health care environment always provides new things to learn, new challenges for performance. There is an intellectual content to the work. One can continue to grow professionally without surcease. The highly educated nurse can always find new areas of interest, or she can herself do research to contribute to the knowledge of her field. In essence the first-line manager has the opportunity to work with bright and interesting people whose motivations are, by and large, altruistic.

Another rewarding factor is the patient side of the equation. Many affective rewards in health care work come from human beings who are grateful for the care they receive. Emotional rewards, on a one-to-one basis, are common when one does a job well.

Other aspects of the health care environment can be more fraught with problems. Just as working with good people is one of the chief benefits of the health care environment, so coping with frustrated, burned out, or incompetent employees can become a major drawback of first-line managing. The health care industry is labor-intensive, which means that people, not machines, constitute the chief tools of the manager. Where there are more people, there are more problems. Yet an automated assembly line with few problems would, by comparison, seem dull to most people who elect nursing as a career.

A nursing education sensitizes the manager to dealing with people, but dealing with people who must get the job done is not the same as dealing with patients. When with a patient, the nurse is concerned primarily with human needs. When dealing with staff, the manager must be sensitive both to human needs and organizational needs. The relationship is more complex. Ideally, an effective manager helps employees to reach their own goals while simultaneously serving organizational goals.

There are many problems in today's health care organizations that tax the capacities of the humans who serve in them. Nurses have always experienced the emotional press of working with people who are sick, traumatized, dying. Burn-out (however labeled) is always a possibility in such an emotion-laden situation. To this inherent problem the care environment adds the overlay of organizational intrigues.

Nurses have traditionally felt the pressures of being caught between physician, patient, and institutional demands. The present upheaval in the health care field has complicated and intensified those pressures, while creating new ones. Cost containment measures that often decrease human and other resources to critical levels; extensive administrative monitoring procedures; the shift in patient populations toward sicker patients whose care is more difficult to render—these are only a few of the pressure-increasing changes.

In such an environment it is particularly important that the first-line manager possess some conceptual framework of management that will enable her to consider her role and responsibilities in an organized and dispassionate manner. Concepts of management are tools that facilitate getting the job done. The more understanding that the manager has of how people work in organizations, the more effective she is likely to be.

MAPPING THE DOMAIN

Scott gives a useful interpretation of the various management approaches in the guise of organization theory.[1] His approach is, loosely, historical. He divides organization theories into three major groups: classical, neoclassical, and modern. These three domains serve as a useful framework for categorizing one's knowledge of the organization and the behavior of persons within it.

According to Scott, "classical" theory takes the perspective of formal organization. Hence the procedures of management have to do with understanding the formal organization as it might appear on its organization chart—who reports to whom, who is responsible for which tasks. "Neoclassical theory," in contrast, focuses on the human relations within the organization—how managers and workers behave, or should behave. Scott's "modern" school focuses on a systems approach to organization theory. To update Scott's classic work (first published in 1961) would require addition of the contemporary management theory that focuses on productivity, marketing, and strategic planning.

Classical Theory

Principles of management arising from the classical theory have to do with division of labor, scalar and functional processes, structure, and span of control. They prescribe how the work of an organization is distributed and meted out.

The Organization Chart

The easiest way to obtain the overall perspective of work distribution for any organization is to examine its organization charts. In an acute care setting work is often divided according to the various professional services and business functions. Each subunit, in turn, has its own pattern of organization. The most common pattern in the acute care setting is for nursing to manage its own professional services. The manager in charge of nursing, by whatever title (vice president, director), is typically responsible for all nursing services offered within the institution.

That pattern is not invariable, however; there are highly decentralized organizations in which professional services are dispersed. In such an organization, the nurses in ambulatory clinics might be accountable to administrators of the clinics rather than to a centralized department of nursing.

The organization charts are the graphic representations of the institution. Since the acute care hospital is one of health care's most complex organizational forms, it will be used as an illustration here. Most organization charts are positional—that is, they are organized by title and rank. Figure 15-1 demonstrates this construction. Notice that the controlling organizational principle here is time (days, evenings, nights).

Figure 15-2 shows an organization in which the controlling principle is geographic, and Figure 15-3 shows one in which the division has been made strictly on the basis of function. In practice, two or more principles may be used together to derive an organizational design. The aim is to find what works best in a given organization.

For most first-line managers in acute care, the principle that determines responsibility is geography. A head nurse, for example, usually has one or two geographic patient care units for which she is responsible. Community health managers may also have geographical territories, though these are usually defined on the basis of where the client lives rather than where the agency's buildings lie.

A small organization may have a single organization chart. More commonly, several charts (at various levels of managerial authority) will be necessary to

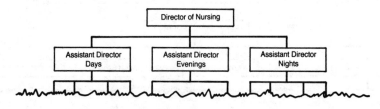

Figure 15-1 Positional Organization Chart

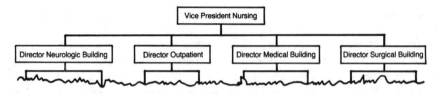

Figure 15-2 Organization Chart Based on Geographic Locations

describe a complex organization. In most cases a nursing division or department will compose its own chart to explain the distribution of its work.

The organization chart, whatever the bases for its work distribution, is a document that illustrates in pictorial form the hierarchical chains of authority. Figure 15-4 shows how the line of command is indicated in the diagram. Each box on the diagram shows a managerial position that is responsible for all boxes (positions, functions) branching from it at lower levels. The hierarchy of command is demonstrated in this line pattern.

In a line position, the employee is accountable to the persons above them on the organization chart and responsible for the persons (positions) beneath them. A line position is directly in the chain of command, from the highest-placed administrator to the lowest-level employee.

In addition to line positions, there are others that fall into the *staff* category. The staff position, in contrast to the line job, has only indirect responsibility to or for others in the line of command. The power of a staff position is an extension of the authority of the immediate superior of the person in the staff slot.

Figure 15-5 illustrates two staff (S-1 and S-2) positions. Notice that these incumbents are not in the direct, downward path of authority. They derive their positional authority from their boss, but indirectly (often in a coordinative manner). Staff position S-1 is held by an accountant responsible for the nursing budget.

Notice that the next level in the organization (next boxes off the direct line of authority) are assistant directors of nursing. The person holding the S-1 staff position is not technically "superior" to the assistant directors, although he or

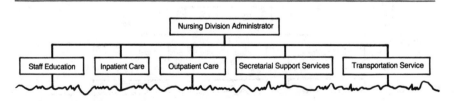

Figure 15-3 Functional Organization Chart

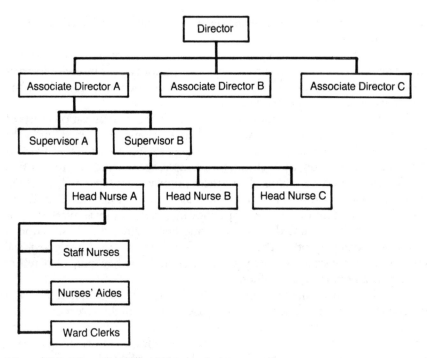

Figure 15-4 Hierarchical Line of Command

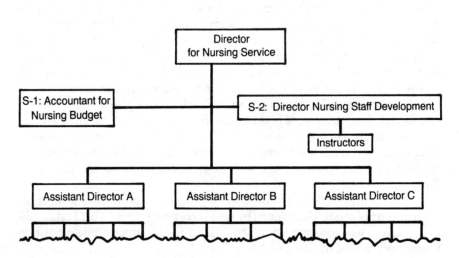

Figure 15-5 Line and Staff Patterns Mixed

she might have a major influence on how the budget within which they work is devised and managed.

Some positions have both staff and line authority. Position S-2 illustrates this. The staff development director has line authority over inservice instructors but a staff relationship with the community of nurses for whom the programs of inservice are planned.

The first-line manager should have access to all of the organization charts of her institution. She should know where her position and her staff "fit" with the rest of the organization. It is interesting to see how nursing work is distributed. In an acute care setting, for example, the nursing division is often divided into patient care units. The patient population is separated according to some classification scheme, such as medical and surgical cases on different units. Larger institutions use more specific categories; cardiovascular cases, for example, may be separated from endocrine ones. Often the classification is based on a criterion other than nursing. In the illustrations just given, the criteria were physician specialty categories, though they may also reflect corresponding nursing specialties.

In a community nursing program, the division of labor might follow a different principle. For example, geographic territory might have more importance than patient diseases or conditions because of travel necessities for staff. Even here, however, other principles might be employed in creating departments and units of operation. For example, there might be functional units that overlap as to geographic districts. An agency might have one department responsible for patients needing complex nursing care and another department managing patients who need care provided by a nurse's aide or homemaker.

Some aspects of nursing work call for departments other than patient-dictated specialties. In the acute care setting, for example, there may be such departments as inservice education, intravenous therapy, or even an office of nursing personnel management in a large institution. Seldom does a complex institution create all of its departments on the same principle. It is an issue of practical mix: What kinds of units are needed to get the work done?

Scalar division reflects the number of levels through which the work is distributed. For example, a highly centralized organization might have the following levels along the main vertical line of authority: director, associate directors, supervisors, head nurses. A decentralized organization, in contrast, might reduce this to two levels, with head nurses reporting directly to the director.

Span of control reflects the number of positions reporting to a superior. Span of control can be determined by simply counting the number of subordinate "boxes" with direct accountability lines to the superordinate position immediately above the boxes.

Issues of structure have to do with the relationships of positions and functions within an organization. In nursing organizations most relationships are those of line and staff, as discussed. Some organizations employ a third structure: a matrix design. In this design, positions are created that do not follow the principle of "unity of command," which dictates that each employee should have one and only one immediate superior. Such an arrangement is evident in the hierarchical line pattern shown in Figure 15-4.

The matrix organization, however, allows for more complex work relations. Table 15-1 shows a matrix organization. Notice that an employee in this design might have two (or maybe more) bosses. In this example the head nurse is responsible to two superiors: the supervisor and the clinical specialist whose patients are cared for on her unit.

Matrix organizations, like all others, have strengths and weaknesses. Employees may feel "caught" between the conflicting demands of two bosses. Other employees have been known to play one boss against another. When the interpersonal relations among all parties are excellent, a matrix allows for creative and productive new ways of organizing and achieving goals. The system thus has major vulnerabilities and offers unique opportunities. It always lacks, however, the simple clarity of the more usual hierarchical design.

Operational Principles

Span of control is one of the important management principles in the classical model. Span of control refers to the number of persons reporting to a single supervisor (the manager at any level). The span of control should ideally be such that the supervisor can give adequate supervision to all subordinates without being underused or unnecessary.

Several things help determine the ideal span of control in a given situation. First, the expertise of the subordinates must be considered. A manager with inexperienced subordinates cannot manage as many as if they were experienced, and so the span should be decreased if subordinates need a lot of direct supervision. Similarly, the more complex and unique the work being done, the smaller the desirable span of control. In contrast, if the work is repetitive and easily learned, and/or if the subordinates are experienced and competent in their jobs, a supervisor may be able to regulate a large number of subordinates with relative ease.

Another important principle of classical theory concerns scalar organization. Ideally there should be no more levels in an organizational hierarchy than are absolutely necessary. The greater the distance between the chief executive and the lowest worker, the more likely it is that the executive will be out of touch and unable to exercise effective control.

Table 15-1 Matrix Design

	Head Nurse, 3 West	Head Nurse, 3 East	Head Nurse, 4 East	Head Nurse, 4 West
Clinical Specialist (Cardiovascular)	X	X	X	X
Clinical Specialist (Respiratory)	X	X	X	X
Clinical Specialist (Rehabilitation)	X	X	X	X
Clinical Specialist (Endocrinology)	X	X	X	X

X = Staff nurses

Span of control and scalar levels interact. If one assumes an absolute number of employees in a given institution, this relationship is easy to see. If each supervisor has a large number of subordinates, there will be fewer scalar levels in the organization than if the opposite were true. An organization with few scalar levels is called a "flat" organization. With a wide span of control, fewer levels are necessary; a narrow span of control necessitates more levels and a "tall" organizational structure.

In nursing's past there have been preferences for both narrow and wide spans of control, flat and tall organizations. For example, over a decade ago there were attempts to promulgate increased scalar levels with a narrower span of control. This was labeled as the "consultative model." The theory was that a nurse supervisor with only a few subordinates could be a true teacher and consultant for those few. At present, the opposite model is usually advocated, with fewer levels and with each supervisor responsible for more subordinates. In acute care this model reaches its ultimate form when head nurses report directly to the director of nursing (only two layers and a broad span of control).

The head nurse with 24-hour responsibility for her unit, incidentally, usually breaks all the norms set by management texts for span of control. The number of subordinates under her is extremely high. Sometimes this is mitigated by an unofficial matrix organization in which evening and night supervisors act for the head nurse, i.e., substitute as the boss on offshifts. Sometimes such arrangements end up using matrix tactics such as coordination between the head nurse and the offshift supervisors to arrive at evaluations for employees.

In essence, the classical model of organization is not a single model but an amalgam of many theories. Most of these theories arose early in the history of management as a studied discipline. What ties these theories together is their belief that the key to management lies in the formal organization of the institution and the problems that are inherent in the organizational structure.

Neoclassical Theory

Neoclassical theory, according to Scott's taxonomic scheme, includes a large cluster of management theories that sought to compensate for the limitations of classical theory by looking at human relations within the organization. This general approach to management entails application of psychological or sociological principles to the work setting. The behavioral sciences introduced new foci to the study of management: the informal structure, interactions among work groups, leadership behaviors, conflict and its management, decision making, worker alienation, motivation, delegation, supervision, and power relationships, to name a few. Many of these elements are discussed elsewhere in this book.

While classical management theories deal primarily with organizational structure, neoclassical theories focus on humans and their interactive processes. Hence these two schools may be seen as complementary to each other rather than opposing. Both the organizational entity and its workers are important in a comprehensive view of management.

The uniting link among the various neoclassical theories is their shared focus on people as the essence of an organization, and on dynamic human processes rather than structure. Since the first-line manager may not have too much say about the way in which her organization is structured, the behavioral emphasis of neoclassical theory may have special significance for her.

Scott's neoclassical category covers a long period during which diverse management theories evolved. These theories are almost *too* diverse to be meaningfully classified together, except for their focus on people. Many take opposing positions. For example, one can find contrasting theories concerning conflict as an organizational principle. Some theories assume that conflict is bad and explore ways in which a manager can control and eliminate conflict in the work environment. Other theories advocate the selective use (and even creation) of conflict by the manager; these theories stress the power of conflict as a motivator and as a means to get the best production from workers. While such theories reach opposite conclusions as to management tactics, they can be seen to share the common neoclassical elements. That is, they focus on human behavior in organizations and on the ways in which a manager can manipulate human behavior to the desired ends. A few sample theories will be discussed here to illustrate the process-oriented, behavioral focus of neoclassical management thought. They are a small collection from an extensive literature.

Two major thrusts are distinguishable in neoclassical theories. Some focus on managers; others focus on workers. Still other theories concentrate on how the traits or behaviors of the two groups interact.

Studies of the Leader

Early studies exploring the leader (or manager) often tried to associate certain leadership characteristics with productivity and good management. These studies sought to identify the most important human traits of a good leader. The underlying premise was that if one could identify the traits of good leaders, then one could learn how to find them and promote them to positions where their leadership skills could be used. The diversity found in the traits of studied leaders led to abandonment of this approach. Now many theorists claim that leadership and/or management can be learned.

One of the most interesting behaviors addressed under the study of leadership behavior was that of problem solving/decision making. This subject will be used as an illustration of the leader/manager focus in neoclassical theories.

Problem Solving by the Manager

Problem solving is not the only skill needed by the manager, but it is certainly a primary one. To oversimplify, management is the successful balance of two behaviors: solving problems and achieving goals. Some eras, some situations require the focus to shift more toward one of these poles; other eras and other organizational circumstances reverse the emphasis. There is no permanent balance. The effective manager develops a sensitivity concerning which behavior requires the most attention at the moment.

While much management literature has addressed the process of problem solving (or decision making), the best formulation of the process still rests with the description given by the philosopher and educator, John Dewey. In Dewey's conceptualization, problem solving is the process by which people think; it is the pattern underlying one's logic.[2]

Problem solving for Dewey is specific; that is, it begins with a given problem for a particular person. The problem presents itself in a way that is anything but distinct. The problem is simply an obstruction, mental or physical, that presents itself to the individual—some undefined situation that keeps one from moving on. Often it may be perceived as an itch, a nagging puzzlement. Suppose, for example, that a head nurse sees a patient's irregular lab result on a test. It surprises her; somehow it doesn't "fit" with her expectations; it becomes an intellectual obstruction—a problem.

Notice that the laboratory report itself is not a problem. It became a problem only when it was conceived as such by a particular person. It is the head nurse's problem. If she had simply checked to see that the report was available and in the chart, it would not have given rise to a problem (unless it hadn't been there).

Having experienced the problematic itch, however, the head nurse begins the next step of problem solving: She tries to clarify the problem. Why, she asks herself, does the lab value surprise her? Why doesn't it seem right? In order to clarify the problem, the head nurse surveys the "environment" surrounding the problem. She does this in an attempt to define the problem more specifically. The environment surrounding this particular problem is not a "given" but consists of those elements that she thinks might be connected with the obstruction. In this case, the environment might consist of many things—how the patient looks, how the patient reasons, the patient's abilities, the patient's diagnosis, the patient's other lab results.

Suppose the head nurse examines all this. Now she is ready to define her problem in a more satisfactory way. The lab result, she tells herself, is in opposition to all the patient's clinical signs. Now she has a situation defined in a way that is more delimited than the original itch, but it may not yet be enough. She may not be certain of her assertion. This may lead her to study the patient's diagnosed condition in a text book (there may be things she doesn't know about the disease) and to study the lab variable (perhaps it has other meanings than those with which she is familiar). In other words, she expands or changes the "environment" of the problem as her inquiry leads her further.

However she does it, the head nurse keeps going back and forth between the environment of the problem and the formulation of the problem until she is satisfied that she has specified the problem. The anomalous laboratory report might even lead the nurse to question the physician's original diagnosis; it might lead in all sorts of directions. Let's assume in this case that her first analysis still holds: The test result is antithetical to everything else in the patient's status and diagnosis.

Now that she has a firm problem definition, she begins to search for solutions. The difference between problem definition and solution seeking is not absolute or rigid in problem solving. The whole process is a messy back-and-forth motion in which information gained at every stage may change both the problem formulation and the places where answers are sought.

In this particular case, notice that solving the head nurse's problem won't "resolve" an action situation; it won't prevent patient falls, it won't improve the patient's condition. But it will resolve the nurse's intellectual problem—the nagging uneasiness caused by the sense that all the evidence does not fit. Let's suppose that, once the problem has been defined, several solutions present themselves to the nurse. In a more formal process we might call these hypotheses. She starts with the most likely explanation and works her way through the options until she finds a solution that solves the problem (removes the obstruction).

In our example, we'll assume that the head nurse is fortunate: Her first proposed solution turns out to be accurate. Her tentative hypothesis takes the head nurse to the laboratory, where she inquires into laboratory processes and the processing of reports. She discovers that a medical technology intern was just dismissed for falsifying reports to cope with a heavy work load. She discovers that this technologist supposedly ran the reported test on her patient. She orders a repeat test on which the patient falls within normal limits for the problem variable.

A simple case, a definitive solution. But notice how far afield the nurse is from her initial investigation, from the "environment" in which she sought the initial definition of the problem. If her first hypothetical solution had not worked, then she would have had to move on to her second conjecture.

Notice that in this conception of problem solving, the problem only exists when it is perceived. The person's definition of the situation as problematic makes it so. The way she searches the environment will determine how she casts the problem. The problem definition will dictate the sorts of solutions that are sought. Her vision or lack thereof will determine the number and the quality of the solution considered.

Management literature of the neoclassical era had its own descriptions of problem solving. Many of these approaches used Dewey's process as a model. Simon's work on decision making in management inquired how effective managers were in their problem-solving activities. Unfortunately, his description of typical managerial decision making was not reassuring. Simon found that managers tended to classify problems along established dimensions and to make only a limited search for alternatives. Most managers, he found, constructed a simplified model of the real problem situation based on past experience and a particularized view of the problem stimulus. Decisions were usually made with incomplete knowledge of the consequences of the selected alternative, and not all possible alternatives were considered. Managers, said Simon, mostly used solutions that they had used in the past; the typical manager had a limited number of rules, programs, and actions that directed decision making.[3]

Later in the neoclassical period, Janis and Mann continued the study of managerial problem solving. Their work resulted in a number of recommendations to the manager concerning his problem solving. They suggested that the problem solver ask himself the following questions:

- Was a wide range of alternatives canvassed?
- Was the full range of objectives and values to be fulfilled canvassed?
- Were the costs weighed—positively, negatively, and in relation to the consequences for each alternative?
- Was there a search for new information concerning each alternative, and for new alternatives?
- Was new information assimilated and subjected to expert judgment?
- Were the consequences of all alternatives re-examined before a final decision was made?
- Were provisions made to implement courses of action for each contingency, each risk in the decision?[4]

Notice that in these examples of problem solving there was an abrupt shift from a focus on problem clarification to a concentration on analysis of the solution alternatives. The artificial simplicity of these examples may have had the effect of making problem solving seem mechanical and simple rather than the complex, "messy" process that it is.

Problem solving was only one leadership behavior studied in the neoclassical era. Other phenomena included leaders' use of power; their interpersonal strategies; leadership styles; identification and classification of the tasks to which they gave their attention; as well as their relationships with others, from board members to workers.

Studies of Interactions between Manager and Worker

Another thrust of neoclassical theory investigated the leader in relation to the worker. Several historically important studies in these manager-worker relations will be mentioned here.

The work of McGregor served as a bridge between studies of leadership and followership because it looked at the manager's attitude toward the worker. McGregor derived and described two contrasting management philosophies expressed by various managers.[5] These philosophies comprised two different sets of managerial beliefs concerning workers. The philosophy held by the manager, so McGregor asserted, radically affected how he managed people. McGregor's philosophies became famous as Theory X and Theory Y.

Essential beliefs of Theory X reflected skepticism about why people work and how they behave in the workplace. These beliefs included:

- People dislike and avoid work if possible.
- Direction, coercion, and control are needed to obtain performance.
- People try to avoid responsibility.
- Personal goals inherently conflict with company goals.
- It is unreasonable to have high expectations of people.

Theory Y represented an opposite pole of managerial beliefs about workers. The Theory Y manager believed that

- Work is natural; people generally enjoy it.
- People are capable of self-direction and self-control.
- People seek and enjoy responsibility.
- Personal goals can be achieved through company goals.
- It is reasonable to have high expectations of people.

It was evident that a manager with the latter theory had a different orientation to his role than did the manager who believed Theory X. The manager holding Theory Y was more concerned about his workers and their job satisfaction; the manager holding Theory X, in contrast, focused on the tasks to be done rather than on the workers doing them.

McGregor's work started a long series of investigations that polarized management concerns between the worker and the task. Some authors essentially advocated a management focus on one pole; others developed contextual theories indicating when one focus was appropriate and when the other should dominate.

Blake and Mouton's work along these lines was another important management classic. They, like so many others in the neoclassical era, looked at the manager's perspective on the worker and on the tasks to be done. Where other researchers (from the work of McGregor onward) had taken an either-or approach to these two elements, however, they ended the dichotomy.

Blake and Mouton constructed a model for management based on two interacting factors: the focus of the manager on work output and the manager's orientation toward people. In this management grid each factor was placed on a continuum with ratings from one to nine. A manager was tested on each variable. A manager with a score of nine would rank high on that variable, i.e., a high level of concern with output or a high degree of caring about his workers.

Blake and Mouton found that the two variables were not incompatible, as had been previously assumed, and that the best managers were those who tested nine-nine, not nine-one, one-nine, or even five-five. Hence they asserted that getting the job done effectively was not antithetical to being concerned about the welfare and satisfaction of one's workers.[6]

Notice the shift that occurred over time. In McGregor's studies, approaches to workers and tasks were seen as unconscious attitudes held by managers, philosophic perspectives that were assumed rather than deliberated. Others, including Blake and Mouton, came to see these variables as factors that could be purposefully manipulated by managers to achieve their own ends.

Studies of Workers

Studies of workers in the neoclassical mode are well represented by the famous example of the Hawthorne studies. This research set out to see how workers would perform when the circumstances of the work environment were systematically modified. Whether the circumstances were modified favorably or adversely turned out to be less important than the simple fact that the workers were made to feel special simply because they were being studied. The role of psychology in interpreting worker behavior was established for all time by this finding.

Human motivation and job satisfaction were studied extensively, and Herzberg's work was one of the classics in this line. Herzberg found that the factors creating job satisfaction and those creating job dissatisfaction were not opposites but separate entities. He found, for example, that the satisfying factors in a job related to work tasks, whereas dissatisfaction related to the work environment. Poor salaries, short lunch periods, or cramped office space could create dissatisfaction (Herzberg called these "hygiene factors"). Good salaries, long lunch periods, and spacious offices, on the other hand, did not generate contentment. What gave people satisfaction were performance factors such as opportunities to manifest talent, the sense of having turned out a good piece of work, and recognition of work achievement (Herzberg called these "motivation factors").[7]

Studies of workers have focused on several factors, primary among them being job satisfaction variables. Motivation and the effects of various work designs were also studied. Worker involvement in managerial decision making was another area of concentration, and the use of psychological profiles to match worker with job also resulted from the focus upon the worker.

Many of the things that a first-line manager needs to learn to be effective were studied during the heyday of neoclassical theory. Management of people is particularly important in a labor-intensive field such as health care. When the work environment is fraught with problems and stresses, focus on the human dimension of management becomes even more crucial.

Modern Theory

Scott's classification of organizational theories has been useful in this discussion, but his use of the term "modern" must be seen in context. His frame of reference is no longer contemporary. Scott's "modern" category essentially comprises the systems theories that emerged following the neoclassical studies. Focus in this time was on the logic of the systems design. The development of computerization probably encouraged this highly rational, highly systematized view of management.

As happens at the end of every era, the limitations as well as the benefits of a theory or set of theories become clear with the passing of time. The systems model is still of great utility today. Its limitations are also evident in retrospect. A systems model makes certain assumptions about what is known, what is certain, what is stable. The limitations of the model have become clear in the contemporary era, when those "knowns, certainties, and stabilities" are not always available.

A Systems Model

A systems model is one useful way to conceptualize management. Since the system design is the same, whatever the subject matter of the model, it will be described here as it might apply to the job of a first-line nurse manager in an acute care health facility.

A system is a set of interrelated and interdependent parts (outcomes, processes, or structures) designed to achieve a goal or set of goals. Goals dictate the system's central processes, that is, the activities that turn the raw material (input) into the finished product (output). In Figure 15-6, the system gets its raw materials from the surrounding environment and returns its finished product to that environment. In the context of nursing management one might assume improved patient health to be the major nursing goal; sick people, the input; well (or improved) people, the output; and nursing actions that effect change, the central processes.

A systems model can also be applied when a given nursing process is the goal. For example, one might have the goal that all staff nurses be able to perform emergency cardiopulmonary resuscitation. The input, in this case, would be the nurses' skill in the procedure before intervention; the central process (thruput), an educational intervention; and the output, the nurses' skill in the procedure after the education. Similarly, a goal relating to organizational structure might be to achieve a given staffing ratio per patient. Here, the input would be the ratio before intervention, the central processes would be new scheduling and staffing plans and strategies, and the output would be the ratio subsequent to implementing the new plan.

The chief characteristics of a systems model are:

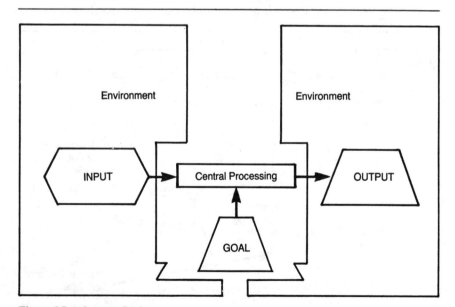

Figure 15-6 Systems Design

1. The system has three major parts: input, central processing, and output.
2. The nature of the central processes is prescribed by the desired goal. Processes are planned to achieve the desired goals.
3. The environment places constraints on the system, because it determines what raw materials are available as well as what happens to the finished product.
4. The system may have alternative central processes in order to cope with variations in the raw material or in the resources available within the system itself (central processing).

A nursing unit, for example, has the goal of caring for various "raw materials"—that is, patients, unique individuals with a variety of illnesses or conditions. The goal of the nursing unit may remain constant, but the central processing may vary, depending on the particular patients on the unit at any one time. Hence the central processing may be adapted to changes in the "raw material."

Similarly, changes in central processing may take place when resources of the system suffer alteration. For example, a nursing unit may switch from a primary care assignment to a functional one during an acute shortage of staff. Nevertheless, the goals of the system remain constant.

An effective systems model requires still another component—a cybernetic loop to establish communication and control (Figure 15-7).

The properties of a cybernetic system can be summarized as follows:

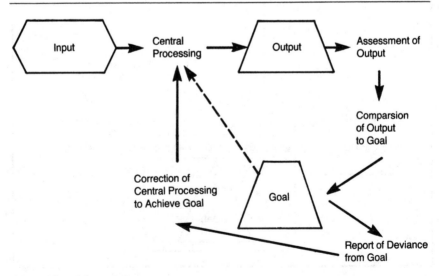

Figure 15-7 Cybernetic Loop

The system has the capacity to sense departures from the desired output. For this to happen, the system must first know what output is desired. A clear description or measure of the goal is necessary in order to have a basis for comparison, and the product of the system must be assessed, measured, or described in a similar manner. If the product cannot be characterized in the same way as the goal, there is no way to compare them. One must be able to tell precisely how the two factors (goal and product) differ.

The system is able to prescribe action to correct deficiencies in the product. When differences between the product and the goal can be identified, the system must be able to determine or hypothesize the source of that difference, and it must then formulate a strategy to correct the disparity. In other words, the system must relate the outcome to the central processing that caused it. The cybernetic system, therefore, prescribes corrective actions. In some cases those actions may be obvious; in others, the system may have to explore proposed alternative actions until successful ones are discovered.

The system allocates resources and efforts to implement the proposed corrective actions. The proposed corrective actions must be feasible, and they must be implemented. Otherwise, the prescription is meaningless.

The system has the capacity to sense results of the change in processing. Here one is back to the first step; the system again measures output (the new output) against the original goal.

One might illustrate the cybernetic function in relation to an inservice education program. Suppose, for example, that a given patient outcome, safe use of crutches, is measured by the number of patient falls and accidents occurring while patients use crutches. Suppose also that the set standard has been exceeded: More falls and injuries are occurring than should be tolerated. The cause has been diagnosed as staff ignorance of procedures for safe use of crutches. For this case the systems model, including a cybernetic loop, might look like that in Figure 15-8.

In this example, the change in central processing (offering an educational program) improved the output but did not reach the set goal. Hence the cybernetic system calls for changes in central processing. These changes might include refinements in the educational program (creating a more effective program), or they might involve a noneducational tactic, e.g., a change in administrative policies concerning the way patients on crutches are managed on the units.

Another example illustrates the use of alternative paths to achieve the same goal. Suppose that the goal is a decrease in patient injuries resulting from falls from beds. One head nurse might achieve the goal by improving the use of safety devices (bedrails, safety straps, and nets). Another might achieve the same goal not by increasing patient restraints but by increasing the safety of the

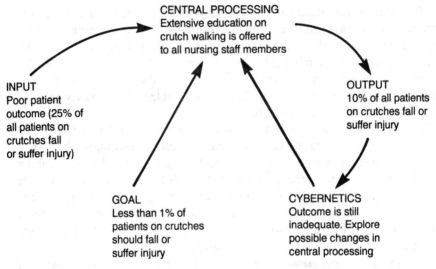

Figure 15-8 Cybernetic Function in an Educational Program on Crutch Use

environment in which they ambulate (carpeting instead of hard flooring, additional handrails, fewer unstable pieces of furniture, lower beds).

Both head nurses might bring their injury rate down to the acceptable norm. How does one judge which approach was best? Human values will enter into the determination, as will cost.

Quality Assurance As a Systems Application

Quality control programs employ a systems model for purposes of ensuring patient care effectiveness. Some forms of quality control have always been used in nursing: accident reports, employee appraisals, nursing rounds. Patient care audits and formal quality assurance systems with their own evaluation tools are now formalized in every institution. Essentially these systems use the cybernetic controls described in the previous section. Quality assurance systems are addressed elsewhere in this book, and the uses of such systems will not be repeated here. We will, however, look at the quality control system *qua* system.

Specifically, we will look at some of the common errors made when using a quality assurance system. Quality control is useless if any part of the system is missing or inaccurate; success is ensured only by careful design. Something can go wrong with each system component.

Setting Standards: A standard is useless if it is set too high. A standard that cannot be met simply sets people up for failure. Similarly, a standard is too low if it is always achieved without effort; in the case of nursing, it is not truly directive of practice. Standards may also be inappropriate. They may wrongly entail matters outside of the nurse's control, or they may be invalid—i.e., fail to measure what they purport to measure. A good nursing standard is one that represents the best patient outcome that can realistically be achieved through the influence of nursing in a given care delivery setting.

Evaluation: Evaluation cannot succeed unless standards are operationalized for careful and consistent measurement. Accurate measurements of standards must be incorporated into valid and reliable tools that are used to make the evaluations. The system must be able to document carefully the relationship between standards and patient outcomes (i.e., between the goals and the output). Patient outcomes and the standards must both be amenable to measurement or precise description.

Adjustment: To adjust a system when standards are not achieved one must know the linkages between central processing and outcome. Sometimes assumed linkages prove false. (Such situations identify areas for nursing research.) Moreover, adjustment requires not only knowing what factors cause certain outcomes but also obtaining the power, resources, and wherewithal to make the requisite changes. It isn't enough, for example, to know that a problem could be solved with a certain product if the funds don't exist to acquire that product.

Not all failures in adjustment are due to deficient resources, however. Sometimes a system is simply too rigid to encourage necessary change. Other systems are too fluid, producing changes too rapidly for evaluation to keep up and assess what is happening.

A systems model may serve as a quality control design for any subject area to which one cares to apply it, from patient care to education, from management practices to staff motivation. The applications are endless. The systems model is of most use in a stable organization. Conditions must persist long enough for the measurement systems to be devised and used, and adjustments implemented. The model is highly rational; that is, the answers it provides should be the same for whoever uses the model.

Computers and the Systems Model

Computers, whose logic is not dependent on the qualities of their users, epitomize the application of a systems design. In the computer system, input, thruput, and output are highly prescribed. Computers are only as good as the systems programmed into them; nevertheless, they enable us to handle masses of data in ways that were simply not possible for earlier generations.

Sometimes the problem with computerized systems is that they give the manager more data than she can understand. The first-line manager must develop ways to interpret the output of the computer systems that affect her work. Often this involves devising matrices and formulas by which data can be summarized and interpreted.

When an institution is contemplating the purchase and installation of any computerized system, it is vital that nursing's evaluation of the system be obtained. The first-line manager can participate by identifying the sort of data that would be of value to her if they were collected. Often it is on the nursing unit that the use of the computerized system is most intense. The first-line manager must take an early and persistent interest in system purchase and design decisions.

Not all decisions can be made by computerized systems, but decisions and delegations that are highly prescribed can be done efficiently by computerized systems, freeing managers for decision making in the domains that cannot be quantified for processing by the computer. Computers are especially valuable in decision situations where a large number of variables must be considered simultaneously. A staffing program is an example of such a situation. When people are dissatisfied with the results of a computer program (such as a computerized staffing schedule), the cause is not usually the fact that the program is computerized but that variables have been wrongly included, omitted, or prioritized in the controlling program. Modifying the program, rather than discarding it, is usually the answer.

Computers are discussed more fully in Chapter 14. First-line managers work in settings that use computers more and more. The trick, of course, is to make the machines work for the manager.

SUMMARY

This chapter has reviewed some of the historical approaches taken to the development of management as a discipline. Scott's division of classical, neoclassical, and modern has been used to organize broad theoretical foci of general historical periods. The reader must appreciate that this chapter is a brief and inadequate representation of the development of management as a discipline. Thus it might serve to stimulate further inquiry and education in the field. Further, the reader is reminded that some of the more recent management approaches are examined in other chapters of this book.

NOTES

1. W.G. Scott, "Organizational Theory: An Overview and an Appraisal," in *Classics of Organization Theory*, edited by Jay M. Shafritz and Philip H. Witbeck (Oak Park, IL: Moore Publishing Co., Inc., 1978), 274–290.

2. J. Dewey, *Democracy and Education* (New York: The Free Press, Macmillan, 1966), 150.

3. H.A. Simon, *Administrative Behavior* (New York: The Macmillan Company, 1957), 79–109.

4. I.L. Janis and L. Mann, *Decision Making: A Psychological Analysis of Conflict, Choice, and Commitment* (New York: The Free Press, Macmillan, 1977), 11.

5. D. McGregor, *The Human Side of Enterprise* (New York: McGraw-Hill Book Company, 1960), 33–57.

6. R.R. Blake and J.S. Mouton, *Making Experience Work: The Grid Approach to Critique* (New York: McGraw-Hill Book Company, 1978), 88–90.

7. F. Herzberg, "One More Time: How Do You Motivate Employees?" *Harvard Business Review* 46, no. 1 (1968): 53.

BIBLIOGRAPHY

Douglass, L.M. *The Effective Nurse: Leader and Manager.* 3rd ed. St. Louis: C.V. Mosby Co., 1988.

Jernigan, D.K. *Human Resource Management in Nursing.* Norwalk, CT: Appleton & Lange, 1988.

Kron, T., and Gray, A. *The Management of Patient Care: Putting Leadership Skills to Work.* 6th ed. Philadelphia: W.B. Saunders Co., 1987.

Lewis, E.M., and Spicer, J.G., eds. *Human Resource Management Handbook: Contemporary Strategies for Nursing Managers.* Rockville, MD : Aspen Publishers, Inc., 1987.

March, J.G., ed. *Handbook of Organizations.* Chicago: Rand McNally and Co., 1965.

Marriner-Tomey, A. *Guide to Nursing Management.* 3rd ed. St. Louis: C.V. Mosby Co., 1988.

Nadler, D.A.; Tushman, M.L.; and Hatvany, N.G. *Managing Organizations: Reading and Cases.* Boston: Little, Brown & Co., 1982.

Shafritz, J.M., and Whitbeck, P.H. *Classics of Organization Theory.* Oak Park, IL: Moore Publishing Co., Inc., 1978.

Stogdill, R.M. *Handbook of Leadership: A Survey of Theory and Research.* New York: The Free Press, Macmillan, 1974.

Young, L.C., and Hayne, A.N. *Nursing Administration: From Concepts to Practice.* Philadelphia: W.B. Saunders Co., 1988.

chapter 16

Staffing and Assigning of Nursing Personnel

The goal of a good staffing system is the effective use of nursing resources. The recent introduction of DRGs under a prospective payment system has accelerated the development of several staffing methods based on a nursing patient classification system (NPCS). The classification system provides documentation substantiating nursing resource allocations in relation to patient needs.

Staffing systems, nursing patient classification systems, and implementation of a variable billing system are closely related, and they directly affect the functions for which the nurse manager is responsible. It is for this reason that these topics are discussed in the same chapter.

Several definitions will be helpful to the first-line manager in discussing related issues. A *nursing patient classification system* is a process of grouping patients into categories according to their perceived nursing care needs.[1] *Variable billing* for nursing care separates nursing costs from the room and board charges; the number of nursing care hours per individual patient is identified and appears as a separate item on the bill. A valid and reliable patient classification system is likely to provide a sound basis for variable billing.[2] *Staffing* is the creation of a plan to determine how many nursing personnel of which classifications will be needed for a given nursing unit on each shift. *Scheduling* is the ongoing implementation of the staffing pattern by the designation of individual personnel to work specific hours and days on a given unit. *Assignment* is the manner in which the total work of the nursing unit is distributed among the present staff members on a given shift.

NURSING PATIENT CLASSIFICATION SYSTEMS

Most nursing departments have in place some type of NPCS to classify patients according to their nursing needs. Traditionally, staffing was determined by patient census and nursing hours per patient day. In 1984 the Joint Commission on Accreditation of Hospitals (as it was then known) established Nursing Standard III, which required nursing units to have a staffing system based on patients' nursing care requirements.[3]

The NPCSs in use range from a simple four-point scale with which staff nurses estimate the level of care to sophisticated data-driven systems that determine nursing intensity based on the linkage between DRG, patient acuity, and nursing hours per patient day. The need for a reliable NPCS took on greater importance with the implementation of prospective payment and DRGs. Nursing departments facing cost containment efforts are utilizing NPCSs to measure nursing intensity levels and their relationship to nursing resources and DRGs. With shortened hospital stays and sicker patients now the norm, nursing intensity and productivity factors are forcing many nursing departments to cost-out their product and charge patients variably for nursing care.

The literature abounds with various instruments available for classifying patients. There are basically two types of patient classification systems used—prototypes and factor evaluations. Prototype instruments identify categories based on profiles that describe characteristics of a typical patient and his nursing care needs. Each category represents a different level of nursing care intensity required by the prototypical patient. In the factor evaluation, critical indicators of care (e.g., activities of daily living) are identified and assigned weights. The total of all individual items determines the overall ranking and indicates the patient category.

Giovannetti stresses the importance of understanding the differences among instrument designs: "The type of instruments is central to the question of comparability of classification information between facilities and in many cases between units within a facility. Some types are more amenable to the determination of a skill level, while others may be more useful in terms of patient placement."[4] The diverse methodologies behind such systems are a drawback. A study by the Prospective Payment Assessment Commission (ProPAC) found that "differences across studies in definitions and methodologies limited the comparison of results."[5] It was further decided that developing norm-based nursing intensity adjustments for DRGs would not be warranted. This highlights the need for nursing to develop a better understanding of the differences between patient classification systems and to define commonalities that express the relationship between nursing skill, nursing hours per patient day, and patient outcomes.

Ledwitch has described six key characteristics of a valid patient classification system: (1) It determines the patient's required level of care according to key indicators on the actual care delivered; (2) it has the capacity to determine staffing needs associated with the level of illness in patient groupings; (3) it includes all aspects of nursing time according to uniform standards; (4) it has the ability to generate trend data, i.e., the number of patients in each acuity classification; (5) all levels of nursing are involved in supporting the system, including monitoring to ensure validity and reliability; (6) there is a common data element to allow linkages to other hospital systems such as accounting.[6]

Not all institutions may have the financial means to purchase and install a computerized NPCS. Such a complex system requires a facility with adequate computer resources to support its development and installation. Clearly, first-line nurse managers require orientation and training to the NPCS if data are accurately to reflect the reality on the unit.

One concern when implementing an NPCS is interrater reliability. Whatever the design, all classification systems require individual judgments by those who use them, and there is bound to be some variation. However, teaching, monitoring, and reinforcement reduce errors and increase the quality and accuracy of the data.[7,8]

Staff members must be well prepared by a clear teaching plan for the introduction of a system. Sometimes a failure to understand the purpose of an NPCS may lead nurses to inflate their ratings for fear that staff may otherwise be reduced. A system is only as good as the data entered. As the saying goes, "Garbage in, garbage out."

The NPCS is often one tool used in nursing's attempts to be seen as a revenue-generating department rather than a cost center. The ability to define nursing's financial contribution to an organization clearly gives nursing management greater control over patient care resources and, based on revenues, a greater role in developing hospital policy. As Sovie and Smith point out: "[Nursing] cannot control costs if we do not know what they are; and to know our costs, we must price our product or charge for nursing care."[9]

NPCSs reflect nursing care demands and average hours of nursing care for patients in each category. Ideally the care hours determined by the system match the care required by the patient as well as the care actually rendered. However, this might not always be possible. Discrepancies are likely to occur during periods of short staffing, when the number of actual personnel falls below the planned staffing schedule. This may present a problem when classification data are used as a basis for variable billing practices.[10,11]

In addition, Sovie and Smith advise that staff document in the patient record that the nursing care as measured in the patient group was given. This is important for periodic audits verifying that the care billed for was indeed received.[12]

Linking nursing care requirements to DRGs may be a desirable goal, but thus far studies indicate that nursing care requirements vary considerably within DRGs.[13] A long-standing criticism of DRGs is their lack of sensitivity to severity of illness measures. Atwood, Hinshaw, and Chance conclude that

"Just knowing a patient's DRG does not solve the problem of being able to predict the complexity of nursing care needed, the amount of staffing needed or the amount to charge the patient."[14] The prospective reimbursement policy makes it especially important for nursing to measure its actual costs per patient and to detect and monitor any negative budgetary effects.

STAFFING DECISIONS

Many nursing organizations hire staff based on unit staffing patterns; others do not have an initial constant staffing plan. The latter will be examined separately as "variable staffing." The present discussion deals with those organizations that implement a permanent staffing pattern. Staffing patterns in nursing services are usually a compromise among three factors: (1) the staffing pattern desired by the nursing organization, (2) the staffing that the economics of the institution can support, and (3) the personnel available in a given community. When the desired staffing pattern is constricted by factors 2 or 3, the nurse manager must be able to assess accurately what assignment methods she can use and what levels of care she can supply in view of her actual staffing situation.

To assess the actual staffing, however, the manager should have a desired staffing pattern against which to compare it. Thus the first step in staffing is to determine the staffing pattern needed to attain the objectives of the nursing department or unit. Determination of a desired staffing pattern, unfortunately, involves so many variables that it is not possible to produce a satisfactory formula to assist the nurse manager in making a staffing determination. Some of these variables are listed in Table 16-1.

Identifying Staffing Needs

The first step in determining a desirable staffing pattern is to identify staffing needs for the functional nursing unit. To calculate staffing needs, most nurse managers use a combination of tradition, staff feedback, and staffing theory. Where a patient acuity classification system is used, scores are converted to nursing manpower calculations, and a unit manpower "average" is determined and included in staffing calculations.

Ramey[15] is one of many authors who have identified the steps necessary for a scientific calculation of staffing needs. These steps usually include:

- Determining in behavioral terms the kind of care the institution desires to offer

Table 16-1 Variables That Affect Staffing Patterns

Patient factors:

• Level, complexity, and duration of care needs

• Types of patients served: their conditions, illnesses, age groups, and other specific selective factors

• Numbers of patients and fluctuations in numbers

• Socioeconomic factors influencing health needs

• Patient expectations for care

Environmental factors:

• Physical layout of institution and patient units

• Number of patient beds

• Facilities and services offered

• Equipment and supplies available

• Supportive services from other divisions and departments

• Supportive services from other agencies

Staff factors:

• Number and mix of nursing personnel

• Hours and rotation policies

• Job descriptions and role functions

• Personnel policies

• Education and experience levels of personnel

• Competitive markets for staff in community

• The work ethic of staff members

Nursing and institutional objectives:

• Level and type of care institution desires to give patients

• Selected care assignment patterns

• Services, educational and other, that institution desires to give personnel

• Nursing administration supportive services

• Developing a system to measure the quality or quantity of care given. (The selection of quality, quantity, or a combination of both will depend upon how the institution defines its kind of care.)

• Developing a system to relate the care measurement to a patient classification system

• Developing a job description for each level of nursing personnel

• Developing a system to record time not attributable to direct patient care activities (inservice education, personnel evaluation, counting narcotics, waiting for elevators, giving reports)

• Developing a system to calculate how proposed changes in the environment (change in supplies, altered physical plant, new operational systems in other divisions) will affect nursing time

• Using available resources to calculate projected patient days for the period of staffing

• Calculating average task hours per unit for each shift classification of personnel.

If all of these systems are created and the calculations are accurately computed, the staff projections will be accurate provided that

- units continue to get patients who need the same general amount of care;
- projected patient days prove to be accurate;
- no great change occurs in either nursing or medical methodologies;
- systems of assigning staff members are not changed;
- physical plant and equipment remain the same or as calculated in the formula;
- other divisions and departments do not change their systems so as to change the ways they interrelate with nursing.

Since the scientific method rests on many assumptions, it may have little practical advantage over the reasoned estimate of a head nurse. The scientific method may, however, be a useful validation process for substantiating desired changes in staffing.

In the abstract, one can think of a staffing pattern as a sequential process of determining patient needs, systems to meet those needs, and the personnel necessary to run those systems. Unfortunately, it is not possible to separate these steps in making the calculations. There is no such thing, for example, as a patient needing four hours of direct nursing care per shift. There *is* such a thing as a patient needing four hours of direct nursing care under a given system of care, with these supplies, in this environment. As soon as one begins to quantify patient care, one does so on the assumption of a given operational system. Thus calculating the patient need hours already assumes an operational nursing system.

Changes in the physical plant will also affect nursing hours according to the nursing systems in operation. For example, suppose a laundry chute was relocated from the end of a long hall of patient rooms to the middle of the hall. There is no way to give an accurate total of nursing time "saved" by this physical alteration. If the nursing system is such that each nurse carries linen to the chute on completion of each patient's morning care, making one trip per patient, then the time savings might be great. If, however, the nurse uses several large portable units to hold laundry, thus making only two or three trips to the chute for the total floor of patients, the savings of nursing time might be negligible.

The same variability holds for determining the use of staff. If one tries, for example, to calculate how many hours of RN care and how many hours of nursing assistant care a patient needs, one is again making pseudoscientific calculations that do not necessarily reflect the reality of the situation. Such calculations are done on the basis of assigning levels to tasks. If a patient is sick enough, "lower-level" tasks such as feeding and bathing may become higher-level tasks, thereby invalidating the calculating system. In addition, tasks assigned to personnel of different levels may not only vary greatly from institution to institution but within the same institution as well.

Determination of staffing needs is thus based on existing and proposed operational systems. Even a "scientific calculation" cannot account for this mixture of needs, systems, and personnel. While calculating staffing needs is probably a good learning experience, the nurse executive who devises staffing patterns on the basis of her own experience and that of her administrative staff should not feel apologetic.

Fluctuations in Staffing Needs

In evolving a staffing pattern the nurse executive must provide for periods of average activity and adjust for periods of increased or decreased activity. Usually this can be done by means of three separate staffing plans: the regular staffing plan, the floating staffing plan, and the emergency staffing plan. The regular staffing plan is based on the average activities of each work unit. The floating staffing plan is designed to compensate for two variables: increases in patient activities and absences among the regular staff members due to illness or other contingencies. The organization that is unable to maintain a float staff has to have a larger regular staff. The emergency staffing plan bolsters the number of staff to meet atypical emergencies. Some institutions that give all employees vacations during the summer months, for example, use the emergency staffing plan at that time. Few institutions are able to adjust staffing for periods of decreased activities, although institutions that have a monopoly on hiring of health personnel (due to the absence of other employing agencies in the area) may be able to send employees home when the workload is light.

In building a functional staffing system it is clear that systems that are applicable to a constant environment cannot be applied to an environment in continual flux. Health institutions, therefore, require a staffing system that is remarkable for its flexibility.

One solution to staffing an inconstant environment is to staff for maximal anticipated activity. Most nursing divisions, however, function under an economic reality that prevents such abundant staffing. Usually staffing is planned to cover the average activity, but planning for the average activity pattern must be accompanied by contingency planning to meet periods of increased activity.

Contingency planning for periods of increased activity usually involves two strategies: internal movement of staff personnel and the call-in of extra staff. Internal movement entails transferring regular staff members from their home units to the unit with an overload or using a float staff. Call-in staff can be provided by the use of a reserve pool of part-time workers, by development of a regular on-call duty shared by regular personnel, by reliance on external agencies, or by the use of double shifting and overtime for regular personnel. None of these systems is entirely satisfactory.

The most common contingency adjustment for increased activities is the transfer of staff members from a less busy patient unit to the unit experiencing an overload. Moving staff from one unit to another, however, threatens the unity of the work group and often causes the transferred worker to feel resentful and insecure. Such transfer policies employ a conception of workers as interchangeable parts. Work groups do not function that way, however; they build group identities, work ethics, work patterns, and discrete social systems. If workers are transferred from the group too often, they are likely to quit. In addition to group and individual psychological factors, some patient units require specialized functions and skills that transfer personnel cannot supply.

The use of a float staff is a partial solution to increased activity needs, but it presents its own set of problems. The usual difficulty in establishing a float staff is finding the right persons for it. An ideal float staff is one composed of full-time workers who like the challenge of working with different types of patients and in different settings. The problem, of course, is the scarcity of nurses and other workers who enjoy this challenge. The vast majority of workers seems to prefer the stability of working with a known group of patients and staff.

Many institutions, therefore, employ a float staff consisting of part-timers and/or personnel waiting for permanent unit positions to become available. Unfortunately, part-timers and new personnel are the workers least likely to succeed at meeting the changing demands of float positions. The institution that desires a good float staff should evolve a reward system that recognizes the unique difficulty of float work.

With regard to call-in options to meet increased activity demands, a reserve pool of part-time workers is the best solution. If an institution is lucky enough to have a regular group of nurses who will work on call, it is indeed fortunate.

When such a reserve pool is not available, some institutions rotate on-call hours among their regular personnel. This is frequently done for specialized areas, such as the operating room or coronary care unit, where specialized skills are required. On-call systems have the disadvantage of being costly, since most employees receive a base on-call pay whether or not they are called in to work.

The use of agency nurses is usually the least satisfactory way to supplement staffing. Such individuals are not oriented to the institution and should not realistically be expected to function in the kind of pressure situation that exists when activities to be done exceed the capacity of available staff.

Use of the institution's own personnel with double shifting and overtime poses two problems. First, it is extremely expensive; second, it pushes staff members beyond normal psychological limits, decreasing their efficiency and safety.

Another mechanism for increasing staffing flexibility with minimal aggravation to staff is the companion-floor system. In this arrangement two floors serve relief functions for each other. Staff members are oriented to the alternative floor and given the assurance that, if they are transferred, it will be to the familiar companion floor.

Whenever possible, instead of moving staff to accommodate activity it is preferable to move the activity to accommodate staff. Since patients are the source of nursing activities, this method calls for systematized patient placement. When patients rather than staff are considered to be the mobile factors, they need not be shifted from floor to floor in order to balance activities. Instead, a gatekeeping function is performed during patient admission. A patient acuity classification system is used to determine cumulated patient care hours per unit; upon admission, patients are assigned to units according to their anticipated care needs and that unit's status regarding patient care hours. This gatekeeping activity requires the following four support systems:

1. a system that covers several units to which each patient may potentially be assigned;
2. a system in which available medical information is adequate for an intelligent admissions nurse to estimate future patient care needs;
3. a system that provides the admissions nurse with a concise report on the activities status of each floor at any given time;
4. a system that empowers the admissions nurse to make the placement decision, unhampered by physician or patient floor preferences.

Variable Staffing

Variable staffing is an alternative to the permanent staffing pattern. This method does not make assumptions about care units and their patients. With a variable staffing pattern, needs are determined daily, based on current input data from patients on each unit. This eliminates problems that arise when staffing is based on a normative prediction of patient needs, and conditions different from that prediction occur. With variable staffing the pattern of staff can change daily. Staffing of the whole institution rather than of the unit is held constant, and staff are distributed on each shift according to variable staffing calculations arising from the patient acuity classification system.

Variable staffing combines staffing and scheduling into a single step. Work hours are scheduled, but unit placement is not planned ahead. Staffing is planned only as far as the number of personnel for the whole institution per shift. Variable staffing is a mathematical solution to the problems inherent in scheduling on a staffing pattern, but it does not necessarily solve all human problems. Many staff members do not like to participate in the system because it breaks down permanent work groups. Staff may feel like interchangeable cogs in a big machine. Many prefer the consistency of working on a single unit with a single patient population. Thus, while variable staffing can solve problems of workload imbalance, it may create a less-than-desirable environment for the worker.

Daily Workload Irregularities

Even when the workload is adequately distributed among the respective nursing units, there is another imbalance that affects nursing staffing. This is the problem of irregular distribution of tasks within a work shift. The day shift is probably most susceptible to this work problem. When peaking of activities occurs, it is necessary to overstaff in order to have adequate coverage for the peak hours, which means that there are also periods when personnel do not have enough to do.

Efficiency dictates that the nurse manager investigate ways and means to decrease peaks and valleys in the workload. Careful analysis of the nursing care delivery systems often reveals ways in which tasks can be redistributed to even out the workload. Redistribution may include reallocation of tasks within a shift or among various shifts.

Why, for example, must so many institutions squeeze all bathing activities into the busiest morning hours? With a little planning, bathing can be distributed over both day and evening shifts. The manager who plans this change, however, will meet initial resistance from many employees who feel that the institution "owes" them the "loaf time" that occurs during lulls in the work pattern. This same phenomenon is seen in the nursing assistant who objects to taking additional assignments after she has "finished her patients for the day." Exaggerated peaks and valleys in the work flow reinforce this kind of thinking.

Some peaking problems are caused by the impact of other departments. When patient activities must be planned around the hours of other departments, interdepartmental planning may alleviate peaking. For example, some nursing divisions have bargained for staggered visiting hours for physicians in order to schedule physiotherapy in coordination with nursing activities.

Mix of Staff Personnel

Another important decision involved in planning staffing patterns concerns the mix of personnel. The mix must be determined for the regular, float, and emergency staffing plans, but the most important decision, of course, is that affecting the regular staffing. The nurse manager must decide how many RNs, LPNs, nursing assistants, and/or other workers are to staff her nursing unit.

Such decisions may be partially dictated by who is available in the community. Clearly the kinds of patients to be cared for also influence such decisions. Efficient use of personnel and quality of care are the basic criteria for determining mix. Usually mix is determined by trying to match the number of tasks at each level with the number of workers at that level. In such task-oriented planning the number of professional nurses is in direct proportion to the complexity of patient tasks.

With this system, adjustments are made on the basis of levels of tasks. Assuming that the management is adequate, if one finds the RNs racing to complete tasks while the nursing assistants have "nothing left to do," the unit needs to move toward staffing with more professionals. On the other hand, if RNs are found distributing linen and cleaning up utility rooms, the mix may call for redistribution toward more nursing assistants and fewer RNs.

Some managers believe that use of the task criterion to estimate levels of staff personnel is not the way to attain maximum efficiency. Managers who favor professional staffing give the following argument: When many lower-level personnel are scheduled there is an increased need for supervising, directing, and checking. This need for management alters the role of the professionals, since time spent on management is not spent on direct patient care. Therefore, staffing with higher-level personnel, whose role concepts and education prepare them for self-direction, achieves more and higher-quality patient care with fewer personnel. Reducing the amount of supervising, directing, and checking to be done enables fewer nurses to do more nursing, and the decrease in number of staff compensates for the use of higher-paid workers.

Two additional factors support the move toward heavily professional staffing. One is the increasing complexity of nursing technology, which decreases the usefulness of employees with low levels of technological skill. The second factor is an ironic one: Some unions have been so successful at raising the salaries and limiting the job activities of nursing assistants that they have made the nursing assistant position less functional from the perspective of the hiring nurse executive.

In addition to the mix of personnel for patient care, the mix of nursing and nonnursing personnel must be considered. The use of unit managers or unit secretaries is common to most health institutions, freeing the professionals for actual nursing care. This division of nursing and nonnursing functions on the unit has probably solved more problems than it has created, but the division has occasioned some difficulties in coordination. Such difficulties can be forestalled by recognizing and taking preventive measures against potential conflict situations.

It is relatively easy to separate nursing activities from support services, so problems seldom occur with role definition along these parameters. Indeed, when nonnurse personnel function efficiently and effectively, one finds great opportunities for professional nursing. Difficulties occur when the unit management staff performs below par. The services of unit management can be compared to supply lines that serve an army. Soldiers on the battlefield give little thought to such support until the ammunition fails to arrive; suddenly, support services have a direct and critical effect on their ability to fight.

The nurse is in a similar position. The stocking of sterile supplies, for example, is not really important to her until she cannot obtain materials to do a dressing; then the supportive services do indeed become critical to her ability to nurse. After this occurs, she will be unlikely to forget the importance of stocking supplies to nursing care.

When unit management services are perceived clearly as means to the ends of nursing care, the division of functions is effective and everyone works toward the same goals. A problem arises, however, when a unit manager develops a sense of his or her job as an end in itself. This can easily happen, and persons who take extreme pride in their work may be more susceptible to this fault than less conscientious workers.

Compared to the world of the nurse, the world of the unit manager is orderly, routinized, and relatively stable. Unit managers deal with inanimate objects that stay where they're put (except when nurses move them); they have supplies that are used up at regular rates (except when nurses unpredictably use "too much" of an item at one time); they have supply charges that can be processed using clearly defined standard operating procedures (except when a nurse forgets to write down which patient used the supply); and they receive temperature readings that can be transferred routinely to patient charts (except when nurses are slow to record them on the temperature board).

It should be clear that, from the perspective of the unit manager or secretary, the biggest obstacle to doing the job is the professional nurse. This obstacle is particularly frustrating if the manager sees the job as an end in itself. A conflict of styles is almost inevitable. On the whole, the unit manager has a job with a high degree of task routinization and a low level of technology; the nurse, on the other hand, has a job with highly varied tasks and a high level of technology. The nurse cannot develop routinized behavior when patient needs, priorities, and surrounding events cannot be predicted from one minute to the next.

If the unit manager sees his or her job as one of helping the nurse to cope with this irregular environment, the relationship between nurse and manager can be effective; such managers can take pride in their ability to assist professional staff to cope with exigencies of all kinds. Unit managers are most likely to develop such a cooperative job orientation when they report to the head nurse.

When a unit manager is coequal with the head nurse, means (support systems) tend to be equated in value with ends (nursing care). Managers in such a system may try to substantiate the equality of their position by adapting the environment to the needs of their own job, with its low technology and routinized tasks. This creates the problem of two bosses demanding that the same environment conform to the needs of diverse work perspectives. The problem with such an arrangement is not a confusion of tasks but a confusion of means with ends.

The power conflict is further exacerbated when an institution hires bright, ambitious persons as unit managers. They, not unexpectedly, fail to find the routinization of their tasks to be challenging. Since their duties fail to live up to their conception of what a manager does, they readily turn their attention to power plays for control of the unit.

A relatively simple solution to these potential problems is to make the unit manager directly responsible to the head nurse. In this way, better nursing care will remain the objective of the support staff as well as of the nursing staff.

Appropriate staffing decisions concerning the numbers of secretaries or unit managers to be hired can be made by simple assessment of the kind and number of non-nursing tasks to be completed on each nursing unit.

Scheduling Staff for Staffing Patterns

As difficult as it is to determine staffing patterns, filling those patterns can be an even greater problem. Anyone who tries to staff a given patient unit for seven days a week soon discovers that the seven-day week was created to confound managers, especially in a society where the five-day work week predominates. Suppose that one desired to fill one RN position, on one patient unit, for one shift, for every day of the year—365 working days over fifty-two weeks. Suppose that institution's RNs work five days per week, take four weeks of vacation, and have eight paid holidays per year. This means that each RN works 232 planned days per year. The mathematical problem is clear: One full-time RN is not enough, while two RNs are too many (464 planned days).

The next obvious step is to see whether three RNs could share two staffing positions—728 planned staffing days compared to 696 actual working days.

So three nurses do not quite fill two positions, although there is less discrepancy between planned and actual days than in the two-for-one plan. A further discrepancy arises, however, when one tries to fit these work days into given weeks.

Using three full-time RNs in an average week, with no holidays or vacations, produces the following pattern:

X = days worked in the week

RN A	X	X	X	X	X		
RN B			X	X	X	X	X
RN C	X	X	X			X	X

This pattern reveals that on one day each week the unit is overstaffed. When calculating to fill the 728 planned staffing days, this means that one day per week is "wasted" out of the 696 working days of the three RNs.

There are, of course, solutions to this problem. One is to accept the loss and credit it toward inservice education time. When this is done, overstaffing for all patient units is made to coincide on the same day, and "extra" staff members are placed in educational programs. This is not really excessive inservice time, because, with holidays considered, each RN would have fewer than eight planned inservice days per year.

Another solution is to use the overstaffing to solve internal variations in workload. In this procedure, one makes certain that overstaffed days do not coincide over all units. The "extra" RN can then be transferred to the unit with the heaviest patient activity. (The problems inherent in constant employee transfer have been discussed earlier in this chapter.)

An ideal solution to the overstaffing problem presented in this example would be to find a nurse interested in working only four days per week. Attainment of this ideal is not always possible.

Still another solution to the overstaffing problem is to balance the excess staff scheduling against a deficient staff scheduling pattern. When four workers fill three positions, a deficiency occurs:

Worker A	X	X	X	X	X		
Worker B			X	X	X	X	X
Worker C	X	X				X	X
Worker D	X	X	X	X			X

With four workers (e.g., LPNs) for three positions, one deficiency occurs per week. Thus a floor that had the good luck to have a staffing pattern requiring two RNs and three LPNs per day could minimize losses by seeing that the day with the "extra" RN was the same day on which one LPN would be missing.

Notice that this sample schedule "fit" was attained by having complete freedom for placement of days off. In this pattern, the RN would have every third weekend off, and the LPN would have only one weekend off out of every four. When an institution must "bid" in a competitive market for staff, it may have to offer more frequent weekends off, further confounding the staffing problem. When rotation of shifts is required, another variable enters into staffing. Variable staffing, of course, alleviates these scheduling irregularities but entails problems of its own, as already mentioned.

These examples of staff scheduling illustrate only some of the complexities involved in determining work days. They should be adequate, however, to demonstrate that literally hours could be spent on scheduling every week by head nurses or supervisors. When the scheduling process is complicated by holidays, vacations, and personal requests, the task becomes mammoth.

Many institutions find cyclical scheduling to be the best solution. Mutually adaptive (i.e., coordinated) schedules are produced for the workers of each patient unit; these schedules extend over a set number of weeks. With the completion of the cycle, the employee group begins again with the first week of the cycle. This repetition of the pattern enables employees to calculate days off months and even years in advance. In some of these systems, each employee has the same work pattern, the variation being produced by alteration of the weeks of the cycle. In most plans, cyclical patterns are different for different workers. Since some patterns may be seen as more desirable than others, there must be a system to determine who gets priority rights in selecting patterns. Most cyclical, repeating patterns are based on four-, six-, or eight-week blocks.

When available, staff scheduling by computer is even more satisfactory than the usual cyclical form. The computer has more flexibility, because any number of variables can be fed into the staffing calculation. Worker preferences and constraints can thus be factored more easily into a work schedule. Most nursing organizations have developed more flexibility concerning the work schedule than was true in the past. Today's nursing organization may have several different plans with associated benefits to enable people with real time constraints to continue to work. For example, a student who could not rotate nights or evenings might continue to work on one of the alternative scheduling plans.

STAFF ASSIGNMENT SYSTEMS

There are four staff assignment systems in common use: functional, team, modular, and primary care. Multiple variations and combinations of these systems are practiced. In this section, three criteria are used in assessing an assignment method: (1) administrative efficiency, (2) patient needs satisfaction (effectiveness), and (3) staff needs satisfaction.

Functional Assignment

In theory, the functional assignment method offers the greatest administrative efficiency because of its division of labor according to specific tasks. There is a treatment nurse, a medications nurse, a bedside nurse, and so forth. Each employee has a clearly defined set of tasks that is different from the assignments of others. There is thus little likelihood of confusion over who will do what, and minimal time is spent on coordinating activities among staff members.

The functional system, while highly efficient, is usually rated low on the criterion of patient needs satisfaction because of its regimentation. Patients' needs can be overlooked if they fail to fit into the "compartments" of the functional system. For example, the patient who needs limited human contact will not have this need met in the functional assignment system.

This criticism of the functional method should not be accepted without close examination, however. It is certainly true that the regimentation of duties into rigid, discrete compartments is likely to result in failures to attend to the issues that do not conform to the classification system. Mature professional judgment on the part of the nursing staff can help compensate for this potential deficiency, however.

In some instances the functional system may have considerable merit in relation to patient needs satisfaction. In an environment where patients have similar needs, regimentation may have its advantages. If anticipated, routine patient needs are built into the task assignment system, it may be that these needs will be met more consistently than by other assignment systems.

One should not overlook the tendency of most nursing units to fall back on the functional system during periods of critical staffing shortage. This clearly indicates that nurses find the functional method to be most effective during pressing shortages and also that no system of assignment should be judged out of context. A system's success or failure depends to a great extent on the circumstances in which it is used.

Nursing theorists also rate the functional system low with regard to staff satisfaction. The prescribed division of labor gives each worker repetitious and thus potentially boring tasks. In addition, the worker does not have the satisfaction of seeing a "complete" piece of work, that is, a patient who gets well because of the worker's singular efforts.

Such judgments are based on an abstract analysis of the work design and an assumption about what people like. There are, it is true, many instances of staff dissatisfaction under functional nursing plans. It is also true, however, that many staff members are best satisfied by this task-oriented system. Some workers are simply more secure in repetitive, task-oriented jobs.

Team and Modular Assignments

The team method of assignment evolved as an attempt to increase patient and staff satisfaction, even at the cost of administrative efficiency. There are several reasons for this potential loss of efficiency. Each staff member is confined to the care of a limited group of patients. When the mobility of staff is decreased, there is a loss of overall unit efficiency. Another source of inefficiency in team assignments is the increased time spent on coordinating delegated work. Since individual assignments are less regularized than under the functional method, supervisors spend more time checking up on workers.

Not all experts agree that the team system is less efficient than the functional method. Many believe that the closer interaction among staff members provides an esprit de corps that compensates for time expended in conferences and work coordination. Most advocates of the team system, however, base their support on the increased satisfaction of patient and staff needs.

The basic premise of team nursing is that if a nurse has responsibility for one-half or one-third of a unit's patients she can know more about each patient than if her responsibility is to all patients on the unit. Given a smaller number of staff and patients to work with, the nurse can better match staff abilities and patient needs in care assignments. In addition, she can provide more direction for each worker on the team. Effectiveness of care is the anticipated outcome. Theoretically, patients' needs are better met by the team system because they are cared for by a limited number of personnel who know them better. Needs that could be missed under the functional system are carefully identified by the team method.

Increased effectiveness in care, so it is reasoned, results not only from identification and satisfaction of patient needs but from the opportunity for closer and more therapeutic patient-nurse relationships. These gains in effectiveness, however, may be somewhat offset by the increased likelihood of errors. The worker doing multiple different tasks is much more likely to make a mistake than is the worker who is repeating the same task over and over. In almost all cases the team assignment system is associated with a patient-oriented rather than task-based division of labor. Each staff member is likely to be doing many different tasks for a limited number of patients rather than a single task for a large number of patients, as occurs under functional methods. Since this system increases the likelihood of error, much more time must be devoted to monitoring task assignments.

Theoretically, staff members should derive greater job satisfaction from team than from functional assignments, due to increased guidance and better matching of assignments to their skills. In addition, by working with fewer patients the team members have a clear sense of their own contribution to patient outcomes.

Modular nursing is "more of a good thing." If giving the nurse a team is more effective than giving her a whole unit, then giving her a smaller module of patients should be even better than giving her a team. Most arguments for or against team nursing can be applied to the modular method. Again, a little more efficiency is lost because staff mobility is reduced even more than under the team method. The smaller size of the team, however, permits closer monitoring of care than is the case with team nursing, thus probably decreasing the percentage of care errors and increasing the chances that patient needs will be identified.

Primary Care Assignments

The premise of primary care nursing is different from that of the team and modular methods. Under primary care each patient is assigned to one professional nurse for the patient's total hospitalization.

The focus of primary care nursing is on who plans the care more than who does the care. The RN may be assisted in the care of her patients by other staff members assigned through various systems. Often a modular-type assignment is used, but this is not invariable. In this system each professional nurse has a selected number of patients, and she is responsible for all nursing care planning for these patients. Usually this care planning is seen as a 24-hour responsibility, and the primary nurse may be called at irregular hours for important changes in her patient's nursing needs.

Administrative efficiency is lost by limiting each nurse's knowledge and mobility to the care of only a few patients. The system does permit, however, the mobile use of other staff members. In addition, the detailed written care plans may help increase the efficiency of these other workers.

On the other hand, it is likely that the primary nurse will generate more nursing orders than would appear under any other system. Any efficiency gained through clarity of orders and mobility of lower-level personnel is likely to be lost through the increased work requirements. Efficiency is clearly sacrificed for increased care effectiveness in this system.

One source of increased efficiency, however, may be the elimination of many positions in the chain of command. The physician and other health workers are encouraged to deal directly with the primary nurse. Less time must thus be spent passing on orders—a result that may also improve effectiveness by decreasing the number of care errors that occur with multiple relays of orders.

Effectiveness of care is apparently improved by the primary care mode. The system claims a high score on the criterion of patient needs satisfaction because each patient has a "private nurse planner." The method ensures that at least one staff member has a vested interest in the patient's case, and the patient's problems are more likely to be identified and resolved under this system. Another source of effectiveness, the probable decrease in care errors, has already been mentioned.

Primary care represents an attempt to establish an accountability system for the professional nurse. Each primary nurse can be held accountable for her own patients' progress and care. This is not possible when care is shared among many workers.

Theoretically, primary care should increase the RN's satisfaction with her career because now she has "products"—that is, patient outcomes that are directly the result of her own work and decisions. This form of assignment allows the nurse to operate at the peak of her professional capacity. This system is not overly concerned with the satisfaction of staff members other than the primary nurse, though they may also benefit from her clear nursing orders and guidance.

In real-life situations staff and patient needs satisfaction is greatly dependent on the preparation of the nurse for a primary care role. A nurse who is not secure in nursing care planning will feel threatened by primary care assignments. In addition, the patient whose primary nurse is not capable is much worse off than the patient who, under team or functional nursing, is exposed to many nurses, any one of whom might plan for the patient's needs. In primary nursing, therefore, the success or failure of the system depends entirely on the selection of nurses for the primary role.

Comparison of Assignment Systems

The role of the staff nurse differs greatly from assignment system to assignment system. In functional care, the nurse mainly organizes and sequences a number of given tasks. Her job in the functional system is to complete these tasks on time. A large part of her job involves organization and management.

Team nursing makes patient needs analysis and problem solving a bigger part of the job of the staff nurse; it increases her sense of responsibility for patient outcomes. Team nursing does not decrease the staff nurse's need for organization and management, however. Since her tasks are now more variable, this aspect of her role actually increases. Whether she is a team leader or a team member, she has more kinds of tasks to organize than under the functional system. Not only does she have more of her own work to organize, she must also coordinate her assignments with those of other team members.

Modular nursing, by cutting down the size of the functional unit, cuts down on organizing of tasks and increases the focus on patient care. Primary care further decreases organizing of tasks for the staff nurse and increases her focus on patient care.

The role of the head nurse also varies within the four major assignment systems. In functional care, the head nurse is a manager in the strict sense; only she has the overall view of the whole unit, and only she is responsible for seeing that all the "pieces" of work are delegated and completed. Since many different nurses are likely to see each patient under the functional system, however, the head nurse can be fairly sure that any gross defects or omissions in care will come to someone's attention. Her evaluation activities are thus usually limited to two or more nursing rounds a day.

Under the team system, the head nurse delegates many of her day-to-day management duties to team leaders. This should allow her more time for long-term planning for patient care and staff education needs. From the head nurse perspective, the team system should be ideal; she has optimal distribution of management tasks and a minimal number of persons requiring close assistance and evaluation (two or three team leaders). This ideal is seldom realized, however, for the head nurse soon discovers that a whole new set of duties devolves upon her.

The head nurse's assistance to and evaluation of team leaders turns out to be more complex than her relations to staff under a functional system. The head nurse must observe and evaluate team leaders' organizing, coordinating, and technical nursing skills as well as their interpersonal relationships. The team leader is typically a nurse who has had little preparation for the management role. Thus the head nurse is required to teach management as well as nursing skills under the team system, since team leaders must be taught how to make appropriate assignments, how to assess staff capabilities, and how to handle the authority of their positions.

A factor that increases the complexity of teaching management skills to team leaders is the inherent difficulty of managing patient-based care as opposed to task-based care. The team leader's job in patient-based care is actually more complex than the job of the head nurse in task-based care; it calls for far more coordination and cooperation with others, it involves more problem solving, and it requires greater involvement with both staff members and patients.

Under the team system, the head nurse cannot evaluate the effectiveness of the care on her unit simply by seeing that all tasks get done. The amount of time that the head nurse spends observing, teaching, and evaluating is greatly increased under the team system. The head nurse can no longer assume that someone will "catch" care deficiencies. Now only one-half or one-third of her professional staff are likely to see any given patient. The head nurse's evaluation activities must increase to ensure the safety and adequacy of care. Daily rounds are no longer adequate as the only assessment device.

The same points hold for modular and primary care systems. As these systems limit the patient's contacts to fewer professional nurses, the head nurse must accordingly assume the role of clinical care evaluator. In the extreme of primary nursing care, it is vital that the head nurse evaluate the care planning of each nurse. If a primary care nurse makes an error in judgment, it is not likely to be corrected unless the head nurse discovers it.

In the evolution from functional, through team and modular, to primary care systems, the head nurse role evolves from that of organizer and manager of tasks to evaluator of clinical care and teacher of nurses. These role variations clearly demand different abilities. Hence an excellent head nurse under one assignment system may be a poor head nurse under another.

SUMMARY

Staffing and assigning of personnel are major responsibilities of the first-line manager. All staffing and assigning strategies have their good points and their limitations. System selections should be made with due consideration to the unique circumstances of the organization in which the first-line manager works.

Goals that drive selection include patient safety and service, accurate matching of nursing resources to patient care demands, flexibility in use of staff, ability to meet individual personal needs of staff members, ability to satisfy professional goals of the nursing staff, equity and fairness for all employees, simplicity of system management, and cost effectiveness.

When they are well managed, staffing, scheduling, and assignment systems may be virtually "invisible" in the organization. When they are poorly managed, they become everyone's concern; patients, staff, and organization all suffer.

The first-line manager needs to make informed choices in the methods that she selects, whether the choices are made independently, in consultation with her staff, or in peer management groups. How the work is organized can have a direct effect on its quality and quantity.

NOTES

1. P. Giovannetti, "Where Do We Go from Here?" in F.A. Shaffer, ed., *Patients & Purse Strings* (New York: National League for Nursing, 1986), 349.

2. M.D. Sovie and T.C. Smith, "Pricing the Nursing Product: Charging for the Nursing Care," *Nursing Economics* 4, no. 5 (September/October 1986): 218.

3. Joint Commission on Accreditation of Hospitals, *Accreditation Manual for Hospitals—1985* (Chicago: Joint Commission on Accreditation of Hospitals, 1984), 97–98.

4. Giovannetti, 352.

5. K.F. Price and E.T. Lake, "ProPAC's Assessment of DRGs and Nursing Intensity," *Nursing Economics* 6, no. 1 (January-February 1988): 13.

6. L. Ledwitch, "Expanded Utilization of the Patient Classification System," in J.C. Scherubel and F.A. Shaffer, eds., *Patients & Purse Strings II* (New York: National League for Nursing, 1988), 150.

7. M.A. Tarnicale, "Patient Classification: Cutting the Margin of Human Error," *Nursing Management* 17, no. 10 (October 1986): 49.

8. J. Unger, "Building a Classification System that Works," *Journal of Nursing Administration* 15, nos. 7, 8 (July/August 1985): 20.

9. Sovie and Smith.

10. Giovannetti, 356.

11. M. Dijkers, T. Paradise, and M. Maxwell, "Pitfalls of Using Patient Classification Systems for Costing Nursing Care," in F.A. Shaffer, ed., *Patients & Purse Strings* (New York: National League for Nursing, 1986), 9.

12. Sovie and Smith, 219.

13. M.D. Sovie, M.A. Tarnicale, A.W. Vanputee, and E. Stunden, "Amalgam of Nursing Acuity, DRGs, and Costs," *Nursing Management* 16, no. 3 (March 1985): 34.

14. J.R. Atwood, A.S. Hinshaw, and H.C. Chance, "Relationships among Nursing Care Requirements, Nursing Resources, and Charges," in F.A. Shaffer, ed., *Patients & Purse Strings* (New York: National League for Nursing, 1986): 117.

15. I. Ramey, "Eleven Steps to Proper Staffing," *Hospitals* 47, no. 6 (1973): 98–104.

BIBLIOGRAPHY

Adams, R., and Duchene, P. "Computerization of Patient Acuity and Nursing Care Planning." *Journal of Nursing Administration* 15, no. 4 (April 1985): 11.

Alivizatos, M.S. "A New Concept in Scheduling for Nurses." *Supervisor Nurse* 12, no. 2 (1981): 20.

Becker, E.R., and Foster, R.W. "Organizational Determinants of Nurse Staffing Patterns." *Nursing Economics* 6, no. 2 (March-April 1988): 71.

Berry, V.I., and Reichelt, P.A. "Using Routine Collected Data for Staffing Decisions." *Hospitals* 5, no. 22 (1977): 89.

Boyer, C.M. "The Use of Supplemental Nurses: Why, Where, How?" *Journal of Nursing Administration* 9, no. 3 (1979): 56.

Clark, E.L. "A Model of Nurse Staffing for Effective Patient Care." *Journal of Nursing Administration* 7, no. 2 (1977): 22.

Eusanio, P.L. "Effective Scheduling—The Foundation for Quality Care." *Journal of Nursing Administration* 8, no. 1 (1978): 12.

Fisher, D.W., and Thomas, E.A. "A 'Premium Day' Approach to Weekend Nursing Staff." *Journal of Nursing Administration* 4, no. 5 (1974): 59.

Gallagher, J.R. "Developing a Powerful and Acceptable Nurse Staffing System." *Nursing Management* 18, no. 3 (March 1987): 45.

Ganong, J.; Ganong, W.; and Harrison, E.T. "The 12-Hour Shift: Better Quality, Lower Cost." *Journal of Nursing Administration* 6, no. 2 (1976): 17.

Hamilton, J.M. "Nursing and DRGs: Proactive Responses to Prospective Reimbursement." *Nursing & Health Care* 5, no. 3 (March 1984): 155.

Higgerson, N.J., and Van Slyck, A. "Variable Billing for Services: New Fiscal Direction for Nursing." *Journal of Nursing Administration* 12, no. 6 (May 1982): 20–27.

Kaye, G.H., and Krol, S. "The Nursing Shortage: This Time Traditional Responses Won't Work." *Supervisor Nurse* 12, no. 7 (1981): 13.

Kelly, P.A., and Lambert, K.L. "The Effect of a Modified Team Approach on Nurse-Patient Interaction and Job Satisfaction." *Journal of Nursing Administration* 8, no. 4 (1978): 3.

Kirby, K.K. "Issues in Nursing Resource Management: Past and Present." *Nursing Economics* 4, no. 6 (November-December 1986): 305–308.

Kirby, K.K., and Wiczai, L.J. "Budgeting for Variable Staffing." *Nursing Economics* 3, no. 3 (May-June 1985): 160.

Kirby, K.K., and Wiczai, L.J. "Implementing and Monitoring Variable Staffing." *Nursing Economics* 3, no. 4 (July-August 1985): 216.

McCarthy, D. "Primary Nursing: Its Implementation and Six Month Outcome." *Journal of Nursing Administration* 8, no. 5 (1978): 29.

Marram, G. "The Comparative Costs of Operating a Team and a Primary Nursing Unit." *Journal of Nursing Administration* 6, no. 4 (1976): 21.

Marriner, A. "Variables Affecting Staffing." *Supervisor Nurse* 10, no. 9 (1979): 62.

Norby, R.B.; Freund, L.E.; and Wagner, B. "A Nurse Staffing System Based Upon Assignment Difficulty." *Journal of Nursing Administration* 7, no. 9 (1977): 2.

Osinski, E.G., and Powals, J.G. "The Cost of All R.N. Staffed Primary Nursing." *Supervisor Nurse* 11, no. 1 (1980): 16.

Somers, J.B. "Purpose and Performance: A Systems Analysis of Nursing Staff." *Journal of Nursing Administration* 7, no. 2 (1977): 4.

Spitzer, B. "Making Primary Nursing Work." *Supervisor Nurse* 10, no. 1 (1979): 12.

Williams, M.A. "Quantification of Direct Nursing Care Activities." *Journal of Nursing Administration* 7, no. 8 (1977): 15.

Williams, M.A. "When You Don't Develop Your Own Validation Methods for Patient Classification Systems." *Nursing Management* 19, no. 3 (March 1988): 90.

Williams, M., and Murphy, L. "Subjective and Objective Measures of Staffing Adequacy." *Journal of Nursing Administration* 9, no. 11 (1979): 21.

Vail, J.D.; Morton, D.A.; and Rieder, K.A. "Workload Management System Highlights Staffing Need." *Nursing & Health Care* 8, no. 5 (May 1987): 289.

Zander, K.S. "Primary Nursing Won't Work . . . Unless the Head Nurse Lets It." *Journal of Nursing Administration* 7, no. 8 (1977): 19.

chapter 17

Systems of Measurement for Nursing Care

Much effort has been devoted to evaluating the quality of health care delivery. The heightened interest in quality stems largely from concerns about the effects of new incentives to control costs under a prospective payment system. Health policy analysts and health care providers are watchful that the availability of fewer resources to treat patients in hospitals and alternative care delivery settings does not compromise the quality of care rendered.[1]

However, there may be questions about what is meant by "quality," for quality is one of the most difficult concepts to define, measure, and evaluate. Donabedian, in describing the "epidemiology of quality," refers to "duality."[2] By this he means that discussions of quality health care must refer to two sets of populations: providers and clients.

There is a growing acknowledgment on the part of health care observers that consumer satisfaction is one of the outcome measures that is critical in evaluating quality.[3] Structure and process are well-established determinants in any measurement system, but the recent focus of quality research has been on outcome criteria, including morbidity and other measures of health status.[4]

The concern with quality is extending into all areas of the health care system. Until recently quality assurance programs had been largely confined to acute care facilities—an approach that did not reflect the reality that individuals receive care across a continuum extending from prevention through acute care to rehabilitation or home care. Quality assurance is now on the agenda as a priority for all providers of health care. Nurses, as the prime care givers, are in a critical position to affect quality; they need to be aware, therefore, of how their activities are measured by quality control mechanisms.

NURSING QUALITY CONTROL SYSTEMS

The nursing quality control system resembles a quality control system for any other field or occupation. It is a system set up to measure the quality of the product of the organization—in this case, nursing care. Typically, quality control systems focus on goals for a given group of patients who hold in common some health state, disease or injury, care need, or nursing therapy. The nursing care plan may be thought of as the comparable quality control format for the individual patient. Slee identifies three essential components of any quality control program: standards, surveillance, and corrective action.[5]

Selecting the Type of Standard

The setting of standards or criteria for a given patient group is the first step in structuring an evaluation system. In setting standards one can choose to appraise nursing activities from the perspective of structure, process, or outcome.[6]

Structure Standards

If one looks at the criteria applied by most accrediting agencies in nursing— such as the American Nurses' Association, the National League for Nursing, and the Joint Commission on Accreditation of Healthcare Organizations—it is apparent that these groups have selected structure as their primary focus. The following four questions and statements taken from accreditation questionnaires of the three cited agencies illustrate the point:

1. Is a registered nurse responsible for planning, evaluating, and supervising the nursing care of each patient?
2. Are written care plans used?
3. The nursing department provides training programs and opportunities for staff development.
4. There is a system for recording accurate and objective observations of patients in the clinical record.

Structural standards are directed toward assessing the protocols by which nursing care is organized and managed—that is, the arrangements by which nursing care is delivered. Such standards address organizational structure, the established ways of operating, and the delivery systems of the organization.

Structure-based criteria are designed to identify necessary, but not sufficient, conditions for quality care. It might be necessary for a registered nurse to plan patient care, but the fact that care is planned by a registered nurse does not guarantee that the planning is in fact done well. Written care plans may be necessary for good care, but writing such plans down does not in itself ensure that they are adequate. The movement toward standardized care plans is one effort to meet structure-based quality assurance criteria. Criteria based on structure stipulate conditions under which it is likely that good nursing will take place, but such criteria do not in fact assess nursing quality. Structural criteria address themselves to the way in which the organization is systematized; they evaluate the administrative processes that arrange the work.

Process Standards

Process standards provide a second perspective on care delivery; they measure aspects of the nursing process itself. "Nursing process" here refers to the activities of the individual nurse, the actual interactions between the nurse and the patient. The nursing process takes place within the providing structure, but it refers to the mode of actually delivering care rather than to the structure by which care delivery is organized.

The primary difference between process and structure-based standards can be demonstrated by the conversion of two of the previous structural criteria into representative process standards.

- *Structural standard:* Are written care plans used?
- *Related process standard:* Is the written care plan appropriate for the patient? Does it demonstrate consideration of the patient's personal, disease-related, and therapy-related needs?
- *Structural standard:* There is a system for recording accurate and objective observations of patients in the clinical record.
- *Related process standard:* The charting shows evidence of relevant observations of patient progress, of response to therapy, and of completion of orders.

Process standards assess the performance of specified and prescribed nursing activities. They evaluate the level of adequacy at which indicated activities have been performed. A critical difference between structural and process standards is that the process standard requires a professional judgment to determine whether a criterion has been met. Anyone can determine whether care plans are used (structure), but only a nurse can judge whether a given care plan is proper for a given patient (process). In this case, nursing's increasing reliance on standardized care plans may satisfy the structural criterion, but unless the plans are individualized the process criterion will not be met.

This element of judgment does introduce the possibility of some differences in ratings, but such differences can be decreased by expressing each criterion in clearly defined and specific terms.

Outcome Standards

The outcome standard takes yet another perspective; it measures the patient's health outcome. The difference between process and outcome standards can be illustrated by conversion of a process standard to an outcome standard:

- *Process standard:* Nurse applies dressings without contaminating the sterile field (process of nursing).
- *Outcome standard:* Patient does not develop a wound infection (patient result).

Outcome standards represent the ultimate goals of nursing, for, if the patient outcome is not satisfactory, it matters little what nursing process was used or what organizational arrangement supported the therapy. Nevertheless, outcome alone is inadequate as a basis for quality control. If, for example, one discovers that a large number of patients are experiencing wound infections, one must look at both the nursing process and the organizational structure to find the cause and to institute the cure. All three perspectives are essential in problem solving and as a basis for future planning.

In nursing, outcome standards can be difficult to isolate. One has to be able to determine how much of the patient's health outcome is due to nursing, how much is due to medicine, and how much is due to other factors. Typically the patient's health outcome is the result of multiple interacting factors of which nursing is only one. Nevertheless, if nursing has a significant effect on a given health outcome, standards may be set for it.

Outcome standards are usually set for groups of patients that may logically be expected to share health goals. For example, one can easily set a standard that all obstetric patients must learn appropriate feeding and handling techniques for newborn infants. Similarly, one might set a standard that leg amputees must learn the procedures of safe crutch walking. For all patients with surgical incisions, one might set the standard of first-intention wound healing.

Common outcome standards can be developed for patients grouped by similar diseases and injuries or by similar incapacities. They can be identified for all juvenile diabetics (similar disease) or for all paraplegics (similar incapacity), regardless of the source of the disability. A sample taxonomy for the selection of patient groups is shown in Table 17-1.

In spite of the complexity of design problems, evaluation systems are created and the results studied in most institutions. The Joint Commission has suggested a format for institutions that do not wish to create their own model. This format is predominantly oriented to medical diagnosis. While some nurses do not choose to use a medically oriented model, it is important to note that the elements that nursing shares with medicine, the simple criteria of

Table 17-1 Taxonomy for Selecting Patient Groups

Grouping Criterion	Examples
Disease	All new diabetic patients Cardiac patients
Like treatment	Preoperative patients All patients on renal dialysis
Like needs	Patients with immobility Patients with decreased vision
Geographic criterion	All patients in this hospital All patients on this unit
Life stage	All geriatric patients All teenagers
Illness stage	All patients needing intensive care All self-care patients

morbidity and mortality, are the easiest to evaluate. Documentation is available for intensive coronary care nursing that directly correlates survival rates with appropriate nursing measures.[7] Since survival is the primary objective for the coronary patient during the critical phase, such documentation provides a standard of measurement that lends itself to clear statistical validation. Such clear and singular outcomes are not possible for all health conditions, however, and this fact complicates many attempts at measurement.

Studies of outpatients at health maintenance clinics also allow comparison between the professions of medicine and nursing. Where selected patient groups are divided between physician clinics and nurse clinics, nurse-run clinics have been shown to produce equal or better outcomes for outpatients on health maintenance status.[8] Newer studies tend to confirm these conclusions; they indicate the value of nursing on an outcome basis for groups of patients who could be managed by either profession. Outcome studies provide a way for nursing to assess its contributions to both joint and independent ventures of patient care.

For the majority of patients, however, treatments are mixed and outcomes are complex or highly individualized. To use outcome standards given these conditions means that one accepts the following assumptions:

- Some health outcomes are primarily attributable to nursing.
- Some health outcomes are partially attributable to nursing.
- Regulation of nursing actions can produce statistically improved health outcomes for patients in these categories.

The statistical approach is important here, for no single outcome can be ensured. For example, suppose it is determined that nursing makes a critical difference in the number of surgical wound infections. Clearly this does not mean that nurses are responsible for all wound infections. Nor does it mean that the infection of any given patient can be attributed to nursing. The patient might develop such an infection for a variety of reasons: the physician's poor technique during surgery, the intern's poor technique in changing the dressing, ineffective sterilization of dressings, the patient's own interference with the dressing, or poor nursing technique. Improving the nursing technique should produce a statistical change in the number of wound infections, but not the elimination of all infections.

Relationship among the Three Types of Standards

The relationship among the three perspectives of evaluation (structural, process, and outcome) can also be important in effecting appropriate change. Failure to meet an outcome standard may indicate a need for a change in the nursing process; failure to meet a nursing process standard may indicate a need to change organizational structures. For example, if several patients develop postoperative infections (negative outcome), it may be that nurses need to examine the process of caring for wounds. If nurses are lax in techniques of distributing medications, it may be that the nursing structure creates pressures to take improper shortcuts. Thus results of assessments from one perspective (structural, process, or outcome) may have implications for another perspective.

The following evaluations of a cardiac resuscitation illustrate that all three perspectives can be used to describe the same event:

1. Outcome evaluation: Patient survived, suffered no irreversible brain damage, received no physical trauma such as cracked ribs. Patient understands what happened and has worked through the reaction to the event.
2. Process evaluation: Appropriate verification of the state of cardiac arrest was made. Cardiac massage and resuscitation were begun immediately. Procedures followed were accurate as to mechanics and rates. Air passages were initially checked for obstruction. Patient was placed on a hard surface.
3. Structural evaluation: Cardiac board and mechanical respirator were ready-at-hand in the treatment room. Respirator was equipped and ready for immediate use. Cardiac resuscitation team arrived within three minutes. Prearranged standing orders enabled them to provide defibrillation and medication at once.

SELECTING THE CONTENT TO BE EVALUATED

After the type of standard has been selected for an evaluation project, the next step in establishing a quality control system is to identify the areas to be evaluated. In designing outcome standards, one tries to identify some conceptual framework that covers the totality of the subject matter. When this is possible, standards are more likely to be comprehensive than when they are merely identified on an ad hoc basis.

Process standards may be limited to direct patient care or expanded to cover other nursing functions, such as recording, assigning, or maintaining equipment. The scope will depend on the objectives and needs of the institution. Since the evaluation process can be time-consuming, quality control is often limited to evaluation of the nursing process alone, excluding administrative factors. Like outcome standards, process standards should be organized according to some conceptual framework. This may be reflected in the department's concept of nursing. The following list shows particulars in three areas of nursing care that could be used as a basis for structuring a process-oriented quality control instrument.[9,10,11]

1. Nursing care:
   (a) sustenal
   (b) remedial
   (c) restorative
   (d) preventive

2. Nursing problems:
   (a) preserve body defenses
   (b) prevent complications
   (c) re-establish patient in outside world
   (d) detect change in body's regulatory system
   (e) implement prescribed therapeutic and diagnostic activity
   (f) provide comfort

3. Nursing care as process:
   (a) observation
   (b) inference
   (c) validation
   (d) assessment
   (e) action
   (f) evaluation

The particular structure selected is not as important as that a structure *be* selected. Too many control checklists lack organization and simply present a random list of standards.

CONSTRUCTING THE STANDARDS

After the content to be measured has been selected, the next step in the process is that of constructing the relevant standards. Since outcome standards are the most difficult to compose, these will be reviewed in detail.

The first problem in setting outcome standards is reaching consensus on the meaning of a "standard." Two contrasting definitions are frequently used in nursing literature: (1) a criterion of excellence or attainment; (2) a baseline against which to measure the event or behavior. Using the first concept, a standard is written in terms of the optimally desired outcome; using the second concept, the lowest acceptable level of outcome is described. While there is no "right" or "wrong" definition of a standard, it is essential that a group reach a consensus on the purpose of the standard it chooses to use.

It is important when composing outcome standards to set realistic goals. Standards set for given time periods must represent accurate nursing prognoses for the given patient base. Not only must the standards be appropriate to the given patient base, they must reflect a realistic level of care at the given institution. If standards are set at a level far above that which can be reached realistically, they will serve only to frustrate staff members.

Standards must also reflect the level of nursing care for which resources are available. This economic factor again forces the nurse planner to consider standards from a realistic perspective. For what level of care does the institution provide resources?

One problem with constructing outcome standards is that health outcomes change over time. There are distinct stages of illness for certain impairments; for others, there is a gradual progression from the initial illness to the final outcome. The setting of reasonable standards requires that times be specified at which outcomes will be measured.

Some conditions virtually set their own critical measurement points. For example, most nurses would agree that postpartum patients should be assessed at the completion of the delivery phase, on the first postpartum day, and on the day of discharge. Other conditions may require more arbitrary setting of times for outcome assessments.

In formulating outcome standards, it is helpful to classify them along three different axes:

1. the attainment or avoidance option
2. the performance or state-of-being option
3. the absolute or relative option.

Consideration of these axes can help in planning adequate and uniform measurement tools.

On the first axis an outcome standard is either a state to be attained or a state to be avoided. For example, the standard "maintains normal urinary output" gives a desired attainment. On the other hand, the standard "does not develop a bladder infection" represents an avoidance standard. Some nursing authors prefer to deal strictly with attainment standards; others use both types. Avoidance standards can be converted into attainment standards. The avoidance standard cited above can be converted into a statement such as "maintains bladder's normal microbial status," which represents an attainment standard.

The second axis for outcome standards indicates whether the outcome is something the patient does or a state the patient exhibits. For example, "walks on crutches with a four-point gait" is a performance standard. "Maintains intact skin surfaces," on the other hand, is a state-of-being standard. When evaluating patient performance, it is necessary to differentiate standards that indicate the ability to perform from those that require the act itself rather than the ability. Ability to demonstrate full range of motion of the shoulder joint is an adequate measurement of shoulder mobility. The patient's ability to self-inject insulin accurately, however, may not be an adequate measure if the patient tends to inject doses irregularly. Here the action itself rather than the ability must be measured.

The third evaluative axis determines whether the standard is absolute or relative. The standard "all skin surfaces remain intact" is an absolute standard. In contrast, a relative standard may show progression rather than absolute attainment. An example might be "The patient following a cardiovascular accident increases the ability to depress a hard rubber ball with the weakened hand." This standard is relative because it measures in relation to the patient's own past performance rather than to a particular and absolute norm of strength.

Every outcome standard can be classified in terms of these three axes. It is often useful to classify the standards of a given measurement tool in order to find the biases and predilections of the author. For example, many such tools have a disproportionate number of performance standards and an inadequate number of state-of-being standards. Perhaps this can be traced to the fact that most nurses are comfortable with behavioral (performance) objectives, but states of being do not conform to the same grammatical pattern.

One basic challenge of composing clear outcome standards is to know when one really has an outcome standard rather than a process standard. Probably the easiest way to judge whether or not a standard measures a true outcome is to apply two rules that tell when it does *not*:

1. When the understood or stated subject of the standard is the nurse, the organization, the patient's family, an event, or anything other than the

patient or some aspect of the patient's being, it is not an outcome standard.
2. When the statement says what someone other than the patient does, it is not an outcome standard. (Example: Patient is turned frequently.)

Another question about standards concerns the specificity with which they should be stated. There is no absolute answer to this question. The specificity of standard statements is closely related to the scope of content covered by the evaluation tool. If the tool covers a limited area, the standards can be given in specific and concrete terms. For example, if the evaluation tool is measuring all alcoholic patients in the stage of delirium tremens, it is possible to state the desired outcomes in great detail. State-of-being standards clearly cannot be stated in behavioral terms, but they can be stated with similar specificity and descriptiveness.

As the scope of content of the evaluation tool broadens, the nature of the standards must change as well. Suppose, for example, that one were to try to write outcome standards using the Mager form for obstetrical patients on the third postpartum day. One could easily produce a list of 200 to 300 such standards. Clearly this form of evaluation becomes unwieldy and impractical. For situations such as this, it behooves the evaluator to reduce the standards to a manageable number, even if they are more general in nature.

Standards of this general sort should be few enough in number that they do not overwhelm the evaluator. To the degree that it is possible, they should be worded so as to be similarly interpreted by different evaluators. While the behavioral type of measure refers to only one behavior, the general standard described here may cover many different actions. For example, "The new mother knows how to feed her infant" includes many different actions, from milk preparation to the actual feeding process.

There are two ways to assist the evaluator in the use of general standards. One way is to list the specific components of the standard. Not all standards lend themselves to this treatment, however, simply because not all standards have parts that can be isolated and defined. When a general standard does not lend itself to enumeration of component parts, the second way is to list for the evaluator several examples that illustrate the standard's attainment.

Frequently a general standard is accompanied by the statement of a rationale. Unfortunately, so-called "rationales" often turn out to be mere explanations of the standard. Appropriately used, a rationale is a justification, not an explanation; it tells why a statement is important enough to be chosen as a standard; it is not a restatement of that standard.

FORMATS FOR QUALITY CONTROL TOOLS

Once the standards have been determined, a general format for the form itself must be prepared. The principal rule to follow is to keep the format simple, easy to use, and easy to interpret by all users. Some common formats are shown in Figure 17-1.

Format 1 is the least likely of the five shown to produce diverse opinions among raters; however, each standard must be defined very precisely. Format 2 has the disadvantage of showing greater variation among raters. Format 3 has the same disadvantage but may be useful if the institution wants to quantify the answers. Quantification has the advantages of promoting competition among nursing units and of permitting a nursing unit to surpass its previous grade. Format 4 has the advantage of stability, for even if the "average" changes in an institution, the form is still applicable. Format 5 is the most difficult to construct, but it permits identification of specific levels of nursing care. However, one must consider whether enough descriptions exist to make accurate classification possible. In Figure 17-1, for example, two variables are given in the third statement of Format 5: teaching and learning. This may confuse the issue. For example, how would one classify the patient who received thorough teaching yet did not show minimal learning?

SOURCES OF EVIDENCE

Once the standards and format of the quality control system have been determined, the next step is to identify the sources of evidence. Primary and secondary sources are usually combined; but, where possible, primary sources are preferable. A primary source gives the rater direct knowledge concerning the standard. For example, if a standard is "Patient receives adequate oral hygiene," the rater goes to the primary source, the patient, to observe for this standard. For the standard "Emergency equipment is complete and ready for use" the observer again goes directly to the primary source, that is, evaluates the equipment first-hand.

Not all standards lend themselves to immediate observation techniques, however. "Promotion of independence" might require a careful evaluation of nursing notes (secondary source) over a period of time. Some standards entail both primary and secondary sources. For example, "Adequate hydration is maintained" might call for direct observation of the skin turgor with secondary observation of the intake and output records.

The patient's chart is a frequent secondary source. Indeed, the evaluation of nursing care via the chart is often either included in the quality check or

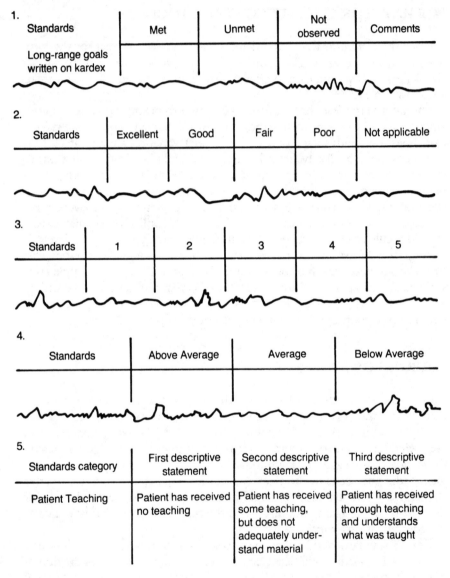

Figure 17-1 Formats for Standards

instituted separately as a nursing chart audit.[12] Another source often used is the patient response (satisfaction or dissatisfaction) to the nursing care. It is important that a group forming a quality control check determine in advance how relevant patient satisfaction is as evidence of professional care. The wording of questions to patients is quite important. Some questions can be worded so as to elicit primary responses: "Did the nurse discuss your surgery with you the day before the operation?" Others cannot be given similar weight: "Are you generally pleased with your nursing care?" The following sources of evidence are those most frequently used in quality control checks: charts, rounds, records, nursing care plans, patient interviews, nurse interviews, and interviews of other health personnel.

Even if a standard is similarly understood by all evaluators, there still may be questions as to what source of evidence would reveal its attainment. Suppose that five evaluators all agree on the meaning of the following standard for blind patients in a rehabilitation unit: "Ambulates safely in known territory." It is still conceivable that without further direction they might evaluate the same standard by five different methods, such as:

1. noting the patient's performance on the standard as recorded in the patient's chart
2. asking several nurses about the patient's ambulation
3. asking the patient about his or her ambulation
4. observing for several days while the patient ambulates on the unit and grounds
5. giving the patient a specific test, such as "go to the solarium and get X."

Clearly some of these evaluation methods are better than others, but the point is that sources of evidence must be clearly identified if standards are to be judged equitably.

FACTORS THAT INFLUENCE THE QUALITY CONTROL SYSTEM

Many other issues may influence both the quality control form and its implementation. The director of nursing care needs to define her precise purposes in using a quality control system. Formulation and implementation of a quality control system can be an educative experience for superiors and head nurses. If staff development is one of the primary objectives of the quality control system, the staff should develop its own system. A group can learn much by devising, revising, and testing its own evaluation tool. If, however, the director is more interested in accurate patient care feedback, she may wish to enlist more expertise in the development of a valid system.

Another legitimate purpose of the quality control system is to motivate nurses toward better patient care. Competitive benefits have already been mentioned. The quality control system is also useful in spotting areas of general weakness and may thus be used as a diagnostic tool by staff education departments.

SURVEILLANCE AND FEEDBACK SYSTEMS

Once the standards have been completed, consideration must be given to setting up the surveillance system. It is important that the quality control form be used in a systematic way. One needs to determine who will evaluate what at what times. Answers to these questions must be based on the institution's needs, but the following guidelines have proved useful in some organizations:

- Schedule evaluation visits at periodic, but unannounced, intervals. The surprise visit is more likely to reflect the normal pattern of nursing care.
- Not all patients need to be evaluated; a sampling technique is quite satisfactory.
- Patient sampling may be done at random, or patients may be selected on the basis of those requiring the most challenging nursing care.
- Persons should serve on the evaluation team long enough to become thoroughly familiar with the evaluation process.
- If evaluation members split the work, each member should grade the same portion of the instrument on all units evaluated.

The third area of quality control identified by Slee is that of corrective action. A quality control system is useless if proper and immediate feedback is not offered to the nursing units involved. It is, however, more productive to have the staff view quality control as a challenge rather than as a punitive club held over their heads.

Nurse managers and staff can be more easily counseled to see the program as a diagnostic tool if they have an integral part in its operation.

For the director, a measure of the quality of nursing care gives a scientific basis on which to calculate nursing personnel needs. She can determine the point beyond which increased staffing alone fails to improve care quality, as well as the point at which care begins to decline due to personnel shortages.

The feedback from process and outcome standards differs. Process standards immediately identify the deficient nursing process, but that is not the case with outcome standards. Outcome measures reveal what is going wrong in the patient's progress, but they do not reveal what is wrong with the nursing process or how to correct it. Outcome standards, therefore, serve as starting points for research into the nursing process, because they do not assume that traditional nursing measures are the proper solutions to patient outcome problems. The research design for determining the cause of an undesirable patient outcome requires use of the scientific method—formulation of hypotheses, identification of all possible variables, and systematic manipulation of variables until the cause of the undesirable outcome is identified and a corrective solution is found.

SUMMARY

Creation of an effective quality control system can be summarized in the following seven (oversimplified) steps:

1. Have a purpose: WHY?
2. Decide which areas to evaluate: WHAT?
3. Identify standards: HOW MUCH?
4. Select a format and construct the tool: HOW?
5. Set up a surveillance system: WHO, WHEN, WHERE?
6. Set up a feedback system: HOW?
7. Develop a system for change: WHY, HOW?

Whether or not the first-line manager is personally involved in the construction of quality assurance measures, she needs to understand the principles underlying their construction. She should be able to tell whether a system and its instruments are valid or flawed. She needs to be able to interpret results from quality assurance measurements on her unit, and she needs to share these results with her staff.

Quality control reports are a major source of data for measuring one's success in the first-line management role. Quality control instruments should measure all aspects of the manager's performance. Good patient outcomes are the essence of effective nursing care. Effective nursing practice is a prerequisite for achieving good patient outcomes. Efficient management of the unit enables effective nursing practice. A well conceived quality assurance system will give the manager feedback on all these aspects. A well conceived quality assurance system can direct the manager in improving patient care, staff performance, and the organization of her unit.

NOTES

1. J. Heinz, "The Effects of DRGs on Patients," *Business and Health* 3, no. 8 (July/August 1986): 17–20.

2. A. Donabedian, "The Epidemiology of Quality," *Inquiry* 22, no. 3 (Fall 1985): 282–292.

3. A.R. Davies and J.E. Ware, "Involving Consumers in Quality of Care Assessment," *Health Affairs* 7, no. 1 (Spring 1988): 33–48.

4. W.L. Roper and G.M. Hackbarth, "Commentary: HCFA's Agenda for Promoting High-Quality Care," *Health Affairs* 7, no. 1 (Spring 1988): 91.

5. V.N. Slee, "How to Know if You Have Quality Control," *Hospital Progress* 53, no. 1 (January 1972): 38.

6. A. Donabedian, "Some Issues in Evaluating the Quality of Nursing Care," *American Journal of Public Health* 59, no. 10 (October, 1969): 1833.

7. L.E. Meltzer, "CCU's Can Save Thousands of Lives; Nurse Is Key Factor In Success," *Hospital Topics* 49, no. 9 (1971): 26.

8. C. Lewis and B. Renski, "Nurse Clinics and Progressive Ambulatory Care," *New England Journal of Medicine* 277, no. 23 (1967): 1236.

9. G. Pardee et al., "Patient Care Evaluation Is Every Nurse's Job," *American Journal of Nursing* 7, no. 10 (1971): 1958.

10. D.E. Brodt, "A Synergistic Theory of Nursing," *American Journal of Nursing* 69, no. 8 (1969): 1674.

11. V.K. Carrieri and J. Sitzman, "Components of Nursing Process," *Nursing Clinics of North America* 6, no. 1 (1971): 115.

12. B.J. Curtis and L.J. Simpson, "Auditing: A Method for Evaluating Quality Care," *Journal of Nursing Administration* 15, no. 10 (October 1985): 14–21.

BIBLIOGRAPHY

Barney, M. "Measuring Quality of Patient Care: A Computerized Approach." *Supervisor Nurse* 12, no. 5 (1981): 40.

Bloch, D. "Criteria, Standards, Norms—Crucial Terms in Quality Assurance." *Journal of Nursing Administration* 7, no. 7 (1977): 20.

Clinton, J.F.; Denyes, M.J.; Goodwin, J.O.; and Koto, E.M. "Developing Criterion Measures of Nursing Care: Case Study of a Process." *Journal of Nursing Administration* 7, no. 7 (1977): 41.

Coyne, C., and Killien, M. "A System for Unit-Based Monitors of Quality of Nursing Care." *Journal of Nursing Administration* 17, no. 1 (January 1987): 26–32.

Davis, A.I. "Measuring Quality: Development of a Blueprint for a Quality Control Assurance Program." *Supervisor Nurse* 8, no. 2 (1977): 17.

Doughty, D.B., and Mash, N.J. *Nursing Audit.* Philadelphia: F.A. Davis Co., 1977.

Hastings, C. "Measuring Quality in Ambulatory Care Nursing." *Journal of Nursing Administration* 17, no. 4 (April 1987): 12-20.

Hegedus, K.S. "A Patient Outcome Criterion Measure." *Supervisor Nurse* 10, no. 1 (1979): 40.

Hegyvary, S.T., and Haussmann, R.K.D. "Monitoring Nursing Care Quality." *Journal of Nursing Administration* 6, no. 9 (1976a): 18.

Hurwitz, L.S., and Tasch, V. "Developing a Quality Assurance Program." *Supervisor Nurse* 8, no. 6 (1977): 50.

McNally, F. "Nursing Audit: Evolution Without Pain." *Supervisor Nurse* 8, no. 6 (1977): 40.

Meisenheimer, C.G. *Quality Assurance: A Complete Guide to Effective Programs.* Rockville, MD: Aspen Publishers, Inc., 1985.

Mowry, M.M., and Korpman, R.A. "Automated Information Systems in Quality Assurance." *Nursing Economics* 5, no. 5 (September/October 1987): 237–244.

Osinski, E.G. "Developing Patient Care Outcomes as a Quality Measure of Nursing Care." *Nursing Management* 18, no. 10 (October 1987): 28.

Purgatorio-Howard, K. "Improving a Quality Assurance Program." *Nursing Management* 17, no. 4 (April 1986): 38–42.

Rinke, L.T., and Wilson, A.A. "Client-Oriented Project Outcomes." *Caring* 7, no. 1 (January 1988): 25–29.

_____. "Quality: Will It Make or Break Your Hospital?" *Hospitals* 60, no. 11 (July 5, 1986): 54–58.

Schmadl, J.C. "Quality Assurance: Examination of the Concept." *Nursing Outlook* 27, no. 7 (1979): 450.

Selvaggi, L.; Ericksen, L.; Keon, P.; and MacKinnon, H.A. "Implementing a Quality Assurance Program in Nursing." *Journal of Nursing Administration* 6, no. 7 (1976): 37.

Tescher, B.E., and Colavecchio, R. "Definition of a Standard for Clinical Nursing Practice." *Journal of Nursing Administration* 7, no. 3 (1977): 32.

_____. "The Relationship of Nursing Process and Patient Outcomes." *Journal of Nursing Administration* 6, no. 9 (1976b): 18.

Wandelt, M.A., and Ager, J. *Quality Patient Scale*. Detroit: Wayne State University Press, 1970.

Weinstein, E.L. "Developing a Measure of the Quality of Nursing Care." *Journal of Nursing Administration* 6, no. 6 (1976): 1.

chapter 18

Employee Performance Appraisal

Three separate aspects of the employee evaluation process are examined in this chapter. The first aspect comprises the structural elements of performance appraisal: purpose, criteria, and measuring systems. Next, the use of appraisal for improving employee performance is reviewed through a sample interview system. Lastly, some of the interpersonal factors of interviews—both techniques and stumbling blocks—are discussed.

THE EVALUATIVE PROCESS

The use of periodic employee performance evaluation is common practice in nursing management. It is also a chronic problem area that often evokes negative responses from both the person being evaluated and the person doing the evaluation. The nature of the problem is twofold. One reason why the process often miscarries has to do with the uses to which the performance evaluation is put. A list of potential uses might include the following: employee motivation; improvement of performance; recognition of accomplishments; establishing work standards; improving communications; letting employees know where they stand; providing a permanent record of employee performance; identifying education needs; and providing a documented basis for retention, promotion, transfer, demotion, dismissal, or salary adjustment.

Most institutions use a single employee evaluation procedure to serve several of these purposes, and this initiates the problem. It is highly unlikely that a single structure can be devised to meet such diverse and possibly incompatible purposes. A document that is used as a basis for withholding a raise, for example, seldom serves as a source of motivation. The tendency to try to make one form and one event serve multiple and incompatible purposes virtually guarantees that none of the potential benefits of evaluation will be realized.

The solution to this problem is to develop separate evaluation procedures for separate purposes. If an employee knows, for example, that an evaluation session is only for the purpose of identifying educational needs, the employee is likely to be frank about deficiencies. If the employee thinks, however, that the same information will be documented in a personnel record and included in future employment references, the employee's responses are not likely to be as honest.

While the concept of separate evaluation procedures for separate purposes is logical, few managers have the time to conduct multiple evaluations for each employee. In light of this fact, it is reasonable to try to combine compatible functions in one evaluation process. In some instances, however, institutional policies may foist incompatible purposes onto the same evaluation process, regardless of the rater's intentions. One principle that should always be maintained is that the employee must clearly understand the purpose(s) that the evaluation is meant to serve.

Trait versus Event Language

The second reason why employee evaluation often goes awry has to do with the nature of the evaluation process itself. Many evaluation forms address traits of the employee. Since this procedure seems to pass judgment on the character of the individual being evaluated, it is not surprising that the employee finds it threatening to self-esteem. Categories such as initiative, appearance, quality of work, quantity of work, competence, interpersonal relationships, and quality of judgments are statements about the individual, not about the events in which the individual participates. Poor scores on such traits typically result in the employee's adopting a pattern of defensiveness and self-justification or in a withdrawal from real communication.

The use of trait categories also places the evaluator at a disadvantage, for trait language represents a summary opinion derived from an observation of multiple behaviors. If the employee disagrees with the judgment of the evaluator, the employee is likely to ask for examples. If the evaluator is unable to recall specific incidents, the evaluator looks inept. Even if the evaluator is able to produce illustrative events, there is still no guarantee that the evaluator and the employee will place the same interpretation on those events. For example, what the evaluator sees as behavior that shows failure to apply basic nursing principles may be interpreted by the employee as creative behavior. When using trait language, there is no way to resolve different interpretations of the same behavior. The result is an unproductive interview that ends in a mutual stand-off.

The solution to this problem is to revise evaluation systems so as to use event language rather than trait language. Employee behaviors can then be compared against stated criterion behaviors. Criterion behavior statements take such forms as "Evolves appropriate care plans for assigned patients," "Prepares patients for discharge by adequate teaching programs," and "Assigns team members according to their credentials and abilities." This form of statement relieves the evaluator of the burden of interpreting behaviors as character traits. The evaluator need only compare the actions of the employee with the actions described in the desired criteria. Fewer disagreements occur between employee and evaluator when the only type question is about what did in fact happen rather than about what that event "meant."

Identification of criterion behaviors is the first of several steps required for structuring an evaluation system that uses event language. Criterion behaviors will not be the same for individuals filling two different positions. The staff nurse and the nursing assistant are expected to demonstrate different behaviors; therefore, they have to be measured against different criteria. Criterion behaviors should be included in each job description as well as in the evaluation form. The criterion behaviors are those most important to job performance, and they should be measurable.

In wording, the behavior statements should be explicit so that they will have the same meaning for all readers. Each statement should identify the expected level of performance in precise behavioral terms. Both the job description and the evaluation tool, if well constructed, will reveal what is considered to be most important for the given role. The following statements are the criteria selected by one institution for evaluation of staff nurses:

- Accurately assesses patient care needs.
- Sets realistic short- and long-term patient goals.
- Plans appropriate nursing care measures to reach identified goals.
- Demonstrates competency in implementing nursing care.
- Documents nursing care plans.
- Evaluates effectiveness of nursing care in relation to goals.
- Modifies care plans as needed to reach goals.

Some institutions prefer greater detail in their criteria than that given here. In any case, the criteria should be stated as desired behaviors, not as traits of the individual.

Construction of the evaluation tool also involves selection of a format. An essay response to each criterion gives the rater the greatest freedom; such a response can include illustrations of actual employee behaviors. On a forced-choice format, the rater must decide for each item whether the employee has met or has failed to meet the behavioral standard. It is also possible to create graduated criteria, numerical or verbal, to estimate the degree to which the individual has met each criterion. The introduction of the subjective element (degree of attainment) does, however, tend to offset some of the advantages gained by use of factual event language.

The next step in instituting an event-based system is the preparation of the employee for the evaluation process. Employees have a right to know what behaviors are expected of them. The job description is discussed with each individual at the time of employment, and it may be supplemented with more detailed materials during the orientation process. In addition, a copy of the actual evaluation form should be given to the new employee at the time of hiring. Then the employee has every chance to orient work behavior to the desired standards during the period for which performance will be measured.

To measure the employee against the stated behavioral objectives, the evaluator keeps anecdotal records of the employee's behavior. Such records should not be interpretive comments such as "Miss X did sloppy work today." Instead, they should describe the behavior: "Miss X left used linen on the floor until 2:00 P.M. and failed to remove a completed breakfast tray from the patient's room until lunchtime." Such behavioral specifics will help to avert arguments over meaning during the evaluation conference.

The manager should routinely set aside time for evaluation activities; this is a vital part of her management function. She may find it easier to select one behavior daily for evaluation; she can then note how all staff members of a given job classification conform or fail to conform to that behavior. This process may give a better distribution of observations than one can gain by trying to evaluate one employee, on several criteria, on the same day.

Planned evaluation periods are also more likely to reveal the typical behavior of employees. Without planned observations and recordings, the evaluator is likely to remember only those unpleasant, though possibly infrequent, occasions when an employee makes mistakes.

Rating Errors

In filling out the evaluation form, the rater needs to be cognizant of common rating defects. The following rater distortions occur frequently:

- *Halo effect.* The individual whose performance in several known areas is good is assumed to perform well in other, unknown areas.

- *Recency effect.* Recent issues weigh more heavily with the rater than do events that occurred earlier in the evaluation period.
- *Problem distortion.* One poor performance weighs more heavily with the rater than do multiple good performances that went unnoticed, since they created no problems.
- *Sunflower effect.* The rater grades all her employees too high because of a feeling that she has a "great team."
- *Central tendency.* The evaluator tends to mark everyone as average, especially if she is unsure of the real performance on a particular criterion.
- *Rater temperament effect.* Raters manifest differences in the strictness or leniency with which they rate employees.
- *Guessing error.* Some raters guess at behavior rather than record that particular observations were not made.

A related issue is the question of who should evaluate an employee. The ideal rater is the manager to whom the employee reports. For a staff nurse or a nursing assistant, this manager is usually the head nurse; for the head nurse, the rater is usually a supervisor. Evaluation is best handled by the management level closest to the employee, because that manager has the most extensive first-hand knowledge of the employee's performance. This choice of raters also helps to reinforce the appropriate lines of authority. If a supervisor evaluates the employees who work under a head nurse, for example, it undermines the head nurse's ability to control her personnel.

The so-called "peer evaluation," in which employees evaluate each other, places responsibility unfairly in the hands of a staff member. It is difficult for a staff nurse, for example, to give a fair but low grade to a coworker whom she may have to ask for assistance in the future. In most cases, the peer review leads to inflated evaluations so as to preserve productive work relations. In addition, one may perceive this approach to be an abdication of management responsibility.

Another issue is the question of how often to evaluate personnel. The more often evaluation can be performed, the less stressful the situation becomes; moreover, frequent evaluation takes on the character of guidance rather than of judgment. Yearly evaluations are clearly too far apart to have a vital impact on behavior patterns, and the very infrequency of the event causes high anxiety levels in employees.

CHANGE-ORIENTED EVALUATION

Evaluation interviews can have many different purposes. The interview that is aimed at improving employee performance will be discussed here. For a performance appraisal to have the effect of improving job behaviors, several things must occur for the employee. The employee must (1) learn which behaviors are desired, (2) learn which of his or her behaviors fail to meet the desired pattern, (3) learn how to change a behavior toward the desired pattern, and (4) leave the interview determined to change the behavior. These four requirements form the basis of the successful evaluation interview; none of them can be omitted.

Identifying the Desired Behaviors

The first requirement is that the employee be acquainted with the desired behaviors. A good way to accomplish this is to begin the evaluation interview by reviewing the employee's job description, in order to locate and explore differences in interpretation and attitude between the manager and the employee concerning the job. Even when an employee has been in a position over a long period, mutual exploration of the employee's role and its expected behavioral components can be beneficial.

Another useful technique for identifying different interpretations of a job is for both the manager and the employee to prepare for the interview by listing and ranking the key functions of the employee's job. A comparison and discussion of differences between their key-function lists will help the manager and the employee to understand each other better. Differences, whether about job content or assumed importance of tasks, will help the employee to see which functions the manager views as most important. Seeing the employee's list will help the manager better to understand the employee's work behavior. Obviously one should not review a job description prior to requesting a "spontaneous" list of key functions, because the memory of the job description would preclude spontaneous generation of the employee's internalized key functions.

Identifying Behaviors That Fail To Meet the Desired Pattern

The second requirement for a change-oriented evaluation interview is that the employee must learn how the employee's behaviors fail to measure up to those desired by the manager. For this to occur effectively, a radical deviation from the typical evaluation interview is required. In the typical interview the employee's behavior is the focus of the evaluative process. The employee sits passively while the manager describes things that the employee did correctly and incorrectly. In this context, the employee understandably interprets the mention of things done correctly to be mere "sugar coating," intended to make the recitation of shortcomings more palatable. This "right-versus-wrong" mechanism transforms the evaluation process into a kind of trial during which the employee simply hopes that the good will outweigh the bad. This type of evaluation is not likely to change the employee's behavior, because the interest of the employee is focused totally on the final "verdict"—i.e., on how the jury weighted the conflicting evidence. The most that can happen is acceptance or rejection of the judgment. Where evaluative balance sheets are required by the organization, the manager might do well to complete this task in a routine manner but to separate it from the work-counseling interview.

In order to satisfy the second criterion of a productive evaluation interview, therefore, it is clear that the balancing-out approach should be avoided. The simplest way to do this is to eliminate one side of the balance—the good side. This is not to imply that the good is forgotten or ignored; it means merely that it is not appropriate content for an interview that has the purpose of improving performance.

Since this type of evaluation interview does not follow the usual pattern, the employee will need to be oriented to the nature and purpose of the counseling interview. The employee must know beforehand that the purpose of the interview is to improve job performance, not to recognize successes. Thus, for both the best employee and the least effective one the evaluation interview has the same purpose and structure: to probe for ways to improve performance.

How the identification of behaviors to be changed is managed in the interview will depend greatly on the insight, objectivity, and motivation of the employee. If the employee is capable of objective self-evaluation, the performance deficiencies can be identified through reciprocal interaction between manager and employee. When an employee is not capable of objective self-evaluation, it is up to the manager to identify behavioral deficiencies clearly.

One of the ironies of the evaluation process is that the better the employees are, the more likely they will be to identify their own deficiencies; less capable employees are less likely to see their own defects. Capable employees are usually adept at identifying performance areas to be improved, because they measure themselves against internalized standards. Less capable employees are more likely to require someone else to identify their deficiencies. Regrettably, in some instances the manager will simply have to assert that specific behaviors must be changed, without meaningful self-insight having occurred.

It is not prudent to identify all the deficiencies of an employee; only those that are to be changed first should be cited. It is unlikely that an employee will be able to work effectively on more than one or two behavioral changes at a time.

With employees whose performance is satisfactory, the manager may find it most productive to let them select their own behaviors for improvement. With other employees, the manager may have to specify the behaviors that most seriously impair their work. There may be instances when an exceptionally poor employee has more than one or two behaviors that must be changed immediately if the employee is to be retained in the position. While it is probably unrealistic to expect that this individual will be able to make so many behavioral changes at once, at least the interview serves to document that the required changes have been communicated to the employee.

Like any other system, the change-oriented employee evaluation must be used with judgment. The system works best with two types of employees: self-motivated achievers who enjoy working toward a goal, and workers who clearly need guidance and direction from an authority figure. It is always possible, however, that a very good employee is not interested in making any performance changes. In this case, the manager would be wise to alter the evaluation system if she wants to retain the employee. When an employee has, in effect, asserted that only so much will be done on the job and no more, the manager must accept that stand and then decide whether or not to keep the employee on that basis.

In identifying behaviors to be changed it is important that the manager not be overzealous in trying to impose some "ideal employee image" on a worker. It is unrealistic to expect exactly the same behaviors from all employees. The manager who singlemindedly insists on ideal performance will rob herself of many of the best talents of her staff. For example, one nurse may approach her work with zest and enthusiasm, and another may approach her work with cautious, steady planning. Both of these contrasting behaviors may result in valuable contributions to the total work group. The manager should focus on developing the talents and abilities inherent in the employee's makeup. If the manager and the employee together identify behaviors to be improved, these individual considerations can be taken into account.

Identifying How To Change Behaviors

The third requirement for a productive change-oriented interview is that the employee must understand how to change a behavior toward the desired pattern. Too often managers believe that this can be done merely by pinpointing an undesirable behavior and directing the employee to change it. This is seldom effective. It is important that the employee and the manager clearly identify the new behaviors that the employee will be expected to exhibit. These behaviors must be described, action by action. For example, if the manager and the nurse employee agree that the nurse will now distribute her medications on time, the agreement does not give the nurse any help. It does not tell her how to modify the behaviors that cause her to distribute drugs chronically late in the first place.

A time limit should be set by which the employee can be expected to have practiced and assimilated the new behavior. Some behaviors, of course, cannot be allowed to develop gradually, but these are in the minority. Usually the employee can be given a grace period during which to concentrate on effecting the change in behavior.

Motivating toward Improvement

The last requirement for a successful change-oriented interview is that the employee must leave the conference determined to change an undesirable behavior. For many individuals, participation in the setting of the behavioral goals will alone provide this motivation. If the process of employee evaluation is seen as a means whereby the manager assists her employee to find easier ways to function, the process will be seen as supportive, not judgmental. If the employee feels that the manager is sincerely trying to help, this will serve as motivation to adopt the agreed-upon behavioral changes.

There are many false conceptions about motivation, the least valid of which is that it can be supplied from the outside. Motivation is an internal phenomenon; an individual either is or is not motivated to achieve a given goal. It is not possible for the manager to motivate a person who does not want to be motivated. Some individuals can inspire others in such a way that they become motivated, but the manager should not have to rely on charisma. While it is not possible to supply motivation, it is possible for the manager to require certain behaviors as conditions for holding a job, receiving a raise, or getting a promotion. Control mechanisms can be used to ensure that the employee will leave the interview with the knowledge that, in order to hold the job or obtain a raise or promotion, a behavior must be changed.

With an exact idea of what is expected, and with a time limit set for behavioral change, the employee will understand that the interview has not been a mere rhetorical exercise. To ensure that the time limit has meaning, the manager should hold one or more follow-up conferences during and at the end of the projected period. It is a good idea to close the evaluation interview by setting the date for the follow-up conference and by affirming that the purpose of that conference will be to evaluate progress toward the change(s) in behavior.

The evaluation interview designed to improve employee performance by identifying deficiencies is only one kind of change-oriented interview. With some employees the manager will prefer to build on strengths rather than to correct weaknesses; this is the way in which a successful employee can be sincerely commended. When a manager is interested in the special knowledge or abilities of an employee to the extent that she helps the employee to build on these talents, recognition is inherent. The manager's interest provides much more employee satisfaction than does the abstract "reading off" of a list of virtues in the typical employee evaluation interview.

GUIDELINES FOR COMMUNICATING IN INTERVIEWS

In conducting the employee evaluation interview, the manager can be assisted by a few basic guidelines. The first is to hold a two-way communication. This means that the interview must be planned to involve active participation from the employee, not just "tell and sell" from the evaluator. The manager can ensure two-way communication by preparing a number of good questions to ask the employee, questions that will require thought and discussion.

The key-function comparison scheme mentioned previously is an example of an activity that creates two-way communication. In order to make the interview mutual, the employee should be advised to prepare for the evaluation just as conscientiously as does the manager. Both parties should not only identify key functions and work problems but also make suggestions and pose questions relevant to the employee's performance. If the manager is mature and experienced in her role, another way to establish two-way communication is for the two individuals to discuss their mutual expectations of each other.

Whenever possible the manager seeks agreement concerning deficiencies and goals. However, the interview should not be reduced to a bargaining session. The manager may need to assert her authority when the employee is not in agreement; employee acceptance is desirable, but not always possible.

Another requirement for the interview is that the manager must make absolutely clear what she means. For example, if the interview is a last warning before a potential dismissal, she must make certain that the employee understands the situation. Some employees use defense mechanisms to interpret as casual conversation that which the manager means to be a final warning. In all instances it is useful for the manager to follow the conference with a letter to the employee summarizing the interview, the problems discussed, and the goals set. When an interview serves a disciplinary function, it is absolutely essential that this written follow-up be done. While disciplining an employee is never an easy task, the use of an event-focused evaluation system makes the job less difficult.

Interview Traps

One of the best ways to maintain good communication during an evaluation interview is for the manager to avoid falling into common interview traps. These traps include:

- conducting a one-way conversation
- interrupting the employee's thoughts, explanations, or questions
- criticizing the employee rather than the performance
- smoothing over real deficiencies and problems too quickly
- failing to investigate facts before expressing opinions
- passing the buck by claiming that one's corrective measures originate "higher up"
- allowing the interview to fall into charge-countercharge cycles
- allowing the interview to fall into charge-excuse cycles
- allowing the interview to deteriorate into a social visit.

During an interview the manager continually evaluates what is happening in the interaction. She must recognize what she is doing as well as what the employee is doing in order to avoid traps and to keep the interview productive. One basic rule for the manager is to keep her response options open. For every statement made by an employee, there are numerous ways to respond.

Unconsidered responses tend to fit into one of two typical patterns. The first pattern is to respond with a judgment of the employee's statement. In an interview situation, this response creates a trial-like atmosphere. The second common pattern of response is direct reaction to the content of the employee's statement. There are many times when this is an appropriate response, but there are also many times when other responses are better.

To illustrate some response options, consider the following interview that has fallen into a charge-excuse cycle:

Head Nurse: ". . . also, you failed to give Mrs. Jones her passive exercise all last week."

Staff Nurse: "You are thinking about last Thursday, and that day she was so upset she wouldn't let anyone touch her."

Head Nurse: "I'm not thinking just of Thursday. You didn't exercise her weak side on Friday either."

Staff Nurse: "On Friday her doctor did that spinal tap and took all morning at it. No one could have gotten in there to exercise her."

Head Nurse: "But nothing occurred on Friday afternoon, and you still didn't exercise her."

Staff Nurse: "But I was taught that patients were to lie flat and quiet after a spinal tap to prevent a headache."

This head nurse has fallen into a deadly trap, for the staff nurse can probably find an excuse for any charge the head nurse can level. The head nurse has in each case responded to the content of the staff nurse's statement. As long as she continues this, she will neither break the cycle nor make her point.

To break off this unproductive cycle, the head nurse needs to recognize that such a pattern takes two to keep it going. As soon as one participant refuses to play, the cycle is interrupted. One simple solution is for the head nurse to admit that this line of conversation is unproductive and break it off to move to another topic.

A better option might be to answer the last response with a question or suggestion that directs the employee out of the cycle: "Why don't you review for me your plans for Mrs. Jones last week. Maybe we can explore what happened to them."

Alternatively, the head nurse might switch from content-directed charges to feeling exploration. She could direct a question to the staff nurse concerning her feelings about the patient, Mrs. Jones. Another choice would be for the head nurse to point out that Mrs. Jones's care is only part of a larger problem and then return to that, instead of haggling over one instance of behavior. Another useful response option is for the head nurse to call the staff nurse's attention to the excuse pattern of her responses. They might then explore why this pattern dominates her explanations of her work. Numerous paths can be taken to restore the interview to a productive session. The critical factor is simply that the manager must recognize the defective communication pattern and try a constructive response option.

Other Interview Processes

Managers often use the evaluation interview to encourage changes in employee attitudes. It is impossible to work with attitudes that are expressed in trait language, such as "You are hostile," "You are racially prejudiced," "You are headstrong and impulsive." One logical way to proceed toward creating a desired attitude change is to identify the behavior or behaviors that give evidence of the trait. To tell an employee, for example, that she is impulsive does not tell her how to change that trait, nor does it make her wish to change. It is possible, however, to identify behaviors that both demonstrate impulsiveness and impair the work process. It is quite legitimate to require that an employee change a nonfunctional work behavior.

Ideally a manager tries to create in an employee a positive attitude toward a suggested behavioral change. In some instances, however, the best way to change attitudes is to change behaviors first. When attitudes are firmly entrenched, this approach may be appropriate. Once individuals are routinely doing a particular act, they are likely to develop positive attitudes toward that act. Many nurse managers, for example, have tried to build a "favorable attitude" toward written nursing care plans before requiring them on the nursing units. However, the favorable attitude may still fail to develop, no matter what steps the manager takes to induce it. On the other hand, the nurse manager who firmly and consistently requires that care plans be written by each staff nurse finds that, after a short period of time, attitudes toward writing the plans have become positive.

Managers often have difficulty knowing when and how to end an interview. While there is no absolute rule for timing, almost any interview can easily be contained within an hour. If a manager holds longer conferences, she is likely to be doing one of two things: (1) turning the interview into a social visit or (2) belaboring the same essential points. Both of these patterns are to be avoided.

A good way to end the interview and give it a sense of completion is for the manager to summarize the events of the interview. She can briefly identify the problems discussed, the agreements reached, the goals set, and the proposed behavioral changes. This summarizing activity has two functions: First, it gives the employee a final chance to compare her interpretation of the interview with the interpretation of the manager. Differences in understanding may thus be revealed and settled. Second, the summarization clearly announces to the employee that the interview is at an end.

There is no easy way to learn interview skills. The manager who uses a post-interview self-review, however, will improve her skills considerably. She should analyze each interview immediately after it is finished, while the dialogue, including her responses to employee statements, is still fresh in her mind. Learning to recognize her weaknesses in interviewing will help the manager to guard against these deficiencies in future conferences. The manager who develops skill in evaluative interviewing will be rewarded by improved employee-manager relations and by improved work performance from her staff.

SUMMARY

Employee performance appraisal is a must for an effective organization, yet an evaluation system is fraught with hazards if it is poorly conceived. Similarly, the effects of employee evaluation and counseling can be detrimental if they are not managed with skill. In order to make evaluation work for her rather than against her, the first-line manager must learn the skills required in personnel appraisal and counseling. She must also work to see that her organization has the proper instruments and systems to make the appraisal effort pay off.

When an effective system of employee appraisal is applied by managers skilled in the performance of appraisal and counseling, then poor staff performance can be corrected and good staff performance enhanced. It is important to note that both the system for appraisal and the methods for doing the individual appraisals and counseling are important factors in achieving the goals of the system.

The new nurse manager often avoids completing performance evaluations or does the task superficially because it involves passing judgment on others. For the nurse who has been taught to be nonjudgmental (of patients), the task may be uncomfortable. The best way to get over hesitancy concerning this vital function is to learn to do it well. After all, the first duty of the manager is to direct others in the performance of their work. Learning to be effective in performance evaluation and counseling is going a long way toward achieving that end.

BIBLIOGRAPHY

Behrend, B.L., et al. "Articulating Professional Nursing Practice Behaviors." *Journal of Nursing Administration* 116, no. 2 (February 1986): 20–24.

Bernhardt, J., and Schuette, L. "P.E.T.: A Method of Evaluating Professional Nurse Performance." *Journal of Nursing Administration* 5, no. 8 (1975): 18.

Brief, A.P. "Developing a Usable Performance Appraisal System." *Journal of Nursing Administration* 9, no. 10 (1979): 7.

Cunningham, L.S. "The Art and Science of Promotion." *Journal of Nursing Administration* 6, no. 1 (1976): 37.

del Bueno, D. "Performance Evaluation: When All Is Said and Done, More Is Said Than Done." *Journal of Nursing Administration* 7, no. 10 (1977): 21.

_____. "Implementing a Performance Evaluation System." *Supervisor Nurse* 10, no. 2 (1979): 48.

Dracup, L. "Improving Clinical Evaluation." *Supervisor Nurse* 10, no. 6 (1979): 24.

Gauerke, R.D. "Appraisal as a Retention Tool." *Supervisor Nurse* 8, no. 6 (1977): 34.

Goodykoontz, L. "Performance Evaluation of Staff Nurses." *Supervisor Nurse* 12, no. 8 (1981): 39.

Haar, L.P., and Hicks, J.R. "Performance Appraisal: Derivation of Effective Assessment Tools." *Journal of Nursing Administration* 6, no. 7 (1976): 20.

Lawson, B.N. "Evaluation—A Sorry Procedure." *Supervisor Nurse* 9, no. 9 (1978): 32.

Marriner, A. "Evaluation of Personnel." *Supervisor Nurse* 7, no. 5 (1976a): 36.

_____. "Discipline of Personnel." *Supervisor Nurse* 7, no. 11 (1976b): 15.

Marshall, J.R., and Schau, E. "An Evaluation Process for Nursing Assistants." *Journal of Nursing Administration* 6, no. 8 (1976): 37.

McNamara, E.M. "The Caring Employer Helps the Troubled Employee." *Hospitals* 50, no. 20 (1976): 93.

Meyer, A.L. "A Framework for Assessing Performance Problems." *Journal of Nursing Administration* 14, no. 5 (May 1984): 40–43.

Nauright, L. "Toward a Comprehensive Personnel System: Performance Appraisal—Part IV." *Nursing Management* 18, no. 8 (August 1987): 67–77.

Robertson, P., and Knutson, K.E. "Disciplinary Conference Letter." *Supervisor Nurse* 7, no. 3 (1976): 10.

Schuler, R.S. *Personnel and Human Resource Management* (Third Edition). St. Paul, MN: West Publishing Co., 1987.

South, J.C. "The Performance Profile: A Technique for Using Appraisals Effectively." *Journal of Nursing Administration* 8, no. 1 (1978): 27.

Stull, M.K. "Staff Nurse Performance: Effects on Goal-Setting and Performance Feedback." *Journal of Nursing Administration* 16, nos. 7, 8 (July/August 1986): 26–30.

West, N.; Ayers, M.; and Sudbury, J. "An Objective Appraisal Instrument for Nurses." *Supervisor Nurse* 10, no. 3 (1979): 32.

Index

A

Accreditation of educational programs
as professional goal, 54-55
Actions, delegation of, 169
Adaptive mode of management, 62-65
Administration of policies as first-line
manager responsibility, 103-104
Agency nurses
for increased activity, 269
use of, liability problems with, 130
Alcohol abuse, nurse suspected of,
managing, 133-138. *See also* Impaired
nurse
American Academy of Nursing (AAN),
52
American Hospital Association (AHA),
50
American Medical Association (AMA),
50-51
American Nurses' Association (ANA),
51, 52
Anticipation of content in message
reception, 111
Artificial heart, ethical quandaries arising
from, 142
Assignment, definition of,
262

B

Baseline safety guide for resource-
driven model of care, 39-41
Behavior(s)
desired, identifying, in change-
oriented performance appraisal, 307
failing to meet desired pattern,
identifying, in change-oriented
performance appraisal, 307-309
how to change, identifying, in change-
oriented performance appraisal,
309-310
human, directing and controlling,
188-189
Billing, variable, definition of, 262
Budget
personnel, 215
planning of, 218-219
supply, 216-217
Budgeting, 212-219. *See also*
Budget
cost containment in, 217-218
expense types in, 214-217
incremental, 213-214
rudiments of, 213-217
zero-based, 214
Burnout, 161-162

Note: Pages appearing in italics indicate entries found in artwork.

Business
    health care as, 5-6
    of nursing, 209-220
        budgeting in, 212-219. *See also*
        Budget; Budgeting
        structuring, 186-188

C

Call-in staff for increased activity, 269
Capital, expenses, 214-215
Change
    continuity or, 206-207
    effecting, 200-206
    implementing, resources for, 202-206
    logistics of, 206
    psychological aspects of, 200-202
    resistance to, 201-202
Change-oriented evaluation, 306-311
    identifying behaviors failing to meet
        desired pattern in, 307-309
    identifying desired behaviors in, 307
    identifying how to change behaviors
        in, 309-310
    motivating toward improvement in,
        310-311
Classical theory of organization, 240-247
    operational principles in, 245-247
    organizational chart in, 241-245
Clinical ladders, 57
Committee(s)
    feedback mechanisms of, 178
    function of, 179
    interdivisional, 184-185
    leadership skills for, 185-189
    membership on, 177-178
    powers of, 176-177
    productivity of, 178-179
    structure and function of, evaluation
        of, 176
    standing, 180-182
Communication
    collateral relations in, with nurse
        colleagues, 119-122
    directional flow of, 115-116
    in employment performance appraisal
        interviews, guidelines for, 311-314

face-to-face, 113
as first-line manager responsibility,
    101-102
forms of, in communication, 113-115
function of, 108
groups and, 116-126
    collateral relations in, 117-126
        with health professionals, 118-119
        with patients as consumers,
        122-123
        with support services, 117-118
        with physician colleagues, 123-126
    support services and negotiated
        order model in, 117-118
mediated, 113, 114
message content and, 112-113
methods of, 109
model of, 107-109
receiver of, nurse manager as, 111-113
sender of, nurse manager as, 109-111
structure of, 108-109
Companion floor system for increased
    activity, 270
Competence, staff, assuring, nurse
    manager's responsibilities for, 130-131
Computer scheduling, 276
Computers, 232-234
    systems model and, in modern theory
        of organization, 259-260
Consent, informed, 141
Consumer(s)
    impact of cost containment on, 4-5
    marketing to, 6-7
    patients as, collateral relations with,
        122-123
Consumer orientation in health care,
    29-32
Content, anticipation of, in message
    reception, 111
Context, managers, 238-240
Continuing education, 56-57
Continuity, change or, 206-207
Cost-benefit analysis, 74-75
Cost containment, 217-218
Cost-effective management, 209-212
Cost effectiveness model of financial
    planning, 74

Customer satisfaction, quality service and, 229-230
Cyclical scheduling, 276

D

Decentralization, delegation and, 172-173
Decentralized organization, role of first-line manager in, 97-98
Decision(s)
  delegation of, 168-169
  staffing, 265-278. *See also* Staffing, decision(s) on
Decision making, 196-197
  definition of, 193
Delegation, 167-174
  of action, 169
  content of, 169-170
  of decision, 168-169
  elements for, 167-169
  modes of, 170-172
  process of, 171-172
  of responsibilities, 168
  special problems of, 172-174
  structures for, 170
  of tasks, 168
  24-hour, 173-174
Delivery systems, alternative, growth of, 13-14
Departments, other, materials and services provided by, 225-227
Design groups, 182-183
Development, staff, as first-line manager responsibility, 102
Diagnosis-related groups (DRGs)
  classification system, 4
  hospital utilization patterns and, 12
  management changes and, 63-64
Direct expenses, 217
Direction of personnel, 174
Double shifting for increased activity, 270
Drug abuse, nurse suspected of, managing, 133-138. *See also* Impaired nurse

E

Education for excellence, 55-58
Effectiveness, managerial, 73-75
Effectiveness models of management, 77
Efficiency, managerial, 73-75
Efficiency models of management, 77
Employee performance appraisal, 302-315
  change-oriented evaluation in, 306-311. *See also* Change-oriented evaluation
  evaluative process in, 302-306
  interviews for, communication guidelines for, 311-314
  rating errors in, 305-306
  trait versus event language in, 303-305
Entrepreneurial mode of management, 65-66
Environment
  changed, nursing in, 16
  control of, in problem solving, 198-200
  institutional, organization of, 15-16
  managed-care, 14-15
Equity issue in health care, 143-144
Ethical issues in health care, 143-144
Ethical quandaries, explosion of, 142-143
Evaluation
  as first-line manager responsibility, 102
  motivation and, 162-164
Event language versus trait language in employee performance, 303-305
Expenses
  capital, 214-215
  direct, 217
  operating, 215
  overhead, 215

F

Factor evaluations for classifying patients, 263

Feedback systems in quality control,
298-299
Financial models, 74-75
First-line management, strategies
planning and, 69-70
First-line nurse manager, 93-105
effects of organizational structure on,
97-98
goals of, 23-85. See also Goals
management by, 167-190. See also
Management
in management of staff, 99
professional relationships of, 96-97
responsibility(ies) of, 99-104
for administration of policies,
103-104
for communicating and motivating,
101-102
for ensuring patients' welfare,
102-103
for measurement and evaluation,
102
for planning and organizing,
100-101
for setting objectives, 99-100
for staff development, 102
role of
analysis of, 93-99
ethical implications of, 141-146
legal implications of, 129-141.
See also Legal responsibilities
resources of, 98-99
as sender/receiver of communication,
109-116
strategic planning by, 69-70
supervision by, 150-164. See also
Supervision
Float staff for increased activity, 269
Functional staff assignment, 277-278

G

Goals
effectiveness as, 73-75
efficiency as, 73-75
leadership tone and, 27-29
of nursing division, 20-21

nursing theory, 42-44
patient care standards and, 41-42
patient ideologies and, 32-42
productivity as, 75-84. See also
Productivity
professional nursing excellence and,
46-58. See also Professional
nursing excellence
strategic planning and, 66-70
Goal-driven models of care, 35-36
Goal-oriented management, 60-66
adaptive mode of, 62-65
entrepreneurial mode of, 65-66
planning mode of, 60-62
Government, administrative branches
of, related to health care knowledge
of, need for, 47-48
Group(s)
based on organizational position and
job function, 183-184
design, 182-183
for management, 175-185. See also
Committee(s)

H

Head nurse. See also First-line nurse
manager
Health care
as business, 5-6
home, emergence of, 4
home, technology in, 231-232
marketing of, to consumer, 6-7
quality issues in, 7-8
Health Care Financing Administration
(HCFA), 7-8
Health care professionals
collateral relations with, 118-119
impact of changes on, 8-10
Health maintenance organizations
(HMOs), 7, 13-5
group model for, 14
independent practice associations as,
13-14
network model for, 14
Health-related organizations,
participation in, 48-51

Heart, artificial, ethical quandaries
arising from, 142
Home health care
emergence of, 4
nurses for, nurse manager's
responsibility for, 130-131
technology in, 231-232
Hospitals, marketing services of, 7
Human behavior, directing and
controlling, 188-189

I

Ideology(ies)
nursing, goals and, 33-35
patient, goals and, 32-42
Impaired nurse, management of, 133-138
intervention in, 134-136
re-entry in, 136-137
responsibility of nurse manager in, 137-138
Improvement, motivation toward, in
change-oriented performance
appraisal, 310-311
Incremental budgeting, 213-214
Independent practice associations
(IPAs), 13-14
Indices, productivity, 77-80
Informed consent, 141
Institutional environment, organization
of, 15-16
Institutional policies, legal issues and,
138-140
Interdivisional committees, 184-185
Interviews, employment performance
appraisal
communication guidelines for, 311-314
processes in, 313-314
traps in, 311-313
Inventory control, 223-224
Issues, on-the-job, 144-146

J

Job
description of, 151-152
design of, versus staff skills in
supervision, 151-153

Job function, groups based on,
183-184
Job stress, 161-162
Joint Commission on Accreditation of
Healthcare Organizations, 49
Joint roles in nursing, 121

K

Knowledge, nursing, programmed
versus unprogrammed, 90-91
Knowledge workers, supervision of,
150-151

L

Language, event versus trait in employee
performance, 303-305
Leader, studies of, in neoclassical theory
of organization, 248-249
Leadership skills, committee,
185-189
Legal responsibilities
institutional policies and, 138-140
liability and, 131-133
in managing impaired nurse,
133-138
to and for organization, 129-140
to patients, 140-141
safeguards for, 131
for staff competence, 130-131
Legal safeguards in nursing practice,
131
Liability, nurses', 131-133

M

Managed-care environment, 14-15
Management
of change, 192-207. *See also* Change;
Problem solving management
concepts of, 238-260
context of, 238-240
cost-effective, 209-212
by exception (MBE), 63
first-line, strategic planning and,
69-70

of materials, 222-227. *See also*
Materials management by objective
(MBO), 61-62
effectiveness/efficiency and,
73, 74
organizational theories in, 240-260
of people
committee leadership skills in,
185-189
delegation in, 167-174. *See also*
Delegation
direction in, 174
groups in, 175-185. *See also*
Committee(s); Groups
personnel, productivity and, 83-84
problem solving, 192-200. *See also*
Problem solving management
of product line, 228-229
of staff by first-line nurse manager,
99
of technology, 230-234
Management models, effectiveness/
efficiency and, 73-74
Manager
first-line nurse, 93-105. *See also*
First-line nurse manager
problem solving by, in neoclassical
theory of organization, 249-252
and worker, interactions between,
studies of, in neoclassical theory of
organization, 252-253
Marketing to consumer, 6-7
Materials management, 222-227
inventory control in, 223-224
staff involvement in, 224-225
Materials provided by other departments,
225-227
Measurement as first-line manager
responsibility, 102
Measurement systems for nursing care,
285-299. *See also* Quality control
Mentoring in orientation of new staff,
156-157
Message content in communication,
112-113
Message reception, problems of,
111-112

Models
of care
goal-driven, 35-36
resource-driven, 36-39
financial, 73-74
management, 73-74
Modern theory of organization, 254-260
quality assurance as system
application in, 258-259
system model in, computers and,
259-260
systems model in, 254-258
Modular staff assignments, 278-279
Motivating toward improvement in
change-oriented performance
appraisal, 310-311
Motivation, 159-164
burnout and, 161-162
evaluation and, 162-164
in facilitation of work, 160-161
as first-line manager responsibility,
101-102
job stress and, 161-162
recognition and, 162-164

N

Narcotic abuse, nurse suspected of,
managing, 133-138. *See also*
Impaired nurse
National context, 3-10
National Health Council, 48
National League for Nursing (NLN),
51, 52
Negotiated order model for relations with
support services, 117-118
Neoclassical theory of organization,
247-254
problem solving by manager in,
249-252
studies of interactions between
manager and worker in, 252-253
studies of leader in, 248-249
studies of workers in, 253-254
Neonatal technologies, new, ethical
quandaries arising from,
142

Nurse(s)
  as colleagues, collateral relations
    with, 119-122
  effects of health care changes on, 8-10
  liability of, 131-133
  newly licensed, orientation of,
    154-155
  part-time, supervising, 157-159
Nurse manager. *See also* First-line nurse
  manager
Nursing
  business of, 209-220. *See also*
    Business of nursing in changed
    environment, 16
Nursing division, 16-17
  goals of, 20-21
  objectives of, 19-20
  philosophy of, 18, 19, 20
  purpose of, 18-19, 20
Nursing ideology, goals and, 33-35
Nursing knowledge, programmed versus
  unprogrammed, 90-91
Nursing organizations, participation in,
  51-53
Nursing patient classification systems
  (NPCS), staffing and, 262-265
Nursing practice, legal safeguards in,
  131
Nursing research, professional excellence
  and, 57-58
Nursing theory, goals and, 42-44
Nursing Tri-Council, 52

O

Objectives
  of nursing division, 19-20
  setting of, as first-line manager
    responsibility, 99-100
Operating expenses, 215
Organization(s), 12-21
  classical theory of, 240-247. *See also*
    Classical theory of organization
  emerging systems of, 13-21
  health maintenance. *See* Health
    maintenance organizations (HMOs)
  health-related, participation in, 48-51

of institutional environment, 15-16
  legal responsibilities to and from,
    129-140
  modern theory of, 254-260. *See also*
    Modern theory of organization
  neoclassical theory of, 247-254. *See
    also* Neoclassical theory of
    organization
  nursing, participation in, 51-53
  nursing division in, 16-17
  professionals, goals of, 53-55
  traditional systems of, 12-13
Organizational structure, effects of,
  on role of first-line manager, 97-98
Organizing as first-line manager
  responsibility, 100-101
Orientation of new staff, 153-159
  mentoring in, 156-157
  for newly licensed nurses, 154-155
  preceptor programs in, 155-156
Outcome standards for quality control,
  288-290
Overhead expenses, 215
Overtime for increased activity, 270

P

Part-time nurse, supervising, 157-159
Patient(s)
  as consumers, collateral relations
    with, 122-123
  legal obligations to, 140-141
  placement of, to balance nursing
    activity, 270
  rights of, 140
  welfare of, ensuring, as first-line
    manager, 102-103
Patient care, standards of, 41-42
Patient ideologies, goals and, 32-42
Peer review organizations (PROs), 8
  in nursing, 47
Perceptions, control of, in problem
  solving, 197-198
Performance appraisal, employee,
  302-315. *See also* Employee
  performance appraisal
Personnel. *See* Staff

Personnel budget, 215
Personnel management
  productivity and, 83-84
  real versus ideal, 89-90
Philosophy of nursing division,
  18, 19, 20
Physicians
  as colleagues, collateral relations with,
    123-126
  effects of health care changes on, 8-10
Planning
  as first-line manager responsibility,
    100-101
  strategic, 66-70
    first-line management and, 69-70
Planning mode of management, 60-62
Policies, administration of, as first-
  line manager responsibility, 103-104
Preceptor programs in orientation of
  new staff, 155-156
Preferred provider organization (PPO),
  14
Pride, sense of, motivation and, 159-160
Primary care staff assignments, 279-280
Problem, definition of, 193-195
Problem solving management, 192-200
  control of environment in, 198-200
  control of perceptions in, 197-198
  criteria for assessing alternatives in,
    196
  decision making in, 196-197
  definition of terms in, 193
  generating alternative solutions in,
    195-196
  implementing selected alternatives in,
    197
  problem definition in, 193-195
Process standards for quality control, 287
Product line management, 228-229
Productivity, 75-84
  committee, 178-179
  indices of, 77-80
  tactics to encourage, 80-84
    personnel management as, 83-84
    structures as, 81-83
  work atmosphere and, 81
Products, selection of, 227-228

Professionals, health care
  collateral relations with, 118-119
  impact of changes on, 8-10
Professional nursing excellence
  clinical ladders and, 57
  education for, 55-58
  goals of professional organizations
    and, 53-55
  health-related organizations and, 48-51
  on job, 55-58
  nursing organizations and, 51-53
  nursing research and, 57-58
  social accountability and, 46-48
Professional organizations, goals of,
  53-55
Professional relationships for first-line
  nurse manager, 96-97
Professional staff, managing, challenges
  of, 150-151
Prospective payment system (PPS), 4
  community health care repercussions
    of, 130
  cost-effective management and, 210
Prototype instruments for classifying
  patients, 263
Psychological aspects of change, 200-202
Purpose of nursing division, 18-19, 20

Q

Quality assurance as system application
  in modern theory of organization,
  258-259
Quality control
  content for evaluation in, 291
  evidence for, sources of, 295
  factors influencing, 297-298
  feedback in, 298-299
  standards for
    constructing, 292-294
    outcome, 288-290
    process, 287
    selecting, 286-290
    structure, 286-287
  surveillance in, 298-299
  systems for, 285-290
  tools for, formats for, 295, *296*

Quality issues in health care, 7-8
Quality of life, ethical quandaries arising
  from, 143
Quality service, customer satisfaction
  and, 229-230

R

Rating errors in employee performance,
  305-306
Receiver of communication
  nurse manager as, 111-113
  skills for, 112
Recognition, motivation and, 162-164
Relationships, professional, for first-line
  nurse manager, 96-97
Research, nursing, professional
  excellence and, 57-58
Resistance to change, 201-202
Resources, 87-315
  communication, 107-127. *See also*
    Communication
  of first-line nurse manager, 98-99
  for implementing change, 202-206
Resource-driven models of care, 36-39
  baseline safety guide for, 39-41
Responsibility(ies)
  delegation of, 168
  of first-line manager, 99-104. *See also*
    First-line nurse manager,
    responsibilities of
Rights, patients', 140

S

Scheduling, definition of, 262
Selectivity in message reception, 111
Sender of communication
  nurse manager as, 109-111
  role of, thinking ahead into, 112
Service(s)
  provided by other departments,
    225-227
  quality, customer satisfaction and,
    229-230
Skills
  leadership, committee, 185-189

receiving, in communication, 112
staff
  assessment of, in supervision,
    152-153
  versus job design in supervision,
    151-153
Social accountability of nursing, 46-48
Society, nursing and, 46-55. *See also*
  Professional nursing excellence
Solutions, alternative, in problem solving
  assessing, 196
  generating, 195-196
  implementing selected, 197
Staff
  assignment systems for, 276-282
    comparison of, 280-282
    functional, 277-278
    modular, 278-279
    primary care, 279-280
    team, 278-279
  competence of, nurse manager's
    responsibility for, 130-131
  development of, as first-line
    manager responsibility, 102
  direction of, 174
  involvement of, in materials
    management, 224-225
  management of, first-line nurse
    manager, 99
  mix of personnel in, 272-274
  new, orientation of, 153-159
  performance of, appraisal of, 302-315.
    See also Employee performance
    appraisal
  professional, managing, challenge
    of, 150-151
  scheduling of, for staffing patterns,
    274-276
  skills of
    assessment of, in supervision,
      152-153
    versus job design in supervision,
      151-153
Staffing, 262-282
  adjustments in, for increased activity,
    268-270
  decision(s) on

daily workload irregularities in, 271
fluctuations in staffing needs and,
268-270
identifying staffing needs for, 265-268
mix of staff personnel in, 272-274
scheduling staff for staffing patterns
in, 274-276
variable staffing and, 270-271
definition of, 262
nursing patient classification systems
and, 262-265
patterns of, scheduling staff for, 274
plans for, 268
variable, 270-271
Standing committee, 180-182
Standard(s)
of patient care, 41-42
professional, upgrading, as proffesional
goal, 53-54
for quality control
constructing, 292-294
outcome, 288-290
process, 287
relationship among, 290
structure, 286-287
Strategic planning, 66-70
effectiveness/efficiency and, 73, 74
first-line management and, 69-70
Stress, job, 161-162
Structure(s)
for delegation, 170
organizational, effects of, on role of
first-line manager, 97-98
productivity and, 81-83
Structure standards for quality control,
286-287
Substance abuse, nurse suspected of,
managing, 133-138. *See also*
Impaired nurse
Supervising part-time nurse, 157-159
Supervision
motivational component of, 159-164.
See also Motivation
nature of, 151
orientation of new staff in, 153-159.
See also Orientation of new staff
staff skills versus job design in, 151-153

Supply budget, 216-217
Support services, collateral relations
with, 117-118
Surveillance systems in quality control,
298-299
Systems model in modern theory of
organizations, 254-258
computers and, 259-260

T

Tax Equity and Fiscal Responsibility Act
(TEFRA), 3-4
Team nursing, staffing systems and, 280-282
Team staff assignments, 278-279
Technology(ies)
in home care, 231-232
managing, 230-234
medical, adaptive mode of
management and, 64
new, ethical quandaries arising from, 142
Tone, setting of, by leader, 27-29
Trait language versus event language in
employee performance appraisal,
303-305
Transfer of staff for increased activity, 269
24-hour delegation, 173-174

V

Variable billing, definition of, 262

W

Work, facilitation of, manager in, 160-161
Worker(s)
knowledge, supervision of, 150-151
studies of, in neoclassical theory of
organization, 253-254
and manager, interactions between,
studies of, in neoclassical theory of
organization, 252-253
World context, 310

Z

Zero-based budgeting, 214